SIBERIA

RUSSIA

FINLAND

Results of the
Balkan Wars:
1912-13

Petrograd
(St. Petersburg)

ESTONIA

LIVONIA

URLAND

LITHUANIA

To Serbia

To Rumania

To Montenegro

To Bulgaria

To Greece

Minsk

Dnieper

OLAND

Kiev

UKRAINE

GARY

Sea of Azov

CASPIAN SEA

RUMANIA

Bucharest

BLACK

SEA

Sofia

BULGARIA

Constan-
tinople

ASIA

MINOR

ECE

Athens

Crete

Cyprus

THE RISE OF MODERN EUROPE

A SURVEY OF EUROPEAN HISTORY
IN ITS POLITICAL, ECONOMIC, AND CULTURAL ASPECTS
FROM THE END OF THE MIDDLE AGES
TO THE PRESENT

———————

EDITED BY

WILLIAM L. LANGER

Harvard University

THE
GREAT
ILLUSION

1900–1914

BY

ORON J. HALE

University of Virginia

ILLUSTRATED

1817

HARPER & ROW, PUBLISHERS

New York, Evanston, and London

To the Memory

of

A. F. H.

CONTENTS

ILLUSTRATIONS

The illustrations, grouped in a separate section, will be found following page 142.

MAPS

INTRODUCTION

Our age of specialization produces an almost incredible amount of monographic research in all fields of human knowledge. So great is the mass of this material that even the professional scholar cannot keep abreast of the contributions in anything but a restricted part of his general subject. In all branches of learning the need for intelligent synthesis is now more urgent than ever before, and this need is felt by the layman even more acutely than by the scholar. He cannot hope to read the products of microscopic research or to keep up with the changing interpretations of experts, unless new knowledge and new viewpoints are made accessible to him by those who make it their business to be informed and who are competent to speak with authority.

These volumes, published under the general title of *The Rise of Modern Europe*, are designed primarily to give the general reader and student a reliable survey of European history written by experts in various branches of that vast subject. In consonance with the current broad conception of the scope of history, they attempt to go beyond a merely political-military narrative, and to lay stress upon social, economic, religious, scientific, and artistic developments. The minutely detailed, chronological approach is to some extent sacrificed in the effort to emphasize the dominant factors and to set forth their interrelationships. At the same time the division of European history into national histories has been abandoned and wherever possible attention has been focused upon larger forces common to the whole of European civilization. These are the broad lines on which this history as a whole has been laid out. The individual volumes are integral parts of the larger scheme, but they are intended also to stand as independent units, each the work of a scholar well qualified to treat the period covered by this book. Each volume contains about fifty illustrations selected from the mass of contemporary pictorial material. All noncontemporary illustrations have been excluded on principle. The bibliographical note appended to each volume is designed to facilitate further study of special aspects touched upon in the text. In general every effort has been made to give the reader a clear idea of the main movements in European history, to embody the monographic contributions of research workers, and to present the material in a forceful and vivid manner.

Professor Hale's volume spans a relatively short but exceptionally pregnant period of European history. As he remarks in his preface, the appalling catastrophe that broke over the world in 1914 has stamped the initial years of the twentieth century as the "prelude to war" or the "road to disaster," thereby obscuring what we now can see as a period unusually rich in ideas and full of promise for both good and evil. It was an age of prosperity and progress; it was also one of brilliant achievement in science and technology; and yet again it was one of smoldering unrest presaging radical changes in Western society. It stands to reason that such periods of incipient crisis and upheaval confront the historian with formidable challenges. Professor Hale deserves much credit for the skill with which he has both analyzed and integrated strange and diverse forces of the budding century. This fresh and stimulating reevaluation of the prewar years adds a distinguished volume to *The Rise of Modern Europe* series.

WILLIAM L. LANGER

PREFACE

A distinguished French historian, the late Marc Bloch, tells of a student's paper that contained this sly or naïve statement: "It is well known that the eighteenth century begins in 1715 and ends in 1789." One can imagine another student writing: "It is well known that the nineteenth century begins in 1815 and ends in 1914." Such a view indeed is widely held, but the assumption underlying this book is that the years from 1900 to 1914 were not simply the sunset of the nineteenth century—or the last act in a Victorian play—but rather a period that clearly belongs to the twentieth century, and one in which our present-day concerns and achievements had their beginning. Wherever the historian of my generation delves in this epoch he encounters his own present. To be sure the period was one of seedtime rather than of harvest; in science, in art and literature, in technical advances, in economic growth and development, indeed in almost every respect, these were gigantic years in which Europeans gained enormously in knowledge, wisdom, wealth, and power. Discoveries and developments originating in these decades were later to revolutionize the world.

The significance of the epoch is well illustrated by the emergence of a new appreciation of the universe and the world of nature. First among theoretical physicists, then among the philosophers of science, and finally through them to a wider public, the implications of Max Planck's quantum theory and Einstein's relativity turned men's minds away from the Newtonian conception of the universe and the belief that nature functioned like a great machine. Discontinuity, indeterminancy, and the relativity of space, time, and mass developed a competing, and eventually a dominating, image of nature.

Also in the political sphere the period had its revolutionary aspects. The year 1905 witnessed the first Russian revolution, the victory of a modernized Japan over one of the great powers, and a diplomatic revolution in the relations of the principal European states. The Boer War, the Russo-Japanese War, and the public exposure of conditions in the Congo manifestly marked a turning point in the history of Western imperialism. Internally, or domestically, the mystery of economic growth began to replace social injustice as the dominant theme in economic history, and the transition from wealth to welfare, which distinguishes the nineteenth from the twentieth century, became an acknowledged social goal. The fact that the leaders in the various fields of endeavor—Freud, Max Planck, Bergson, Diesel, Max Weber, J. J. Thomson—all experienced life in two centuries was a characteristic feature of these years and constituted as it were a bridge between two worlds which science and technology were rendering ever more dissimilar. The automobile, the airplane, the gene theory, abstract art, and the first wireless signal flashed across the Atlantic were germinal achievements of the first decade of the 1900's.

The posturing of the "decadents" at the turn of the century should not be given undue weight, for the real mood was broadly optimistic and anticipatory. Some pessimists envisioned a "shipwrecked Europe," but most observers were convinced that they lived in an age of peace and progress and that there would be more prosperity to come. The "road to disaster" theme, so often applied to these years, is a highly retrospective construction. No one, including this author, whose youthful years fell before 1914, really anticipated the approaching chaos of our times. I have therefore tried to avoid mistaking the natural optimism of youth and the contrasting sadness of later years for a cosmic transformation.

This volume in *The Rise of Modern Europe* series was undertaken originally by the late Professor Sidney B. Fay. Professional demands, and finally the infirmities of age, made it impossible for him to complete the assignment. The profession is thereby the loser. Professor Fay generously made available to me the drafts of chapters he had written. They mainly dealt with those aspects of the era in which he was the master—diplomatic history. Helpful though his manuscripts were, they were not such that they could be integrated with my own work, as I had hoped they would be. I benefited also from reading Professor Langer's unpublished Lowell Lectures, delivered in 1941, on the intellectual and social background of the two world wars in our century. My further debt to him as an experienced editor and masterly critic is likewise gratefully acknowledged.

A complete listing of obligations incurred in the preparation of this volume would be inordinately long. I am in a sense a hostage to the many scholars whose special knowledge and researches have been digested and incorporated in my work. Footnotes and bibliography both reveal the extent of this indebtedness. Facetiously I might say that mistakes of fact or interpretation are not mine but the responsibility of these many specialists!

I am deeply indebted to the Institute for Advanced Study, Princeton, New Jersey, for support and hospitality during the session 1963–64, when intensive work on this volume began; and to the University of Virginia for a semester's leave and financial support to complete the task of writing and revision. A supporting grant from the American Philosophical Society is also gratefully acknowledged. The staffs of the Firestone Library, Princeton, and Alderman Library, University of Virginia, deserve special thanks. Professor Freeman J. Dyson, of the Institute for Advanced Study, guided me patiently through the chapter on "Scientific Revolution." Frederick F. Ritsch, of Converse College, reviewed several of the chapters and made helpful suggestions for improvement; and graduate assistants Larry D. Wilcox and Harry Ritter gave valuable assistance in preparing the bibliographical essay and typing the manuscript. Friends and colleagues—William A. Jenks, Enno Kraehe, Woodford McClellan, and Alexander Sedgwick—cheerfully responded to my plea for aid in collecting suitable illustrations. I acknowledge with pleasure the kind permission given to publish privately owned photographs and illustrations of works of art by Mrs. R. W. Ladenburg, Princeton, Mrs. Lisa Arnhold, New York City, Mrs. Ayala Zacks, Toronto, Canada, and Frau Martha Dix, Hemmenhofen, Bavaria. The person to whose memory this book is dedicated gave, as always, cheerful understanding and encouragement.

ORON J. HALE

January 1, 1970
Charlottesville, Virginia

THE GREAT ILLUSION
1900-1914

Chapter One

BEGINNING THE TWENTIETH CENTURY

I. AN END AND A BEGINNING

BY the year 1901 Europe's nineteenth-century promises had become substantial realities: the nation state, constitutional government, and a predominantly secularized and industrialized society. Europe had also gained a position of world predominance, which was then lost in the course of the twentieth century as a result of two catastrophic wars. In 1914 Europe stumbled into a civil war, and the civil war grew into a world war. The First World War was a great divide, a watershed in world history. It produced an irreversible shift in the axis of world power, which was registered historically in the relations of states, the loss of empires, and radical changes in the distribution of national power. Such agreement on the significance of the First World War does not extend to the period that preceded it—the decade and a half that elapsed between the beginning of the century and the bursting of the storm.

A view frequently advanced is that these years were simply the tag end of the nineteenth century, which really ended in 1914. A favorite period with the social historian and the pictorial press, it is often presented as a rapturous summer before the "guns of August" began to boom. The French call it "la belle epoque," the British "the Edwardian era," with all kinds of evocative overtones. To Stefan Zweig it was the "Age of Golden Security" and "a sweet time to be alive"; and Winston Churchill reminds us that the "Old World in its sunset was fair to see." For the Marxist-Leninist historian Liashchenko, it is a period of "parasitic or decaying capitalism" antecedent to the "socialist revolution." Gerhard Masur, in his brilliant *Prophets of Yesterday,* employs the moving image of a small telltale cloud hanging over a volcano on a beautiful summer afternoon. But historical periods are rather like men, in one respect—they are assessed at their end for achievements, values, and significance. If the end is bad then all the positive accomplishments are likely to be forgotten. So it is with the period 1900–1914.

I

Opposed to these nostalgic views and retrospective assessments is the indisputable fact that most Europeans in 1900 saw themselves not at the end of a played-out era but at the beginning of a new century full of hope and promise. Certainly, this was the mood of the great crowds that gathered on Unter den Linden, in Trafalgar Square, and in the Place de la Concorde at midnight, December 31, 1900, to roar *Prosit Neujahr,* or *Bonne Année,* or Happy New Year. For them the twentieth century began on schedule, and the notable achievements and developments in science, art, technology, and economic life that marked the years before the First World War gave color and substance to their confident belief. However viewed, the period has its distinct identity.

A man who identified himself with the twentieth century was Alfred Harmsworth, editor and proprietor of the *London Daily Mail,* who arrived in New York on December 30, 1900. It had been arranged with Joseph Pulitzer that Harmsworth, always the center of a "stunt," should take over the management of the *New York World* for twenty-four hours to demonstrate "what is wanted in the newspapers of the Twentieth Century."[1] This he did on the following Tuesday, the first day of the new year and the new century.

Harmsworth's appearance coincided with the publication of replies to an inquiry sent by the *World* to a number of prominent Americans and Europeans. The question posed was: "What, in your opinion, is the chief danger, social or political, that confronts the coming century?"

Émile Zola's reply was a copyright article headlined: "What happiness has the Nineteenth Century brought to humanity; what is the outlook for the new century?" Zola cataloged so extensively the ills of mankind, spiritual and bodily, that he slighted the happiness theme and did not consider at all the question posed by the New York editor. Élie Mechnikoff, the noted Russian-French biologist, who somewhat prematurely was credited by sensational journalists with having invented a "long-life elixir," cheerfully chronicled the great advances in biology and medicine which would soon extend human life to seventy years and more. Even without the "long-life elixir," he declared,

1. "The young man of genius who has revolutionized European journalism within four years will take entire charge of the morning *World* for one day to show his idea of what the Twentieth Century newspaper should be." *New York World,* January 1, 1901.

"centenarians will be plentiful and hearty along the shady, broad streets of the next century."

Most of the respondents in identifying "the chief danger, social or political," spoke from the standpoint of their interests or profession. Hermann Adler, chief rabbi of Great Britain, thought that the greatest danger was the recrudescence of racial and national antipathies; the Chinese ambassador—doubtless with the Boxer War in mind—singled out "the growing covetousness of individuals and nations"; Max Nordau most feared "individualism as preached by the madman Nietzsche"; the Bishop of Raphoe (Ireland) viewed "education without religion" as the greatest danger; while Dean Farrar thought it was drink. Arthur Lee, member of Parliament and a big navy man, said that the greatest danger lay in the possibility that some combination of European powers might "destroy the supremacy of the Anglo-Saxon race." Conan Doyle, Max O'Rell, and Max Beerbohm cited "the irresponsible press" as the greatest danger; and William Jennings Bryan, Cardinal Gibbon, and Joseph Arch thought the greatest danger would come from "mammon worship" and the increasing influence of wealth. A considerable number of respondents thought that imperialism, militarism, armaments, or war itself would constitute the gravest danger in the new century. Among the notables who plucked this string were W.T. Stead, Andrew Carnegie, James Keir Hardie, John Dillon, Frederic Harrison, and Walter Besant. Concluding the résumé of replies and predictions, and discounting the pessimism, the buoyant editor declared: "The *World* is optimistic enough to believe that the twentieth century . . . will meet and overcome all perils and prove to be the best that this steadily improving planet has ever seen."[2] This sense of a boundless future was strong among all Western leaders in 1900, and it brought zest and assurance to the cities and cultures of men. It was a time of incredible innocence: War was unlikely; social reform was every man's duty; and progress was inevitable. Poet, priest, statesman, scientist, industrialist, labor leader, or social reformer—few foresaw the grandeur and the misery that would characterize the twentieth century.

2. *New York World,* December 30, 1900, and supplement. Less optimistic but still positive were the serious academic assessments such as *An der Wende des Jahrhunderts: Versuch einer Kulturphilosophie* (Freiburg i.B., 1899), by the sociologist and philosopher Ludwig Stein.

It was a period dominated by the heirs of Samuel Smiles and Karl Marx.

2. IMPERIALISM: MYTHS AND REALITIES

The number of respondents to the *World's* inquiry who thought the greatest danger confronting the new century was militarism, imperialism, and organized violence doubtless reflected the concern generated by the colonial wars just concluded or still in progress—the Spanish-American War, the Boer War, and the Boxer Rebellion in China, which was a war as well as an antiforeign revolt. The causes of intensified European imperialism, its manifestations and consequences in the areas of impact, and the theories that developed to explain this new trend in world history received extensive treatment in the preceding volume in this series.[3] Here we need to consider three principal aspects of the phenomenon of imperialism on the eve of the First World War. First, recent theories and explanations of imperialism must be examined; second, the current literature requires evaluation; and third, note must be taken of how imperialism contributed to the situation that produced a war in 1914.

One wonders if "imperialism," because of looseness of definition, is a word that scholars ought to use. Richard Koebner has made a thorough investigation of the origins of the term and its modern usage. He shows that the accepted meaning changed substantially in the course of time until the turn of the century when the English economist and publicist J. A. Hobson gave the word the political and economic connotations which it henceforth bore. This ideological transformation emerged, as Koebner states, during and immediately after the Boer War, and "it originated in England."[4]

J. A. Hobson was an original thinker and challenging writer. His *Imperialism: A Study*, published in 1902, is a milestone in the literature of world politics. As an economist Hobson had propagated theories critical of free enterprise capitalism and its low social yield to the mass of the people. In his "economics of distribution," which in some respects anticipated J. M. Keynes, oversaving for capital investment led to underconsumption and unjust distribution at home, while accumulated

---

3. Carlton J. H. Hayes, *A Generation of Materialism* (New York, 1941), pp. 216–41, 306–22, 336–40.

4. Richard Koebner and H. D. Schmidt, *Imperialism: The Story and Significance of a Political Word, 1840–1960* (Cambridge, Eng., 1964), p. 249.

capital, seeking a higher return, was exported to undeveloped areas where it produced the phenomenon of modern imperialism. Thus capital exports kept domestic wages and standards of living low. In 1899, on the eve of the Boer War, Hobson was commissioned by the *Manchester Guardian* to go to South Africa as a special observer and reporter. What he thought he saw there of the causes of the war led him to relate his economic views to the kind of aggressive and conspiratorial enterprise undertaken against the Boers. In colonial adventures such as the Spanish-American War and the Boer War, so he concluded, predatory capitalists seeking higher returns on their investments united with colonial enthusiasts and nationalists in wars of conquest and exploitation. This was the central theme which Hobson generalized into a convincing theory of imperialism.[5]

Although Hobson was not a Marxist, even an economic determinist, his central ideas were adopted by revolutionary socialists and incorporated eventually into the Marxist-Leninist canon as a valid explanation of the crisis of capitalism and its certain extinction. Rudolf Hilferding gave it an important position in his *Finance Capitalism* (1910), as did Rosa Luxemburg in her *Accumulation of Capital* (1913). Lenin in his tract *Imperialism, the Highest Stage of Capitalism* (1916) explained the war of 1914 in terms of imperialism and confidently prophesied the end of the capitalist age. All three Marxist theorists acknowledged their indebtedness to Hobson.

Today the Leninist conception of imperialism, modified and extended, has become religious dogma, although the Hobsonian foundation has been almost completely demolished. This has come about through broad and intensified research in the economic aspects of British imperial activity between 1870 and 1914. Mention has been made of Professor Koebner's examination of the changing meaning of the term "imperialism." As to its validity as Lenin used the concept, he bluntly says: "Lenin's theory of imperialism was suitable for propaganda among the half-educated whose power of criticism was not fully developed."[6] One of the most devastating analyses and exposures of

5. Hobson, *Imperialism: A Study* (Ann Arbor, 1965), Chap. VI, "The Economic Taproot of Imperialism"; also Hobson, *Confessions of an Economic Heretic* (London, 1938), pp. 62–63.

6. *Imperialism: The Story and Significance of a Political Word*, p. 282. Also important is Koebner's article "The Concept of Economic Imperialism," *Economic History Review*, 2d ser., II (1949), 1–29. One of the first to examine Hobson's thesis critically

Hobson's facts and methods is the extensive article by the British scholar D. K. Fieldhouse.[7] Of Hobson's models and his use of the statistics of British capital exports, he concludes that Hobson "performed an intellectual conjuring trick." Sophisticated studies such as A. K. Cairncross, *Home and Foreign Investment, 1870–1913,* and Ragnar Nurkse, *Patterns of Trade and Development,* published in 1953 and 1959 respectively, pointed strongly in the same direction. A different approach to the problem of Britain's imperial expansion was made by the scholars R. E. Robinson and J. Gallagher, in their *Africa and the Victorians* (1961). In a careful examination of British decision-making in each acquisition of African territory, these authors found few capitalists, less capital, and not much pressure from the alleged traditional promoters of colonial expansion. Cabinet decisions to annex or not to annex were made usually on the basis of political or geopolitical considerations. Altogether the literature rebutting the Hobson-Leninist dogma is so convincing that one can say with D. K. Fieldhouse: "the noes have it."[8]

Further studies of European colonial activity outside the areas of British interest tend also to shift the emphasis from the economic motive to a plurality of motives. Here again old familiar figures come into view—the explorer-adventurer, the trader, the missionary, the engineer, the scientist, the colonial-minded patriot, and the humanitarian. A recent scholarly study of French colonial expansion by Henri Brunschwig concludes that economically the French empire contributed little to the development of the homeland. Investments in the colonies amounted to only 3 or 4 billion francs of a total of 50 billion invested abroad. Algeria was the only colony that attracted settlers because there French farmers could continue to produce grain and wine for markets already glutted. Brunschwig concludes that the French colonies were never economically viable; they were not a na-

---

was William L. Langer, in his article "A Critique of Imperialism," *Foreign Affairs,* XIV (1935), 102–15, followed by E. M. Winslow, *The Pattern of Imperialism* (New York, 1948).

7. "Imperialism: An Historiographical Revision," *Economic History Review,* 2d ser., XIV (1961), 187–209.

8. Other authoritative critiques are: David S. Landes, "Some Thoughts on the Nature of Economic Imperialism"; and Richard J. Hammond, "Economic Imperialism: Sidelights on a Stereotype"; in the *Journal of Economic History,* XXI (Dec., 1961), an issue devoted to the topic: "Colonialism and Colonization in World History."

tional necessity but were born of national feeling after the humiliation of 1870.[9]

Nationalism and humanitarianism were the principal ingredients of colonial enthusiasm and activity at the turn of the century. In Britain, France, Germany, the United States, and later, Italy, it was belief in the mission of a civilized people to share its culture with the less fortunate races that produced public support for colonial enterprises. It was the feeling of pride in undertaking this as a national task and not leaving it to others that provided the incentive for the pursuit of empire. These two convictions were responsible for the "clear consciences" which Western peoples still enjoyed between 1900 and 1914. They stilled all criticism, excused all exposed evils and wrongdoing, and in the end won the day. The greatness of France, of Britain, of the United States, of Germany—the civilizing mission was one of the tests and the proof of such greatness.[10]

Further support for the dominance of nationalistic and humanitarian drives in colonial expansion is afforded by the examples of Italy and Russia, neither of which had surplus capital or manufactures to export, and yet they were among the most aggressive in pursuit of colonial objectives. Italy took to imperialism almost as soon as she was unified as a means of enhancing her national prestige. The concept of contiguous territory was also a motivating factor in many instances of expansion, as was national security. The development of sea power started the feverish search for naval bases. A great upsurge of Christian missions also played an important part. As one expert noted, missionaries functioned in a dual capacity—converting Westerners to imperialism and natives to Christianity. Colonies, moreover, were valuable status symbols. A disorganized and nearly bankrupt state like Portugal stubbornly refused to sell any of her colonial territories. Overseas possessions were valued symbols of a great past or of a country's place in the present world.

While the humanitarian motive combined with national pride to reinforce the general belief in colonial "good works," at least two

9. Henri Brunschwig, *French Colonialism, 1871–1914: Myths and Realities* (New York, 1966), pp. 135–38, 182.

10. *Ibid.*, pp. 167–81. "Anyone who thinks that colonial imperialism was simply a case of capitalists snatching at profits from lucrative territories and of defenseless populations, has no idea of what it was all about."

episodes, thoroughly aired in the European press, served to stimulate some second thoughts about imperialism. Both concerned the treatment of indigenous peoples, the one in the Belgian Congo the other in German Southwest Africa. Leopold II of Belgium, one of the most astute entrepreneurs and capitalists of his generation, had taken the initiative in the exploration and development of the Congo Basin. In the Berlin Act of 1885, the powers had approved the establishment of the Congo Free State under a firm guarantee that it would be maintained as an area of free trade and free enterprise. Leopold as sovereign would have sufficient territory for the exercise of his humanitarian and administrative energies while the British, French, and Germans would develop the country and reap the benefits—or so they thought.

As might have been anticipated it did not work out this way, for Leopold concentrated on the economic exploitation of the region and in so doing flagrantly violated the free trade and enterprise stipulations of the original Berlin Act. His concessions policy, his rubber and ivory monopolies, and his restless rooting around for investment and development opportunities aroused ill will and envy in financial and colonial circles in Britain, France, and Germany. By no means all the motives that inspired the anti-Congo agitation in these countries were humanitarian.[11]

The Congo experiment in international trusteeship encountered stormy weather when critical reports by British consular officials attracted the attention of the press and produced unpleasant publicity for Leopold and his administration. Leopold's implacable critic was the English reformer E. D. Morel, who organized the Congo Reform Association, with an active coordinate "league" in Germany and a branch in Switzerland. In the publicity that emanated from Morel's organizations the Congo administration was harshly criticized for restrictions on trade, the exclusive concessions granted to development companies, the native lands policy, and the system of forced labor for the operation of the plantations and the collection and movement of products. The "atrocities in the Congo," which became a staple of the sensational press, scandalized and outraged humanitarians in England and on the Continent. Morel's campaign continued relentlessly until 1908 when, by international agreement, Leopold's personal rule was ended and the

11. J. Willequet, *Le Congo Belge et la Weltpolitik* (Brussels, 1962), pp. 33–35, and *passim*. Based on archival records, this is one of the most important studies published in recent years on the pre-1914 colonial movement.

Congo state transferred to Belgian sovereignty. Reforms instituted by the Belgian minister of colonies, Jules Renkin, promised to eliminate the most serious abuses, but they also eliminated the profits derived from the administration by the former sovereign authority. Thereafter, until the war, the deficit in the budget of the Belgian Congo amounted to three francs per capita annually for all Belgian citizens.

Another series of exposures that tarnished the image of European colonialism and caused some second thoughts about the whole matter concerned the German colonial system, especially as it functioned in German Southwest Africa. The revelations and charges, which were aired in the Reichstag and the press, originated with the young Center party deputy Matthias Erzberger. The charges with respect to inefficiency and favoritism in administration, mistreatment of natives, and the concessions policy led to the replacement of the minister of colonies, cancellation of a number of concessions and contracts, and a general reform of the German colonial system.[12]

Did the prewar colonies "pay"? Books have been written to show, one, that they did, and two, that they did not. Roughly, with regard to trade and commerce, some "paid" but most did not. Britain derived a fabulous income from India in the period 1875 to 1914, when India's imports increased almost 500 percent and exports about 350 percent. The Netherlands East Indies also paid handsomely. But Germany's colonial trade amounted barely to one-half of 1 percent of her total foreign commerce. France's colonies did somewhat better. In the period 1909–13 colonial imports and exports amounted to 10 percent of France's total foreign trade. To small countries, such as Belgium and Holland, colonial trade was relatively more important than to the great industrial powers. Broadly, however, costs of administration, protection, and services considerably exceeded the value of trade and raw materials produced by the colonies. Togoland, for example, was the only self-supporting German colony, and the Philippines administration cost the United States considerably more annually than the original war with Spain.[13]

---

12. Klaus Epstein, *Matthias Erzberger and the Dilemma of German Democracy* (Princeton, 1959), pp. 52–60; G. W. F. Hallgarten, *Imperialismus vor 1914,* 2 vols. (Munich, 1963), II, 31–39, 73–76.

13. M. E. Townsend, *European Colonial Expansion Since 1871* (New York, 1941), pp. 379, 520; Brunschwig, *French Colonialism,* p. 90; and the careful analysis of Jean Stengers: *Combien le Congo a-ti-il-coûté à la Belgique* (Brussels, 1957).

Toward the end of the nineteenth century, colonial policy makers began to perceive that often colonies were more valuable as producers of raw materials than as market areas. This shift from emphasis on trade to development and exploitation of natural resources required substantial capital investments as well as more financial aid in the form of loans, administration costs, and defense.[14] Since colonial budgets showed annual deficits, it is not surprising that a certain "colonial weariness" set in. And yet no one advocated abandoning these unprofitable enterprises which were a burden on the taxpayer at home. All were banking or speculating on the future when their colonies would pay. So occuption and police forces were provided, railroads and other technical installations were built, administrative services were established, hospitals and schools were constructed so that a local labor force could be trained. As this went on, the colonial dependencies were to some extent modernized and equipped with capital assets instead of simply being exploited for their resources and their labor. In the perspective of modern history, imperialism was the principal vehicle for the spread of Western culture, science, and technology to the non-European parts of the world. And even more, during the decade and a half before 1914, native revolts and colonial scandals were driving home to Western leaders the idea that reconsideration of the methods of dealing with dependent peoples was in order. Considerations of native welfare under trusteeship began to replace colonial exploitation.

There remains to be considered the specific question asked at the beginning of this section on imperialism: Was it a principal cause, direct or indirect, of war in 1914? Obviously the acute rivalries that developed among the European powers during the period of rapid overseas expansion—especially in Asia and Africa—contributed to international tensions and ill will. Since imperialism was popular with the voters, there was much clamor in the mass press and in consequence, we must presume, much heartburn, envy, and frustration among the less successful competitors. However, the partition of Africa and the division of a large part of Asia into spheres of influence were

14. Townsend, *European Colonial Expansion,* pp. 589–600. This expenditure on colonies moved a recent critic to comment: "If I were to set up a rival doctrine of economic imperialism to that of Hobson and Lenin, my choice for prophet would be Veblen, the apostle of conspicuous consumption." R. J. Hammond, "Economic Imperialism: Sidelights on a Stereotype," *Journal of Economic History,* XXI (1961), 596.

accomplished without precipitating a general war. Russia and Japan collided in Manchuria, but in Africa only Fashoda and the Moroccan crises seriously endangered peace. In the scramble for overseas investment opportunities the element of competition and rivalry among national groups is often overstressed. The international consortium was frequently more prominent than the national banker.[15] For example, the development of the oil industry was European, and not noticeably national; American and German capital, as well as British, was involved in the south African mining industries; American capital and market interests were prominently represented in the Congo monopolies; French and British capital joined Belgian capital in the development of the Katanga copper mines; French capital participated in Leopold II's Peking-Hankow railroad concession; a British-German group secured the loan and contract for the Tientsin-Nanking line, and a four-party group—British, French, German, and American—shared the contract for the Canton-Hankow-Szechuan line. This same combination gained a monopoly on Chinese government loans, which they held until the Russian and Japanese governments secured admission for their financiers in 1912.

This evidence suggests that it is fallacious to say that imperialism or colonialism equals war, in the Marxian sense. But colonial rivalry did exacerbate national feelings and contribute to international ill will and hostility. But if there was much competition and rivalry before 1914 there was also much international cooperation; and it is a common-sense observation that wars are not ordinarily made in the marketplace.

3. NATIONALISM AND INTERNATIONALISM

Second to imperialism, nationalism is most frequently cited as a force impelling Europe toward war in 1914. Every writer on international relations in the prewar period emphasizes its importance. As a force, how is it to be described and evaluated as Europe entered the twentieth century? H. G. Wells once petulantly defined a nation as "an assembly, mixture or confusion of people which is either afflicted by, or wants to be afflicted by a foreign office of its own, in order that it should behave

---

15. Wilhelm Solf, German secretary of state for colonies, tartly noted that "The good will and patriotism of our capitalists are immense as long as it is not a question of opening their pocketbooks." Quoted in Willequet, *Le Congo Belge,* p. 391.

collectively as if it alone constituted humanity."[16] We can be reasonably certain that Wells had in mind eastern and southeastern Europe, and probably Ireland. In these areas the excesses of nationalism were most clearly displayed. Professor Carlton J. H. Hayes, in the preceding volume in this series, described the transition after 1870 from a liberal and cultural nationalism to a "totalitarian nationalism," which was popular and commonplace, pseudoscientific, realistic rather than romantic, racist and anti-Semitic, and intolerant of national minorities. In Hayes' words, "national self-determination" was halted and gave way to a "determination by superior races."[17] Sir Lewis Namier suggests that nationalism was basically a linguistic creation—a product of the philologist, the folklorist, and the historical romancer. The language chart became the "Magna Charta" and title deed of separate nationality. The drive to make the political map of Europe correspond in every part to the linguistic map did not produce altogether satisfactory results.[18] Indeed, the demand that every little language have a country all its own just about wrecked Europe in the twentieth century and undermined the Continent's position of world supremacy.

In the course of modern history the principal nations of western Europe had sorted themselves out and acquired national unity and identity, the Italians and Germans being the last to achieve this euphoric condition. Only here and there, as in the case of Walloons and Flemings in Belgium, the Irish in the British Isles, and Danes in Schleswig, were there minorities living unhappily under the rule of another national group. Among the peoples of western Europe, where a high rate of literacy prevailed, a strong sense of patriotism, composed of history, traditions, civic education, language, and literature, was inculcated in each rising generation. Many institutions and agencies served this purpose—the government and the bureaucracy, the schools, the military services with their symbols and ceremonies, the churches, the press, and the patriotic societies. National self-consciousness was highly developed and deeply imprinted, but it was not militant and fanatical as it was among the emerging or oppressed peoples of eastern and southeastern Europe.

16. *The Outline of History* (New York, 1921), p. 960.
17. *A Generation of Materialism*, Chap. VII, "Seed-Time of Totalitarian Nationalism."
18. *Vanished Supremacies: Essays on European History, 1812–1918* (New York, 1958), pp. 165–67.

Also in central and western Europe bitterness and resentment generated by military defeat during the wars of unification had considerably abated by 1900. The French especially were thought to be "a nation of patriots" filled with stark desire to revenge the defeat of 1870 and restore Alsace-Lorraine to the fatherland. But not many of the burning patriots of the 1870's survived their century. When Paul Déroulède, founder of the League of Patriots, died in 1914 he was all but forgotten. Although he received a public funeral, he was "a trumpeter who had sounded the charge on battlefields long ago deserted." His name was unknown to a younger generation, and his "Chants du Soldat," from the war of 1870, were too topical to live. A Swiss journalist observed that the memorial post cards hawked at his funeral were issued by a German printing shop![19]

An integrating and state-supporting force in western Europe, nationalism was an unsettling factor in eastern and southeastern Europe. Here three historic empires—Russia, Austria-Hungary, and the Ottoman Empire—held dominion over more than a dozen national and ethnic groups in various stages of cultural, social, and political development. The governing classes, the bureaucracy, officers, and clergy propagated a "state patriotism" in opposition to national patriotism, asserting the primacy of statism over nationalism. Of the ruling peoples the Turks had the weakest hold over their subject minorities, and in the course of the nineteenth century one after another of the national elements gained independence and all were now waiting for the opportunity to annex the remnants of Ottoman territory in Europe. Russia's position was somewhat different. Historically Russia oppressed her own ethnic minorities while encouraging the subject Slav peoples to assert their independence of Turk and Hapsburg.

Austria-Hungary's nationality problems attracted more attention than those of her neighbors; it was regularly predicted that the Dual Monarchy would inherit in the twentieth century Turkey's role as the sick man of Europe. This strife of nationalities and Austria-Hungary's resort to force in combating it was the occasion of the war in 1914. The condition of the Dual Monarchy and its nationality sickness therefore merit some detailed consideration.

The Hapsburg empire held a contingent of every ethnic group

19. *Neue Zürcher Zeitung*, No. 169 (Feb. 4, 1914).

represented in eastern and southeastern Europe. Many of these minorities were separated from a larger national body beyond the frontiers. Penned up, as it were, in the Dual Monarchy they nursed their discontent and became an easy prey to nationalist agitators and propagandists. Italy, Serbia, Rumania, Russia, exerted a magnetic attraction upon their minority kinsmen in the Hapsburg state. These nationalist dissensions subjected a great and ancient empire to intolerable strains in every part of its structure.

Since the constitutional compromise of 1867 the Magyars of Hungary had governed their minorities with a heavy hand. They made few compromises, monopolized the bureaucracy, excluded all but Magyars from parliament, and enforced a rigorous cultural policy of Magyarization. The *Ausgleich* had also placed in Magyar hands a virtual veto over constitutional changes or shifting of the balance among the national elements of the Dual Monarchy. Minorities were treated with more consideration in the German part of the empire, where the monarchy, the Catholic Church, the bureaucracy, and the army served as cohesive elements. Unremitting friction marked the relations between the German and Hungarian parts of the empire. Certain issues, like specters or apparitions, regularly appeared and disappeared in the political mists of the Theiss and the Danube—the army question, tariffs, manhood suffrage, and the language issue. Tariffs and fiscal problems, of joint concern, arose acutely every ten years.

The politics of minority aspirations was a principal preoccupation of all representative bodies in the Dual Monarchy. The loudest and most persistent conflicts before 1914 were four in number: the Poles and Ruthenians in Galicia, the Magyars and Rumanians in Hungary, the Germans and Czechs in Bohemia-Moravia, and the Serbs in Bosnia. Specifically the Poles dominated the Galician Landtag and the provincial council (*Landesausschuss*) and "oppressed" the Ruthenian peasantry. The Ruthenians, ethnically Ukrainians, demanded proportional representation in the provincial Landtag, recognition of their language in courts and schools, civil service jobs, and a university in Lemberg with a Ruthenian faculty and student body. Politics in Galicia consisted of the endless negotiating of "compromises"—giving less than was demanded, and demanding more as soon as one set of demands had been met.

In Hungary the principal nationality quarrel involved Magyars and

Rumanians, the issues being about the same. Immediately after the Balkan wars Count Stephen Tisza negotiated a "compromise" with the Transylvanian party in the Hungarian legislature, but no one was naïve enough to believe that the Magyar government would fulfill the promises promptly or that the Rumanians would not immediately advance a new set of demands. Oftentimes the object of the minority group was to publicize its persecuted position and to win the active sympathy of co-nationals across the frontiers in Rumania or Russia.

Similarly in Bohemia the Czechs had won a preferential position by 1900, but there was never an end to their political demands and complaints. Nothing would satisfy except a restoration of the kingdom of Bohemia with the Czechs "oppressing" the Sudeten Germans. Here the political scene was an unchanging tableau: "German-Czech Compromise," but any compromise concluded by the Czech party leadership with the government in Vienna would result immediately in a party split and the formation of an even more intransigent Czech national party, whose leaders would denounce the "compromise" as a betrayal and advance new and unacceptable demands. The effect of this was to bring the nationality strife into the Reichsrat in Vienna in such a manner as to disrupt and obstruct public business. After the granting of universal manhood suffrage in 1907, the politics of minorities became even more chaotic and obstructive. "Nationality compromises" in the Dual Monarchy is a subject as dreary and never-ending as Home Rule in Britain and electoral reform in France.[20]

The nationalistic discord and distempers, so conspicuous in the Danubian state, produced adverse consequences domestic and foreign. It brought representative government into disrepute, exacerbated national feelings, and gave the impression abroad of a state about to disintegrate from internal strains, and deserving of the epithet "ramshackle Austria." The "oppression" of minorities, real or imaginary, was an abrasive factor in the relations of the Dual Monarchy with its neighbors. Almost every national minority harboring separatist hopes could look abroad for support from fellow nationals living in an

20. The standard works on the ills of the Dual Monarchy are: Oscar Jaszi, *The Dissolution of the Hapsburg Monarchy* (Chicago, 1929); Robert A. Kann, *The Multinational Empire: Nationalism and National Reform in the Hapsburg Monarchy, 1848–1914*, 2 vols. (New York, 1950); Arthur J. May, *The Hapsburg Monarchy, 1867–1914* (Cambridge, Mass., 1951); and the excellent reappraisal of the forces of cohesion and disunity in the *Austrian History Yearbook*, III, pt. 1, 1967.

independent state. Magyar discrimination against Rumanians in Transylvania regularly evoked angry editorials in the Bucharest press and demonstrations in the streets. And the South Slav unity movement promoted by Serbia and backed by Russia was the immediate cause of the Great War.

Nationalism has received more attention from historians than internationalism, national strife more notice than international cooperation. But in Europe before 1914 there was developing such a network of supranational relationships and institutions as to give hope to many that traditional divisions between countries would in the course of the twentieth century sink into insignificance. Not even the most pessimistic predicted that Europe was entering an "era of violence." Developments in five salient fields supported the belief that international cooperation would in time replace national isolation and competition. These areas were economic cooperation, the international labor movement, scientific and cultural cooperation, social legislation and humanitarianism, and the international peace movement. A concrete manifestation of the trend toward cooperation was the impressive number of international organizations that came into existence in the decades immediately preceding the war. Between 1900 and 1914 there were established 304 nongovernmental organizations and 13 governmental bodies.[21] As a period it is unmatched in this respect by any comparable era in our century.

Advances in technology and the growing economic interdependence of nations required coordinated private and governmental action on a diversity of matters—rail transportation and freight forwarding, telegraph and wireless, postal services, control of international rivers, international shipping, navigational charts and signals, public health and police regulations, protection of patents and trademarks, and the enforcement of copyright. The procedure was standardized. Usually one of the smaller states such as Switzerland, with a reputation for disinterested international action, would take the initiative and invite the interested states to send expert representatives to a conference. From their deliberations, if a basis of agreement were developed, a draft convention would emerge which all interested governments

21. F. S. L. Lyons, *Internationalism in Europe, 1815–1914* (Leiden, 1963), p. 14. The number of private international bodies set up between 1815 and 1900 was 164, of governmental organizations 24.

would be asked to ratify. When a specified number had done so, the convention and its prescriptions became internationally binding. An international bureau was usually created to function between conferences or congresses. The most important official organization established in the international field between 1900 and 1914 was the International Institute of Agriculture, founded in 1908 in Rome on the initiative of the indefatigable David Lubin. The International Office of Public Health, established in Paris in 1907 to deal with epidemic diseases such as cholera, had a considerable staff for current operations. The headquarters for most international organizations were located in Paris, Brussels, London, Berlin, Geneva, Rome, and Berne.

The international protection of labor was also an obvious need. But governments were slow to enter this field, which was left largely to private organizations, humane employers, trade unions, and social reform parties. However, in 1900 was founded the International Association for the Protection of Labor, with the International Labor Office as its executive organ. Especially concerned to promote uniformity in labor legislation, this body was so important that in 1919 its duties were taken over by the officially established International Labor Organization. Trade unions began to organize internationally around 1900, and by 1910 twenty-eight trades had established international federations and about 60 percent of all European trade unionists were linked internationally. Periodic congresses were held beginning at Copenhagen in 1901 and ending with the Budapest congress in 1911, at which twenty countries were represented.[22] Closely related to the internationally federated trade unions were the consumers and producers cooperatives which organized the International Cooperative Alliance at a congress held in London in 1895. At the Glasgow conference, held in 1913, more than 4,000 cooperative societies were represented.[23]

International cooperation in business was represented by numerous organizations for the exchange of commercial information, trade statistics, market reports, and tariff rates. Noteworthy was the organization of the International Association of Chambers of Commerce, in 1905, and the International Federation of Permanent Committees for Expositions, in 1908.

22. *Ibid.*, pp. 135–64.
23. *Ibid.*, pp. 193–200.

Of the 400 private or unofficial organizations that came into existence between 1815 and 1914 some were of such weight and importance as to influence directly international relations. Such were, for example, the Interparliamentary Union, the Institute of International Law, and the International Law Association. Among European intellectuals the cosmopolitan tradition was strong and found expression in scientific collaboration in 37 international organizations dealing with pure science and 65 with applied science. Similarly almost every branch of the humanities and the social sciences maintained an international bureau and sponsored periodic conferences. Many of these societies, like the International Union of Esperantist Vegetarians, were doubtless marginal or superfluous. The great upsurge in internationalism is attested by the aggressive propagation of universal languages for easier communication among educated persons. Ordinarily a happy hunting ground for cranks, three such artificial languages were seriously propagated by responsible people—Esperanto, Volapük, and Ido.

Numerous religious, humanitarian, and social reform organizations established international bureaus and sponsored congresses and conferences. The range was broad—temperance leagues, Zionists, missionary societies, the student Christian movement, women's suffrage, public and private charitable societies, and sports organizations, such as the Olympic Games. A landmark in the religious field was the World Missionary Conference held at Edinburgh in 1910, which marked the beginning of the ecumenical movement in the Christian churches.[24]

The capstone of this active propagation of international societies was the establishment in 1910 of a Union of International Associations, sponsored by 137 organizations, with a central office in Brussels. Its principal task, besides coordinating the scheduling of conferences and congresses, was the publication of the *Annuaire de la vie internationale* and the quarterly journal *La Vie Internationale*. The *Annuaire* listed 300 organizations in 1909 and 510 in 1913, which were in their purpose economic, humanitarian, scientific, religious, artistic, and sporting. More than 250 conferences and congresses were scheduled for the years 1912–1914. Obviously much had just been launched, much was not firmly rooted, and much was abandoned or swept away by the war.

24. *Ibid.*, pp. 201–61, 263–85.

But enough of the structure was visible in 1914 to show what kind of a European order men wished to build—if only they had been left in peace!

By its nature international, the peace movement was one of the oldest cooperative enterprises in European public life, and in many respects the last decade of the century was the most successful in the history of the movement. Of the many societies occupying the field, the Universal Peace Congress group was the most prominent and important. Its leadership was recruited from people of the highest social rank with the best credentials—referred to by one of their number as "un groupe du high-life pacifique."[25] These were influential people with entrée to the centers of power and the best sources of information. In their quest for peace through government action—through international law, arbitration, and disarmament—their manifestoes, meetings, and appeals attracted wide attention if not always wide approval. The best-known leader—magnetic, dedicated, untiring—was Bertha von Suttner, an Austrian aristocrat, whose pacifist novel, *Die Waffen Nieder,* was a sensation when published in 1889. Far from a literary masterpiece, the message was greater than the medium. It carried to the target and was translated into eight languages including Russian and Japanese, and circulated more than a million copies.[26]

Bertha von Suttner served for a time as private secretary to Alfred Nobel, the Swedish industrialist whose fortune was derived from the development and manufacture of explosives. She influenced him in the establishment of the Nobel peace prize, and in 1905 she became one of the deserving recipients, the first woman to be so honored. She organized the Austrian Peace Society, which became a model for other national societies, and collaborated closely with Alfred H. Fried, who headed the movement in Germany. She traveled and spoke extensively in the United States, enlisted the interest of Andrew Carnegie in the cause, and made a strong impression on President Theodore Roosevelt. In military circles she was ridiculed and denounced, but she prophesied that "the twentieth century will not end without having witnessed the banishment of the scourge of war from human society." Bertha von

25. *Ibid.,* p. 339.
26. The official English translation, *Lay Down Your Arms,* was published in 1892.

Suttner died in Vienna just one week before the assassination of the Archduke Franz Ferdinand at Sarajevo.[27]

Russia had not been a fertile field for the "war against war." It was therefore a great sensation when Nicholas II, with motives not entirely humanitarian and pacifistic, issued the invitation to the first official peace conference which convened at The Hague in May, 1899. Three principal topics composed the agenda—disarmament, arbitration, and the laws of war. With regard to disarmament nothing concrete was accomplished, but several amendments to the Geneva convention of 1864 on the laws and customs of war were framed and later adopted. With regard to arbitration the conference's work was more enduring— for it resulted in the establishment of the Permanent Court of Arbitration at The Hague, to which governments could voluntarily have recourse for the settlement of disputes. The fact that such a conference had assembled, that it had produced a number of international conventions which were ratified and adopted by the participating governments, was in itself a remarkable advance and a triumph for the friends of international law, mutuality, and peace.[28]

The initiative in convening the second Hague Conference was taken by the Interparliamentary Union, which met at St. Louis in 1904 and there petitioned President Roosevelt to issue the invitation. The Russo-Japanese War intervened, and in 1907 the American President deferred to the Czar, who then issued the invitation. For the first time nearly all the Latin American states attended, forty-five states in all participating. Much the same ground was covered as in the first conference, but the results were disappointingly meager. The limitation of armaments was again shelved—the German delegation generously assuming the onus for this action—and no real advance was made with regard to the delicate matter of compulsory arbitration. Indeed the only positive achievement was the drafting of additional conventions dealing with the use or prohibition of certain weapons, and the general rules of war. Hailed as steps toward "humanizing war," these slight achievements could not disguise the fact that the 1907 conference was an anticlimax to the hopes raised by the first Hague Conference.

27. *Memoirs of Bertha von Suttner: The Records of an Eventful Life*, 2 vols. (Boston, 1910).

28. For summary accounts of the first Hague conference see Carlton J. H. Hayes, *Generation of Materialism*, pp. 322–27; and Lyons, *Internationalism*, pp. 342–54.

The proliferation of international organizations, the dedicated activity of the peace societies, the convening of the Hague conferences, and the establishment by Andrew Carnegie of the Carnegie Endowment for International Peace in 1910 scarcely offset the darkening situation that developed in the relations of the principal powers between 1900 and 1914. Of lesser wars and crises there was an unending succession, and their nature was such that statesmen and molders of opinion were little inclined to seek security in arbitration and disarmament but rather to cultivate the national ego and develop to the limit the nation's potential for war. Europe at the turn of the century was composed of a galaxy of proud, independent, and highly competitive nations led by men whose sense of collective Europe was at the lowest ebb in a century. The international elite was grossly outnumbered by the nationalist multitudes.

4. MILITARISM AND ARMAMENTS

Preparation for war in the interest of national defense was a paramount function of modern states. Excessive emphasis on this aspect of national life was popularly described as "militarism," and this has been cited as one of the basic causes of the First World War. Did the piling up of armaments, the excessive emphasis on military preparedness, the "rattling of sabers" in international negotiations, veritably contribute to the outbreak of war?

From 1815 to 1870 the internal security role of armies was stressed equally with national defense; after 1870 priorities shifted and the external role was emphasized to a greater extent than the internal mission. National security, national honor, and national interest became identified in a unique manner with the armed forces of the national state. As nations became wealthier they spent more on national defense. Science, technology and industrialization contributed to national wealth and made possible a greater diversion of material and human resources to the military establishments. After 1870 universal military service became established throughout the Continent. The superiority of the mass army over the long-term professional army was thought to have been conclusively demonstrated in the wars of 1866 and 1870. In quick succession universal military service was adopted by Austria in 1868, by France in 1872, by Japan in 1873, by Russia in 1874, and by Italy in 1875. By 1900 the system was established in almost all countries except Britain and the United States. Not every male citizen or subject was trained to arms—in Germany only about half of each annual class was inducted and trained before passing into the reserve. Because of her stationary birth rate and devotion to equality, France inducted and trained a higher proportion of each annual class than any other country. Thus more men were trained to arms than ever before, while the untrained were subject to conscription in the event of a national emergency. When fully mobilized under such a system a modernized country could support about 10 percent of its population in the armed forces. No such armed hordes had ever been seen on earth as were mobilized in 1914.[29]

Identifying completely with the national state and inspired by patriotism, men served proudly in the armed forces and taxpayers bore willingly if not joyously the increasing costs of security. How this burden grew and affected the individual taxpayer is shown in the following table.[30] The doubling, in most instances, of the costs of defense be-

PER CAPITA COSTS OF MILITARY AND NAVAL ESTABLISHMENTS
(IN DOLLARS)

	1870	1890	1914
British Empire	3.74	4.03	8.53
France	3.03	4.87	7.33
Germany	1.33	2.95	8.52
Italy	1.44	2.63	3.81
Russia	1.34	1.32	2.58
Austria-Hungary	1.16	1.56	3.48
United States	1.98	1.06	3.20

tween 1890 and 1914 is strikingly apparent, but the individual taxpayer's burden in 1914 was modest compared to today's demands. However, national and individual incomes were proportionately smaller in the prewar period. The actual portion of national income expended on defense by the European powers between 1900 and 1914 averaged slightly less than 5 percent; in 1937, by comparison, it was 9.9 percent. The sharpest increase occurred in the years 1912–1914 with the feverish expansion of military forces that followed the Italo-Turkish and

29. Hoffman Nickerson, *The Armed Horde, 1793–1939* (New York, 1940), pp. 198–200.
30. Quincy Wright, *A Study of War*, 2 vols. (Chicago, 1942), I, 670–71.

Balkan wars. Protests at the "crushing burden of armaments" expressed both the relative pain felt in the pocketbook nerve and the abhorrence of war and violence felt by idealists and pacifists.

Turning now to the military establishments supported by the taxpayers, we observe a considerable uniformity in structure and design. Industrial workers and peasants filled the ranks, peasants and lower middle class supplied the noncommissioned officers, and the upper bourgeoisie and the aristocracy filled the officer corps. During the nineteenth century the military career, hitherto a preserve of the aristocracy, had been opened to the middle class. Even in Germany, by 1873, 62 percent of the infantry lieutenants came from the bourgeoisie, which also supplied the artillery and the technical services. Even greater changes in the social origins of the German officer corps occurred between 1900 and 1914.[31] The stereotype of the Prussian Junker officer and the existence of a high military caste has always been considerably exaggerated.

France came nearest to realizing the idea of a nation in arms—a goal never actually attained by any country in peacetime. France in 1900 was not the defeated and dispirited France of 1870. With the Russian alliance had come a rebirth of confidence, which was soon reinforced by the entente with England. The "new spirit" found expression, after the challenge of the first Moroccan crisis, in significant army reforms—a two-year service term, the expansion of the reserve system, and the elimination of almost all exemptions from military service. Because of her lagging birth rate the French reservoir of young men of military age was much smaller than the German. A massive 80 percent of each annual class had to serve—more than in any other country—and even then to meet the military manpower requirements was a strain. When the Germans greatly expanded their forces in 1913 the French had no choice but to go over to a three-year service term and to extend the military obligation in wartime to twenty-eight annual classes.[32]

31. Karl Demeter, *The German Officer-Corps in Society and State* (New York, 1965), p. 267. Table showing social origins of officers enrolled in higher military training institutes and schools in 1899 and 1913.

32. Of the major powers requiring universal military service, the number under arms per 1,000 of able-bodied males between ages twenty-one and sixty in 1900 was: France, 58.4; Germany, 48; Russia, 43.6; Austria-Hungary, 34; Italy, 30.2. Gerhard Ritter, *Staatskunst und Kreigshandwerk,* 2 vols. (Munich, 1954–1960), II, n. 15. The colonial manpower reserve was an important factor in France's national defense planning. Con-

France was no showcase for militarism. The fear of military dictatorship was deeply ingrained, and a number of safeguards were built into the government structure. In this respect the *Conseil supérieur de la défense nationale* was a symbol of the supremacy of the civil over the military authority. Composed of the minister president as chairman and the ministers of war, marine, foreign affairs, colonies, interior, and finance, it was the highest decision-making body in matters of national defense. Further, to prevent the rise of a Bonaparte, or another Boulanger, a regulation required the concurrence of the cabinet for the assignment of a general to a corps command for more than three successive years. These and other safeguards made it extremely unlikely that the French army could ever become a "state within a state."[33]

Historically Prussia was a military monarchy, and this character was transferred to the Bismarckian Reich. The conflict of civil-military authority, it was thought, could not arise since the Kaiser in his person constitutionally represented the highest military as well as civil authority. Technically as "Oberster Kriegsherr" he would exercise supreme command and at all times coordinate military and political requirements. For a Bismarck and a William I this was a practical constitutional arrangement, but under their successors it was an absurd fantasy. In fact the coordination of political and military policies and actions was never more deficient than under William II between 1890 and 1914. On the role of the military in national life little need be said. The pride that Germans took in military service, the prestige won by the armed forces in the wars of unification, and the constitutional position accorded the military establishment are all well known and documented and require no detailed exposition.[34]

The security of Britain and her empire depended upon a zealously guarded naval supremacy. The challenge to that supremacy is a theme reserved for treatment in later chapters. As for civilian control over the armed forces, that authority had not been challenged in modern times. In public esteem and fiscal support the British army ran a poor second

scription was imposed upon the natives in Tunis and Algeria, and substantial forces were raised on a voluntary basis in France's other colonies.

33. Ritter, *Staatskunst und Kriegshandwerk*, II, 31–34.

34. See Gordon A. Craig, *The Politics of the Prussian Army, 1640–1945* (New York, 1955), Chap. VI, "The State Within a State, 1871–1914"; and Alfred Vagts, *A History of Militarism* (New York, 1937), pp. 197–221.

to the navy. The men in the ranks were regarded and treated as mercenaries; the officer corps provided sinecures for younger sons of the aristocracy and squirearchy. The British army had more officers in proportion to the troop establishment than any other army in Europe. There were no tactical units or staffs trained above regimental level. Such an army was suitable only for coastal defense, garrison duty, and small colonial wars. The Boer War was taken as a national warning by the British. The humiliating reverses shocked the country and stirred political authorities to institute reforms.

The army was greatly improved during the war, but it was the diplomatic developments—Britain's entry into the alliance system—that revealed the dimensions of her military problem: the fashioning, no less, of a modern army capable of participating in a Continental war. Acting on recommendations of the Esher Committee, substantial reforms in the command and administrative structure were accomplished by the Balfour government. The Committee of Imperial Defense, as a high-level coordinating body, and the rudiments of a general staff structure were also established at this time. Further reforms and the erecting of a reserve system on a volunteer basis was the contribution of the Liberal government under the direction of the secretary for war, Richard B. Haldane. The Esher reforms and the raising of the Territorial Force were not achieved without a major propaganda effort appealing to the people to "repent and reform" and to substitute the rifle range for the cricket field.[35]

Like Prussia, the Russian state externally had the appearance of a military monarchy. Supreme authority, military and civil, resided in the person of the Czar, who regularly appeared in uniform and was at all times attended by military adjutants and high military dignitaries. The Russian army, modeled on the German, was a massive force, although its deficiencies were more conspicuous than its strengths. After the adoption of universal military service the periodic induction and release of conscripts created an immense reservoir of mediocre trained manpower. Hence the designation most often applied to the Russian army—the "steam roller." In numbers, including its reserve components, it vastly exceeded any other European army. However, as late as 1909, 38 percent of the recruits were illiterate and the educational

35. Ritter, *Staatskunst und Kreigshandwerk*, II, 46–66; and Cyril Falls, "The Army," in Simon Nowell-Smith (ed.), *Edwardian England* (London, 1964), pp. 517–45.

level of the junior-grade officers was shockingly low. Two basic essentials of an effective national army were lacking: first, a modern armaments industry; second, an educated patriotic people identifying themselves with the state. In fact, the army was not popular with the Russian people, as it was in Germany or in France under the Third Republic. If the Russian army had a historic mission it was the conquest of Austrian Galicia and the "freeing" of the Balkan Slavs. Defeat in the Russo-Japanese War and the revolution of 1905 so reduced Russia's power that any military undertaking was not to be thought of for an extended period. By the Czar's decision, priority was given to restoring the navy; not until 1909, with the appointment of W. A. Sukhomlinov as minister for war, was modernization and expansion of the army taken seriously in hand. Sukhomlinov's reform program was greatly facilitated by the economic prosperity which Russia experienced after 1909. In 1913 Russian rearmament was caught up in the fever of military expansion that gripped the whole continent during the last two years before the war.[36]

No lengthy description of the Austrian military establishment is necessary. Like Germany and Russia, the highest military and civil authority was wielded by the king-emperor, Francis Joseph. Austria was the least militaristic of the continental powers. She inducted and trained the smallest percentage of each annual class of recruits; she ranked fifth in per capita expenditure for defense; and in 1914 she stood in fourth place in the size of her land forces, ahead of Italy and England. In the higher commands Austrians rather than Hungarians predominated; the multinational character of the ranks was accounted a weakness. It cannot be charged that Austria participated in the armaments race. In matters of organization, training, and weaponry the Austrian army stagnated until 1906 when Conrad von Hötzendorf became chief of the general staff. Restless, driving, resourceful, he was the central figure in renovating and expanding the armed forces. Between 1906 and 1914 some of the results of neglect were overcome, but ironically in 1914 the government that resorted to force in the first instance was least prepared to fight a major war.[37]

Returning now to the question with which this section opened: Are

36. Ritter, *Staatskunst und Kriegshandwerk*, II, 98–109; W. A. Sukhomlinov, *Erinnerungen* (Berlin, 1924), pp. 278–82, 330–50.

37. Oskar Regele, *Feldmarschall Conrad* (Vienna, 1955), pp. 150–226, *passim*.

militarism and immense armaments to be accounted important causes of the war of 1914? Indirectly, yes, but not in the way critics of militarism ordinarily think. Armaments themselves cannot cause war. Nations did not normally arm in order to fall upon their neighbors and despoil them but usually because it was felt that national security or national interests were at stake and armaments were the best assurance of survival. It was basically fear of aggression that made men willing to support defense budgets and serve in the armed forces. The great danger to peace lay in the progressive escalation of armaments in the effort to achieve a sense of national security. But what produced a sense of security in one state engendered fear in the neighboring state, which in turn increased its military forces. Thus armaments instead of giving security often bred further insecurity.

More immediate than this psychological factor was the influence of the military on political decisions and the failure to coordinate military planning with foreign policy. This aspect of civil-military relations is a main theme in Gerhard Ritter's monumental *Staatskunst und Kriegshandwerk* (Statesmanship and the Military Craft). He shows how often general staff planning lacked coordination with political policies and, as in 1914, produced some nasty surprises. He concludes that the decisive cause of the failure to preserve peace in 1914 was the subordination of the political establishment to the military leadership.

Retrospectively the years from the beginning of the century to the beginning of the war have been described most frequently as a period of "armed peace," when Europe, by implication, was marked as a City of Destruction. But these ills—nationalism, militarism, imperialism—were they realities or only dark shadows on a bright landscape? Overwhelmingly, contemporary spokesmen for humanity predicted a glorious century of continued progress and improvement. We now turn to some of those aspects of the early twentieth-century scene that inspired such hopes.

Chapter Two

THE PEOPLE AND THE LAND

I. POPULATION AND POPULATION MOVEMENTS

THE world's greatest resource is people; history is the record of how people made themselves at home on this planet and using its resources developed a succession of civilizations and cultures. How many people participated in this planetary enterprise at various stages could never be determined with a great degree of accuracy. Counting and recording were arts that developed relatively late even among advanced peoples. However, by 1900 most European states took a regular census of the population and recorded vital statistics. In previous centuries this was an ecclesiastical obligation, which in the course of the nineteenth century was taken over by the civil authorities, except in Russia, where the Orthodox Church continued to record vital statistics. Population figures and vital statistics, always imperfect and inadequate in the eyes of statisticians and demographers, were certainly more reliable than those of previous centuries. Also, where Europeans colonized, and in Asia and Africa where they governed native populations, an effort was made to enumerate populations and maintain statistics. In 1911, for example, a general census was taken in the British Empire, including the commonwealths and dependencies.[1] But outside Europe and its overseas colonies, the population figures commonly offered for Africa, Asia, and Oceania were at best rough estimates.

The heaviest concentrations of the world's population were in Europe and Asia, with Europe in 1900 estimated to have 24.9 percent and Asia 58.3 percent of the world's population, with the remaining 16.8 percent assigned to North and South America, Oceania, and Africa. The arresting feature of Europe's demographic history was the rapid expansion of population which began in the eighteenth century and continued unabated through the nineteenth and into the twentieth.

---

1. J. A. Baines, "The Census of the Empire," *Journal of the Royal Statistical Society,* new ser., LXXVII (1913–14), 381–441.

The population of Europe was estimated at 266 million in 1850. By 1900 it had reached 401 million, and by 1910 it was estimated at 447 million. Within the European area the rate of growth varied considerably. It was highest in eastern and southeastern Europe and lowest in southwestern Europe—France, Italy, Spain, Portugal. Northwestern Europe fell between the two extremes.[2]

Europe's population continued to increase, although the birth rate declined or remained stationary. Infant mortality and the incidence of fatal disease were strikingly reduced, and under greatly improved conditions of life people lived to an older age. Other favorable factors too were operating: there were no major wars; better food, clothing, and shelter maintained and prolonged life; improved sanitary conditions reduced epidemics; and medical knowledge and services began to affect ever larger segments of the European population. The decline of the death rate—now the major factor in Europe's population growth—was not uniform throughout the Continent. It began to decline in northwestern Europe around the middle of the nineteenth century, in southwestern Europe about 1870, and in eastern Europe about 1900.[3]

Since the population continued to expand—Ireland being the exception—the declining birth rate did not excite alarm. Smaller families met with social approval rather than condemnation. The "small family system" made its appearance first in France, became the established pattern for northwestern Europe after 1875, and for southern and eastern Europe around 1900. The limitation of families does not appear to have been the consequence solely of urbanization or industrialization, or an inevitable accompaniment of a high standard of living. Custom and fashion exerted great influence in the limiting of families.[4] Not until after World War I, with its heavy losses in the productive sectors of the population, did demographers and public leaders begin to speak of a "crisis in population." At last it was appreciated that when

2. A. M. Carr-Saunders, *World Population: Past Growth and Present Trends* (Oxford, 1936), pp. 21, 42; W. F. Willcox (ed.), *International Migrations,* 2 vols. (New York, 1931) II, 78–80; *Handwörterbuch der Staatswissenschaften* (Jena, 1924), II, 688. The estimated increase of population for the principal powers in the decade 1900–1910 was: Russia (1897–1911), 29 percent; Germany, 15; Austria, 8.8; Great Britain, 8.4; France, 1.6. For the continent as a whole the population growth rate reached its highest point—1.4 percent annually—between 1900 and 1914.

3. Carr-Saunders, *World Population,* pp. 78–81; M. R. Reinhard and A. Armengaud, *Historie Générale de la Population Mondiale* (Paris, 1961), pp. 226–304, *passim.*

4. Carr-Saunders, *World Population,* pp. 112–16.

the death rate exceeded the birth rate and the difference was not made up by immigration, the nation faced slow extinction.[5]

Another prevailing aspect of Europe's population history was the heavy drain of people through emigration. "The history of mankind is the history of migrations," says one authority. The figure of 50 million Europeans emigrating between 1846 and 1932 has become established as the measure of the great "Atlantic Migration," since the overwhelming majority made their way to North, Central, and South America. The causes and conditions that inspired this mass movement are generally agreed upon: Europeans were for the first time free to emigrate, they were welcomed as settlers and workers in the thinly populated host countries, economic prospects in the homeland were not favorable, and the movement of emigrants was facilitated by cheap transportation and organized recruiting. Whatever may be advanced as motives by individual emigrants and emigrant groups, the fluctuations of the movement after 1875 closely parallel the curve of economic activity and the business cycle. When the demand for labor and settlers in the areas of immigration was high, people went; when it was slack, they stayed at home. Altogether during this period approximately 19 million Europeans went overseas to seek work or to start a new life on another continent.[6]

This mass exodus is the more striking when it is recalled that the first decade and a half of the twentieth century was a period of booming prosperity and economic growth. Why did these people leave the Continent? No valid generalizations about conditions in Europe can be advanced, other than that the emigrants came from those areas that did not share substantially in the economic upsurge of the prewar years. That is to say, they came primarily from the nonindustrialized areas and those that were overpopulated in relation to their resources and opportunities. The movement was stimulated by the big shipping lines,

5. However, the risk of forecasting on the basis of contemporary trends is shown by the chart in Carr-Saunders, *World Population*, p. 129, projecting the population levels for the principal European countries to 1970. The estimates, made in 1932, gave France, for example, a population of 39 million, a decline of 2 million. In fact, the French census of 1964 enumerated a population of 49 million, and in 1969 it stood at over 50 million!

6. Willcox, *International Migrations*, I, 230–31; Carr-Saunders, *World Population*, p. 51; Reinhard, *Histoire Générale de la Population Mondiale*, pp. 307–16. It is difficult to document, but many young men doubtless emigrated to escape military service.

who competed keenly for the emigrant trade, as the airlines do today for the tourist traffic. When men were free to come and go they did so largely in response to employment opportunities. The flow of emigrants between 1900 and 1914 was, like the commodity market, largely self-regulating.

In the nineteenth century the Europeans who expatriated themselves came mainly from northwestern Europe—the British Isles, Germany, and Scandinavia. Around 1885 emigration from southern and eastern Europe increased massively as the "old emigration" began to slacken, and by 1896 the "new" exceeded the "old." By 1900 Italy led all countries in the number of overseas emigrants, the rate being between three and four hundred thousand annually. The British Isles were second with an annual rate of around 300,000, and Austria-Hungary third, with an annual rate of 237,000. Russia, including Poland, held fourth place, followed by Spain and Portugal. Emigration from other European states was in the low thousands.[7]

Rural areas, where large estates predominated or where parcellation had reduced peasant holdings below the subsistence level, were the largest contributors to the stream of emigration. Southern Italy, Poland, Hungary, and Galicia were typical. The new emigration went to fill a labor market and not primarily to settle on the land. Also much of the emigrant labor was repatriated. International migration was a feature of the growing world economy, and its movements correlated closely with the business cycle.[8]

Where did these people go? Just as others had throughout the preceding century, they went mainly to the United States, although the percentage declined in comparison to previous decades—75 percent in 1901–1905, 65 percent in 1906–1910, and 60 percent in 1911–1915. Increasing numbers now went to the Argentine, Canada, Brazil, Australia, and South Africa.

Another important movement of population which took place under one sovereignty was the emigration from European Russia into Siberia and south central Asia. It is estimated that 3 million Russians emi-

7. Willcox, *International Migrations,* I, 230–31, 232; also H. Bunle and F. Leurence, "Les migrations internationales de 1901 à 1920," *Bulletin de la statistique général de France* (Paris, 1921), October.

8. A. Sartorius von Waltershausen, *Die Entstehung der Weltwirtschaft* (Jena, 1931), pp. 445–46, 448–50; H. Jerome, *Migration and Business Cycles* (New York, 1926).

grated thence in the nineteenth century. But what had been a small stream became a great rush after the turn of the century. Between 1900 and 1914, an estimated 3.5 million Russians seeking land and freedom emigrated beyond the Urals.[9]

Another kind of population movement began after 1880, when large numbers of unskilled workers began to move from one European labor market to another. The statistics for these movements before 1914 are of the vaguest kind. But at least a half-million Poles entered Germany annually as seasonal workers on East Elbian farms, and large numbers of Italians emigrated temporarily to Austria, Switzerland, and France, where they engaged in the heavy work of roadmaking, stevedoring, quarrying, construction, and mining. The French census of 1911 reported more than a million alien workers resident in the country. Compared to the postwar restrictions on the movement and employment of alien labor, the barriers throughout Europe prior to 1914 were insignificant.[10]

The right to emigrate and resettle was regarded in the nineteenth century as a natural right of man. Even the czarist government of Russia conceded to its troublesome and unpopular minorities—Jews, Finns, and Poles—the freedom to emigrate. In general, western and central European states took no positive measures to prohibit or restrict emigration, but almost all governments sought through legislation and administrative measures to control the movement. Although the declared objectives were the protection of their emigrant nationals against exploitation, at times these regulations were administered in a manner to restrict the flow of migrants. A considerable bar to the emigration of young men was the requirement that the military service obligation be satisfied before an exit permit could be secured. Major legislation to regulate emigration was enacted by the Scandinavian countries in the 1860's, by Belgium in 1876, by Switzerland in 1888, by Germany in 1897, by Italy in 1901, and by Hungary in 1903. Such measures, however, served to channel and regulate rather than to check or reduce emigration.[11]

9. Donald W. Treadgold, *The Great Siberian Migration* (Princeton, 1957), pp. 31–35; Carr-Saunders, *World Population*, pp. 54–56; Willcox, *International Migrations*, II, 556–58.

10. Carr-Saunders, *World Population*, pp. 145–46; Willcox, *International Migrations*, II, 220–23; Walterschausen, *Die Entstehung der Weltwirtschaft*, pp. 457–58.

11. J. D. Whelpley, "Control of Emigration in Europe," *North American Review*, CLXXX (1905), 856–67; Elizabeth Cometti, "Trends in Italian Emigration," *Western*

The movement of Jews out of eastern Europe was a dramatic feature of the mass emigrations before 1914. Reliable statistics are lacking until 1899, when the United States Immigration Service began to categorize immigrants by religion and ethnic origin. Between 1899 and 1914, 1,500,000 Jewish immigrants entered the United States, an estimated four-fifths of the total migration. Although Italians exceeded Jews in numbers, the latter had the lowest reemigration rate of all the ethnic groups. Sixty-seven percent of the Jews came from the Russian Pale and Russian Poland, and 14 percent from Austria-Hungary, mainly from the province of Galicia.

The exodus of the Jews from Russia was comparable to the flight of the Irish to the New World after the midcentury famine years. While persecution, pogroms, and religious discrimination played a role, the social structure of the Jewish communities and their worsening economic position appear to have been the principal causes of emigration. With a high percentage of petty tradesmen and workers in the consumer goods industries, especially the clothing and textile trades, the Jews were dependent on a large non-Jewish market for their livelihood. Changing economic and political conditions in eastern Europe began severely to restrict the market in proportion to the number of merchants and craftsmen. This accounts for the high number of small tradesmen and skilled workers in the Jewish emigration, which in its occupational aspect resembled a migration of the clothing industry. This factor also largely determined the conditions of their resettlement and employment. The modern garment industry in western Europe and the United States was largely the creation of these skilled workers and tradesmen.

The migration and resettlement of the Jews also resulted in their transformation from a small-town folk to an urban people, from one whose daily life was regulated minutely by their religion to one that now developed a Jewish lay culture that accorded more and more with their new secular environment. In the period of heaviest movement before 1914 they were welcomed as workers and traders in the expanding economy of Europe and America. While they were perhaps not as assimilable as western European migrant groups, there was nothing

Political Quarterly, XI (1958), 820–34; John Cosa, "A Century of Hungarian Emigration," *American Slavic and East European Review*, XVI (1957), 501–14; R. F. Foerster, *The Italian Emigration of Our Times* (Cambridge, Mass., 1924), pp. 3–43, 474–93.

that foretold the hideous revival of anti-Semitism that led to the mass extermination of the Jewish communities of central and eastern Europe during World War II.[12]

Population trends and problems were subjects of deep interest and extensive comment by contemporary social scientists. Mass emigration and a declining birth rate, offset by a declining death rate, which were revealed whenever a national census was taken, afforded social scientists much material for analysis, argument, and prophecy. Most economists and students of population problems during the nineteenth century took their stand as Malthusians or neo-Malthusians—population increasing geometrically must inevitably overtake a food supply that could be increased only arithmetically. The German social scientists, especially, with their penchant for theoretical formulation and disagreement, argued the pros and cons endlessly in their *Schriften* and *Blätter* and *Abhandlungen*. By 1900, however, the balance definitely tipped against the Malthusian doctrine and its implications for Europe. It was largely from the economic developments during the preceding fifty years that contradictory views received support. England had shown that through industrialization and by exchanging manufactured goods for raw materials and foodstuffs a larger population could be supported with a higher standard of living and culture. The experience of Belgium and Holland as manufacturing and trading countries was also instructive; and Germany's achievements were solidly convincing. Through industry and trade she had supported a rapidly growing population without any appreciable emigration since 1890. Although Malthus' "law" may have been valid for the past, it was not applicable to Europe in its present historical stage, it was asserted. A large population afforded greater possibilities of cooperation, division of labor, and variety and volume in the production of goods. The recent history of Europe, the social scientists insisted, was a refutation of Malthus, for a rising standard of living and culture, rather than impoverishment, had accompanied the progressive increase of population. "With every mouth God sends a pair of hands," expressed the optimistic belief that

12. Willcox, *International Migrations,* II, 471–520; S. M. Dubnow, *The History of the Jews in Russia and Poland,* 3 vols. (Philadelphia, 1920), especially Vol. III; L. P. Gartner, *The Jewish Immigrant in England, 1870–1914* (London, 1960); L. Hersch, *Le Juif errant d'aujourd'hui* (Paris, 1913); Jerome Davis, *The Russian Immigrant* (New York, 1922); S. Joseph, *Jewish Immigration to the United States from 1881 to 1910* (New York, 1914).

a large population could take care of itself quite as well as a small one. But a few economists—among them John Maynard Keynes—were beginning to state the problem in more sophisticated terms: Could the growth rate of an industrial economy be kept in balance with the growth of the population?[13]

2. FOOD AND AGRICULTURE IN WESTERN EUROPE

Maintenance of a healthy agriculture and a thriving population on the land was an avowed policy of every European government. Legislators never ceased praising "the simple, invigorating, and healthful pursuit of agriculture." Positive legislation favoring the agrarian economy was also not lacking. Agricultural schools, experiment stations, cooperative credit and marketing organizations, market roads, and protective tariffs were all subjects of favorable legislation. In France and Germany especially, grain, meat, wine, and fats—whatever was substantially produced at home—were accorded protection by maintaining prices well above the world market level. In general, European agriculture, despite overseas competition, made notable progress toward the end of the century and entered a period of prosperity after 1900, when world prices for primary products turned sharply and continuously upward.

By 1900 it is not incorrect to speak of "scientific agriculture." Under the best systems of cultivation fallow land was eliminated, better crop rotations introduced, more natural and artificial fertilizers employed, and improved implements used. Grain, meat, and fibers were now imported in large quantities from overseas, while specialized agriculture—dairying, poultry raising, market gardening, and fruit growing— was practiced on the land close to large urban and industrialized centers. Agriculture, like industry, became scientific and technical as the channels of communication were developed between the agricultural colleges and experiment stations and the people on the land. Here farm papers and journals and official agricultural bulletins, together with "winter schools" and "continuation schools," met important needs. The most advanced agricultural practices were employed in

13. The positions taken by leading economists and sociologists in Germany, France, England, and Scandinavia are summarized in *Handwörterbuch der Staatswissenschaften*, II, 773–812.

Germany, Scandinavia, Holland, and Belgium. German agriculture, as a model, exerted great influence in eastern and southeastern Europe.

British agriculture, based on a unique land system and unprotected by tariffs, lacked the supports which Continental agriculture generally enjoyed. The issue of protection had been decided at midcentury with the repeal of the Corn Laws. "No taxes on food" was a winning political slogan, especially after the enfranchisement of the urban workers in 1867. In the 1870's the railroads and cargo steamers brought heavy imports of foreign wheat and livestock feed at prices well under British costs of production. Shipping costs were the key to the situation. Between 1873 and 1896, wheat rates from New York to Liverpool declined from twenty-three cents per bushel to three cents; Australian wool rates were halved; and wheat and jute rates from India in 1905 were only a fourth of what they had been in 1873.[14] Added to slumping world prices was the most severe and prolonged drought period of the century (1892–95), which left British agriculture in a desperately depressed state.

Painfully, between 1895 and 1914, English agriculture adjusted to an altered position in the national economy. The concentration of landholding and the tenant leasing system made adjustment difficult until the customary leases were made less restrictive and the tenant farmer given more freedom in utilizing the land. What then occurred was another "agricultural revolution." Much marginal land went out of cultivation or was put to pasture; the crop rotation which had been followed in the eastern counties since the days of "Turnip" Townshend was slowly abandoned; wheat was dropped from the new rotations and specialized agriculture slowly emerged. Britain became more a stock and dairy farm and less a grain farm. The introduction of specialty crops led to a substantial expansion of market gardens, orchards, poultry raising, and potato production. The prominence of fish and chips, Brussels sprouts and cabbage, jams and jellies on the British table dates from the turn of the century.

On the human side, drought and depression, low wages, and backward conditions contributed further to depopulation of the countryside. Small holdings and allotment acts, passed by a concerned parlia-

14. Douglass North, "Ocean Freight Rates and Economic Development, 1750–1913," *Journal of Economic History*, XVIII (1958), 537–47.

ment, were ineffective in checking the drift from the land. Free trade had signified the sacrifice of agriculture and the concentration on industry, commerce, and finance. Britain was the wealthiest country in the world, but she was dependent on her neighbors and the overseas territories for a large part of her food supply. Just before the war she was importing 80 percent of her wheat, 75 percent of her edible fats, and 42 percent of her meat. Since the bread on her table depended on the security of the world's shipping lanes, it is easy to understand how all considerations of national defense were concentrated in her navy.[15]

In contrast to England the rural population of France still outnumbered the urban. The trend favored the city, however—61 percent of the population was rural in 1896, declining to 56 percent in 1911. One of several factors that slowed the shift to urban centers was the widespread ownership of land. The revolutionary land settlement had fixed for a century and a half the structure of French agrarian society. France was still a land of small peasant proprietors, the owner-operator representing about 75 percent of the total number of agriculturists who tilled approximately 60 percent of the land under cultivation, the remainder being rented or sharecropped. The French land system included more than 2 million dwarf holdings of two and a half acres or less. These "scrap holders" represented much of the rural labor force, for such holdings, whether owned or rented, were too small to support a family or occupy a cultivator full time. The trend in size of holdings, however, was toward the reduction of dwarf holdings at one end of the scale and of large holdings at the other. The desirable farm was one that would absorb the labor and give support to an entire family.[16] This was rural France.

The variety of soils and climate in the large agricultural area that constituted France made for a broad spread of crops. Wheat was king, but France had the largest cattle inventory of any European country in

15. N. S. B. Gras, *A History of Agriculture in Europe and America* (New York, 1925), p. 198; Raymond P. Stearns, "Agricultural Adaptation in England, 1875–1900," *Agricultural History*, VI (1932), 130–54; Pierre Besse, *La crise et l'évolution de l'agriculture en Angleterre de 1875 à nos jours* (Paris, 1910), *passim;* and for a wealth of statistical material, *Final Report of the Royal Agricultural Commission, Parliamentary Papers*, XV (1) 1897, pp. 44 ff.

16. *The Land Tenure Systems in Europe* (League of Nations Conference on Rural Life, 1939), pp. 15–16; J. H. Clapham, *Economic Development in France and Germany, 1871–1914* (Cambridge, Eng., 1936), pp. 160–66.

proportion to population; dairying flourished, and the variety and quality of French cheeses were justly famous; the lower Rhone Valley was a spacious fruit and flower farm; and the names of the great wine regions—Burgundy, Bordeaux, Champagne, and Provence—were almost sacred. The specialties of French agriculture were the delight of the *gourmet,* a word that has been justly internationalized.

The French remedy for agricultural depression and foreign competition was a stout tariff wall. Beginning with the Méline tariff of 1892, increasing protection was given to wheat, wine, cattle, meat, and butter, to name only the important items. Agriculture was assisted in other ways. The famed individualism of the French peasant farmer did not keep him from seeking the benefits of cooperation. Indeed before 1914, the French agriculturist had developed, with the support of the state, the full range of cooperatives—credit, marketing, and selling, and cooperatives for the purchase of seed, supplies, implements, and breeding stock.

Owing to the diversity of crops and the small holdings, French farmers used a minimum of modern agricultural machinery. After 1900 France began to import substantial amounts of agricultural implements, but these were mainly harvesting machines—mowers, reapers, binders, and steam threshers—used in the hay and grain harvests because seasonal labor was in short supply. Although intensive and extensive agriculture was maintained at a high level, and the small holdings produced a substantial commercial surplus, France's agriculture was not as productive as its neighbors. The yield per acre in staples such as wheat and potatoes was considerably below the average yield in Germany, Holland, Belgium, and England.[17] But this could be counted a small price to pay for her system of landholding, which gave stability to her rural population, kept the people on the land, controlled the movement to the cities, and gave Frenchmen slight cause to emigrate.

The Italian land system combined the English feature of large estates with peasant-owned, or rented, small holdings. Peasant proprietorship was extensive in Lombardy and Venetia, but the major feature of Italian landholding was the separation of owners and tillers of the soil and its cultivation under ancient forms of agrarian contract, which

17. Clapham, *Economic Development of France and Germany,* pp. 172–73, 177–78.

took the form of rent-paying or crop-sharing tenancies. The richest soil and the best agricultural practices were found in the Po Valley and the Venetian plain. The central mountain region, from north to south, was deforested, eroded, and low in fertility. Southern Italy, Sicily, and Sardinia, except in favored areas, were subject to drought, the soil impoverished, and the cultivation primitive. Here dense and growing population pressed hard upon the food resources of the country. Cereals, oil, and wine were the basic diet, and the cultivation of wheat occupied more than half the arable land. About two-fifths of the cereal production was consumed by the producer and his family, and he strove also to be a self-supplier in oil and wine. On the whole, before 1914, the income from land diminished, the tax structure was unfavorable to agriculture, and the government undertook no major programs to support or revitalize the agrarian economy. A bright spot in the drab picture was the considerable development of agricultural cooperatives in northern and central Italy.[18]

"Latifundia Italiam perdidere" was the judgment pronounced by Pliny upon the great landed estates of Italy in his day. While the latifundia had changed substantially, the problem of large estates still persisted in southern Italy and Sicily. Consisting of tracts from 300 to 1,000 acres in extent, unity of ownership and administration of these ex-fiefs was maintained even though the income might be divided among several heirs in each generation. Absentee landlordism was the rule, the estate or parts of the estate, depending upon its extent, being leased to a speculator (*gabellotto*), who in turn leased to peasant laborers or shepherds and made his profits as a rack-renter. A parliamentary inquiry in 1907–1908 showed that in Sicily 787 landlords owned one-third of the total area of the island, which had a population of 3.5 million. Breaking up the estates and distribution of the holdings to land-hungry peasants appeared a rational solution. But in fact they were so situated that water, sanitation, roads, dwellings, and security were nonexistent on these great tracts, making them wholly unsuitable,

18. The standard contemporary work on Italian agriculture is Ghino Valenti, *L'Italia agricola dal 1861 al 1911* (Rome, 1911); Valenti summarized his treatise in two articles, "Italian Agriculture in the Last Fifty Years," in the *Bulletin of the Bureau of Economic and Social Intelligence,* International Institute of Agriculture (Aug., 1912), pp. 199–213; (Sept., 1912), pp. 165–98; the development of cooperatives is treated by G. Costanzo, "The Principal Types of Agricultural Co-operative Society in Italy," *International Review of Agricultural Economics,* XIV (1923), 50–80.

without an enormous investment of capital, for subdivision into single-family farms.

It was here in southern Italy among the 4.5 million peasants—the majority landless agricultural laborers—that conditions were the most wretched and poverty flourished. Emigration was the principal factor of change in the economic life before 1914, in that it reduced somewhat the supply of labor and raised wages. Emigrant remittances and the return of emigrants bringing their savings further stimulated land purchase and agricultural improvement. However, the total economic and social transformation of these blighted areas, requiring enormous public investment, was not taken seriously in hand until after World War II.[19]

If agricultural conditions were deplorable in southern Italy, they were worse in Spain. Under Roman rule Spain had an estimated population density of 60 to 65 per square kilometer; at the beginning of the twentieth century it was barely 38 per square kilometer. In Roman and Arab times Spain was one of the most productive of the Mediterranean lands in the produce of its soil and mines. The Spaniard in modern times had come close to reducing it to a wasteland. Rural overpopulation, excessive subdivision, and latifundia were elements of a "Mediterranean misery" that Spain shared with southern Italy and Sicily. Two-fifths of the land—52 million acres—went uncultivated. Perceptible depopulation of many rural districts moved the government to attempt remedial action. A "Home Colonization Law" went into effect in 1907. This provided for the colonization of small holders upon state and communal lands, and even held out the prospect of acquiring land by confiscation from private owners. Credit and technical assistance were rendered to these communities through local authorities, and after a term of years, if the tenant's performance was satisfactory, he could acquire title to his holding.[20] The Spanish Home

19. The report of the parliamentary committee on the condition of the peasants in southern Italy and Sicily was published in 1910. A summary and updating of the report was made by the director of the inquiry and published in 1923: G. Lorenzoni, "Latifundia in Sicily and Their Possible Transformation," *International Review of Agricultural Economics,* XIV (1923), 316–49; also Lorenzoni, "Recent Agrarian Policy in Italy and the Problem of Latifundia," *ibid.,* XVI (1925), 89–99. The report of the parliamentary inquiry is also summarized in the *Bulletin of the Bureau of Economic and Social Intelligence* (May, 1912), pp. 191–206.

20. Enrique Alcaraz, "The Problems of Home Colonization in Relation to Credit and Co-operation," *Bulletin of the Bureau of Economic and Social Intelligence* (Dec., 1912), pp. 175–94.

Colonization Act was similar to measures enacted in a number of countries before 1914 in response to the peasant's demand for land, the authorities' concern at rural depopulation, and the large landowner's need for a local labor force.

3. LAND TENURE AND UTILIZATION

"The land problem is not one problem but many problems," writes Folke Dovring, the most recent scholar to examine Europe's agricultural position in the twentieth century.[21] Two problems of utilization were outstanding: (1) the social and economic validity of large estates; (2) dwarf holdings and dispersed plots where peasant ownership predominated. These two problems could exist as separated regional phenomena or as interdependent problems in the same region. The areas of large landed estates and overcrowded peasant villages lay east of the Elbe, in East and West Prussia, Pomerania, and Silesia; in Posen, Austrian Galicia, and the Baltic provinces; in parts of Bohemia-Moravia, in Hungary, and in Rumania. In the liberal tenets of the nineteenth century it was firmly established that individual proprietorship of land was superior to any form of tenancy, that the best worker was he who worked for himself. This was reinforced by a kind of social romanticism which found in peasant society the prototype of all human society. (Rousseau was probably its principal source.) The liquidation of manorial servitudes in favor of the peasant occupier was the solution of the land question offered by the French Revolution and in the subsequent land reform legislation of the nineteenth century. Where peasant tenures were numerous and of the heritable type, the serf emerged as an independent proprietor; where estates were large and peasant tenures limited, the estate owner's unencumbered hold on the land was confirmed.

In the literature of agrarian reform much was written about the desirability of breaking up big estates and converting them to family-sized holdings of from 30 to 100 acres, which was held to be sufficient to support a farm family and absorb its labor. Except in the Scandinavian countries and in Ireland, where the compelling force was national and political, little was attempted and even less was accomplished before 1914.[22] From the areas of great estates and latifundia came the streams of people seeking in the cities and overseas the decent

21. *Land and Labor in Europe, 1900–1950* (The Hague, 1956), p. 352.
22. Dovring, *Land and Labor in Europe*, pp. 222–42.

existence that was denied them in the cramped, poverty-stricken peasant villages.

Linked with the problem of creating and maintaining family-size farms as a basis of agrarian society was the existence of fragmented and dispersed holdings in the areas where peasant farming already predominated. This condition probably owed more to inheritance than to the medieval manor system. In accordance with Roman law and the Code Napoléon all children had equal rights in regard to the inheritance of their father's property. This principle contributed to the fragmentation of peasant holdings in a large part of central, western, and southern Europe. Most land legislation accompanying serf emancipation provided for the consolidation of peasant holdings. In Scandinavia consolidation was effected in the course of the nineteenth century; in the Netherlands and Belgium the problem was manageable; and the existence of 2 million dwarf holdings in France bespoke the necessity of consolidation as well as the disinclination to act. Prussian land legislation produced good results in consolidating holdings in north Germany, but fragmentation was a serious matter in Rheinland-Pfalz, Hesse, Württemberg, and parts of Bavaria. In Austria the problem was serious in Upper and Lower Austria, Slovenia, Dalmatia, Bohemia, Galicia, and Bukowina.

Land surveys revealing ownership structure were rare, but a survey made in Austria in 1870 showed only 20 percent of the farms in consolidated blocks. Another census of landholding made in 1902, based on the land registers initiated by Joseph II, showed approximately 56.9 million parcels of land divided among 5.81 million landholders, or about ten parcels per person. The cost and inconvenience of cultivating a farm divided into ten parts and dispersed over an entire commune can be imagined. The shape of many of these holdings, owing to the old strip system, was fantastic. Strips of land four meters wide and four kilometers long were actually on the registers. In Slovenia and Dalmatia the land might belong to one holder, the fruit trees to another, and the cover crop to a third. A comprehensive law for the consolidation and redistribution of land in the rural communes was enacted in Austria in 1883. Two-thirds of the landowners in the commune had to agree before the state would proceed with a general consolidation. The cost of surveying was high, the peasants conservative, and the officials cautious, which is to say that progress was slow in ending the uneconomic distribution and utilization of the land.[23] In Austria and in other states of central Europe consolidation and redistribution of holdings in the village communes resembled in some respects a Penelope's web— what was accomplished in one generation was partially undone through inheritance in the next. In the opinion of one authority in agricultural economics, one-third of Europe's agricultural land at midpoint in the twentieth century was again in need of consolidation.

4. THE AGRICULTURAL LABORER

In Prussia east of the Elbe, large entailed estates, administered by the owner or his bailiff, occupied up to 50 percent of the arable land. Scientific methods with substantial investment of capital made these enterprises agriculturally the most productive in Europe. Rye, wheat, oats, potatoes, sugar and fodder beets, and livestock were the principal products. Here were produced the large commercial surpluses that fed the cities.

Land, labor, and capital were the three ingredients of commercialized agriculture. Land was inherited and capital was available in sufficient amounts during this period of rising prices and productivity. Labor was the most difficult element, not to procure, but to manage. The life of the laborer on the estates devoted to the raising of commercial crops was wholly different from that of his cousin in the factory or in the city. Statistics of hours and wages, of employment and unemployment, and of health and accidents among farm workers do not really tell us much about their personal life. Among farm laborers personal documents are exceedingly rare, even rarer than among those who have stood at the bench or tended the machine. Such a rare document is the memoir written by Franz Rehbein, a self-educated agricultural laborer who, after twenty years as a hired worker on farms and estates in north Germany, eventually became a Social Democratic party official. Although his memoirs, *The Life of a Farm Laborer,* are decorated with socialist formulations and clichés, they are in their solid factual descriptions a rare cultural document of the times.

Rehbein was the son of a poverty-pinched tailor in a small village in

23. Dovring, *Land and Labor in Europe,* pp. 36–60; H. G. Bote, *Bodenzersplitterung und ihr Einfluss auf die betriebswirtschaftlichen Verhältnisse in Deutschland* (Kiel, 1928), pp. 131 ff.; "Restriping of Land in Austria," *Bulletin of the Bureau of Social and Economic Intelligence* (Apr., 1912), pp. 205–14.

eastern Pomerania. The family of six children was left destitute when the father died of tuberculosis without ever having had the attention of a physician. In eastern Pomerania noble estates alternated with helot villages; these were the hereditary lands of the Junker families of Puttkammer, Zitzewitz, Köller, Glasenapp, and Bonin. As the oldest son in the family, Franz Rehbein worked first with his mother in the potato harvest on a large neighborhood estate and when the harvest was over took service as a "farm boy." Children in such families, as his mother sadly remarked, had to be pushed out of the nest as soon as they could "lift a finger." The following year, at age fourteen, the boy signed with a labor recruiter for summer work in a sugar refinery in Holstein. With a large party of local laborers—men and women—he joined the annual exodus of migrant workers from the poverty-stricken villages in the east to west Germany where wages were better and employment more plentiful. These "Saxon migrants" (*Sachsengänger*), since all Germany west of the Elbe was Saxony to them, were replaced for the season by migrant workers from Poland, Galicia, and Hungary, who were content to earn the lower wages paid in East Elbia because there was nothing at all to be earned at home. Told by a fellow migrant that he couldn't possibly do the work that would be required of him as an oxen driver at the sugar factory, and would go home with empty pockets, Franz slipped away from the gang chief in the Hamburg railway station and eventually found summer employment as a cowherd with a "bog farmer" in western Holstein. Thereafter, for twenty years he worked for well-to-do farmers and estate owners in Holstein and Mecklenburg, in the section known as the "Counts' Corner" (*Grafenecke*), where the Bülows, Rantzaus, Reventlows, and Schulenburgs had their patrimonial estates.

Not all his employers and supervisors were stereotyped "oppressors of labor," and all but one or two are described with considerable sympathy and understanding. The rural employer types are well drawn, from the farm owner who was notoriously tight-fisted in money matters—"not in taking it in but in giving it out"—to the manager's wife who incessantly praised the hired men they had last year, "who always ate a very light breakfast." For each position, Rehbein describes the terms of employment, the long hours of work, the unhygienic quarters, the treatment of workers by the owner or supervisor, and the food provided—a monotonous diet of buckwheat groats ("grits"), skim milk, fat bacon, black bread, potatoes, and a barely edible spread, half butter and half margarine. Workers hired for the season or the year and resident on the estate were subject to the antiquated Prussian Servant's Code (*Gesindeordnung*), which subordinated the workers in the strictest manner to the will and whims of the owner or manager. To leave the estate in the evening for a visit to the neighboring village required the overseer's permission. If conditions became intolerable and the worker left before expiration of his contract, he could be arrested and returned to the estate and his pay docked for the days he was absent. A dishonest employer could overcharge for clothing and personal purchases, and in one position Rehbein lost an entire year's wages when the farmer charged him with negligence resulting in the loss of a valuable farm animal. Against such chicanery the "servant" had no recourse at law; nor did this class of worker—numbering more than a million in Germany—have sickness or accident insurance or retirement benefits.

Three years of recruit training and service in the cavalry in Metz was an unenjoyable experience for Rehbein. This interruption of his life raised the question of whether as a farm worker, with no prospect of bettering his position, he should return to the land or join the ranks of unskilled labor in some kind of industrial employment. By now an experienced farm worker, he chose the country and returned to Holstein. At age thirty he married a farm girl in service, only, as was customary, when it became necessary to legalize their relationship before the birth of the first of four children. Residing now in a rural village, Rehbein became a "free" day laborer, which meant that he must earn in daily wages during the spring, summer, and autumn sufficient money to carry his family through the usual period of winter unemployment. Ironical is his description of a meeting of the village farm laborers, called by the county manager (*Landrat*) and the local pastor, to organize a savings society for farm workers—a savings society among heads of families whose annual income never exceeded $150 per year! But this was an age, we must remember, in which everyone was normally poor and the whole bent of economic thought was directed toward saving rather than spending and consumption.

Rehbein's career as a farm laborer ended on a Sunday afternoon in September, when his right arm was mangled in a steam-driven threshing machine and subsequently amputated. At this point, with no workmen's compensation, the certainty of a destitute family, and his wife expecting their fourth child within the week, his memoir also ends.[24]

5. LAND REFORM IN RUSSIA

Compared to enclosures in England, or serf emancipation in central Europe, or the freeing of the slaves in the United States, the emancipation of the Russian serfs and the related land settlement must be accounted statesmanlike and generous. The peasants received about three-fourths of the land which they had cultivated previously as serfs, the landlords were indemnified for the ceded lands, and the state assumed the considerable debt thus created, which was to be liquidated by peasant redemption dues over a period of forty-nine years. To ensure payment of dues and taxes, titles to the peasant lands were vested in the village commune (*mir*) and the lands made inalienable and unmortgagable. For the authority of the landlord over the serf was substituted the collective authority of the communal elders and the heads of the peasant households. By the czarist authorities the land settlement was considered adequate to prevent the peasant households from falling into destitution or decay. The allocation of the communal lands followed customs which had prevailed in the past in many parts of Europe. In the western provinces the cultivated holdings were traditionally hereditary in the households, but in the remainder of the country, which included four-fifths of the peasant families, repartitional tenure prevailed. Here, meadow and pasture were held communally while the farming plots were reallocated at periodic intervals to adjust to the number of households and their changing size. Repartition, it was said, took land from the dead and gave it to the living.

The land settlement of 1861–1864 made no provision for a large increase in population. In the 1860's the population of European Russia was given at 50 million, and in 1914 it was estimated at 103 million. Since life was largely communal and it was the responsibility of the village council to provide land according to the size of households, there were no voluntary restraints on size of families of the kind that a private property system imposed. "Not enough land" was a peasant

24. Franz Rehbein, *Das Leben eines Landarbeiters* (Jena, 1911). Rehbein later found employment as a minor official in the Social Democratic party.

complaint from the day of emancipation. And to say "Russian peasant" was to evoke the phrase "land hunger." An American grain expert traveling in south Russia in 1906 put it thus: "This innocent child of nature . . . knows nothing but land. . . . The only hope that he has, the only light that he can see, the only thing that he can understand, is land. Therefore the State lands, the Crown lands, and those of the big estates haunt the peasant. He wants them with an innocent kind of want, much as cattle hunger for the choicest grass and will get it, too, unless the fence proves too strong."[25]

Shortage of land was not entirely an illusion, but stating Russia's agrarian problem solely in terms of "too little land and too many people," as was done by the peasants and the representatives of peasant interests, was a distortion of reality. At the time of emancipation the average family allotment on the lower Volga was 85 to 90 acres, in the black soil belt 40 acres, and west of the Dnieper 23 to 25 acres.[26] Population growth brought the average allotment down to 30 acres per family, but between 1861 and 1900 the peasants acquired by purchase through the Peasant Land Bank several million acres from estate owners and public bodies. They also farmed a large part of the private estate land on a share or rental basis. In fact, in 1900 the ratio of land to individual agriculturist was still higher in Russia than in any other European country except England. Overall, the land-man ratio was 22.5 acres; and in the black soil region it was 17.5. These ratios compare with 16.5 acres in Scandinavia, 15.25 in France, 16.87 in Germany, 13.5 in Hungary, and 6.75 in Italy.[27] Obviously the peasant problem was not solely lack of land.

What then accounts for the impoverished condition of the peasantry and what was the source of the discontent that set off the revolution in 1905? The impoverishment of the peasantry and the deficiencies of Russian agriculture were the consequences, first, of the heavy tax burden imposed on the peasants; second, the communal system of

25. R. E. Smith, *Wheat Fields and Markets of the World* (St. Louis, 1908), pp. 41–42. But this observer penetrated to the heart of the matter when he commented that the peasants might easily increase the yields produced on their present holdings, and that this would be better than having a little more land to cultivate.

26. V. P. Timoshenko, *Agricultural Russia and the Wheat Problem* (Stanford, 1932), pp. 50–51, 54–56.

27. Dovring, *Land and Labor in Europe*, pp. 66–67, 77, statistical tables on "Land and Manpower."

landholding and farming; and third, the universal backwardness of agricultural techniques.

Crushing financial burdens were placed on the peasantry by the state. They were obligated for the redemption dues, they paid higher taxes than the gentry, they paid zemstvo taxes for local improvements, and they bore the main burden of indirect taxes and import duties on vodka, sugar, kerosene, tobacco, matches, tea, cotton, iron, and other products. A series of poor crops, and arrears of payments and taxes piled up with little prospect of payment. When the redemption dues were canceled in 1905–1906, the delinquent payments exceeded the original total debt because of accumulated interest on arrears at 6 percent![28]

The communal system of landholding and farming presented many features reminiscent of the manorial regime of the late Middle Ages. The fields were unfenced, divided generally into strips, and the peasant holdings were dispersed. Hay and meadow lands were divided in the same manner, and agricultural processes had to be coordinated among all the villagers as the common right of pasturage rested upon the stubble land and the mowed fields. When redistribution of plots was practiced there was no incentive to conserve or improve fertility or make any other kind of investment in the land. To grow a special crop outside the cycle prescribed by the village assembly was impossible. Custom dictated when all should sow and all should reap, and when the village livestock was to be put upon the stubble.

Russia was the largest grain-growing country in the world. From 70 to 80 percent of the crop land was devoted to wheat, rye, barley, and oats. And it might be noted that this was the type of culture most unsuited to small-plot farming in densely populated regions. Generally the three-field system of grain growing was practiced: winter wheat one year, a spring-seeded grain the next, and fallow the third. The more complicated but productive rotations practiced in the rest of Europe—green crops, root crops, and oilseeds—were extremely rare. Specialized agriculture—dairying, poultry raising, market gardening, and fruit—was scarcely practiced at all, and the cattle and pig inventories were proportionately the lowest in Europe. Although Russia had

---

28. G. T. Robinson, *Rural Russia Under the Old Regime* (New York, 1949), pp. 96, 111. Robinson thinks that the most telling evidence for the real distress of the peasantry was the continued accumulation of arrears in dues and taxes.

rich lands especially suitable for grain growing, the yields per acre from peasant farming were only half those of central and western Europe.[29] That "poor people have poor ways" is a country saying, and it aptly applied to peasant agriculture in Russia. There were simply too many peasants who were content, in the words of Bernard Pares, "to scratch the ground with a wooden plow and sit down to live off whatever the harvest may give him."[30] Crushing taxation, inferior technical methods, communal restraints, and lack of capital and initiative, rather than lack of land, impoverished Russia's rural masses.

In 1902, when serious peasant disorders—looting of grain and timber, illegal pasturing, arson, and withholding of rent—broke out in the provinces of Kharkov and Poltava, three separate official commissions were already investigating aspects of the peasant agrarian problem. These focused attention on the institution of the *mir* and the communal basis of peasant society. Suddenly it was agreed by local officials, priests, teachers, and peasant elders that the time had come to abolish the restrictive rural commune. Industrialists also regarded the worker's link to the *mir* as a hindrance to the permanent organization of labor in industry—the peasant worker was always going back to the country to visit his family, or to help with the spring sowing, the summer haying, or the fall harvest. Thus the winds of change were stirring in the Russian countryside when the disasters of the Russo-Japanese War turned them into a hurricane.

Serious disorders broke out in February, 1905, in the province of Kursk south of Moscow, and "soon the greatest agrarian disturbance since the days of Pugachev was under way."[31] Altogether forty-seven of the fifty provinces of European Russia were affected, the regions of the lower Volga and the central black belt suffering most. Beginning with illegal timber cutting, plundering of barns, theft of livestock, and withholding of rent and labor, the movement became more violent and destructive as it spread, reaching a climax in November. Since the peasants were unarmed, they used the torch as their principal weapon "to smoke out the landlords." Peasant violence, fueled with much vodka, was more destructive of property than of lives, as landlords and

29. Timoshenko, *Agricultural Russia and the Wheat Problem*, p. 276.
30. *Russia and Reform* (London, 1907), pp. 442–43.
31. Robinson, *Rural Russia Under the Old Regime*, p. 155.

bailiffs finding themselves without protection fled from the areas of turmoil and danger. Disturbances slackened during the winter but began again in the spring. With the return of the armed forces from the Far East, military control was imposed in the most turbulent districts. Special military field courts were established where the provincial governors requested it, and summary executions by hanging became everyday occurrences. During the next eighteen months more than 3,000 persons were executed under court orders. How many were killed in the punitive actions carried out by troops is not known. Twenty thousand peasants were banished to northern Siberia.[32]

The carrot as well as the noose was used to master the agrarian revolt. In November, 1905, the government announced cancellation of the redemption debt and promised that more land would be made available to the peasantry. Subsequently the Nobles' Congress, the congresses of zemstvos and municipalities, the All-Russian Peasants Union, and the revolutionary parties all endorsed agrarian reform and advanced conflicting proposals as to how the peasants should be given more land and on what terms. This issue deadlocked the government and the first Duma.

P. A. Stolypin, appointed prime minister in June, 1906, cut the Gordian knot when he dismissed the Duma and initiated the program of land reform which is associated with his name. Cold as a fish, ruthless and self-confident, Stolypin undertook to modernize Russian agrarian society as S. Y. Witte had sought to modernize industry and business. His program had these features: the replacement of the communal land system by individual land ownership; the consolidation of plots to form unitary farms and facilitate better cultivation; the sale of more land to the peasants; and a massive program of peasant emigration to Siberia. Of the measures relating to landed property, the decree of November, 1906, and the law of June, 1910, which embodied and expanded the earlier decrees, were the most important. They provided, first, that in communes in which hereditary household tenure prevailed the peasants would acquire title to the land they tilled; second, where periodic redistribution was practiced a majority vote by the village assembly could dissolve the commune and convert the land to private ownership; third, any peasant as an individual could withdraw from

32. *Ibid.*, pp. 197–98.

the *mir* and secure title to his holding; finally, by majority vote the members of the commune could effect the exchange and consolidation of plots to form unitary farms. Land commissions, with the state bearing the considerable cost of surveying, were authorized to carry out the work of consolidation. As part of the package, more land from state and imperial domains was made available and the Peasant Land Bank expanded its purchase of private holdings for resale to individual cultivators.

Judgments on the Stolypin program vary widely. Marxist and Populist historians describe it as a failure or minimize the achievements. However, it cannot be denied that the Stolypin laws revolutionized land tenure in Russia. The work of surveying, the preparation of registers, and the issuance of title deeds were time-consuming; but from 1906 to 1916 between seven and eight million households—approximately two-thirds—converted their holdings from communal to private property. The consolidation of plots was more complicated, costly, and time-consuming; and in some areas encountered peasant opposition. However, by 1916 a million and a quarter households—about one-tenth—had exchanged their dispersed plots for consolidated holdings. There is no doubt that the peasant response was positive, and there was real point to Stolypin's remark to Bernard Pares in 1910 that land reform "cannot now be stopped with cannon."[33] A fair and final judgment on the Stolypin reforms might be that they were not "too little" but that they were "too late."[34]

One right which the peasant acquired in 1906, which he had never before possessed, was the unrestricted right of removal and resettlement. He could now sell his allotment in the village and take a new holding elsewhere. Many dwarf holders, especially, took advantage of

---

33. Treadgold, *The Great Siberian Migration*, p. 157.

34. The following cover the facts and appraise the Stolypin reforms: Robinson, *Rural Russia Under the Old Regime*, Chap. XI; G. Pavlovsky, *Agricultural Russia on the Eve of the Revolution* (London, 1930); A. D. Bilimovich, "The Land Settlement in Russia and the War," in A. N. Antsiferov and others, *Russian Agriculture During the War* (New Haven, 1930), pp. 305–43; and the excellent summary in Treadgold, *The Great Siberian Migration*, pp. 36–63; P. I. Liashchenko, *History of the National Economy of Russia* (New York, 1949), pp. 729–53, gives the Marxist-Leninist interpretation. On the gigantic task of land consolidation—what the Germans aptly call *Flurbereinigung* (field-clearing)—see the excellent contemporary article, without ideological tears, "General Outline of the New Russian Land Reforms," in *Bulletin of Economic and Social Intelligence* (Nov., 1913), pp. 119–34; (Jan., 1914), pp. 132–60.

this opportunity. With a view to relieving just such rural pressures the Stolypin government promoted a program of emigration and settlement on the vacant agricultural lands of Siberia. The peasant response was impressive. Between 1906 and 1914 nearly 3 million peasant farmers moved with government help from the most congested provinces to the new lands in Siberia. The movement reached its peak in 1908–1909, when more than 700,000 in each year made the move.[35] Thereafter, until the war, the average was 300,000 annually. "Land of our own" was a powerful magnet to the Siberian emigrant, as it was to the American homesteader in Washington, Idaho, and Montana.

Insofar as the agrarian structure was concerned, the trend in Russia after 1905 paralleled that in central and western Europe—a reduction of dwarf holdings at one end of the scale and a decline in the area of large farms at the other; a rational consolidation of plots and an increase in the middle range of enterprises, which produced for a special market and were of a size to support a family and fully employ its labor. The course was visibly toward what Marxists disparagingly described as the "small commercial kulak farm." The land reform program also had social and political goals; Stolypin hoped that it would bring social stability to the mass of the people, inculcate greater respect for what was "mine and thine," and by creating a conservative class of peasant proprietors give the monarchy and the state a stronger foundation.

For Russian agriculture the period 1907–1914 was one of significant progress and increasing prosperity. Land reform and resettlement, new products and improved techniques, larger capital investment, and the general rise in world prices all combined to lift Russian agriculture to new levels of prosperity. An immense work was accomplished by the zemstvos during this period in the areas of education, public health, and the spread of agricultural knowledge. Beginning in the western provinces the primitive three-course grain cycle was gradually replaced by modern rotations, new crops, and more intensive cultivation. The improved techniques found application on peasant farms as well as on large estates. The result of these improvements is seen in the substantial increase in production of such crops as sugar and fodder beets, potatoes, sunflower seed, flax fiber, and clover. In fact, Russian agricul-

35. Antsiferov, *Russian Agriculture During the War*, pp. 322–24; Treadgold, *The Great Siberian Migration*, pp. 146–49, 153–83.

ture reached a level of production in 1913 which had not been restored twenty-five years later.[36]

A significant index of modernization and capital investment in Russian agriculture was the increased purchase and use of improved farm implements and machinery. Domestic production of agricultural machinery rose in value from 10 million rubles in 1900 to 60 million in 1913, and imports, mainly from Germany, England, and the United States, increased from 15.9 million rubles in 1900 to 59.5 million in 1912. Farm machinery was one of the most rapidly expanding industries in prewar Russia. In 1908 a representative of the U.S. Department of Commerce visited the largest implement-producing company, located in Kharkov. It employed 1,200 men, the capital was German, the machinery and tools American, and "the general manager was a wide-awake, pushing, Vienna-born Englishman."[37]

Despite increasing crop diversification, Russia remained basically a grain-producing country, covering with her large export surplus the increasing requirements of western Europe. As a wheat exporter she took the lead from the United States in 1904–1905, and in the decade before the war she was the largest net exporter of wheat, barley, oats, and rye. Russia furnished to the export market nearly three-fourths of the barley, nearly half the oats, a third of the rye, and one-fourth of the wheat. England, Germany, Italy, and the Netherlands were the principal buyers.[38] When the war closed the door of the Russian granary in 1914, the event touched off a scramble for supplies in the world's grain markets such as had never been seen before.

36. Antsiferov, *Russian Agriculture During the War*, pp. 45–82; Timoshenko, *Agricultural Russia and the Wheat Problem*, pp. 139–50.

37. Roland R. Dennis, *American Agricultural Implements in Europe, Asia, and Africa* (Washington, D.C., 1909), p. 69; Timoshenko, *Agricultural Russia*, pp. 212–13; Arnold Bonwetsch, *Der Handel mit landwirtschaftlichen Maschinen und Geräten in Russland vor dem Kriege* (Berlin, 1921).

38. Timoshenko, *Agricultural Russia*, pp. 479–86. In the period 1909–13, the peasant farms produced four-fifths of the wheat marketed, the large estates one-fifth.

Chapter Three

TECHNOLOGY AND ECONOMIC GROWTH

I. THE RETURN OF PROSPERITY

IN the opinion of economic and business leaders the best thing about the nineteenth century was its passing; the prospects for the new century seemed much brighter. From 1873 to 1896 the national economies, although they had shown considerable growth, were more often in the doldrums. Throughout this period of the Great Depression—the name it bore until it was robbed of this distinction by a greater depression—the long-range trend of prices for primary products and manufactured goods was steadily downward; land values, interest rates, and wages also declined. Money was tight, the investment rate low, and each time, as in the early eighties and early nineties, when it seemed that an upward trend was beginning, hopes were blighted by a new slump. However, in 1896 a rising trend set in, and by the turn of the century there were sanguine indications that the corner had been turned and a sustained advance had begun. Except for the brief recessions of 1901 and 1908, the period was marked by advancing prices, rising money wages, full employment, and an economic growth rate that was unsurpassed until the 1950's.

In consequence of the Great Depression social and economic affairs had been forced upon the attention of governments and political parties to a degree that had not prevailed before. Mr. Gladstone spoke for an older generation when he declared that unemployment was a subject not within the competence of the House of Commons. The Great Depression weakened the laissez-faire spirit, created the atmosphere in which socialism took deep root among industrial workers, led to the abandonment of free trade and resort to protection, encouraged the expansion of municipal and state ownership, and forced upon the state the role of defender of many of the exposed interests and classes. In all this there was of course no central planning but a great many piecemeal expedients designed to break out of the long economic decline

54

and gain a new buoyancy—tariffs, tax relief, and support of economic ventures overseas.[1]

By 1900 Europe was the center of a booming world economy. The export of capital from western Europe, which had been at a low ebb during the Great Depression, was resumed at a higher rate, and between 1904 and 1914 reached massive proportions. Although some of this golden flow was channeled to unproductive government loans, armaments, and sultans' palaces, the greater part—certainly more than 60 percent—went into the development of natural resources, transportation, electrical utilities, petroleum, trade, and local industries. European investors considered carefully the factors of security and profit before laying out their money—although they might take a "flyer" in something like Bay State Gas or the San Antonio Land and Irrigation Company. When we observe the difficulties encountered today in providing underdeveloped countries with needed capital, we must conclude that the performance of the pre-1914 "parasitic capitalist" is much in need of reevaluation.

Basic to the economic boom, of course, was the increase in population, a rising standard of living, and a soaring demand for all kinds of goods and services. If we were to single out one industry that was a pacemaker, one that demanded large amounts of capital, it would be the electrical industry—lighting, municipal transportation, and power. Every city of any significant size was made unsightly by marching rows of power poles and transformers, festoons of wire, clattering trolley cars, and thundering undergrounds. In the quarter-century before 1914 the electrical industry played the role in economic growth that the railroad played in the nineteenth century. Older industries, such as textiles, coal and steel, shipbuilding and machinery, were greatly quickened and expanded. In the consumer goods industries the pacemakers were soap and margarine. The added thrust of the oil industry, of the exciting new motorcar industry, of rubber products, and of chemicals and pharmaceuticals registered sharply on the chart of economic growth. Gold mining in South Africa, rubber plantations in Malaya and the East Indies, oil wells, refineries, and storage plants

---

1. Hans Rosenberg, "Political and Social Consequences of the Great Depression of 1873–1896 in Central Europe," *Economic History Review*, XIII (1943), 58–73; A. E. Munson, "The Great Depression in Britain, 1873–1896: A Reappraisal," *Journal of Economic History*, XX (1959), 199–228.

in Mexico and the Caribbean, and everywhere the extension of railway lines—all were promising and drew heavily on the capital resources of Europe. Although Thomas Mann chronicled, in this period, the decline and fall of the merchant House of Buddenbrooks, and Galsworthy the disintegration of the Forsytes, we should remember that this decade saw also the blooming of the house of Siemens, of Lever, Bosch, Mond, and Rockefeller, and of Nobel, Solvay, and Du Pont.

2. ELECTRICITY COMES OF AGE

At the turn of the century Europe was experiencing one of those discontinuous leaps forward in technology and invention which had marked industrial progress since the mid-eighteenth century. Electricity, petroleum for lighting and fuel, the internal combustion engine, the automobile and the airplane, refrigeration, the wireless telegraph, and motion pictures appeared as marvels of applied science affecting directly the lives of millions of the earth's inhabitants.

The foundations of the electrical industry were laid between 1880 and 1900, but practical application had developed slowly. Werner Siemens proudly announced, as early as 1867, that "Technical science now has the means of generating electric current of unlimited strength, cheaply and conveniently, at any place where driving power is available."[2] The first practical application, after the telegraph and telephone, was in arc lighting in railway stations, arcades, streets, and public buildings. Edison's incandescent electric light was the sensation of the international Electrical Exhibition in Paris in 1881, and in the same year Siemens put in operation the first experimental electric tramway in Lichterfelde, a suburb of Berlin. Emil Rathenau, an imaginative young engineer, met Edison at the Paris exhibition and entered into an agreement with him to form a German Edison Company to develop electric lighting, using American patents and experience. Rathenau's company worked closely with the Siemens firm, principal manufacturer of telegraphic equipment, in the early years of their enterprise. Rathenau developed contracts and franchises for electric lighting while Siemens manufactured the equipment and tended to the installation. In 1886, Rathenau and his associates severed their ties

2. Georg Siemens, *History of the House of Siemens,* 2 vols. (Freiburg, 1957), I, 79. The occasion was his appearance before the Berlin Academy of Sciences, where he described his perfected electromagnetic generator.

with Edison and organized the Allgemeine Elektrizitäts Gesellschaft (AEG) as the principal promoter of central power stations and lighting systems, and shortly thereafter began to manufacture their own equipment, with the exception of the large generators, which they continued to purchase from Siemens. Soon a third firm, Schuckert and Company, backed by south German capital and skill, made its appearance in the electrical manufacturing field. The German banks were generous in providing capital, municipalities were eager for electric lighting and tramways, and the new industry grew like Jack's beanstalk.[3]

In the development of electric lighting and traction, Germany and the United States made fast starts and became the principal manufacturers and installers of equipment. British scientists had made basic contributions to the field of electricity, but in its practical application Britain lagged woefully. Legislation enacted in 1882—the Electric Lighting Act—was so restrictive and disadvantageous for promoters and investors that little capital flowed into the new industry. Britain like France became an importer rather than an exporter of electrical equipment.

The first power plants were central stations, which meant that current was provided for a small area of a city from generators driven by steam engines. The multiplication of such stations in the heart of a city presented knotty problems of construction and operation; and transmission of current over greater distances from outside the city was a technical problem which frustrated engineers for two decades. On August 25, 1891, the mayor of Frankfurt-am-Main opened an electro-technical exhibition by throwing a single switch which bathed the grounds in light from a thousand lamps and set hundreds of motors and machines humming. Proudly he announced that the current had been brought to Frankfurt over a distance of 110 miles from a hydro-electric plant on the Neckar River. This was the first long-distance high-tension transmission line (15,000 volts), built under the direction of the brilliant young Munich engineer Oskar von Miller.[4]

Electrification of city tramways now forged swiftly ahead. Capital flowed like water into these enterprises, and manufacturing establish-

3. Felix Pinner, *Emil Rathenau und das elektrische Zeitalter* (Leipzig, 1918), *passim*.
4. Siemens, *History of the House of Siemens*, I, 111–23. Oskar von Miller was the founder of the great technical museum (Deutsches Museum) in Munich.

ments were expanded and new ones launched. Siemens and Halske, which was about even with Rathenau's General Electric, expanded at home and established branches in England, Austria, Russia, France, Italy, and Belgium. In one year the concern received inquiries about installations of power and streetcar systems from thirty cities on three continents. In 1901–1902 they had 88 power stations under construction. The rate of building by all companies was such that by 1910 every large city in Europe and North and South America had been supplied with electric power for lighting and municipal transportation. The stimulus to the European, and especially the German, economy was considerable. Electrification required quantities of steel, copper, cables, fabrics, steam engines, and construction materials. It gave work to thousands of men in mines and factories and on the construction sites. The electrical industry operated like an enormous motor which moved Europe's economy forward at an increased speed.

It is not surprising that pressure and enthusiasm should have produced speculation and overexpansion. In 1901 came the inevitable reaction—a big slump in the shares of electrical companies, disastrous prices in the equipment sector, and bankruptcies of the weaker companies. Under pressure from investment banks the larger firms drew together to limit competition, curtail production, and stabilize prices. From the number of failures and mergers came what the economists describe as "duopoly," two giant concerns dominating an entire industry—the German General Electric Company and the Siemens-Halske-Schuckert concern.[5]

By 1907 the industry in Germany had recovered from its reverses and was again expanding rapidly. The electrification of Europe proceeded along two lines: In the Alpine regions of France, Italy, Austria, and Switzerland, hydroelectric plants were constructed and the power carried hundreds of miles by transmission lines to light the streets and dwellings, propel the tramcars and trains, and turn the wheels of mills and factories. In these regions "white coal" substituted for black. In central and western Europe thermoelectricity was produced by steam plants, where coal was plentiful and falling water absent.

The House of Buddenbrooks failed for lack of a suitable heir; the House of Siemens was fortunate in that for three generations it was blessed with sons and nephews of remarkable technical and business

5. *Ibid.,* I, 194–97. About the same time the General Electric Company and the Westinghouse Company achieved industry predominance in the United States.

ability, men who retained unshakeable control of their enterprise in war, depression, and inflation, through revolution and numerous mergers, operating at the same time in an industry that was technologically always in a condition of flux.[6]

Nothing contributed more to the amenities, comfort, and safety of urban life at the turn of the century than electric light and transportation. It is impossible to recapture the public enthusiasm for this child of science which had lingered so long in the laboratory but which now emerged as the hope of the twentieth century. Understandably, writers began to refer to the nineteenth century as the "Century of Steam" and to the new century as the "Age of Electricity."

3. FROM ENGINES TO AUTOS AND AIRPLANES

Electricity was more flexible and versatile than steam, and it yielded not only power but also heat and light. Compared to the steam engine the electric motor was a dwarf; it could be used as a small power plant wherever current was available. For municipal transportation and small workshops, for passenger and freight elevators, and for cranes, hoists, and ventilating systems the electric motor was an ideal power unit. Its only rival was the internal combustion engine.

A French engineer, Jean Étienne Lenoir, received a patent in 1860 for the first gas engine that possessed practical value. But the commercial history of the gas engine really began in 1876 when Dr. N. A. Otto patented a single-cylinder four-cycle engine of between one and two horsepower, which by 1900 was manufactured, sold, and used all over the world where a small power plant was needed—to pump water, grind grain, saw wood, run a small dynamo, and power the machinery in a small workshop. Where a small power unit was needed it had many advantages over the steam engine—lower cost, low weight per horsepower, safety, speed in starting, and portability.

Gottlieb Daimler was the chief designer and constructor at the Otto engine works in Deutz, a suburb of Cologne. When Daimler left the Otto firm and moved to Stuttgart, he began to develop an engine for the specific purpose of propelling a carriage on the common roads.

6. The range of the Siemens enterprise in 1914 is indicated by its principal departments: Railway Signaling Department, the Incandescent Lamp Works, Traction Department, Department for Lighting and Power, the Turbine and Generator Department, the Electric Motor Division, the Telephone Equipment Works, and the Marine Department, which provided the electrical systems and gear for the new German navy. On the growth of the company, see *History of the House of Siemens,* I, Chaps. X, XII, XIX.

Otto's four-cycle engine was not an oil engine but used illuminating gas as fuel, and the igniter had to be activated with a blowtorch. Daimler developed a multiple-cylinder motor, a gasoline carburetor, and an improved ignition system. The result by 1900 was a four-cylinder high-speed engine capable of 900 to 1,200 revolutions per minute with an unheard-of weight ratio of 88 pounds per horsepower. Daimler had opened up a field in which the steam engine could not compete. In 1885 Daimler patented his engine in France and his first motorcar in Germany. Six months later Carl Benz of Mannheim also received a patent for a "gas motor driven vehicle."[7] Daimler's engines had a strong progressive effect upon automobile development in France, England, and the United States. It was difficult to promote the automobile in Germany, and for the first ten years of operations the Daimler company built motors, which were sold mainly to French automobile producers. In 1901 the company unveiled the first of its Mercedes series, which outperformed all competitors in numerous tests and trials in succeeding years.

Until the beginning of the century France was the leader in developing the motorcar, as its nomenclature reminds us—automobile, chassis, carburetor, differential, tonneau, limousine, etc. The French inventor and designer Émile Levassor developed the arrangement of units and driving mechanism that became standard in all motorcars—the engine cradled in the frame, the friction clutch, transmission, power train, and differential. In 1894 a Paris newspaper organized a trial run for motor vehicles of all kinds—steam, electric, gasoline—from Paris to Rouen and return. More than a hundred vehicles started, but only fifteen completed the race; all the best performers were gasoline-powered with Daimler engines. In 1895 the run was extended from Paris to Bordeaux, and in 1900 the Gordon Bennett Cup races were instituted to stimulate interest and competition. Organized automobile clubs and annual motorcar shows in principal cities also served to propagandize this novel and attractive child of the age of technology.

Britain lagged in adopting the automobile because of antiquated ordinances that prohibited powered vehicles on public roads. Repeal of

---

7. In 1898 Robert Bosch of Stuttgart produced a reliable electric ignition system for the high-speed automobile and airplane engine—the Bosch high-tension magneto. The lowly spark plug, a part of the system, has changed hardly at all since it came from Bosch's engineering department, the work of his designer Gottlob Honold. Theodor Heuss, *Robert Bosch, Leben und Leistung* (Tübingen, 1946), pp. 85–219.

the law in 1896 was celebrated by a motorcar test run from London to Brighton, which has been commemorated in the delightful film *Genevieve*. With English associates a branch of the Daimler company was established in England, and soon British engineers were designing and producing their own excellent cars—Napier, Vauxhall, Humber, Rolls-Royce, Wolseley, and Austin. King Edward acquired his first motorcar in 1901, and the Prince of Wales followed with a purchase in 1903; Lord Salisbury and his nephew Arthur Balfour also became motoring enthusiasts. Soon it was high fashion and personally smart to own and drive an automobile. By 1914 the automobile had displaced the horse-drawn vehicle as the private carriage of the wealthier classes. Also by 1911 horse-drawn trams, heavy drays, and hansom cabs were largely replaced by motor vehicles on London streets. Optimistic observers thought that the effect of the omnibus, taxicab, and motor truck would be to reduce congestion on the streets by quickening the movement of a large volume of traffic. It was confidently asserted that speeding the movement of London traffic to five miles per hour was equivalent to doubling the width of the main streets![8]

Although Britain had the largest number of registered motor vehicles in Europe, France remained the center of the motor industry until 1914. In the United States the utilitarian aspect of the automobile was emphasized from the beginning. However, the ridiculous Selden patent, granted in 1895 and upheld by the courts until 1909, together with the absence of metaled roads between cities, retarded automobile manufacture and development. The breaking of the Selden patent by Henry Ford and the protection given by the Dingley tariff—45 percent ad valorem on foreign motorcars—made the industry more attractive to venture capital. By 1910 there were 200 manufacturers producing 200,000 cars annually. When the Ford Motor Company, organized in 1903, put its Model T car on the market it offered a serviceable vehicle adapted to country roads for the low price of $550. The lesson that Ford taught America was quickly learned: the "auto" was a useful thing and something for everyone to own.

Many contemporaries who were fully in the stream of scientific and

---

8. *Encyclopaedia Britannica*, 11th ed. (1910–11), article on "Motor Vehicles." On engines and motorcars, in general, Eugen Diesel, *From Engines to Autos* (Chicago, 1960), is one of the best; Saint John C. Nixon, *The Invention of the Automobile* (London, 1930), is brief but reliable; also sketches of Benz and Daimler in the *Neue Deutsche Biographie*.

technological optimism also thought that soon they would have a "flying machine" that would carry them through the air as the automobile carried them over the roads. The engines developed for the motorcar, with their relatively high ratio of power to weight, made powered flight a realistic goal. A number of pioneers had made scientific and practical contributions to the design of a heavier-than-air machine that could take off, land, and be steered in the air. In 1900 the two active centers of interest and experimentation were Dayton, Ohio, where the bicycle makers, Wilbur and Orville Wright, were experimenting with gliders, and Paris, where an active Aero Club was sponsored and supported by many of the same men who were promoting the automobile industry. Free ballooning was a popular sport, and French technologists and inventors expected that powered flight would also be a French achievement.

The automobile was Europe's gift to the United States; the airplane was America's first spectacular technological gift to Europe. How the Wrights built and experimented with gliders and then proceeded to powered flight in 1903 has become a folk legend. Their patient and persistent experimental work yielded high returns. They did everything the Europeans neglected. They built experimental gliders and thoroughly mastered the technique of flying them; they studied the principles of the air screw and built experimental propellers; they first used borrowed engines but finally constructed their own. After building several models the Wrights were able to make sustained circular flights of twenty minutes' duration at a height of 300 feet. Concerned about patents and the material rewards of their invention, the Wrights were quite secretive about their experimental flights. When press reports of their achievements began to appear, they gave up flying entirely between 1905 and 1908. Rumors of the accomplishments of Orville and Wilbur Wright were received skeptically in Europe—especially in France, where interest in flying was greatest and where numerous experimental machines were being constructed and tested. These were of all kinds ranging from machines with some possibilities of flight to the utterly fantastic. One multiple-wing affair looked like a flying venetian blind! It never left the ground. The most prominent experimenters in France were the expatriate Englishman Henri Farman, Louis Blériot, and Léon Levavasseur, France's leading engine and aircraft designer. However, the techniques and mechanisms of flight control developed by the Wrights were not understood or applied by the French pioneers. None of them became experienced glider pilots; they attempted to go direct to powered flight and they failed. The best they accomplished were short "hop flights" of barely more than a minute's duration. They thought of the airplane as a machine which could be powered through the air and steered like an automobile or a motorboat.

In 1908 the Wrights made their first public flights, ending all doubts about their claims and achievements. Wilbur made the first European flight at Le Mans on August 8; Orville gave the first public demonstration in the United States at Fort Meyer, Virginia, in September. Numerous experimenters and members of the Aero Club gathered at Le Mans, skeptical and anticipating a failure. What they witnessed was eye-opening. They saw Wilbur Wright take off, fly, bank, circle, and return to point of departure. Two days later he made two more short flights, one a figure eight, the other three complete circles. It was an amazing demonstration especially of lateral control through the use of ailerons, which the French designers had ignored. With ailerons on the wings the machine could be tilted sharply, banked, and turned tightly without losing lateral stability to the point of crashing. Wright flew like a birdman rather than the driver of a powerful motorcar. Between August and December, Wilbur Wright made more than a hundred flights in France, sixty of them with passengers. Of his long flights, one lasted two and a half hours. In the spring of 1909, demonstrations were made in Rome, and in September–October Orville Wright made a series of flights from Tempelhof field in Berlin. The Crown Prince of Prussia was an eager passenger on one of the flights, and the Kaiser spoke enthusiastically about the possible military uses of the new invention.[9]

While the Wright brothers' achievements in the United States faded into a welter of lawsuits over patents, European designers worked to put their revelations as to construction and control into practice,

9. The best work on the development of the airplane is Charles H. Gibbs-Smith, *The Invention of the Aeroplane* (New York, 1966), pp. 66–68, 77–84, 143–53, 171–209; and Elsbeth R. Freudenthal, *Flight into History: The Wright Brothers and the Air Age* (Norman, Okla., 1949), pp. 173–223; Fred C. Kelly, *The Wright Brothers* (New York, 1943), is a popular account; M. W. McFarland (ed.), *The Papers of Wilbur and Orville Wright,* 2 vols. (New York, 1953), is basic.

achieving now steady improvement. In 1909 the airplane can be said to
have established itself as a practical invention. This was impressed
upon the public mind of Europe by two spectacular events: Louis Blériot's flight across the English Channel on July 25, and the first international aviation meeting at Reims, August 22-29. All the best
machines and pilots, except the Wrights, assembled at Reims, and most
records were broken. Glenn Curtiss won the Gordon Bennett Cup for
speed with a record 47 miles per hour. New records for distance, alti-
tude, and passenger carrying were established. The Reims meeting, like
Blériot's spectacular achievement, was well publicized. It was demonstrated beyond question that the better experimental planes would fly,
that they could carry two men at more than forty miles per hour in
comparative safety, that the machines could be adequately controlled
and handled and kept in flight for periods exceeding two hours.
Europe was well launched in the air age.[10]

Insofar as automobiles and airplanes were concerned, the steam
engine and the gasoline engine were not in direct competition. This
was not so with the oil-burning diesel engine, which was exhibited to
the mechanical world at the Paris fair in 1900. Patented by Rudolf
Diesel, a brilliant mechanical engineer, in the early nineties as "a
rational heat engine," the machine was developed in the experimental
shop of the Augsburg-Nürnberg Machine Company (MAN) in
Augsburg and financed jointly by the Krupps and MAN. The first
experimental model performed satisfactorily in 1895, but the development of a reliable and marketable engine required more time and great
expenditure of funds. In return for financial support during this period
Diesel assigned the manufacturing rights in Germany and Austria to
Krupp and the Augsburg firm. But he sold the manufacturing rights
for Russia to Emanuel Nobel, nephew of the Swedish industrialist
Alfred Nobel; the rights for Britain and the Empire he sold to a
Scottish engineering firm, and he made similar arrangements with
French, Belgian, and Swiss machine builders. The American rights
were sold for a million marks to Adolphus Busch of St. Louis, who
organized the Diesel Motor Company of America. Altogether the
manufacturing rights yielded a fortune of about 5 million marks. As
engineer, promoter, and salesman, Diesel was unmatched, but as an

10. Gibbs-Smith, *The Invention of the Aeroplane,* pp. 168-70, 210-19, 319-40.

investor and capitalist he suffered shipwreck and disaster. He built an imposing residence in the Bogenhausen district of Munich, invested and lost heavily in real estate, and suffered further losses in oil ventures in Galicia. Attempts to develop his engine in new directions—the locomotive and the automobile engine—were in advance of their times and yielded no financial return. On the verge of bankruptcy in 1913, he disappeared from a Channel steamer while crossing to England from Antwerp, presumably a suicide. All his assets went to satisfy the creditors.[11]

The diesel engine was more economical and efficient than the steam engine or the gasoline engine. It operated on kerosene or crude oil, fuel could be stored in a small space, and the engine required no stoking and very little attention or maintenance. Whether Diesel's engine was the "rational heat engine" described in the original patent or simply a modification of the Otto motor was much discussed at the time. Certainly it differed from the latter in its basic principle if not in its principal mechanisms. Using the piston and cylinder, the diesel motor achieved such high compression that the cylinder head ignited the fuel charge which was injected by a compressor. The gasoline motor was essentially an explosion motor—the gas charge being exploded by an electric spark; the diesel engine was a combustion motor converting heat into power with high thermal efficiency, giving a smoother flow of power with significantly less strain and wear on the moving parts. It was also much more reliable, since the complicated electrical ignition was entirely eliminated.[12]

Because of the high cost of gasoline in Europe and the advantages of the diesel engine over steam power for many purposes, it was developed and adopted much more rapidly in Europe than in the United States, where gasoline was comparatively cheap and coal generally plentiful. The first diesel engines were single-cylinder stationary power plants, but the licensees were soon constructing multi-cylinder engines of 1,000 horsepower or more. Marine engines were developed for river barges, tugs, and small ships. The first diesel-powered cargo vessel, the

11. Eugen Diesel, *Diesel: Der Mensch, das Werk, das Schicksal* (Hamburg, 1937), *passim;* W. Robert Nitske and Charles M. Wilson, *Rudolf Diesel: Pioneer of the Age of Power* (Norman, Okla., 1965).

12. Rudolf Diesel, *Die Entstehung der Diesel-Motors* (Munich, 1912); Edward Cressy, *Discoveries and Inventions of the Twentieth Century* (London, 1915), pp. 67–72; B. J. Von Bongart, *Diesel Engines* (New York, 1945).

Selandia of 5,000 tons, was commissioned by a Danish shipping line in 1911 and operated efficiently until 1942. In larger vessels, especially ocean liners, and in stationary prime movers, steam power experienced a rebirth through the successful development of the steam turbine and the oil burner. In military technology the diesel motor found a place as an ideal power plant for the submarines of World War I. The diesel locomotive and the high-speed automobile and tractor engines were postwar developments.

Steam, electricity, gas, and oil engines constituted a formidable array of power producers for the more efficient performance of the world's work. Electricity gave rise to the electrical industry, the gasoline engine to the motorcar industry, the diesel engine to specialized engineering works. The stimulus to employment, investment, and capital goods production derived from these industries explains in part why the period from 1900 to 1914 was one of impressive economic growth and progress. Another stimulus to economic growth, which affected not only Europe but the entire world economy, was the petroleum industry, which forged into prominence as the essential supplier of fuel for the new internal combustion engines and as an aggressive rival to coal as a source of heat and power.

4. EXPANSION OF THE OIL INDUSTRY

Until the internal combustion engine appeared, petroleum was valued chiefly for the illuminating oils which it yielded through the distillation process. Where gas and electricity were not available—that is, outside of towns and cities—it was still the principal source of artificial light. Writers could still be rhapsodic about illuminating oils:

In all the far corners of the earth . . . they add to the light of day and well-nigh double the hours that man can give to his labours. They supplement the beams of the Arctic moon, and dispel the gloom of the tropical night. They illuminate the sick room and diminish the terrors of darkness. In a thousand and one ways they contribute to man's comfort, and aid him in the fight against time and circumstance.[13]

Between 1900 and 1914 petroleum vaulted into world prominence as a primary product which yielded not only the valuable illuminating oils but also gasoline, industrial solvents, lubricants, and oil for boiler

13. Cressy, *Discoveries and Inventions of the Twentieth Century*, p. 27.

fuel. The United States produced about two-thirds of the world's supply, the Baku field on the Caspian about one-third, and the Netherlands East Indies deposits were just beginning to be exploited. "Black gold" may have been an exaggeration, but oil was now sought and treasured with all the intensity that characterized a gold rush.

Together with its affiliated marketing companies, the Standard Oil Company dominated the industry on four continents. The Nobel brothers undertook to develop the Baku wells for the distribution of kerosene in Russia. Here the pipeline from well to refinery, the railway tank car, and the oil burner for small tank ships on the Caspian made their appearance. The Rothschilds became interested in Russian oil production and helped to finance the railway and pipeline from Baku to Batoum, and to build the refineries at the Black Sea port. All this with a view to bringing Baku lamp oil to the Mediterranean and western European markets. Ordinarily kerosene was shipped in fifty-gallon barrels, and to the retail trade in five-gallon tins, two to a wooden case. The empty tins were highly prized and put to many uses in Asia and Africa—as an all-purpose receptacle and as a building material. In 1885 the English firm Armstrong, Whitworth Company built the first steam-driven tanker for the transport of bulk oil and oil products. Operated by a Hamburg shipper, the *Glückauf* made its first round trip to the United States in 1886. In a short time thirty tankers were built or building, and the bulk shipment of oil and deposit in storage tanks, whence it was delivered to dealers, effected a revolution in the oil trade.[14]

In the last decade of the century Standard's position in the oil trade was threatened from several directions. Marcus Samuel, with his base in London, organized the Shell Transport and Trading Company and with the largest tanker fleet in the business began to bring oil from Batoum and distribute it in the European market. In 1892, after much political maneuvering, the Suez Canal was opened to the transport of bulk oil shipments and the Shell company began to market Russian kerosene in south Asia. Standard Oil was now challenged in the Asian market by the Royal Dutch, the Shell company, and the Rothschild's

14. F. C. Gerretson, *History of the Royal Dutch,* 4 vols. (Leiden, 1953–57), I, 207–12; R. J. Forbes and R. O'Beirne, *The Technical Development of the Royal Dutch Shell* (Leiden, 1957), 527–41; Sir Boverton Redwood, *Petroleum and Its Products,* 2d ed. (London, 1906), *passim;* R. Henriques, *Bearsted: A Biography of Marcus Samuel* (New York, 1960), Chap. V, "The Beginnings of Shell, 1896–1899."

Bnito company. In the ensuing price war, the three independents, under the leadership of Henri Deterding of the Royal Dutch, formed a unified marketing concern and successfully defended their position against the giant American company.[15]

Gasoline, one of the unwanted by-products of the refining process, was often dumped into rivers or burned at the refinery site. It had only a limited market in Europe as a solvent and cleaning fluid, and this demand was met entirely by Standard Oil at a very high monopoly price. The demand for gasoline in 1895 was about what it had been in 1875. Then came the automobile craze and the gasoline market literally exploded. The Sumatra oils, worked by the Royal Dutch company, produced a high percentage of gasoline and a low yield of kerosene, hitherto considered a disadvantage. It now became profitable to ship gasoline from the Netherlands East Indies to Europe. In the spring of 1902, the first ship loaded with Sumatra gasoline in fifty-gallon steel drums arrived in London. The Royal Dutch and Shell companies then extended their Asiatic marketing agreement to Europe—the Shell company operating in Britain and France, the Royal Dutch taking the remainder of the continent. The consortium's storage and distribution facilities were established at Rotterdam, which soon became the leading oil port in Europe. Standard Oil, still dominant in the kerosene trade, increased its gasoline volume in Europe but was unable to meet the growing demands of its customers, and was shortly purchasing a third of its European supply from the Royal Dutch Shell group.[16]

Standard Oil Company's position—or more correctly, that of its subsidiary, the Anglo-American Oil Company—in the kerosene market in Europe was unassailable; but the Royal Dutch Shell group held first place in the booming gasoline trade. The heavier oil distillations, which were used for fuel, were just beginning to find a market as oil-burning devices were developed and improved.

Oil for fueling ships and locomotives did not spring into prominence overnight. Efficient and economical burners took years to develop, and

---

15. Gerretson, *History of the Royal Dutch*, II, 173–201, 229–50.

16. *Ibid.*, 253–57. In 1907 the Royal Dutch and Shell companies merged, with the former holding the majority interest, and with Henri Deterding as managing director. Marcus Samuel's Shell company was in such straits that a merger seemed the only alternative to liquidation. (R. Henriques, *Bearsted*, pp. 567–94.) In 1910 the consortium acquired the Rothschild holdings in Russia.

coal, one of the world's greatest resource industries, was not easily displaced, especially in Europe, where there was an abundance of coal but little oil. However, the manifest advantages of oil for passenger liners and naval vessels—cleanliness and great saving of space, time, and manpower—won for it strong support among designers and shippers. A powerful convert to fuel oil was Sir John Fisher, first sea lord of the British Admiralty, and in his drive to bring the navy to the highest level of technological efficiency the conversion from coal to oil had a high priority.

The objections raised in some quarters were indeed weighty. Britain supplied the coal and operated the bunkering system on most of the world's sea lanes. Britain's economic interests as well as her sea power were deeply involved. Fuel oil was foreign; coal was native. An oil-burning navy would require a dual bunkering system. Britain, who controlled only 2 percent of known oil reserves, would be dependent upon others for her vital fuel supply. Marcus Samuel worked mightily to make Shell the principal supplier of the British navy, but he failed because the Shell group was really controlled by the Dutch. The Imperial Commission on Oil and Fuel Supply advised against becoming dependent on international suppliers, and the British government proceeded to acquire a controlling interest in the Anglo-Persian Oil Company as a source of supply for the British navy.[17]

By 1914, 45 percent of Britain's naval tonnage had converted to oil. Other governments followed Britain's example; oil became an object of international politics and foreign offices, and oil companies formed business partnerships to ensure national control over adequate supplies. Oil thus became a strategic war material, like so many blessings conferred by science and technology upon an undeserving mankind.

5. CHEMISTRY AND INDUSTRY

"Science in the service of man" was a theme that inspired a host of optimistic writers before 1914. This was not all fantasy but a conviction arising from the many applications of science which had changed the material conditions of life and raised appreciably the European standard of living. Regardless of what the "pure" scientist might say about expanding the boundaries of knowledge, the public lived in the

17. Gerretson, *History of the Royal Dutch*, IV, 281–94; Henriques, *Bearsted*, pp. 551–90.

Baconian tradition that it was the business of science mainly "to find out useful things." Until the end of the previous century, with some exceptions, metallurgy, cements, ceramics, glass, pigments, fuels, dyes, detergents, pharmaceuticals, and fermentation products developed as empirical arts without much regard to theoretical foundations. This line of development reached its limits at the beginning of the twentieth century. Henceforth, new industries, and many old ones, were based on scientific advances in chemistry, biology, electronics, geology, and geophysics.

Chemistry made the greatest number of contributions. While the discovery of physical laws may result in revolutionary applications, as in the case of atomic physics, the chemistry of elements, substances, and compounds has always had the prospect of practical application and economic reward. A research chemist making an important discovery reaped a professional reward by publication of findings in an appropriate journal, but if the discovery appeared to have practical application in technology or industry he would probably patent it. An examination of the periodical *Chemical Abstracts* before 1914 shows that the proportion of chemical patents to free published papers was about one in three or four. In organic chemistry the proportion of patents was even higher. The organic chemist always worked with one eye cocked toward the patent office. Chemistry had become a scientific reservoir that nourished a larger and larger segment of industry and gave buoyancy and thrust to the European economy.

Synthetic dyestuffs and pharmaceutical products were the first major industries to emerge from the chemical laboratory, although agriculture, petroleum, and some consumer goods industries were also heavily dependent upon the science of chemistry. Synthesized in 1880, synthetic indigo, the king of dyestuffs, had supplanted the indigo plantation, and by the end of the century the German chemical industry was supplying from 80 to 90 percent of the world's dyestuffs. Electrolysis was another basic chemical process that received wide application in industry, notably in the production of aluminum, sodium, and zinc, and in the process of electroplating. Independently, in 1886, an American, Charles M. Hall, and a French metallurgist, Paul L. T. Héroult, developed the process of electrolyzing aluminum oxide. The process was patented in France and the United States by the respective inventors, and before many years a laboratory curiosity costing eight dollars per pound became an industrial product selling for twenty cents per pound.

Another basic chemical process that received wide application in industry was discovered by the French chemist Paul Sabatier (1854–1941). The hydrogenation process achieved through the use of catalysts was the result of many years of experimentation and was finally perfected in 1900. What Sabatier showed the manufacturing chemist was that hydrogen could be combined with a great diversity of substances by a simple process at very low cost. Scarcely was his discovery made known than numerous patents were taken out by other people with the object of applying his discovery to manufacturing processes. One of the applications was basic in the creation of new industries—the hydrogenation of oils into higher melting or "hardened" fats, which made possible the production in great volume and at low cost of soap, shortening, and margarines. Whale oil, cottonseed oil, and oils from other seeds and nuts were the basis of the booming soap industry. Margarine produced by hydrogenation of oils gave the industrial working classes, who could not afford high-priced butter, a highly nutritive and palatable substitute spread. Margarine consumption was not limited to the industrial population. Agricultural Denmark had the highest per capita rate of margarine consumption because the Danish dairymen exported their butter and milk products and substituted margarine in their own diet. By 1914 Lever Brothers had organized a giant international soap concern—their only rival being Procter and Gamble of Cincinnati—while the Dutch firms Jurgens and Van den Bergh, in alliance with Lever, were the principal producers and distributors of margarine in England and on the Continent.[18]

The search for synthetic rubber was less of a success story. Wild rubber had sufficed for all industrial and consumer needs until rubber tires for bicycles and automobiles created an insatiable demand for the raw product. In 1910 raw rubber sold for forty cents per pound and the search for a synthetic substitute engaged a host of industrial chemists. The chemical code of rubber was finally broken and a synthetic substitute developed in both Britain and Germany. But success in the laboratory did not mean success in the factory. The substitute was costly to produce. The development of rubber plantations in Indonesia, Malay,

18. Charles H. Wilson, *The History of Unilever*, 2 vols. (London, 1954), II, 24–77, 97–148; also H. R. Edwards, *Competition and Monopoly in the British Soap Industry* (Oxford, 1962), pp. 157–71. Using a British patent, Procter and Gamble built the first hydrogenation plant in the United States, in 1908. The principal product was Crisco, heavily advertised as "the vegetable shortening," in competition with lard. Alfred Lief, *"It Floats": The Story of Procter & Gamble* (New York, 1958), pp. 103–8.

and the Congo greatly reduced the market price of natural rubber; and
the development of a competitive synthetic product was delayed for
twenty years. Another chemical achievement with great practical value
was the synthesis of ammonia by Fritz Haber, professor at the Technical College in Karlsruhe, in 1909. The Badische Analin und Soda
Fabrik successfully undertook the industrial development of the process. Cheap synthetic ammonia was basic in increasing the supply of
chemical fertilizers, and in the production of explosives for mining,
construction, and military purposes. The work of Friedrich Bergius in
the hydrogenation of heavy oils and coal to produce liquid fuel began
in 1910, although the industrial exploitation of his processes was a
postwar development.[19]

Germany's position of predominance in the chemical industries was
due not solely to the brilliant achievements of her universities and
technical colleges, but also to the organization of research within the
industries. If Germany had a secret weapon in the area of technology it
was the industrial research laboratory and research team. Originating
in the dyestuffs industry, product research was well defined and
developed by 1900 and was spreading to other highly technical fields
such as glass, optics, pharmaceuticals, and electronics. The electrical
and chemical industries, the offspring of science, were two of the
brightest jewels in Germany's industrial crown.

6. "EUROPE, THE WORLD'S BANKER"

New industries, born of the union of science and technology, required much capital for their development and growth. But these
requirements were met from available investment sources and from the
profits of the industries themselves. (Successful oil and chemical
concerns paid fantastic dividends in good years.) At the same time
Europe generated large amounts of capital to finance the development
of non-European regions. Britain, France, and Germany were the
principal lenders, although Switzerland, Holland, and Belgium also
generated some export capital. Foreign lending was at a low ebb
during the Great Depression but revived in the 1880's and began a

19. John J. Beer, *The Emergence of the German Dye Industry* (Urbana, Ill., 1959),
pp. 49–93; Ludwig F. Haber, *The Chemical Industry During the Nineteenth Century*
(Oxford, 1958), pp. 121–36, 169–80; Eduard Faber (ed.), *Great Chemists* (New York,
1961), sketches of Adolf von Baeyer, Emil Fischer, Fritz Haber, and Carl Bosch.

sustained rise in 1896. French lending reached its peak in 1906–1910, when it amounted to 4.5 percent of national income. British capital exports, which fell off appreciably during the Boer War, doubled after 1906, reaching an unparalleled 8.5 percent of national income in 1913.[20]

Britain's Continental investments, principally in railroads, had been largely redeemed by 1900. Well before the turn of the century her capital exports went mainly to the Empire and the "pioneer lands," where so many promising prospects had faded and hopes had been deferred. Now they were fulfilled. During the period of heaviest investment, from 1904 to 1914, the bulk of British capital went to the Empire, the United States, and Latin America.[21] British capital was mainly development capital; about 60 percent of foreign loans went into railways, the remainder into public securities, construction, land development, and mining. As Herbert Feis noted, the British investor had a strong preference for "the steam shovel, the locomotive, the plough, and the miningshaft."[22]

The effects of capital export on the domestic economy was much discussed in every lending country before 1914, and especially in Britain. To a social economist, such as J. A. Hobson, foreign investment was a kind of sink for "the frozen income of the super-rich," and the principal cause of imperialism. To this school heavy capital export was also a sign of oversaving and underconsumption. These "social economists" advocated distribution of excess income through either increased wages or social services.[23]

Although Hobson's views gained currency in socialist and labor circles, they do not stand up under critical analysis. A. K. Cairncross, who has examined the evidence dispassionately, concludes that foreign

20. Charles P. Kindleberger, *Economic Growth in France and Britain* (Cambridge, Mass., 1964), pp. 13, 61–68.

21. Sir George Paish, "Great Britain's Capital Investments in Individual Colonial and Foreign Countries," *Journal of the Royal Statistical Society,* new ser., LXXIV (1910–11), 167–87. This is one of the few statistically reliable examinations of British overseas investments before 1914.

22. Herbert Feis, *Europe, the World's Banker* (New Haven, 1930), p. 26; also Paish, "Great Britain's Capital Investments," p. 198. In 1906, Charles Speare, an American investment analyst and writer, visited the principal European financial centers to survey the market for railway securities. London was the most receptive market for new issues, the principal purchasers being British life insurance companies and managers of large trust funds. Charles Speare, *American Securities in Europe* (Philadelphia, 1906), p. 6.

23. J. A. Hobson, *Imperialism: A Study,* 2d. ed. (London, 1905), pp. 70–80; also, *Confessions of an Economic Heretic* (London, 1938), pp. 42–92, *passim*.

investment did pay in social gains as well as in economic return, and that it was advantageous to the national economy. British capital exports went mainly into productive enterprise, financed the expansion of British foreign trade, stimulated the export industries, and assured the homeland of a large supply of foodstuffs and raw materials.[24] Britain did not become a *rentier* country to an excessive degree, but continued to live from her manufactures and trade. Interest payments on overseas investments tended to remain in the country of origin, where they were reinvested. Nor was Britain the sole gainer; the other industrial trading countries benefited from the developing markets and the increasing supply of essential products.

France in proportion to her national income was a large exporter of capital. Less industrialized than Britain and Germany, France nevertheless generated each year about 3.5 billion francs in savings that found their way to the Paris money market. When a Frenchman saved 500 francs he became an investor. This accumulation was the result of a fanatical sense of saving, that "pinching meanness" which French authors have described in so many novels of family life. Since the French economy grew slowly, the domestic capital demand was limited. Thus what was saved was largely available for foreign investment at rates lower than those in any other European capital market. Being both conservative and credulous, French investors favored fixed interest securities of national, state, and local governments. The Paris money market was made to order for the ministers of finance of East European states, struggling Balkan governments, and Mediterranean potentates. For them Paris was a pot of gold to which they returned again and again for another handful. The conference rooms of the French investment banks were quite as familiar to foreign statesmen as the reception rooms of the Quai d'Orsay.

French lending was strongly influenced by political and diplomatic considerations, and governmental control was exerted more rigorously than in any other lending country. German securities were excluded from the French market after 1870, while Russian bonds were bought

24. A. K. Cairncross, *Home and Foreign Investment, 1870–1913*, Chap. IX, "Did Foreign Investment Pay?" Sir George Paish concluded: "Anyone who looked through the trade figures for the last sixty years would find that the exports went up and down in almost exact proportion to our willingness or unwillingness to invest capital." Paish, "Great Britain's Capital Investments," p. 200.

by French investors as a patriotic duty. French loans to Russia, public and private, amounted to an estimated one-quarter of the total of foreign investments, or 11.3 billion francs in 1914. The bulk of French long-term loans were made in Europe—Russia, Sweden, Turkey, Egypt, Spain, Portugal, and the Balkan states. Latin America, where French investments were increasing, received more capital than the French colonies. Altogether France's long-term foreign and colonial investments increased from 28 billion francs in 1900 to 45 billion in 1914.

Being loans mainly to governments, a great part of France's investments were lost as a result of war and revolution. Not a franc was recovered of the Russian debt, and the loans to Turkey, Greece, Austria, and the Balkan states were repudiated. "In all, France lost two-thirds of the net total of her foreign investments, or about six times the amount of the German indemnity of 1870."[25]

Germany had two or three needs for every spare mark. Capital was needed for spurting industries, for financing foreign trade, for housing a growing population, for public utilities, for massive social services, for government expenses, and especially for the costly army and navy. To a surprising degree the German economy generated the capital to meet these requirements, but there was little left over for lending abroad. Berlin was not a favorable market for foreign bonds and obligations. Interest rates were high, the German bankers who controlled the credit system were discriminating, and domestic needs were given priority. Probably less than a tenth of all capital savings went into foreign loans before the war. Karl Helfferich, director of the Deutsche Bank, estimated German foreign investments at not more than 20 billion marks in 1911, a figure he thought "rather too high than too low."[26]

In the matter of capital accumulation and investment the German banks—especially the big four, the Deutsche Bank, Diskonto-Gesellschaft, Dresdner, and Darmstädter—played an expedient role. Each

25. Cairncross, *Home and Foreign Investments,* pp. 223–24; Feis, *Europe, the World's Banker,* pp. 35–59; and the pioneer analytical work on foreign investments, A. Sartorious von Waltershausen, *Das Volkswirtschaftliche System der Kapitalanlage im Auslande* (Berlin, 1907), pp. 381–420.

26. Karl Helfferich, *Germany's Economic Progress and National Wealth, 1888–1913* (New York, 1913), pp. 13, 112. Estimates by reputable authorities vary as much as 50 percent.

had its special field of activity and its close and continuing connection with various segments of industry and business. These banks functioned not only as ordinary deposit and lending institutions but also as underwriters and brokers for their large business and industrial clients. "They floated [their companies], issued new shares, gave credit accounts and manifold loans, delivered them of daughter companies, performed surgical operations in crises, and provided for decent obsequies at the liquidation."[27] When German capital was placed abroad it was usually in the service of German industrial and trading enterprises. Of this policy the German shipping lines, the Rumanian oil industry, the Anatolian railway concessions, and the Siemens electrical and tramway companies in Italy, Austria, and Latin America are significant examples.

German foreign investments were geographically scattered. Austria-Hungary, Russia, and Turkey were the principal European recipients of German capital; and overseas, Canada, the United States, and Latin America were the main areas of investment.

Among the small states of Western Europe, Switzerland, the Netherlands, and Belgium were substantial lenders of capital. Estimates vary, but in 1914 Switzerland's long-term foreign investments were probably not less than 1.5 billion dollars, Holland's about one billion, and Belgium's about a half-billion. Swiss capital was invested in the United States, Italy, Germany, and Russia, frequently in industries such as cotton and lace that were well established at home.[28] The Swiss were also large investors in the electrical utilities of northern Italy.

Holland was a country with very little poverty, a country in which nearly everyone had some capital to invest in home or foreign securities. Dutch capital was directed primarily to the development of their colonies in the East and West Indies, but Dutch investment companies were also large holders of Russian and American securities. Reputedly conservative with regard to bonds, the Dutch investor would gamble wildly in low-priced speculative stocks. More American shares were

27. W. F. Bruck, *Social and Economic History of Germany from William II to Hitler* (New York, 1962), p. 84.

28. A Swiss holding company—Aktiengesellschaft für Russische Baumwoll-Industrie —owned the controlling interest in several large Russian cotton spinning and weaving companies. Another Swiss company—Schweizerisch-Amerikanische Stickerei-Industrie— controlled a substantial part of the lace, embroidery, and tapestry manufacturing industry in the United States.

traded in Amsterdam than in any other European city, including London.[29]

Belgian capital was almost wholly utilized at home and in support of her industrial export trade. Investment in the development of the mineral resources in the Congo was just beginning on the eve of the war. The Union Minière du Haut Katanga was organized in 1906 and produced its first ton of copper in 1911. Thereafter, Belgian capital found in the Congo an expanding field of investment.

Foreign and overseas investment of European capital was an essential factor in raising the world's economy to unprecedented levels. To a considerable extent capital moved like commodities, in response to conditions of supply, demand, and profitability. Conservatively estimated, Europe's foreign and colonial investment in 1913 was in the neighborhood of 35 to 40 billion dollars. Although some of the lending was unproductive, by far the greater part went into the development of the resources, trade, and industry of undeveloped areas. Nor is it just or correct to describe this as "colonial exploitation." The economic growth of primary producing areas depended on European capital and the European market. This was the cardinal feature of the world economy before 1914.

7. CARTELS AND THE CONCENTRATION OF INDUSTRY

Out of the simple joint stock company, providing for limited liability of shareholders, emerged the complex business forms of twentieth-century capitalism. The abbreviations Ltd., Inc., Soc. Anon., and GmbH. became worldwide in their usage and signification. Joint stock enterprise created a new kind of property and a new class of property owners. A man's possessions were no longer his land, house, tools, and livestock, with his cash in a stocking hidden under a mattress. If he belonged to the possessing classes he was also likely to be a stockholder or bondholder.

Enterprises originating as simple partnerships were usually incorporated if they grew to substantial size, incorporation being invariably required by bankers as a condition for lending capital for expansion. Graduation to "big business" status produced the increasingly familiar pyramidal-shaped organization in which the parent concern became a holding and financing agency surmounting a series of "operating

29. Speare, *American Securities in Europe*, p. 10.

companies" which were located without much regard to national frontiers. National tariff systems encouraged or forced the establishment of branch manufacturing companies in foreign countries, with local capital frequently participating. Obviously the European business community was optimistic about international peace and the inviolability of private property.

As Europe moved into the age of "big business," trusts, cartels, syndicates, and pools made their appearance. Indeed it seemed to many observers that economic life in the twentieth century would be completely restructured through trusts and cartels. For the national economist, the lawmaker, the statesman concerned for the public interest, and for individual social and political groups, the flamboyant trend toward monopoly stood in the front rank of interest and concern.[30]

The contemporary literature on this subject is strongly infused with dogmatism and special pleading. Exponents of unrestricted competition denounced monopolistic practices out of hand as a negation of the free enterprise principle undergirding economic progress. Cartels, trusts, and syndicates, they argued, protected high-cost producers and inefficient enterprises; they gouged the consumer and retarded mass production with its consequent savings. Apologists, in rebuttal, recalled Proudhon's paradox that "competition kills competition," and that overproduction and periodic depressions could be eliminated by planning and organization on the part of the industries concerned. Defenders of concerted action and collective controls regarded free competition as economic anarchy and the cartel as a means of achieving order and stability in the market.[31]

By definition, a cartel was a free association of producers for the monopolistic control of the market. The simplest cartel was an agreement among producers with regard to price schedules, production quotas, and market areas. Such agreements largely eliminated the costs of competitive selling, advertising, and a good part of the shipping costs. The arrangement was most effective when it covered a large market area sheltered by a protective tariff.

If the Germans did not invent the cartel they brought it to the

---

30. The richest contemporary source for cartels, trusts, and combinations is the *Kartell-Rundschau,* a fortnightly publication founded in Vienna in 1903. Primarily a reporting publication, it also published theoretical articles. The standard work is Robert Liefmann, *Cartels, Concerns and Trusts* (New York, 1932).

31. Helfferich, *Germany's Economic Progress and National Wealth,* pp. 46–47.

highest stage of development. Originally German industry had as its base many small independent units; concentration and organization of these units for greater efficiency and survival was probably inevitable. Also price fixing in local trades and provisioning, such as beer and baking, was traditional in Germany. In industry cartels made their appearance in the 1870's, experienced a period of active organization in the 1890's, and flourished between 1900 and 1914.[32]

The most highly developed cartel, and the model for many, was the Rhenish-Westphalian Coal Syndicate, organized in 1893, which deliberately assigned production quotas for coal and coke and marketed the output for its constituent members.[33] The German Steel Producers Association, organized in 1904, had a membership of 89 firms and controlled nearly the whole of Germany's basic steel production. Cartel agreements might cover the entire range of products in an industry or just single items produced by a number of companies—incandescent lamps, wire nails, paper, sugar, cement, pharmaceuticals and dyestuffs, alcoholic beverages, glassware and porcelain. One manufacturer with varied output might be a member of several marketing cartels. Nor was cartel membership limited to national producers. Neighboring firms in Belgium, Switzerland, and Austria-Hungary frequently participated in German cartel arrangements.

German syndicates and cartels were often charged with dumping and undercutting in foreign markets while gouging the consumer at home. Such practices were unquestionably resorted to in times of trade depression and glutted markets. It was asserted by one reporter that the German consumer paid cartelized prices on 70 percent of the products he normally purchased.[34]

In free trade England cartels and monopolies did not flourish so ubiquitously. An artificially high price on a basic product invited a flood of foreign imports. Notwithstanding, trusts and price fixing were common. In 1900, for example, Lever Brothers with their "Sunlight" soap held 17 percent of the British domestic market. After failing to

32. There were 210 cartels in 1890, 385 in 1906, and between 500 and 600 in 1911. Werner Sombart, *Der Moderne Kapitalismus,* 3 vols. (Munich and Leipzig, 1928), III, 696. J. H. Heidreich, "Grundlagen der Kartellbildung," *Kartell-Rundschau* (Dec. 12, 1903), pp. 1174–82, examines all the current explanations of cartels and trusts.

33. A. H. Stockder, *Regulating an Industry: The Rhenish-Westphalian Coal Syndicate, 1893–1929* (New York, 1932), pp. 1–17, 39–47, 76–91.

34. E. D. Howard, *The Cause and Extent of the Recent Industrial Progress of Germany* (New York, 1907), pp. 72–73.

form a pool among the principal producers, Lever began to acquire by purchase the controlling interest in competing firms. By 1914 the Lever trust controlled 60 percent of the domestic soap market and was extending its operations to the Continent and throughout the British Empire. Other trusts and combinations dominated the production and marketing of Portland cement, tinplate, industrial spirits, salt, soda, wallpaper, sewing thread, tobacco, paper, and chemicals.[35]

Reflecting the development of a world economy, international cartels, pools, and syndicates flourished before 1914. Production and marketing of a number of natural products favored monopoly and administered prices. Price and marketing agreements were common among oil concerns, diamond and rubber producers, and in the marketing of nitrates, tin, copper, sulfur, and tobacco. An area in which attempts at fixing rates and allocating business were frequently made but which never endured for long was the freight and passenger traffic of the Atlantic shipping lines. More successful was the steel rail cartel, which dated from 1883. Dissolved and reorganized several times, it was firmly established in 1905 with the United States, England, Germany, Belgium, and France as members, with Russia joining later in 1907. In this cartel, as in other international rings, members were protected in the home market and each was allocated an export area free from competition by other members. By 1914 there were about eighty agreements and arrangements operating that could be identified as international cartels.[36]

The growth of trusts and combinations was unquestionably promoted by financiers and investment bankers, whose control over industry and business was rapidly expanding in the prewar years. In Germany, Italy, and the United States, which experienced rapid industrialization, dependence upon investment banks was much greater than in France and England. This control was greatest in Germany, where the banks participated directly in the management of industries whose securities were held by the bank or the bank's customers.[37] The

35. H. R. Edwards, *Competition and Monopoly in the British Soap Industry* (Oxford, 1962), pp. 157–68; Hermann Levy, *Monopolies, Cartels and Trusts in British Industry* (London, 1927), pp. 213–77.

36. Sombart, *Der Moderne Kapitalismus*, III, 695; A. Sartorious von Waltershausen, *Die Entstehung der Weltwirtschaft* (Jena, 1931), pp. 481–89; Liefmann, *Cartels, Concerns and Trusts*, pp. 148–64.

37. In 1910 the Deutsche Bank was represented on the boards of 134 industrial

influence of suppliers and managers of invested capital was invariably exerted to reduce the risk, to limit competition, and to encourage the pool, the cartel, and the merger.

Werner Sombart, writing his classic work on modern capitalism in the 1920's, judged trustification, cartelization, and the control of industry by banks to be signs of an organic aging of capitalism—"The first gray hairs!" Rudolf Hilferding, a leading Marxian economist, developed the concept of "finance capitalism" as a new stage in the evolution of capitalist society.[38] The attention which he gave to the industrial corporation, tariffs, cartels, trusts, and monopolies, and the increasing power of banks over industry, marks his work as a pioneer study. In his view industrial capitalism in a free trade era was being transformed into finance capitalism in an age of monopoly. From this analysis of capitalistic development he projected his theory of imperialism which must lead inevitably to national rivalries, war, and the end of capitalistic society.

Finally, in concluding this survey of the European economy we must ask: Did the capitalist system in its amazing growth, in the decade before 1914, serve social ends? We know the answer that the Marxists attempted to drum into the minds of urban workers; but the visible split in Marxist ranks between the orthodox and the reformists blunted the ideological message. Equally, proponents of laissez-faire capitalism spoke with less dogmatism than formerly, while public policies were clearly evolving toward state action to ensure a juster distribution of the gains from industrialization. In his standard of living, in the hours and intensity of labor, and in the amenities of life generally, the urban worker in 1914 was better off than his grandfather. Although rising prices after 1900 offset real wages, the organized workers were quick to strike, if necessary, for a fairer share of income. In conclusion, we may join J. H. Clapham in his irenic judgment that the socioeconomic system of Europe in the first decade of the twentieth century deserved "no blessing and no cursing."[39]

---

concerns, the Diskonto Gesellschaft on 124, the Dresdner Bank on 102, and the Bank für Handel und Industrie on 101. In 1913–14 the Deutsche Bank was represented on 161 directorates—commercial, industrial, and financial. Sombart, *Der Moderne Kapitalismus*, III, 740–41.

38. *Das Finanzkapital: Eine Studie über die jüngste Entwicklung des Kapitalismus* (Vienna, 1910).

39. *The Economic Development of France and Germany*, p. 407.

Chapter Four

KNOWLEDGE AND SOCIETY

I. SPENCER AND NIETZSCHE

TIME and the historian have given unity to the thought and culture of past centuries—Greek philosophy in the Ancient World, Scholasticism in the Middle Ages, Rationalism in the eighteenth century, and Materialism in the nineteenth. Such a unity cannot be discerned in the opening decades of the twentieth century. Neither religion, nor philosophy, nor any system of political ideas, not even patriotic faith, was dominant or unchallenged. It is rather the pluralities, the conflicts and contradictions, that impress one. Probably the complexity of thought and theory reflected the growing complexity of society and knowledge. One encounters groups adhering to older ideas, beliefs, and values along with those propagating the new and the novel. The landscape of thought was crowded with "prophets of yesterday" and apostles of tomorrow. A salient feature of the scene was the reaction against rigid rationalism, materialism, and scientism. Rationalism in its various phases had never enlisted the mass of men and women who desired a faith that exalted and consoled. Many intellectuals found the reassurance they desired in the philosophy of William James and Henri Bergson—the "new spiritualism," as it was sometimes called. James and Bergson were philosophic, subtly psychological, and intellectually respectable, even popular among the educated and sophisticated. In "Everybody's World" the specialist, as always, was inclined to take his own part for the whole. Thus it was with the scientists. Whether the world was "mind-stuff," pure will, or a stream of experience did not make sense to the factually minded student of nature. Scientists did not especially love metaphysicians—they barely tolerated them. Thus, overlaid and interwoven were a dozen current and competing views as to what the world was made for and how it related to the nature of man.

The challenging of Darwinian determinism and traditional metaphysical systems was in full course at the turn of the century. The new thought placed the emphasis on the psychological rather than the abstract or systematic. The principal manifestations, coming from many directions and varied sources, were doctrines which subordinated truth to utility, the conscious to the unconscious, reason to instinct, and the intellect to the will. There is a visible affinity between Nietzsche's "will to power," Bergson's *élan vital*, William James' "will to believe," and Sorel's social myth. Objective truth no longer held first place.

Indicative of the changing climate was the precipitate decline of the reputation of Herbert Spencer at the time of his death in 1903, and the posthumous acclaim of Nietzsche, who had died in 1900. While Spencer's authority was never great in Continental circles, where Ernst Haeckel preempted the ground he might have occupied, in Britain and the United States Spencer's disciples had not blushed to compare him with Aristotle! Beginning with the *First Principles* (1862), Spencer had continued through biology, psychology, ethics, economics, and sociology, stringing his beads on the single thread of cosmic evolution. At his death, appreciations appearing in learned journals, written by a more sophisticated generation, partook of the apologetic. It was said of Spencer, somewhat unfairly, that specialists regarded him as a great contributor in every other science than their own. Spencer left no lasting message. What killed him off so abruptly as an intellectual force was the glaring contradiction in his basic principles—his fierce defense of individualism and his championship of the evolutionary process, in which the individual fact or unit is necessarily swallowed up in the aggregate whole.[1] The measures he took to perpetuate his work availed little. In his will all rights and property in his books and investments were vested in his trustees, who were charged to maintain in print his *Descriptive Sociology* and all parts thereof for a period "not to exceed the lifetime of all descendants of Queen Victoria . . . and of the survivors of them." After this original prescription for eternal renown the remainder of his estate was divided among a number of learned and scientific societies. Spencer further ordered the publication simultaneously in Britain and the United States of his completed *Autobiography*, and requested one of his trustees, David Duncan, "to write a biography

1. Spencer was opposed to state-supported education and public health measures. See the appreciations by William James and Franklin H. Giddings in *The Journal of Philosophy, Psychology and Scientific Methods*, I (1904), 51–53; and by F. Paulhan, "Herbert Spencer d'après son Autobiographie," *Revue Philosophique*, 64 (1907), 145–58.

in one volume of moderate size."[2] Despite this concern for posterity's enlightenment Spencer's ideas were a badly depreciated coinage.

When Spencer died, Nietzsche was gaining the fame and notoriety that had been withheld during his lifetime. How the literary works of a man like Nietzsche, which are ignored in the author's lifetime, become revived and elevated to the level of uncritical adulation is a mystery of modern culture.[3] Nietzsche, who led a tortured neurotic life, was an obscure and unsuccessful writer when he was committed to a hospital for the insane in 1889. ("At last, the right man in the right place," is probably an apocryphal comment.) Ten years later a reviewer in *The Monist* commented: "He has countless imitators and admirers. No modern German writer of serious literature is so widely read. . . . An English translation of his works is now being published . . . and some of his effusions have actually been set to music."[4] Georg Brandes, the Danish critic and maker of reputations, claimed credit for forcing Nietzsche upon the attention of the literary tastemakers. The literary periodicals took him up first, followed by the serious press and a growing circle of enthusiastic admirers. Soon a cult formed to whom Nietzsche was a spiritual hero and his writings an emancipation and a revelation. Around 1900 he began to draw the attention of academic philosophers, social critics, and moralists.[5]

Literary enthusiasts were prone to ignore his ideas and praise his images, his poetry, and his spirit. Nietzsche's style—imitative of the French aphoristic philosophers, Montaigne, Pascal, and La Rochefoucauld—was so un-German as to cause excitement and wonder. This together with his unrestrained denunciations of contemporary German culture—placing the music of Bizet above Wagner's, for example—assured his popularity in France. The first full-length biography, excluding that of Nietzsche's sister, was published in 1909 by Daniel Halévy, the noted French critic and literary historian. George Bernard Shaw knew his Nietzsche, seized upon the term *Übermensch,* turned it neatly into "Superman," and enshrined it in the Anglo-American

2. *Journal of Philosophy,* I (1904), 84.

3. For a factual account see Crane Brinton, *Nietzsche* (Cambridge, Mass., 1941), Chap. VII, "The Growth of a Reputation."

4. *The Monist,* Vol. 11 (1900–1), 635.

5. The main body of Nietzsche's works includes *Thus Spake Zarathustra* (1883–84); *Beyond Good and Evil* (1886); *The Genealogy of Morals* (1887); and *The Antichrist,* published in 1902 after his death.

vocabulary. And H. L. Mencken's disdain for sweaty democracy must have been reinforced by, if not drawn from, his reading of Nietzsche.[6] It was doubtless the literary enthusiasts who forced Nietzsche upon the attention of academic philosophers and serious students of ideas. The scholarly journals of philosophy, metaphysics, and psychology began to review and note the appearance of books about Nietzsche around 1900, the year of his death. One of the first to insist that Nietzsche was a "philosopher" was the French scholar Henri Lichtenberger, whose *La philosophie de Nietzsche* appeared in 1898. In 1902, Alfred Fouillée, a respected social philosopher, blasted Nietzsche for his "immoral individualism" in his *Nietzsche et l'immoralisme;* and two years later the distinguished political theorist Émile Faguet rendered his opinion in *En lisant Nietzsche.* He dryly concluded that "Nietzsche is certainly not a very original philosopher." In Germany, the distinguished academic philosopher Hans Vaihinger was among the first to give serious attention to Nietzsche as a thinker. Where Vaihinger led others soon followed. In 1905 the *Revue Philosophique* reviewed six German works devoted to the subject of Nietzsche's philosophy.[7] So rapidly did Nietzsche books come from the European presses that a reviewer in 1906 was moved to say that the literature on Nietzsche was already so "copious and encumbering" as to make it necessary for a writer of merit to establish first that his point of view was a fresh one.

In Nietzsche's thought everything is postulated—nothing is discussed on its merits. Often hailed as "the philosopher with a hammer," he assaulted all the ethical, political, and religious idols of his day. He voiced the views of an elite in an increasingly democratic age; he excluded Christianity—a slave morality—from his conceptions of life and society; he denounced "the greatest good to the greatest number" as an injustice to superior persons; altruism was sterile and usually hypocritical; the egoism of a generous personality alone was positive, fecund, and the source of progress; law was organized power, and

6. H. L. Mencken, *The Philosophy of Friedrich Nietzsche* (Boston, 1908).

7. Raoul Richter, *Friedrich Nietzsche: Sein Leben und sein Werk* (Leipzig, 1903); Jakob J. Hollitscher, *Friedrich Nietzsche: Darstellung und Kritik* (Vienna, 1904); Friedrich Rittelmeyer, *Friedrich Nietzsche und das Erkenntnisproblem* (Leipzig, 1903); Arthur Drews, *Nietzsches Philosophie* (Heidelberg, 1904); Oskar Ewald, *Nietzsches Lehre in ihren Grundbegriffen* (Berlin, 1903); Richard Oehler, *Friedrich Nietzsche und die Vorsokratiker* (Leipzig, 1904).

ideas without force were nothing. Nietzsche believed that Western society was decadent and controlled by decadent ideals and values; the aristocrat was closest to his idea of Superman. The will to power and self-assertion was the central theme of Nietzsche's preaching. His immoralism oscillated between banality and insanity.

Although professional philosophers and champions of established values might make a pitiful slaughter of Nietzsche, this did not check the vogue of his ideas and writings. Rebel youth, boulevard philosophers, and literary enthusiasts read him with delight and approval, if not with full understanding. Of his prominent position in the popular or sub-culture of the period there can be no question. In perspective we see Nietzsche as the figure-symbol of a society questioning its established absolutes. Wilhelm Windelband, a distinguished philosopher and contemporary, made this perceptive evaluation: "We meet [in Nietzsche] an individual of the highest culture, and of a thoroughly original stamp, who experiences all the tendencies of the time, and suffers from the same unsolved contradictions by which the time itself is out of joint. Hence the echo which his language has found; hence the danger of his influence, which does not heal the sickness of his age, but increases it."[8]

Nietzsche was intoxicating to the young intellectuals of the 1920's; after that phase waned, his deeper significance for philosophy began to emerge. Today he is claimed by the phenomenologists and the existentialists. Both Karl Jaspers and Martin Heidegger have explored and expanded Nietzsche's significance for the *Zeitgeist* of the twentieth century.

2. WILLIAM JAMES AND HENRI BERGSON

In philosophical journals and academic seminars, and in educated circles where the shaping of contemporary thought was a matter of interest, the doctrines of William James and Henri Bergson incited more interest and controversy than those of any of their peers. Although their philosophical theories are today mainly of historical interest, they were "living thoughts" to educated men before 1914. Whether James and Bergson were "brothers in Pragmatism" was much discussed in the reviews. James embraced Bergson, as he did nearly

8. *A History of Philosophy* (Harper Torchbook ed., 1958), II, 677.

everyone except the neo-Kantians, but Bergson was always coy in his responses. As a new star rising above the horizon, James preceded Bergson. The philosophical doctrine of Pragmatism was the creation of the American philosopher Charles S. Peirce (1839–1914), but it reached its European audience through William James, who infused it—some say "mangled and aborted"—with his psychology and dressed it up in his glowing style. He wrote in a racy vernacular, so different from the "delicate" style of his brother Henry. Pragmatism looked like a genuine American creation, reflecting the milieu from which it came. James' *Principles of Psychology* (1890) was already well known and highly regarded in philosophical and psychological circles. His *Varieties of Religious Experience* (1902), *Pragmatism* (1907), and *A Pluralist Universe* (1909) established his reputation as a twentieth-century thinker and philosopher. And few would disagree with John Dewey's appraisal at the time of his master's death: In American psychology and philosophy "it was James first and no second."

As an exponent of a new philosophy James came to European attention as a result of a paper read at Berkeley, California, in 1898, entitled "The Pragmatic Method." Kantian idealists were affronted when he said: "Kant's mind is the rarest and most intricate of all possible antique bric-a-brac museums; and connoisseurs and dilettanti will always wish to visit it and see the wondrous and racy contents."[9] To James, who noticed "a curious unrest in the philosophic atmosphere of the time," and "the signs of a great unsettlement," all the extant philosophical systems seemed inadequate. Admitting that he was personally discontented, he proposed to throw his description of his own Weltanschauung "into the bubbling vat of publicity."[10]

James' Pragmatism was an extension of Charles Peirce's prescription that to determine the meaning of an idea one must examine the consequences to which it leads in action. Pragmatism did not look to premises but to results; it repudiated "school solutions" with their emphasis on first things, principles, and categories and looked, in James' words, toward "fruits, consequences, facts." James' world was a "world of experience," especially suited to the age of imperialism, the

9. The paper is reprinted in *The Journal of Philosophy, Psychology and Scientific Methods,* I (1904), 673–97.
10. His first brief formulation of Pragmatism, "A World of Pure Experience," is in the *Journal of Philosophy,* I (1904), 533–43.

motorcar, the motion picture, and experimental art. A contemporary caricature of Pragmatism ran like this: "The test of truth is its utility: It's true if it works. . . . If you can't have what you want, don't want it. . . . The universe ultimately is a joint-stock affair: We participate in the evolution of reality. . . . Lies are false only if they are found out: A perfectly successful lie would be tantamount to absolute truth. We must 'will to believe.' "[11] A caricature certainly, but also highly prophetic.

By 1905 Pragmatism was the most hotly debated subject in the philosophical journals. James' views enlisted support in France, England, and Italy, but in Germany, where traditional philosophy was regarded as a national possession, Pragmatism became a term of opprobrium. In Britain it received its weightiest support from F. C. S. Schiller, who headed a group of Oxford philosophers moving toward a split with the orthodox idealist church of F. H. Bradley. Appealing to "the young, the strong, and the virile," they published the collaborative volume *Personal Idealism* in 1902. It marked the first appearance in England of a radically anti-intellectualistic philosophy, and Bradley forthwith excommunicated the entire group.[12] While Pragmatism accorded well with the buoyant optimism of the Edwardian Era, it and the older Idealism soon went down before the logical realism of Bertrand Russell, G. E. Moore, and Alfred N. Whitehead.

Of the many philosophical and religious creeds that were going to bring youth, daylight, and happiness to the twentieth century none was more polished and fashionable than Bergsonism. Born in Paris of French and Jewish parentage, Henri Bergson was a contemporary of Émile Durkheim and Jean Jaurès at the École Normale Supérieure, that unique training school for France's intellectual and political elite. After teaching at the Lycée of Clermont-Ferrand and the École Normale, Bergson was appointed in 1900 to the Collège de France, where, without the burden of students, he wrote his books, polished his metaphors, and delivered his annual course of lectures to large and appreciative public audiences. A magnetic speaker—polished, erudite, and urbane—he lectured on topics from "Plotinus" to "Personality." It

11. H. H. Bawden, "What Is Pragmatism?" *Journal of Philosophy*, I (1904), 421.
12. Bradley's anathema and Schiller's rejoinder were the great events of the philosophical year. See *Mind*, 29 (1904), 309–35, 525–42; and James' genial support of Schiller, *ibid.*, pp. 457–75.

was a mark of distinction and a necessary part of the salon season to attend Bergson's lectures.

His impressive academic reputation rested on three principal works: *Time and Free Will* (1889); *Matter and Memory* (1896); and *Creative Evolution* (1907). In February, 1913, he made the usual American academic tour, lecturing at Columbia, Yale, Harvard, and Princeton. A bibliographical survey showed 126 books and articles published during 1912 dealing with Bergson and his doctrines. He even achieved the distinction of a book entitled *Bergsonism for Beginners* (1913). Abroad in educated circles Bergson's name was probably better known than that of any contemporary French political figure.

Bergsonism, like its Anglo-American cousin Pragmatism, was a revolt against two dominant nineteenth-century systems of thought. First, it was a repudiation of mechanistic systems, derived from misapplied science; second, it was an expression of great boredom with the traditional philosophies—for the most part Kantian in origin—as expounded in the schools. Bergson, who would overthrow the tyranny of positivism and scientism, began as a follower of Herbert Spencer, then reversed his field and became the principal representative of the anti-mechanistic and anti-intellectual positions in current philosophical thinking. Like James and Schiller, Bergson was impressed by "la malaise de la pensée philosophique" at the end of the century. "In all countries, and among a great many thinkers," he wrote in 1905, "the need is strongly felt for a philosophy more genuinely empirical, more closely in accord with immediate needs, than is found in traditional philosophy, elaborated by thinkers who were above all mathematicians. This objective must of necessity involve a rapprochement between pure philosophy and introspective psychology."[13] Bergson attracted a large audience which was equally bored or dissatisfied with the positivism of Spencer and Haeckel and the stale formulations of the academic philosophers—mind and matter, knowledge and consciousness, nature and God, pears and pence.

Bergson was not the shallow creator of an "instant philosophy," but a poetic thinker responding to the needs and opportunities of his age. A bald summary of his thought does him violence rather than justice. The part of Bergson's thought that reached and influenced the public

---

13. Communication to the editor of the *Revue Philosophique*, 60 (1905), 229–30.

may be summarized as follows: Knowledge is simply an instrument of successful action; the ideal of objectivity in the philosophical conception of truth is a mirage; man must look inward to "the stream of consciousness" for the greatest truths; instinct is superior to intellect because it leads to a comprehension of life that intellect can never give; evolution is blindly creative—not mechanistic—like the work of an artist; the *élan vital* is the life force which operates in a way to make evolution creative rather than rigidly recurrent. This can be capped with Bergson's famous simile depicting all life in all time as a great cavalry charge:

As the smallest grain of dust is bound up with our entire solar system . . . so all organized beings, from the humblest to the highest, from the first origins of life to the time in which we are, and in all places as in all times, do but evidence in a single impulsion, the inverse of the movement of matter. . . . All the living hold together, and all yield to the same tremendous thrust. The animal takes its stand on the plant, man bestrides animality, and the whole of humanity, in space and in time, is one immense army galloping beside and before and behind each of us in an overwhelming charge able to beat down every resistance and to clear many obstacles, perhaps even death.[14]

Obviously, it is the *living* man rather than the *thinking* man who is exalted in Bergson's philosophy.

William James praised Bergson's ideas lavishly: "It is like the breath of morning and the song of birds." But Walter B. Pitkin was moved to publish an impish article entitled "James and Bergson: Or, Who Is Against Intellect?" And A. O. Lovejoy dryly remarked that Bergson had indeed presented them with a world in which "at every moment there is 'something doing' and something to do."[15] Bertrand Russell in an extensive analysis of Bergson's works expressed the opinion that "In the rise of this type of philosophy we may see, as M. Bergson himself does, the revolt of the modern man of action against the authority of Greece, and more particularly of Plato. . . . The modern world calls for such a philosophy, and the success it has achieved is therefore not surprising." Russell was especially displeased with *Creative Evolution,* which advanced no philosophic or scientific proof of opinions ex-

14. *Creative Evolution* (New York, 1911), pp. 270–71.
15. *Journal of Philosophy,* VII (1910), 225–31; XI (1914), 667.

pressed but relied on a brilliant style and an astounding fertility in creating, like a poet, analogies, similes, and vivid images. "The number of similes for life to be found in his works exceeds the number in any poet known to me," Russell wrote. Since Russell had found intellect rather more valuable than intuition or instinct in preparing the *Principia Mathematica,* he took Bergson's contrary position to be downright scandalous. Deploring Bergson's emphasis on instinct and intuition at the expense of intellect, Russell concluded: "In the main intellect is the misfortune of man, while instinct is seen at its best in ants, bees, and Bergson."[16]

Neither Pragmatism nor Bergsonism enlisted the support of Benedetto Croce, Italy's leading philosopher and literary critic. He was, however, always interested in news of Bergson, which he received through his regular correspondence with his friend and admirer Georges Sorel. Croce's name is associated prominently with the Hegelian revival, which was also a feature of the *malaise philosophique* before 1914. Hegel, as a star to steer by, had been dimmed or obscured during the second half of the nineteenth century. His revival, as a prop to idealism, was a feature of the intellectual history at the beginning of the century. Croce had been a marginal Marxist, not as a social reformer but as a student of Marx's economic doctrines and philosophy of history. His critique of Marxism, published in 1900, ended this phase of his intellectual development. Historical materialism, it seemed to Croce, made history "a kind of anthology of all proletarian rebellions."[17] In 1903, collaborating with Giovanni Gentile, Croce established *La Critica,* a high-level review devoted to literature, philosophy, and history. It became a principal force in Italian cultural life and a vehicle for Croce's thought and opinion. His major philosophical works—on aesthetics, logic, ethics, and the philosophy of history—were published between 1902 and 1916 under the general title *The Philosophy of the Spirit or Mind.* His study of Marxist doctrines had led him to a closer examination of Hegel, an intellectual experience which he described in *What Is Living and What Is Dead in the Philosophy of Hegel* (1906). The German thinker's dictum that "Phi-

16. "The Philosophy of Bergson," *The Monist,* XXII (1912), 321–47.
17. Quoted in Gerhard Masur, *Prophets of Yesterday* (New York, 1961), p. 267. Croce's *Materialismo storico ed economia marxistica* (Palermo, 1900), was reviewed by Georges Sorel in *Revue Philosophique,* 49 (1900), 551–52.

losophy is history" became the point of departure and the main theme of Croce's philosophy. Croce did not become the acknowledged chieftain of a school of Italian philosophy, but his influence with historians, writers, and savants was substantial.[18]

While philosophers, both academic and popular, promoted their views of man and nature, the working scientists and their achievements could not be ignored. Meetings of academic philosophers included the philosophy of science in their programs, but the papers presented rarely touched on the problems that contemporary science was posing. Despite the efforts of theorists such as Ernst Mach, Henri Poincaré, and Pierre Duhem, who could communicate with speculative thinkers, the gap widened between science and philosophy. Arresting this trend was the basis of an appeal, published in Berlin in 1912, for the formation of a new organization of scientists and philosophers. Asserting the inadequacy of positivism and the impotence of idealism in the field of science, the appeal called for the founding of an association "which shall declare itself opposed to all metaphysical undertakings, and have for its first principle the strictest and most comprehensive ascertainment of facts in all fields of research. . . . All theories and requirements are to rest exclusively on this ground of facts and find here their ultimate criterion." Among the thirty signers, academic philosophers predominated, but the list also included such "Sunday hunters" in the fields of abstract thought as Ernst Mach, Albert Einstein, Sigmund Freud, Jacques Loeb, and the historian Karl Lamprecht.[19] The plan for organizing a society and the launching of a new journal on the principles specified in the manifesto was apparently one of the first war casualties.

18. On Croce, see H. Stuart Hughes, *Consciousness and Society* (New York, 1958), pp. 200–29; Masur, *Prophets of Yesterday,* pp. 264–74; Cecil Sprigge, *Benedetto Croce: Man and Thinker* (New Haven, Conn., 1952).

19. *Journal of Philosophy,* IX (1912), 419–20. Conspicuously missing were Ernst Haeckel and Wilhelm Ostwald, who were propagating Positivism as a religion through their Monistenbund. This division between monists and pluralists was parodied in the nursery rhyme:

Hickory dickory dock!	Hickory dickory doe!
The pluralist looked at the clock;	The Monist looked also;
The clock struck one,	The clock struck ten,
And away he did run;	And he looked again,
Hickory dickory dock!	And said: "It is three hours slow!"

("Mother Goose, Ph.D.," *Century Magazine,* May, 1907.)

Enough of the thinker's world has been brought thus far under review to suggest the variety and complexity of the landscape of ideas. From the metaphysical systems of the *als ob* (as if) and the *Ding an sich* (thing in itself) to the Pragmatism of James and Schiller, from the crude monism of Haeckel to Bergson's plastic formulations, and from the frenetic images of Nietzsche to the cool persuasiveness of Croce, a hundred viewpoints—some only nuanced and some roughly opposed—were offered for intellectual testing and acceptance.

An important market for displaying and testing new wares in modern thought was the International Congress of Philosophy, the first of which was held in Paris in 1900, the second at Geneva in 1904, the third at Heidelberg in 1908, and the fourth at Bologna in 1911. The third Congress assembled at Heidelberg in anticipation of a "ding-dong" battle between Anglo-American Pragmatists and German-led neo-Idealists. To the latter it seemed that barbarism and obscurantism threatened the very citadel of pure Idealism. Two papers on Pragmatism—one by Schiller on the Pragmatist conception of truth, the other by Professor A. C. Armstrong on the evolution of Pragmatism—were presented at a morning session. The hot discussion that developed continued through a special afternoon meeting, with twenty-five participants requesting time to present their views. The most intemperate denunciation of the insidious doctrine came from the German-American Paul Carus, a philosopher of science and editor of *The Monist*. Pragmatism was a "disease," he said, born of the desire for something new and original. "But the truth it contains is not new, and what is new is false." Its propagators, especially James, he said, were really literary figures, who wrote like novelists and were not real philosophers.[20]

In the intellectual debate that enlivened the Heidelberg congress two world views were clearly discernible—the rational tradition and its modes, which lived on in strength and honor, and the antirational trend that was turning to intuition, personality, sentiment, and action. Here the nineteenth century encountered the twentieth. To the former life was thought and truth was absolute; to the latter life was action and truth was psychological.

The life involvement of two spirited young Russian students who

---

20. *Bericht über den III. Internationalen Kongress für Philosophie* (Heidelberg, 1909), pp. 711–40. See also Carus' slashing attack on James and Pragmatism in *The Monist*, 18 (1908), 321–62. However, as James laconically said: "But life wags on!"

attended the Heidelberg sessions reflected this dichotomy. Anna Alexandrovna Oloviannikova was a graduate student in biology and a dedicated Marxist, preparing a dissertation on the instinct of self-preservation in the crab; while Fedor Stepun was a student of philosophy, a neo-Idealist, writing a thesis on the Christian philosophy of history of Vladimir Soloviev. Despite their opposing philosophical positions, when Anna and Fedor met at Heidelberg they courted and married.[21]

3. PSYCHOLOGY AND HUMAN BEHAVIOR

The substance of twentieth-century psychology was drawn from three sources—philosophy, physiology, and medical practice. Philosophical psychology was as old as Aristotle and came into prominence in the modern period with Locke, Condillac, and J. F. Herbart; physiological psychology emerged from nineteenth-century research on the human brain and nervous system. Wilhelm Wundt fused philosophy of the mind with physiology to establish the "new psychology." Trained in medicine and physiology, but with a strong philosophical bent, Wundt established at Leipzig, in 1879, the first psychological laboratory, wrote the first practical textbook on the subject, coined the term "experimental psychology," and founded the first journal devoted exclusively to the new science. Not only did the next generation of German psychologists emerge from Wundt's seminar and institute, but by 1900 fifteen Americans who had received their training in Leipzig were occupying college or university chairs in the United States. Also, by 1900 there were forty-seven experimental laboratories in the world—twenty-five in the United States, ten in Germany, two each in France and England, and one each in Italy, Switzerland, Denmark, Austria, Russia, Canada, Japan, and China.

Wundt and his students concentrated their work almost entirely on perception and sensations—hearing, sight, feeling, taste, and smell. But this kind of psychology, which was predominant until 1900, yielded little information on the higher mental processes. The first breach in the wall was made by Hermann Ebbinghaus (1850–1909), who published his epochal report on memory (*Über das Gedächtnis*) in 1885. Ebbinghaus devised the nonsense syllable and the technique for mea-

---

21. Fedor Stepun, *Das Antlitz Russlands und das Gesicht der Revolution* (Munich, 1961), pp. 111–21.

suring learning and retention. He developed no systematic psychology, for which we may be grateful, but he made a major contribution to the emancipation of psychology from speculative philosophy. "From the most ancient subject we shall produce the newest science" was his favorite quotation.[22]

In France the new experimental psychology found little encouragement; the traditions of medical and philosophical psychology were much too strong to be displaced by any German import. The chair of psychology in the Collège de France was held by Pierre Janet, France's leading psychiatrist, successor to the great Charcot and a recognized authority on hysteria and other mental ailments. Théodule Ribot likewise was a medical psychologist in the French tradition, holder of the first chair of experimental psychology at the Collège de France (1892). Through the *Revue Philosophique,* which he founded in 1876, Ribot sought to keep his countrymen informed of the development of psychology in Germany, Russia, and the United States. Ribot was the first French psychologist to take note of Freud and his theories and to make the readers of his journal acquainted with them. Outside the medical stream most of the psychology offered in French institutions of higher education was strongly philosophical and oftentimes metaphysical. This tradition is well represented by Bergson's work *Le Rire* (1900), which was translated as *Laughter: Essay on the Signification of the Comic.*

If France did not boast a number of psychological laboratories it had a superior one at the Sorbonne headed by Alfred Binet (1857–1911), who was also the founder of the only French journal of experimental psychology, *L'Année psychologique.* Binet's work was spread over a number of fields, but it had a unity of method in measurement and experimentation. He worked much in the schools and with his own children. In 1905 he published a major work on the results of mental testing: *Étude expérimentale de l'intelligence.* In the following year the Ministry of Public Instruction appointed a committee to study the problem of instruction for retarded or subnormal children in the schools of Paris. As a member of the committee Binet was assigned the problem of differentiating retarded from normal children. Together

22. Edwin G. Boring, *A History of Experimental Psychology* (New York, 1929), pp. 310–26, 380–85. Ebbinghaus founded and edited the *Zeitschrift für Psychologie,* the most important psychological journal in Europe at the turn of the century.

with his collaborator, Théodore Simon, Binet devised the first test-scale for measuring normal intelligence or achievement in relation to age. Binet's "intelligence" included memory, reasoning, and judgment. In the first Binet-Simon test, published in 1905, it was established that a three-year-old child of normal capacity would perform successfully on these points: (1) points to nose, eyes, and mouth; (2) repeats sentences of six syllables; (3) repeats two digits; (4) enumerates objects in a picture; (5) gives family name. Applying the tests to retarded children, he was able to define objectively the categories of idiot (mental age two years), imbecile (from two to seven years), and moron (seven to thirteen years). Binet was working on aptitude tests when he died at the age of fifty-four. His work was basic in all subsequent testing in education, industry, and applied psychology. He was also one of the inventors of the questionnaire method in the social sciences. It is no exaggeration to say that Binet effectively opened up the field in which psychology found its greatest practical application.[23]

Another achievement of laboratory psychology in the nature of a major breakthrough requires brief mention. The conditioned response and its significance in behavior was a contribution of the Russian school of physiological psychology. Traditional philosophy on the one hand and physiology on the other were so firmly entrenched in Russia that there was little unoccupied ground for the development of experimental psychology in the Wundtian tradition. Vladimir M. Bekhterev and Ivan P. Pavlov were both physiologists and carried on their early work at the St. Petersburg Military Medical Academy. Bekhterev's investigations of motor reflexes led to the discovery of the conditioned response and in the formulation of the view that habits in behavior were the compounding or deepening of motor reflexes. Bekhterev's research papers, issuing from his Psycho-Neurological Institute, were noted and abstracted in foreign journals, and his *Objective Psychology*, published in 1910, was translated into French and German.[24]

Pavlov's work completely overshadowed Bekhterev's. The leading European authority on glands and the digestive processes, Pavlov had

23. Robert I. Watson, *The Great Psychologists* (Philadelphia, 1963), pp. 300–16; Edith J. Varon, *The Development of Alfred Binet's Psychology* (Princeton, 1935); François L. Bertrand, *Alfred Binet et son oeuvre* (Paris, 1930).

24. N. Kostyleff, "Les travaux de l'école de psychologie russe," *Revue Philosophique,* 70 (1910), 483–507; also Kostyleff, "Bekhterev et la psychologie de demain," *ibid.,* 77 (1914), 147–69.

received the Nobel prize in physiology in 1904. His work on conditioned reflexes, which he pursued for thirty years, grew out of his earlier physiological research. Pavlov's dogs, "conditioned" to salivate to the tick of a metronome, a tuning fork, or the ringing of a bell, are too well known to require elaborate description. In the Pavlov-Bekhterev system, consciousness and introspection were abandoned and every psychoneural act reduced to the schema of a reflex or excitation of the cerebral cortex, which produced an appropriate response. The conditioned response was the most convincing laboratory achievement underlying the behaviorist psychology of John B. Watson, which was so popular in the United States in the 1920's.

To some observing critics, however, it seemed that the results of experimental psychology were below reasonable expectations, and the expenditure of effort out of proportion to achievements. For fifty years experimental and physiological psychology had been hopeful of results which had not been entirely forthcoming. The work on sensations—visual, auditory, tactile—was impressive, and the mechanism of memory and mental testing showed respectable gains. But with regard to psychic functions, such as perception, imagination, and the springs of human behavior, comparable results had not been achieved. Much had been discovered about *mind* but not a great deal about *minds*. Also psychology had not produced a Darwin. Doubt and frustration reached the point where a well-grounded scholar in the field could speak of "the crisis in experimental psychology," a crisis that in his judgment was close to failure.[25] In this atmosphere, in this partial void, the Freudian school began to propagate its claims to universal understanding of the human mind, human behavior, and human society.

The history of Freudian psychology between 1900 and 1914 mainly concerns the development of psychoanalysis as a diagnostic tool and therapeutic procedure for treating certain mental disorders. World War I focused much attention on shell shock and mental illness; and with the translation of Freud's main works into English his ideas began to receive a full literary exposure as an avant-garde Weltanschauung in the 1920's.[26]

25. N. Kostyleff, *La Crise de la psychologie expérimentale* (Paris, 1911).

26. In 1917 Harold Laski overheard a fashionable lady in fox furs ask in a New York bookstore for a popular novel, and as an afterthought: "And give me a couple of Freud's books, please." *Holmes-Laski Letters,* 2 vols. (New York, 1953), I, 100.

Freud became such a cultural hero in America, and the legend of his life was so deeply imprinted, as to lead to misapprehension of his prewar European position and reputation. Professional and institutional conservatism and the hostility of the Catholic Church insulated a large part of the Continent against Freudian philosophy, doctrine, and medical practice. Moreover, in circles where Marxism flourished Freud found no entry.

As a medical fact psychoanalysis began with Freud's collaboration with Josef Breuer, a distinguished Viennese physician, who provided the original insight into the cause and relief of severe neuroses by the achievement of catharsis while the patient was in a hypnotic state. This collaboration led to the publication of a joint work—*Studies in Hysteria*—in 1895. Shortly thereafter the two became estranged and Freud worked alone. The cause of the separation was Freud's insistence on sex as the principal factor in the etiology of neuroses. Their joint publication attracted little attention, sold only a few hundred copies, and remained untranslated. Freud established a private practice, retained his university connection as *Privatdozent* and later professor, and developed his theories and therapy from his experience with patients who came to him for treatment. In 1900 he published *The Interpretation of Dreams,* one of his basic writings. Only 600 copies were printed, and a second edition was not required for ten years. It was translated first into English and Russian in 1913 and into six other languages in the 1920's and 1930's.[27] *The Psychopathology of Every Day Life,* Freud's most popular book, was published in 1904, and the *Three Essays on the Theory of Sexuality,* which rounded out his psychoanalytical doctrines, was published in the following year. Of the latter, only 1,000 copies were printed, but they were not disposed of until 1910, when a second edition was printed, followed by a third in 1915.[28] The *Leonardo da Vinci,* which Ernest Jones describes as the first psychoanalytical biography, appeared in 1910, in an edition of 1,500 copies, a second edition not being required until 1919. In *Totem and Taboo,* published in 1913, Freud sought to establish a connection or resemblance between the customs and fantasies of primitive peoples and the unconscious fantasies of his neurotic patients. *Totem and*

27. Ernest Jones, *The Life and Work of Sigmund Freud,* 3 vols. (New York, 1953–57), I, 360–62.
28. *Ibid.,* II, 286.

Taboo was adversely received by psychologists as well as anthropologists. From this record the conclusion is inescapable that Freud's books and journal publications down to 1914 served but modestly to communicate his ideas and spread his reputation.

Resistance and indifference to Freud's medical and psychological doctrines did not arise entirely from anti-Semitism in the Vienna milieu, or narrow-minded professionalism, or prudery and blindness of fellow scientists. The nature of neuroses, the novel and dogmatic Freudian interpretation, and the verbal complexity of psychoanalytical therapy were just as important in evoking opposition. From his work with severe cases of neurosis Freud consistently found a connection between the patient's symptoms and repressed memories of past incidents, often from childhood and usually sexual. By the method of "free association," which he substituted for hypnotism, the traumatic incidents could be brought from the unconscious to the conscious attention of the patient. This therapy might last from three months to three years. Dreams played a special part, as they were manifestations of the subconscious mind and memory. In sleep the censorship of consciousness was lifted and past incidents came into consciousness in the role of dreams. As one of Freud's followers described it, "The mind is like a city which during the day busies itself with the peaceful tasks of legitimate commerce, but at night when all the good burghers sleep soundly in their beds, out come these disreputable creatures of the psychic underworld to disport themselves in a very unseemly fashion; decking themselves out in fantastic costumes, in order that they may not be recognized and apprehended."[29] It was the role of the analyst to recognize and apprehend the malefactors, expose them, and thus relieve the patient of the source of his mental ailment or physical distress. The malefactor was invariably, so Freud insisted, some sexual disturbance either current or in the past.

Apparently Freud was not discouraged by the indifference with which his books were received. In 1902 he organized the Vienna Psychoanalytical Society, composed of some thirty members, which met on Wednesday evenings to discuss Freud's ideas and their implications. The membership was not exclusively medical but included persons with artistic and literary ambitions and some of a pronounced cultist type who were disciples rather than discerners. Lou Andreas-

29. *Journal of Philosophy*, X (1913), 552.

Salomé, soon a pupil and prominent follower, was of the latter type. With an affinity for genius she collected famous men—Nietzsche, Rilke, Freud.[30] This nonmedical element, and the cultist overtones, made the Freudian movement suspect in professional and scientific circles. The fact that the Vienna group was predominantly Jewish heightened the cultist impression.

A group of Swiss psychiatrists led by Eugen Bleuler and C. G. Jung joined with the Vienna society to hold the first psychoanalytic conference at Salzburg in 1908. Soon an international association, with Jung as president, was organized with national branches in the United States, England, and Switzerland. Psychoanalytical congresses were held at Nürnberg in 1910, Weimar in 1911, and Munich in 1913. The Weimar congress, the most successful, was attended by fifty-five practitioners and interested persons, five from the United States. Three periodicals were founded—the *Psychoanalytical Yearbook* in 1909, the *Journal of Psychoanalysis* in 1910, and *Imago* in 1912, the latter sponsored by Freud personally as a vehicle for nonmedical applications of psychoanalysis.

In 1909 Freud and Jung were invited to the Clark University congress of psychologists, sponsored by G. Stanley Hall, president of the university and a leading psychologist. Freud's lectures, delivered in German, were subsequently published and won him both supporters and opponents. At the next meeting of the American Psychological Association a hot discussion occurred in the section on abnormal psychology, and most of the animus was provided by Freud's recent appearance at Clark University. Often quoted is the alleged remark of William James to Ernest Jones after hearing Freud's lectures: "The future of psychology is in your hands." But James wrote to Professor Mary W. Calkins on September 19, 1909: "I strongly suspect Freud, with his dream-theory, of being a regular *halluciné*. But I hope that he and his disciples will push it to its limits, as undoubtedly it covers some facts, and will add to our understanding of 'functional' psychology. . . ."[31] In fact William James appears to have been more favorably impressed by Jung than by Freud.

As has been noted, the periodical *Imago* was founded to promote the

30. Rudolph Binion, *Frau Lou: Nietzsche's Wayward Disciple* (Princeton, 1968).
31. Jones, *Life and Work of Sigmund Freud*, II, 57; Ralph B. Perry, *The Thought and Character of William James* (Harper Torchbooks, New York, 1964), p. 199.

nonmedical applications of psychoanalysis. The joint editors were Otto Rank and Hanns Sachs, men with academic and literary training rather than scientific and medical. Together they functioned for several years as Freud's literary and publishing assistants. The articles published in *Imago,* which received considerable publicity because of their novelty, were cut to a single pattern—applications of Freudian principles to primitive myths and folklore, to literary figures and situations, to historical characters, religious beliefs, drama, art symbolism, and creative artists. A typical article by E. Hitschmann applied Freudian techniques to an analysis of Schopenhauer, attributing the philosopher's disharmony, pessimism, and ethics to his "psycho-sexual state," which was diagnosed as a "complexus de l'inceste."[32] Even the medical members of the movement contributed in this field, Ernest Jones doing a psychograph of Hamlet.

Although literary Freudians were notably a postwar phenomenon, by 1914 it had become apparent to perceptive persons, such as Théodule Ribot, editor of the *Revue Philosophique,* that "Psychoanalysis had pretensions to be not only a new method of pathological investigation, but also a discipline applicable, beyond the field of medicine, to the affairs of life and to other sciences or arts such as ethics and pedagogy."[33] Freudian psychoanalysis found earlier acceptance among novelists and literary men, as another key to human behavior, than among psychologists and physicians.

On the medical side it suffered severe reverses owing to disagreement and discord within the organized movement. Although Ernest Jones, in his official biography, portrays Freud, not altogether convincingly, as a tolerant and generous leader, his flexibility did not permit amendment

32. Summarized in *Revue Philosophique,* 77 (1914), 108–11. The most grotesque of such studies was Otto Rank's *Das Inzest-Motiv in Dichtung und Sage* (Leipzig, 1912).

33. Ribot, "La memoire affective et la psycho-analyse," *Revue Philosophique,* 78 (1914), 144–61. In this journal, which was broadly international, Freud's name was mentioned in 1900—together with Janet and Breuer—as an authority on hysteria. Articles mentioning Freud and his ideas appeared in 1913 and 1914, and the editor, Ribot, reviewed at length the first comprehensive exposition of Freud's doctrines written for the French public: E. Regis and A. Hesnard, *La Psychoanalyse: Ses applications médicales et extramédicales* (Paris, 1914). The earliest employment, outside Freud's immediate circle, of Freudian concepts in literary criticism encountered by this author is the Harvard prize essay (May, 1911) by Albert R. Chandler: "The Tragic Effect in Sophocles, Analyzed According to the Freudian Method," *The Monist* 23 (1913), 59–89.

or radical reinterpretation of the fundamental tenets of the Freudian structure—the role of the unconscious, the interpretation of dreams, the conception of repression, and the sexual origins of neuroses. On these issues Freud was like flint, and any deviation or repudiation meant a separation from the movement and the master. As with Josef Breuer, so it was also the sexual doctrines that produced the break, first, with Alfred Adler in 1911 and with C. G. Jung in 1912. Adler, president of the Vienna society, together with several prominent members, resigned from the parent organization and formed the Society for Free Psychoanalysis. The break with Jung was more gradual, but the separation became inevitable with the publication in 1912 of Jung's *The Psychology of the Unconscious* (Wandlungen und Symbole der Libido), which made clear his critical deviations from Freudian doctrine and practice. The upshot of it all was the withdrawal of Jung and the Swiss group from the international association and the formation of a new school adhering to Jung's views rather than Freud's. By 1914 the international association was practically in abeyance and three schools of psychoanalysis were competing for recognition. The outbreak of war filled Freud with pessimism: "What Jung and Adler have left of the movement is being ruined by the strife of nations."[34]

Freud insisted that the war and its irrational fury confirmed his interpretation of human nature. Certainly, after the traumatic experience of the world war, Freud's pessimistic view of human nature carried more conviction among reflective thinkers than it had in the "upward and onward" atmosphere of prewar Europe. Pruned of its excesses and fantasies, Freud's work was a contribution to the understanding of human behavior and personality. And finally, in abnormal psychology and mental health, he demonstrated that the subconscious could be explored, that there was a connection between early life experiences and later psychic disturbances, and that awareness of these early experiences promoted mental adjustment and normality.

4. HISTORY AND THE SOCIAL SCIENCES

In the cultural area which John Stuart Mill designated as the "mental and moral sciences" history easily held first place, whether the

---

34. Jones, *Life and Work of Sigmund Freud*, II, 179. *The History of the Psychoanalytical Movement* (1914) was Freud's angry exposure of the heresies of Adler and Jung. What Binet wrote of Charcot might also apply to Freud: "The masters of science are like kings, surrounded by skillful courtiers, who tint the truth."

measure be the output of books, monographs, and journals, or the place accorded history as a subject of instruction in the schools, or the number of university chairs and seminars devoted to teaching and research. While national history was intensively cultivated in the schools as the substance of civic education, at the university level instruction and research covered a broad spectrum from the ancient and classical to the modern. In the faculty of letters of the University of Paris twenty-two positions were assigned to history and the historical sciences. The specialties of the incumbents ranged from methodology and the sciences auxiliary to history to the history of art and music. Besides the traditional fields, which were well covered (medieval history had three positions), Asian history and cultures were assigned two positions, ancient, medieval, and modern church history three positions, history of the Hebrew religion one, and archaeology, medieval and modern art, and the history of music, one position each. Those professors with international reputations included Charles Seignobos, who taught historical method, G. Bloch in Roman history, F. Lot in medieval, Charles Guignebert in church history, Aulard in the French Revolution, and Émile Bourgeois in modern political and diplomatic history. Not many universities boasted such an assemblage of talent, but the cultivation of the historical sciences was a major objective in all institutions of higher learning.

The writing of history flowed in a many-channeled stream, but political, economic, and institutional history predominated; and over it all hovered the spirit of Ranke and the scientific school. A great part of the historical effort in the nineteenth century had gone into the ransacking of archives and depositories and the publication of their contents in great series such as the *Monumenta Germaniae historica,* the *Collection de documents inédits sur l'histoire de France,* the English *Rolls Series* and *Calendars of State Papers,* and the Martens collection of international treaties and conventions. The writing of histories through individual or cooperative effort, based on the great documentary publications, also reached a peak between 1895 and 1914. If it was not stated in the subtitle of these works, it was understood that they were "based on original sources," and the implication was that if they were not so based then they were suspect.

In this genre national histories took first place, but some of extended scope covered European or world history. Of the latter, the *Cambridge Modern History,* initiated by Lord Acton, appeared in fourteen volumes between 1902 and 1912; and the *Cambridge Mediaeval History,* planned by J. B. Bury, began publication in 1911. The Hunt and Poole *Political History of England,* in twelve volumes, appeared between 1905 and 1910; and the Oman *History of England* in seven volumes between 1904 and 1913. In France, Ernest Lavisse edited and published the cooperative *Histoire de France,* in nine volumes, between 1900 and 1911; and the monumental *Histoire de la langue française* began publication in 1905, although it was not completed until 1927. In Germany the *Allgemeine Geschichte in Einzeldarstellungen,* under the editorship of Wilhelm Oncken, was completed in forty-seven volumes shortly before the turn of the century; and the older series, *Allgemeine Staatengeschichte,* gained a new impetus in 1902 when a younger group of scholars began to contribute. In the United States, the *American Nation* series, under the editorship of Albert Bushnell Hart, appeared in eighteen volumes between 1904 and 1918.

Although cooperative enterprises on the grand scale stood in the forefront, the publications of individual scholars were scarcely less important or significant. Noted historians such as Henri Pirenne, P. J. Blok, V. O. Kliuchevsky, M. I. Rostovtsev, A. Aulard, Ludwig von Pastor, Friedrich Meinecke, and Rafael Altamira, to mention only some of the more prominent, were at the height of their productive powers.

The values attributed to history by this generation of scholars may appear today optimistic if not illusory. History revealed the origins and development of the world's cultures, especially Western culture; it showed how social, economic, and political institutions, as well as customs, languages, and literatures had evolved; and it served to instill a healthy patriotism and promote good citizenship. The general cultural and educational values were indisputable. The historical spirit had invaded every field, and historians had a vision of re-creating, of welding together again, the recovered pieces of human history. Comparable to an industrial revolution, there was division of labor and specialization, the fabricating of component parts, and the assembly of units to produce the completed work. As to the value of it all, historians were by and large convinced, as they so often said, that only through knowledge of the past could one understand the present and make intelligent decisions with regard to the future. About the only question that divided historians of the traditional school was whether history was a science or an art, a subject on which there were about as many opinions as there were historians.

A more sophisticated debate on the methodology, substance, and meaning of man in relation to his history was developing in Germany among the philosophers. It gave a new direction to German scholarship and had a delayed impact on historiography and social science in western Europe and the United States. It began with Wilhelm Dilthey (1833–1911) and his repudiation of idealistic philosophy, materialism, and positivism as keys to the understanding of man. Dilthey is important because he sought to give an independent philosophical foundation to the study and interpretation of history. When the dominant aspiration was "to raise history to the level of a science," Dilthey combated the idea with all the logical weapons at his disposal. Neither metaphysics nor scientific laws unified man and nature. Indeed, "Man does not have a nature; man has a history."[35] The world has meaning only through history; and the valid objective of history is not "to tell" or "to explain" but "to understand" (*Verstehen*). The *Geisteswissenschaften* (cultural sciences) should serve to penetrate the human mind; and the target shifts from institutions and forms to the history of ideas and Weltanschauungen. Wilhelm Windelband, Heidelberg's leading philosopher, occupied adjoining ground, and Heinrich Rickert made up the final bill of divorcement between the natural sciences and the human sciences.[36] Difficult and foggy as were their ideas, Dilthey, Windelband, and Rickert nonetheless exerted great influence on the generation of German scholars who were newly launched on their careers. They especially inspired and validated the *Ideengeschichte* of Friedrich Meinecke and Ernst Troeltsch and the sociological school represented by Max Weber and Werner Sombart.

German social science derived its special qualities not only from those who gave theoretical direction to its development but also from the conditions of its propagation. The state, through its universities, provided the setting and the support. There were no chairs or departments of sociology, and even economics was not uniformly established and supported in the institutions of higher education. Sociology, if offered at all, was customarily a part of the philosophy program. Ferdinand Tönnies and Georg Simmel, both important contributors to

35. Quoted in Masur, *Prophets of Yesterday*, p. 163. Also William Kluback, *Wilhelm Dilthey's Philosophy of History* (New York, 1956).

36. *Die Grenzen der Naturwissenschaftlichen Begriffsbildung—Eine logische Einleitung in die historischen Wissenschaften* (Leipzig, 1902). The book cannot be recommended as light reading, but it had gone through four editions by 1921. It was dedicated to Rickert's friend and colleague Max Weber.

sociological theory, held appointments in philosophy; Werner Sombart was professor of economics; Max Weber's first academic appointment was in law, his major appointment in political economy. Similarly Ernst Troeltsch was professor of theology at Heidelberg and Vilfredo Pareto professor of economics at Lausanne. When the German Sociological Association (Deutsche Gesellschaft für Soziologie) was organized in 1913, its membership represented the theoretical interests of diverse scholars rather than the interests of specialists working empirically in an area defined as sociology.

Max Weber was unquestionably the most original social theorist of his generation, and the one whose influence seems to grow rather than decline. Forced by ill health to resign an academic post, he became in 1903 the editor of the most important social science journal in Germany. Experiencing long periods of illness, he nevertheless produced the main part of his work between 1903 and 1914. He turned his attention first to the methodology of the social sciences and then produced the first memorable example of *Verstehende* (Understanding) sociology with the publication in 1904–1905 of *The Protestant Ethic and the Spirit of Capitalism,* the most widely read of Weber's works. Weber judged the Marxian explanation of the development of capitalistic society to be defective and inadequate; and the classical system of economics—profit, rent, wages, and interest—as offering no explanation at all. There must be some other element, some reinforcement, he reasoned, that inspired the modern attitude toward work and economic achievement. Beyond a certain level people would not have labored with such dedicated industry without an incentive that transcended mere economic gain. He found this drive in religion, in the Protestant ethic and the inner-world feeling that derived from Lutheranism and especially from Calvinism. The Reformation by sanctifying work created a climate favorable to the development of capitalism. Although he did not maintain that Protestantism "caused" capitalism, the affinities that he established and stressed suggested a direct relationship. From this pioneer work Weber went on to his great comparative studies of the economic ethics of the world's major religions. Ernst Troeltsch's *The Social Teachings of the Christian Churches and Sects* (1912) broadened and reinforced Weber's suggestive thesis, and it was restated with special reference to Puritanism by R. H. Tawney in his *Religion and the Rise of Capitalism* (1926).

Weber's controversial challenge to Marx on the genesis of capitalism will still inspire an hour's lively discussion in an undergraduate seminar.[37]

Among Weber's contemporaries—Pareto, Sorel, Durkheim, and Sombart—Durkheim, although not the equal of the others in originality and erudition, made a signal contribution to the establishment of sociology as a branch of social science. In 1900 Émile Durkheim (1858–1917) uttered the proud boast that "Sociology is a science essentially French." Working in the tradition of Comte and Spencer, Durkheim and his school accomplished much that supported this claim. He trained a group of able scholars and supporters, founded and edited the best European sociological journal (*L'année sociologique*), and occupied the first university chair of sociology established in France. Son of a Lorraine rabbi, but completely secular in his orientation, he had attended the École Normale with Bergson, Jaurès, and Janet. There he found the instruction and the atmosphere uncongenial —it was too literary and philosophical—and he was graduated next to last place in his class. His first university appointment was at Bordeaux, where in addition to his courses in philosophy he was allowed to give a course in "social science." Called to the Sorbonne in 1902, he held a combined chair of education and sociology. Durkheim's major publications began in 1893 with the appearance of his *Division of Labor in Society,* followed by a statistically based study of suicide in 1897, and concluding with his last major work in 1912, *The Elementary Forms of Religious Life: The System of Totemism in Australia.* None of these works was valued solely for its instructive data but rather more for the theories and methods which they exemplified. Although Durkheim's work has been surpassed in almost every field, he pointed the way and threw considerable light on three areas of contemporary sociological interest: the differentiation of society, social causation, and the bonds and modes of social cohesion.[38]

As a sociologist Durkheim's only rival was Gabriel Tarde, a "left-

---

37. See E. Fishoff, "The Protestant Ethic and Spirit of Capitalism: The History of a Controversy," *Social Research,* XI (1944), 53–77. What is frequently overlooked is that the scriptural relationship of man's bread to the sweat of his brow is not derived from a Protestant ethic but from the Judaic book of Genesis.

38. H. Alpert, *Emile Durkheim and His Sociology* (New York, 1939), *passim;* Floyd N. House, *The Development of Sociology* (New York, 1936), pp. 204–9; and the judicious appraisal in Hughes, *Consciousness and Society,* pp. 278–87.

handed" sociologist, in that he had taken up social science after completing a career as a state jurist. Chief of the bureau of statistics in the ministry of justice, and later professor in the Collège, his earliest writings were in the field of criminology, where his experience as an investigating judge and prosecutor gave him special competence. His early publications helped to demolish the then popular theories of the Italian Lombroso about "criminal types" and the genetic causes of crime. What especially engaged Tarde's interest was the factor of imitation in group life, and especially in antisocial behavior. The *Laws of Imitation* (1890), *The Social Laws* (1898), and *Opinion and the Crowd* (1901) are Tarde's basic works, the last one being the most popular book of its time on "crowd psychology."[39]

Anyone assessing the significance of Georges Sorel will reflect long on whether to classify him with the abstract thinkers or the social philosophers and reformers. He was, in fact, a mixture of both, but since he was a spectator of the workers' movement and not in any way a direct participant, he is best placed with the thinkers. He is remembered for one book—*Reflections on Violence*—and for his later intellectual linkage with Communism and Fascism. Sorel, like Gabriel Tarde, had two distinct careers. Bourgeois in origin, and an engineer by training and profession, he resigned from state employment after twenty-five years to devote his time to study and writing. His education in philosophy, the humanities, and social science was acquired almost entirely from critical reading and isolated reflection. He did not absorb and systematize the ideas of others but analyzed and reacted to all that he read. Original in his thought, he was an intellectual eccentric and very nearly a crank.

After he settled at Boulogne-sur-Seine in 1892 he became a familiar figure in the Bibliothèque National, the public lecture halls of the Collège de France, and the editorial offices of the various reviews to which he regularly contributed. His literary and mental endowments were such as to gain him the acquaintance and respect of Bergson, Croce, and Pareto, and among the younger French intellectuals, the friendship of Charles Péguy, Edouard Berth, and Robert Michels. Among his contemporaries he sought affinity with William James and

---

39. Harry Elmer Barnes and Howard Becker, *Social Thought from Lore to Science,* 2 vols. (Boston, 1938), II, 850–58; House, *Development of Sociology,* pp. 187–93.

Bergson; he seemed uninterested in German philosophy and sociology, and he reacted to Durkheim and Poincaré with skeptical irony.

Sorel began his writing as a marginal Marxist, a critical analyst of Marx's economics and philosophy, and not a pious commentator. He then embraced revisionism, became for several years the "metaphysician of syndicalism," as Jaurès called him, flirted ardently with royalist circles, and then reverted to his commitment to the proletariat. When the Bolsheviks came to power in Russia, he completed his cycle of illusions by saluting Lenin as the leader who had realized his syndicalist myth.

The syndicalist or militant trade union movement, which burst into prominence in France around 1900, inspired Sorel to write the *Reflections on Violence*. The turmoil engendered by strikes was universally condemned even by parliamentary socialists, who favored negotiation and conciliation. To justify the militancy and to give syndicalism an ideology, Sorel published the series of articles that became, as one of his biographers calls it, "a famous and infamous book." Indeed, it was Sorel's only successful book of about a dozen published.[40]

Two of its themes have become a part of social science literature: the concept of the social myth and the virtue of violence. To Sorel the syndicalist's general strike, the Marxist's catastrophic revolution, the Christian's church militant, the legends of the French Revolution, and the remembrance of the June Days are all myths that move men, quite independent of their historical reality. As one of Sorel's disciples (Mussolini) said, men do not move mountains; it is only necessary to create the illusion that mountains move. Social myths, says Sorel, are not descriptions of things, but "expressions of a determination to act."[41] Myths enclose all the strongest inclinations of a people, of a party, or of a class, and the general strike is "the myth in which Socialism is wholly comprised."[42] For Sorel the general strike was a catastrophic conception of socialism, the essence of the class struggle, and the only true Marxist means of effecting the revolution.

40. James H. Meisel, *The Genesis of Georges Sorel* (Ann Arbor, 1951), p. 125. Sorel's *Reflections,* published in Paris in 1908, had gone through four editions and many printings by 1919. It was translated into Italian in 1909, into English in 1914, and into Spanish in 1915. It was also translated into German and Japanese in 1928, and it has had four separate editions in the United States.
41. *Reflections on Violence* (New York, 1961), p. 50.
42. *Ibid.,* p. 127.

Nowhere does Sorel endorse indiscriminate, brutal violence; only violence "enlightened by the idea of the general strike" is unconditionally defended; only violence in the Marxist class war, as Sorel conceived it, is fine and heroic and in the service of "the immemorial interests of civilization." In fact, there is no justification of violence by philosophical argument, but long excursions by an overloaded mind into past history and current events to demonstrate that ethical codes are relative to their time and place. Consistent with this position he could describe the Declaration of the Rights of Man as "only a colorless collection of abstract and confused formulas, without any great practical bearing."[43]

Are alienated intellectuals like Sorel to be held responsible for what was later enacted in their name? Thinkers such as Nietzsche, Bergson, Weber, and Pareto did not relate their philosophical formulations to current political ideologies. But good troops can be enlisted in bad causes. Their ideas may have been "dated and depleted," as Guido de Ruggiero insisted, but when the barbarians arrived on the scene after the war the gates were half open and the defenses weak. For this the "treasonous clerks" do not escape all responsibility.

This chapter began with Nietzsche and closes with Sorel. In between are those philosophers, psychologists, sociologists, and savants whose ideas gave tone and texture to the period. Unity and agreement are lacking; but the marketplace is crowded and the costs of printing were never so low. The work of the historians was probably more of a stabilizing force than that of other cultural practitioners. In no one individual or school are all ideas and trends of the period fully exemplified. The range is too wide: the intellectual repudiation of science and positivism; the enthusiasm for philosophies of action, practice, and experience; the valuing of instinct and intuition above intelligence; the representation of the primitive and barbaric as more revealing of man's nature than religion and enlightenment; the proclaiming of social violence as a higher ideal than social peace; the anti-intellectualism of leading intellectuals; and the increasing isolation of the philosophic liberal—all these attract the observant eye and confound the classifier. In their totality, as well as their variety, these signs announce, as Élie Halévy perceived so clearly, that between 1895 and 1914 one era had ended and another had begun.

43. *Ibid.*, p. 210.

Chapter Five

THE CULTURAL ENVIRONMENT

I. MODERNISM AND THE CHRISTIAN CHURCHES

In the second half of the nineteenth century the authority of traditional Christianity was challenged by two modern developments: the revolutionary advances of science and the historical criticism of the Scriptures and Christian origins. Both weakened the position of the churches, evoked damaging reactions, and led to the desertion of a very large part of the European intellectual and scientific elite. By 1900 many adjustments and concessions had been made, although no true synthesis of theology and the new trends in science and scholarship had been produced. The exasperation of theologians defending traditional positions and the aggressiveness of their rational and scientific opponents had considerably abated, but "modernism," as it was commonly labeled, was by no means a dead issue.[1] Transformations and adjustments were broadly made in the Protestant churches, but during the pontificate of Pius X (1903–1914) every manifestation of modernism was expunged from official Catholicism.

Pius' predecessor, Leo XIII, had constructively expounded Christian alternatives to materialism, agnosticism, and secularism; he had revived the international prestige of the papacy and had sought accommodation with the political, social, and economic changes that had occurred in the nineteenth century. Especially notable was the position taken by Leo XIII in the encyclical *Rerum Novarum* (1891), toward the social and economic issues raised by modern capitalism and industrialization. The encyclical was so prudently drawn and balanced that it was capable of various interpretations on specific points, but its main message was clear: Christian faith comprehended social reform and economic justice.[2] To restore and maintain communication with the

1. On the modernist controversy, see Carlton J. H. Hayes, *A Generation of Materialism*, pp. 131–41.

2. An English Catholic interpreter found it wholly pleasing that it said nothing about votes for the working class; and the injunction to keep the Sabbath holy suggested that it would be un-Christian to start strikes on Sunday, or to conduct strikes at all.

alienated industrial workers became henceforth a major objective of Ketteler in Germany, Meyer in Austria, De Mun in France, Manning and Vaughan in England, Gibbons in the United States, and Moran in Australia. To a greater extent than the Protestant churches, the Catholic Church was able to hold the allegiance of its urban working classes.

The substantial gains made during the pontificate of Leo XIII were jeopardized by the issue of modernism during the pontificate of his successor. If the College of Cardinals had approved overwhelmingly the central policies and concerns of Leo XIII, they would have elected, in 1903, the Cardinal Secretary of State Rampolla, who had been the spirit and instrument of those policies. But when the leader of the Austrian delegation intervened in the conclave to object to Rampolla's election, the choice finally fell on Cardinal Sarto of Venice, who as Pius X headed the Catholic Church until his death in August, 1914.[3]

Pius X's interests and policies were concentrated, in a rather narrow sense, on the pastoral mission of the church. Administrative reforms were vigorously instituted, the religious orders were expanded and energized, training in the seminaries was improved, and the missionary work at home and abroad was given concentrated attention. In Africa and Asia the diocesan organization was greatly expanded in the wake of the missionary movement. Funds were sufficient, if not plentiful, and it was a period of growth and solid achievement. In the field of liturgy and worship the Eucharistic Congresses were raised to the level of world events. Especially brilliant and massively attended were those held in Rome (1905), London (1908), Cologne (1909), Montreal (1910), and Vienna (1912).

Progressive in matters of churchmanship, Pius X assumed a posture of intransigent opposition to everything that was modern in culture, learning, and thought. In syllabus and encyclical he sought to eradicate from Catholic faith and practice all taint of secularism and compromise with learning, science, and social ideas of the new age. This

---

K. S. Inglis, *Churches and the Working Classes in Victorian England* (London, 1963), p. 315.

3. Josef Schmidlin, *Papstgeschichte der neuesten Zeit,* 4 vols. (Munich, 1933–39), III, 12–20. Austrian disapproval of Rampolla resulted from his known democratic sympathies, his support of the Christian social movement, his concern for the Slavic nationalities, and his pro-French leanings.

reached a point of exaggeration where to some observers it seemed that the papacy had wholly repudiated the twentieth century. The image of the Catholic Church as wedded to the past and opposed to modern scholarship, science, and rational knowledge—an image which endured until the middle of the century—was largely formed in the decade before 1914.

The modernist movement, which was more doctrinal than sociological, began about 1890; by 1910 it was dead. It had no schismatic outcome, although a number of prominent theologians were forced out of the church or retired voluntarily. The more prominent modernists— Alfred Loisy, George Tyrrell, Friedrich von Hügel, and Friedrich Heiler—hoped to make the Roman Catholic Church theologically more habitable for those who would accept the results of modern biblical scholarship and historical research. They also disagreed with the official acceptance of Thomism as the only philosophy consistent with Christian faith and knowledge. Previous condemnations of liberal Catholicism had always left loopholes for evasion or maneuver, but the decrees *Lamentibili* (1903) and *Pascendi* (1907) defined and condemned sixty-five propositions or errors concerning intepretation of sacred scripture. The sweeping pronouncement practically put beyond use by the scholar and theologian the modern methods of historical and biblical criticism which had developed during the preceding fifty years. Anyone found tainted by modernism was to be removed from his office or teaching position in seminary or Catholic university. Later, in 1910, an antimodernist oath was imposed on all candidates for holy orders and all clergy exercising ministerial or teaching functions. The organization of diocesan "Councils of Vigilance" was another unlovely aspect of Pius X's campaign against an exaggerated danger.

There was surprisingly little opposition to the antimodernist oath except in Germany, where professors in Catholic theological faculties of the state universities were exempted after a second *Kulturkampf* threatened to erupt. For the leaders of the modernist movement the alternatives were clear-cut: submit, or eat the bitter bread of the unfrocked clerical. Many less prominent members of the clergy in Germany, France, England, and the United States who subscribed to the oath must have deplored the rigorously suppressive measures instituted by Pius X and a small group of zealots in the Curia. The antimodernist crusade postponed for a generation the rapprochement between Catholicism and Protestantism, which was prerequisite to the twentieth-century ecumenical movement.[4]

In matters theological and doctrinal the Protestant churches made the broadest accommodation to the new forces of biblical scholarship, science, and secularism. Historical scholarship and biblical criticism had a transforming influence equal to, if not greater than that of science. Applied to Christian texts and literature, the new scholarship evoked the historical and reduced the supernatural and eschatological. Adolf von Harnack's *History of Dogma* and Auguste Sabatier's *Religions of Authority* are representative of the scholar's synthesis of the new knowledge and the old faith. New encyclopedias of religious knowledge, manuals, and treatises richly set forth and transmitted the fruits of modern scholarship. James Moffatt's translation of the New Testament into modern English, published in 1913, was indicative of the modernizing trend in Protestant circles.

Reassessment of the central figure of Jesus had also been a feature of the modernist movement among Protestant scholars. Beginning with Renan's *Life of Jesus* and David Friedrich Strauss' *Life of Jesus Adapted for the German People,* there had appeared a score or more of "liberal" lives of Christianity's central figure. All emphasized the "Jesus of history," and ignored the "Christ of religion." The first to challenge this popular trend in a notable way was Albert Schweitzer, whose *Von Reimarus zu Wrede* was published in 1906 and translated four years later as *The Quest of the Historical Jesus*. A landmark in historical theology and biblical criticism, Schweitzer's work repudiated the scholar's Jesus as unrelated to the central problem of religion. The attempt to portray him and his message in contemporary terms, to bring him into this world as a great social reformer, as an agitator in history, or as a kind of super-Socrates, was utterly bankrupt and in itself unhistorical. The "half-historical, half-modern Jesus," he concluded, "is a figure designed by rationalism, endowed with life by liberalism, and clothed by modern theology in an historical garb."[5] Schweitzer's matchless

---

4. Schmidlin, *Papstgeschichte,* III, 138–71; A. R. Vidler, *The Modernist Movement in the Roman Church* (Cambridge, Eng., 1934), *passim; New Catholic Encyclopedia,* 15 vols. (New York, 1967), VIII, 350, XI, 409.

5. *The Quest of the Historical Jesus,* tr. W. Montgomery (New York, 1961), p. 399. "The mistake was to suppose that Jesus could come to mean more to our time by

work of scholarship closed one period of Protestant theology and cleared the road for the next—the neo-conservatism of Karl Barth, Emil Brunner, Paul Tillich, and Reinhold Niebuhr.

Church history and theology mainly concerned church scholars, clergy, and seminarians, and was but one aspect of Protestant church life. Churches also had an institutional life, and their raison d'être lay in the religious services performed for their communicants. In the state churches of Germany, Switzerland, Holland, and Scandinavia, constitutional structures were somewhat altered in the direction of a larger role for the congregational laity in church affairs. But the state remained dominant in the appointment of ministers and management of financial affairs. Civil marriage, civil registration of births, and freedom to sever the church connection, however, did not produce the adverse effects predicted by churchmen at the time of their adoption. In Germany the number of withdrawals from church membership—the only escape from the state-levied church tax—between 1909 and 1914 was fewer than 20,000 annually. Such separations occurred mainly in the large cities under the influence of Marxist ideology. Middle-class and rural families preferred not to incur the social stigma attached to separation from the church.[6] Overall, one can say that "state churchism" remained unaltered, which signified that the churches continued to be strongly national, socially conservative, and dependent on the state.[7] Indeed, by some the church was valued principally as a public utility, supporting peace and order in civil society.

This alliance of church and civil authority explains in part the failure of the Protestant state churches—the Catholic Church had a better record—to gain and hold the allegiance of the urban working classes. This was the most formidable problem of the ecclesiastical communities in the industrially advanced areas of Europe. The state churches—Anglican, Lutheran, Reformed—were organized originally

---

entering into it as a man like ourselves. That is not possible. First because such a Jesus never existed. Secondly because, although historical knowledge can no doubt introduce greater clearness into an existing spiritual life, it cannot call spiritual life into existence."

6. When Wilhelm Ostwald, who was associated with Ernst Haeckel in the anti-Christian Monist League, withdrew from the church in Saxony, he had to appear for questioning before a magistrate and the local pastor. Grete Ostwald, *Wilhelm Ostwald—Mein Vater* (Stuttgart, 1953), p. 141.

7. Heinrich Hermelink, *Das Christentum in der Menschheitsgeschichte*, 3 vols. (Stuttgart, 1951–55), III, 157–91, *passim*.

to serve a predominantly agrarian society. Religious facilities did not keep pace with the mushroom growth of urban industrial areas. For long it was believed by churchmen that when more churches were built they would be filled. By 1900 this easy assumption was dissipated. Where new churches were built and pastoral personnel provided, the workers were still absent. Church attendance, it had to be admitted, had become mainly a rural and middle-class custom. In almost all industrialized countries the estrangement of the industrial working classes from formal Christianity is a fact, but one that has not been fully explored or explained. We really know little about the effect of industrialization and urbanization on religious behavior and practices.

Only for England and France do we possess any trustworthy studies of religious customs and attitudes. Whether it was the established church or the nonconformist chapel, their social conservatism repelled the working man. The Church of England was so bound up with the state and with wealth and privilege that as an institution it had little attraction for the urban working classes. Preaching "mercy to the rich and patience to the poor," as Robert Blatchford, the socialist journalist described it, had worn threadbare during the nineteenth century. Nonconformist Wesleyan and Congregational churches were as much opposed to democracy, socialism, and social reform as they were to sin. The Salvation Army, Workmen's Missions, and the settlement houses worked with the "reclaimed poor," but in between the lower middle class and the "poor" were the working classes, who were not reached by the organized churches and missions. Slow to take a positive stand, the churches became identified in the minds of the workers with the forces of opposition and restraint.

Among the middle and upper classes attendance at church was a traditional propriety; among the working classes nonattendance, hostility, and indifference became equally traditional. Social convention kept the urban workers away from the churches, and nonattendance became a sign of class solidarity. For the worker rising out of his class, joining a religious body meant ascent in the social scale and adoption of the middle-class way of life.

In the opening decade of the twentieth century religious interests were unimportant compared to the trade union, the friendly society or lodge, the political party, and the "pub." Sport, racing, drinking, and gambling were the habit patterns of workingmen rather than church-going. There was, however, no ingrained hostility to religion itself. Declared atheism or unbelief was probably rarer among workingmen than among intellectuals. On the Continent Marxian socialism was avowedly hostile to religion as the "opiate" of the people. Not so in England. It is a known fact that the incidence of baptism was declining —it had been for generations—and civil marriage was on the rise, but there was scarcely ever a funeral without some kind of Christian rites.[8]

"Men loyal to the Church were forever denouncing the triumph of irreligion and irreligious men were forever denouncing the triumph of the Church," is an apt description of the politico-religious scene in France by Gabriel Le Bras, a sociologist who has devoted a lifetime of scholarship to the investigation of the religious attitudes and practices of the French people.[9] Was France de-Christianized as some observers maintained? This was one question he sought to answer. Using statistical techniques and taking account of social complexities, Le Bras and his co-workers mapped religious attitudes and practices in France in the 1920's and 1930's. Since religious practices are strongly influenced by inherited habits, we can assume that roughly the conditions described for the later period were prominent before 1914. In the religious map of France the nuances were impressive; some bishoprics and parishes ran to massive conformity and observance, while in others paganism and almost complete de-Christianization prevailed. The areas of greatest indifference, even hostility, were those of the Paris basin, the Rhone Valley, and southwestern France.[10] Among the significant social forces determining religious attitudes and practices were those of urbanization, the influence of a secular state, and the nationalization of Parisian attitudes and customs. The decline in importance of the aristocracy, a

8. Three studies in this field can be described as objectively illuminating: Inglis, *Churches and the Working Classes in Victorian England*, especially pp. 322–36; E. R. Wickham, *Church and People in an Industrial City* (London, 1957)—the city is Sheffield and the author traces the alienation of the working class back to the eighteenth century; G. S. Spinks, *Religion in Britain Since 1900* (London, 1952), has less depth but is a thoughtful work.

9. For a description of the work of Le Bras and associates, see Eva J. Ross, "Modern Studies in the Sociology of Religion in France and Belgium," *American Catholic Sociological Review*, XV (1954), 115–40.

10. Le Bras, *Études de sociologie religieuse*, 2 vols. (Paris, 1955–56), I, 254–66; and map of religious practices, p. 325, showing by departments *Pays chrétiens, Pays indifférents, Pays de mission*. In the latter Protestants were numerous and up to 20 percent of infants were unbaptized.

crisis in the sacerdotal vocation resulting from separation of church and state, the growth of socialism and trade unions—all contributed to change and created substitute forms of social solidarity. Secularized schools and the army garrison, maintained by universal military service, also altered habits and isolated French youth from priestly guidance.

In the reaction to the Dreyfus Affair the French Chamber passed in 1901 the Associations Law, which in its application had the effect of banning Catholic religious orders in France, a serious blow to Catholic schools. The resultant friction with the papacy led in 1905 to the denunciation of the Napoleonic Concordat and the withdrawal of state recognition and support from all religious cults. In the Catholic Church this produced a severe crisis in financing, recruitment of seminarians, and the maintenance of the services of religion. Seven years after separation a very dark picture could be drawn. The church income amounted to 20 million francs, about half the former state budget; and the average annual income of rural priests was between 1,000 and 1,200 francs, scarcely more than the income of an agricultural laborer. There were but 620 priests in Paris and only 80,000 in all of France; and in the French urban population of nearly 8 million, only an estimated 600,000 were practicing believers. On the brighter side some observers thought that separation had produced important benefits. There had been a considerable revival of religiosity, clerics showed more zeal for their work, and the hierarchy now had greater independence in promoting religious programs. Even in Paris some parishes could report that the number of persons requesting the last sacrament had increased fourfold in four years and the number of children confirmed had increased six times in the same period. But one historic thread was forever broken: the idea of a Gallican church was dead. The Catholic clergy in France could now look only to Rome.[11]

Of the religious scene in general before 1914, it can be said that the historic churches retained their standing in rural areas. Among the middle classes church adherence was perhaps more of a social and cultural formality than a religious experience. There was a great deal of accommodation certainly, a rather easy synthesis of loyalties toward

11. C. Brival-Gaillard, report of an inquiry on the religious attitudes of the French people, *La Revue*, No. 13 (July 1, 1913), pp. 1–19; also "Frankreichs katholische Kirche sieben Jahre nach Trennung vom Staat," *Neue Zürcher Zeitung*, No. 212 (Feb. 12, 1914).

church, state, and society; unconditional adherence to all three did not seem contradictory. There was no obvious clash of values to create unbearable tensions, no avowal yet, as later, by intellectuals that they were suffering *Angst,* isolation, nausea, and despair.

2. SUBSTITUTE RELIGIONS—POSITIVISM, MONISM, SOCIALISM

Who were the defectors from the historic churches at the end of the nineteenth century? They were the secularists on intellectual grounds, the industrial working class on social grounds. What did they substitute for religion? That depended upon a multiplicity of factors—tradition, temperament, intellect, education, profession, social class, and economic status. A deceased graduate of the *École Normale Supérieure* left this personal testament, which was published in 1906:

> In the matter of religion, I have never been attached to a dogma or a sect; I have never embraced an organized cult; I have been, in the very ordinary sense of the word, a freethinker. In matters philosophical, I have endeavored to raise myself above materialist and positivist doctrines, not at all because of disdain or hostility, *but because I never found them for myself sufficiently consoling.* . . . I have always held, in what concerns the future life and the immortality of the soul, to the Platonic formulas; it is a good chance to take, it is a great expectation to contemplate! (C'est une belle chance à courir; c'est une belle espérance à concevoir!) [12]

Obviously an irenic intellectual, an educated humanist, speaks in this testament. How many there were who subscribed to this view, and how wide their influence, cannot be determined by any objective means. Among the highly educated, in humanistic university circles, the number was probably not inconsiderable.

Religious attitudes are among those undercurrents of personal life which occasionally come to the surface. Available evidence suggests that a large part of the educated were rationalists whose inherited ideas had been reinforced by nineteenth-century science. William Archer, the English critic and dramatist, reared in a pious family, made for himself a sufficient religion out of "pride in the history of man and faith in his destiny."[13] George Meredith was avowedly agnostic, and Sir Eyre Crowe, assistant undersecretary in the Foreign Office, was aggressively

---

12. *Revue Philosophique,* 62 (1906), 113.
13. C. Archer, *William Archer, Life, Work, and Friendships* (London, 1931), p. 416. Archer was the principal translator of Ibsen's works and an intimate friend of G. B. Shaw.

atheistic. This led one of his associates to circulate these whimsical lines:

> Crowe will tell you 'til you nod,
> Why he does not believe in God;
> But what we'd really like to know:
> Does God Himself believe in Crowe?

Any list of intellectuals prominent in literature, learning, and public life who were avowedly indifferent, alienated, or hostile to traditional religious beliefs would be a very long one indeed.

Rationalists envisaged men perfecting themselves through knowledge, science, or an improved social order. If they tolerated religion at all—and there were grades of approval and disapproval—they did so because it helped to clean up the natural man. Literature and the drama affirmed religious and social emancipation; and a generous idealism often substituted for religious conviction. The sophisticated social scientist made little distinction between religion, myth, and legend—they were all a part of the human complex. In general, among the highly educated, revelation was discredited as a source of knowledge. Experience alone yielded valid comprehension. Religion never got a very fair hearing with the highly educated because they took its historic forms and rites to be the essence of the thing itself.

Biblical scholarship, Positivism, modern geology, biology, and anthropology were all solvents of orthodoxy. Never since the eighteenth century had there been such a quest by a large part of the educated class for a nontheological guide to life. Many fugitives from orthodoxy stopped short of total unbelief by affiliating with a Unitarian church, an Ethical Society, or a secularized organization such as Ernst Haeckel's Monistic League. The Free Masons, the Free Thought Societies, the Union of Free Thinkers, and many similar organizations offered fellowship to rationalist refugees from "superstition" and "darkness." Whether muted or accentuated, they all sought to deify mankind. It was a property of the age. These societies were also distinctly elitist organizations, their membership believing that they were in possession of truths which would one day "uplift and regenerate the masses." Such was the Positivist Church in London, with which Frederic Harrison and F. S. Marvin were associated for many years. This society had taken on the sizable task of "a reorganization of life, at once intellec-tual, moral, and social, by faith in our common humanity." Beatrice Webb attended one of the meetings at Newton Hall with Frederic Harrison and was not favorably impressed. "His [Harrison's] address seemed to me forced—a valiant effort to make a religion out of noth-ing; a pitiful attempt by poor humanity to turn its head round and worship its tail." And another person who made casual contact with the Religion of Humanity averred that he did not "admire the human race sufficiently to worship it."[14] In France, the strife-torn Positivist society kept alive the tradition of Comtean religion—unification of science and society, peace, and a common humanity—although its active membership never exceeded a few hundred converts. But orga-nized Positivism belonged to the nineteenth century; as a significant force in France and England it did not survive the war.[15]

In central Europe the most conspicuous of the substitute religions was the Monistic movement led by Ernst Haeckel, whose fame and position as a scientist was based on his unfaltering championship of Darwinism through decades of controversy. Haeckel's philosophy, which was the foundation of the movement, was derived from Scien-tism rather than Positivism, although Haeckel's closest associate in the Monistic League, Wilhelm Ostwald, can be classified as a marginal Comtean. A controversial figure in scientific circles from which he emerged, Haeckel was an arresting speaker and provocative writer. Lacking Thomas Huxley's depth, he had some of the Englishman's qualities as a propagator of the faith and spokesman for the scientific view of man and his universe. Haeckel was also arrogant, dogmatic, and polemical. His popular *Riddle of the Universe* was a statement and vindication of his Monistic philosophy in which man was completely merged with nature. All dualist philosophers and theologians, past and present, ancient and modern, all distinctions between soul and body, mind and matter, spirit and substance were targets of his denunciation. For Haeckel the God-idea meant matter and energy; religious ideas were mere fancies or fraudulent inventions. Haeckel's book was a compound of fantasy, polemic, and excessive projection from his scien-tific experience, which by 1900 was manifestly depleted. Sir Oliver

14. Walter M. Simon, *European Positivism in the Ninteenth Century* (Ithaca, 1963), pp. 226–27 n.
15. *Ibid.,* pp. 64–70.

Lodge described Haeckel as "a surviving voice from the middle of the nineteenth century. . . ."[16]

In 1906, Haeckel organized the Monistic League (Monistenbund), which began an aggressive propaganda directed to academicians, scientists, intellectuals, technologists, and the educated middle class. Responding to the appeal were such figures as Wilhelm Ostwald, who became the League president; Rudolf Diesel, the engineer; and the Belgian industrialist Ernest Solvay. Annual congresses were held, a League publication was launched (*Das Monistische Jahrhundert*), and branches of the League were established in the principal cities of Germany, Austria, and Switzerland. The stated objective of the League was to purge and purify man's mind of all superstition and theological conceptions and to replace them with a new "world view" derived from modern science. The Monists would "elevate man's conception of himself to the plane of a true and natural dignity," and "give man an insight into the world as a vast, living, striving, conscious organism, of which he is an integral part, realizing the 'kingdom of heaven' during our life on earth."[17] In imitation of Christian practice a Monistic catechism was devised which answered all fundamental questions in terms of science. Some parts of this document, however, seemed singularly unscientific. Article 32 inquired: "How does man look for truth?" And the answer given was: "In a twofold manner: By learning to find out and by believing what is taught him."[18]

Alarmed at the response to the propaganda of the Monistic League, conservative scientists and theologians organized a rival Kepler Society (Keplerbund) to combat the movement led by Haeckel and Ostwald. When Adolf von Harnack attacked Ostwald personally in the Evangelical Church Congress for promoting a Weltanschauung composed

---

16. *Life and Matter—A Criticism of Professor Haeckel's "Riddle of the Universe"* (London, 1905), p. 51. The original title of Haeckel's book was *Die Welträthsel: Gemeinverständliche Studien über Monistische Philosophie* (Bonn, 1900). The book was widely circulated, selling some 300,000 copies before 1914 in the original and in various translations. In the holdings of the University of Virginia library are three copies of Haeckel's book; they were owned respectively by the William W. Corcoran professor of philosophy, the dean of the school of engineering, and the late Senator Miles Poindexter, an alumnus.

17. Otto Herrmann, "The Monism of the German Monistic League," *The Monist*, 23 (1913), 546; a more detailed exposition is Johannes Unold, *Der Monismus und seine Ideale* (Leipzig, 1908).

18. *The Monist*, 23 (1913), 564.

of "beetle legs" and "electrical substances," the Leipzig scientist withdrew from membership in the Evangelical Church, and in so doing set an example for other members of the League.[19] On the occasion of Haeckel's eightieth birthday an international appeal for funds to expand the League was made, but the war intervened and neither the Monistic League nor the Positivist churches could survive in an atmosphere so antithetical to reason.

As a substitute religion, organized socialism enlisted more believers than Positivism or Scientism. Marxism appeared and developed at a time when the vitality and authority of the historic churches were at a low ebb, when science was sharply challenging religion, and when the current of secularism appeared irresistible. To many it seemed that among urban workers socialism would take the place of religion. Marxian thought by 1900 had become something more than a body of economic theory and a philosophy of history. It had acquired many of the passions and popular formulations associated with religion. With a body of doctrine, a priesthood of interpreters, and a host of adherents, socialism assumed many of the aspects of a religious cult. The elements of the Christian message and mission were paralleled in militant socialism—the condition of bondage and oppression suffered by the working classes under capitalism, the message of salvation embodied in Marxist doctrine and prophecy, the vocation of the proletariat, the glamor of universality, and the vision of the classless society in which all the miseries of mankind would be cured. With the zeal of religious converts, apostles of the "good news" denounced the existing order and prophesied a radiant future.

Toward competing dogmas, religious and secular, organized Marxist parties and leaders lacked a sharply defined position. Religion was officially said to be a private affair, but religion had been condemned by the founder as the "opiate" of the people, and party leaders viewed organized and established churches as inherently opposed to socialism.

Only once did the Marxist leadership grasp this nettle, and then only to withdraw. Influenced or challenged by the exodus of leading Monists from the state church, Social Democratic leaders in Berlin initiated a similar campaign among party members. Meetings were called, the bourgeois churches were roundly denounced, and printed forms necessary to initiate withdrawal from the church were dis-

19. Ostwald, *Wilhelm Ostwald*, p. 151.

tributed in large numbers. Despite the publicity and the oratory, the response was meager and the campaign a failure. Why the movement languished was a subject of inquiry by the Berlin correspondent of the *Neue Zürcher Zeitung*. After investigation he concluded that ordinary party members, however indifferent or hostile toward the church, did not want to cut themselves off entirely from this part of their past; the legal steps required were also complicated and could be unpleasant; and many socialists strongly opposed bringing a personal matter so prominently into party politics.[20]

3. EDUCATIONAL PROGRESS AND REFORM

As representative government made persistent gains during the nineteenth century, popular education became a critical public issue. To give the vote to illiterates was held to be exceedingly dangerous. Almost every European government enacted primary school laws during the 1870's and 1880's. Even in England, which lagged in this matter, it was accepted that a minimum of elementary education, compulsory and gratuitous, must be provided by the public authorities for children whose parents could not, or would not, provide it through voluntary schools. The results of this state-directed attack on illiteracy were impressive. Lord Esher noted the effects of the education act of 1870, when he wrote in his diary: "It is pleasant to see the small and dirty boys reading the labels in the shop windows. It is one of the signs of the happier future."[21] By 1900 a state school system was functioning in every country in western and central Europe, and in eastern and southern Europe the obligation was acknowledged even though the positive accomplishments were not in every instance impressive.

A basic competence in reading, writing, and arithmetic was the modest goal of the compulsory primary schools. There was no idea of creating a ladder system so that children of the common people could enter a secondary school and prepare for the university and the professions. The historic secondary schools—Gymnasium, lycée, and English public school—were open only to the sons of the upper, wealthy, or professional classes. This dual system was characteristic of European school establishments everywhere—primary education for the millions,

20. *Neue Zürcher Zeitung,* No. 349 (Dec. 17, 1913).
21. *Journals and Letters of Reginald Viscount Esher,* ed. Maurice V. Brett, 4 vols. (London, 1934–38), I, 21.

while the secondary schools remained the preserve of the privileged or the well-to-do. Two features of the system ensured this separation: the one, that a child could not transfer to the preparatory school after the third or fourth year in the common school; and second, the fees that were generally levied by the secondary schools, which served to exclude the children of all but wealthy or moderately affluent families. In Russia, simply by order of the minister of public instruction, children of "drivers, footmen, cooks, laundry-women, small traders, and other persons similarly situated" were not usually admitted to secondary or preparatory schools.[22] In the German states the common schools educated about 92 percent of the youth; only 8 percent attended the Gymnasium or other secondary schools. Rigorously selective, French secondary schools were *fee* schools and not *free* schools, which explains why that country had the lowest percentage of pupils in secondary schools of any leading Western country.[23] Only in very progressive countries, such as Switzerland, the Netherlands, and Denmark, could the pupils surmount social barriers and move from the primary to the secondary system without confusion and loss of time. Elsewhere the concern to protect the masses from the mental strain of secondary education was nearly universal.

For fifty years educators and government authorities had waged a ceaseless campaign against illiteracy. The literacy rate was a yardstick frequently employed to measure social and cultural progress. A high rate was an achievement to boast about; a low rate a matter for excuses or apologies. The best literacy record was to be found among the peoples of northern and western Europe—Germany, Scandinavia, Switzerland, the Netherlands, France, and Britain. They could boast of an illiteracy rate below 5 percent. In southern and eastern Europe the illiteracy rate was much higher, reaching its peak in Spain and Portugal in the one direction, and in Russia and the Balkans in the other. Greece and Italy, and the Slav and Magyar provinces of Austria-Hungary, likewise had a high percentage of illiterates.[24]

---

22. Paul Ignatiev (ed.), *Russian Schools and Universities in the World War* (New Haven, 1929), p. 31.

23. In 1909 there were only 131,830 students enrolled in secondary schools. David E. Cloyd, *Modern Education in Europe and the Orient* (New York, 1917), p. 108.

24. Around 1900 the estimated illiteracy rates were between 12 and 16 percent in Belgium and Ireland; 30 percent in Greece and Austria-Hungary; about 40 percent in Italy; 60 percent in Spain and Portugal; and from 70 to 80 percent in Russia and

Progress in the reduction of illiteracy, while not moving everywhere at a uniform rate, was nonetheless encouraging. Hungary, for example, was a dark area in the general picture, but the illiteracy rate was reduced from 54.5 percent in 1890 to 47.7 percent in 1900, and to 43.6 percent in 1910.[25] In Italy the problem was strongly regional. Piedmont, for example, had an illiteracy rate of 17 percent in 1901, but in Calabria the rate soared to 78.7 percent. The situation improved with a new and more rigorous compulsory school attendance law, enacted in 1904, and with provision for a large number of evening and Sunday schools for illiterate adults.[26] In the other dark regions of the Continent—notably the Iberian and Balkan peninsulas—meager resources and apathy toward education for the masses blocked any marked improvement.

Illiteracy was a massive problem in Russia, where both church and state had taken a reactionary position on popular education. In 1897, the only general census ever taken in czarist Russia showed that of nearly 23 million children of school age only one-fourth were literate; the literacy rate for females was only about half that for the male population; and in the rural areas barely a third of the males were literate and only one woman in ten. After the 1905 revolution a compulsory primary education act was debated in the first and second Dumas and adopted by the latter, but it was overruled by the government as premature. Nevertheless the number of schools and the financial support of education increased respectably from year to year. The leadership of the local zemstvo authorities in public education was especially noteworthy. In 1914 they were operating 50,000 schools, employing 80,000 teachers, and enrolling 3 million pupils.[27] The late start, the central government's equivocal attitude toward popular education, and the relative paucity of resources all combined to retard mass education in Russia at the elementary level. Although the situation was

---

the Balkan states. See Paul Monroe (ed.), *Cyclopedia of Education,* 5 vols. (New York, 1910–11), III, 382–83; and Ellwood P. Cubberley, *The History of Education* (Boston, 1920), p. 714.

25. *Report of the* (U.S.) *Commissioner of Education,* 1914, I, 748.

26. Cubberley, *History of Education,* p. 611.

27. W. H. E. Johnson, *Russia's Educational Heritage* (Pittsburgh, 1950), pp. 173–75, 192–204; Ignatiev, *Russian Schools and Universities,* pp. 24–27. By 1914 the literacy rate for Russian army recruits was approximately the same as the Italian rate.

rapidly improving in the cities and towns, the peasants, who constituted 85 percent of the population, had scarcely been touched by the
agencies of formal education.

In educational matters the contributions and standings of the small
states should not be overlooked. Switzerland showed the highest per
capita expenditure for education in all Europe; in the Netherlands, as
in no other country, state aid was given to denominational schools—
Catholic, Protestant, Jewish—on a completely equal basis; Denmark
contributed the folk high school and had the best school attendance
record to be found anywhere. In general the schools in the small advanced states were less stratified socially and the road to higher education more open than in the larger states.

A long evolutionary development, beginning with the Reformation
and greatly accelerated in the nineteenth century, saw the school taken
over from the church and made into an effective tool of the state and
society. Significantly, in the Scandinavian countries, in most of the
German states, and in Hungary, Serbia, and Russia, the ministry responsible for education was also responsible for ecclesiastical affairs.
This did not ensure peace and concord. Indeed, the existence of state-
established churches, of religious minorities, and of militant secular
groups made education an area of acute public tension and controversy.
Several solutions or compromises were evolved: continuation of church
schools, with or without state subsidy; a public system in which the
church provided or certified religious instruction as part of the curriculum; or a school system completely secularized and wholly supported
by taxation. Only France followed the American example and developed a completely secular system. However, private schools, in which
religious instruction was basic, were not prohibited. In fact, in 1906 one
in five French children of primary school age attended a private institution.[28]

The German states had a long tradition connecting church and
school. Although the schools were established and operated by local
and state authorities, religious instruction under the supervision of
church officials, Catholic, Evangelical, or Reformed, was compulsory in
the course of study at both elementary and secondary levels. Normally
the elementary schools were segregated on the basis of religious affilia-

---

28. H. G. Good, *A History of Western Education*, 2d ed. (New York, 1960), p. 305.

tion; in mixed communities a nondenominational school (*Simultan-schule*) was customarily authorized.[29]

In England, throughout the nineteenth century, an established church stubbornly blocked the development of a national system of education. What evolved eventually was the unique British device of the financial grant made by the central government to local schools, whether these were Church of England schools or local board schools. In return for substantial subsidies the recipient institutions were required to meet standards set by the Board of Education and to submit to inspection. The same solution was applied when public pressure finally forced the government to enter the field of secondary education. The Education Act of 1902 was much misliked by Nonconformist groups because it continued the grants to church schools, but by 1910 some 1,200 secondary schools supported by local taxes and national subsidies had been established. The historic "public schools" were still the main road to the universities and higher education.

Doubtless the most critical problem in educational affairs at the beginning of the twentieth century concerned the form, content, and structure of secondary education. The issue was much the same everywhere—the question of humanism versus realism, of the classics versus the modern subjects, especially science and modern languages. Altogether it took about fifty years to break the monopoly of Greek and Latin as the sole preparation for university admission and study. In France the Ribot commission of 1898 provided the recommendations which were embodied in the reform measures of 1902. The central feature of this major step in modernization was the establishment in the lycées and colleges of four parallel programs of study, with equal rights and privileges of university admission.

In Germany, and elsewhere in central and northern Europe, the issue presented itself as one of equal rights and privileges among the principal types of secondary schools—the classical Gymnasium, the Realgymnasium (with emphasis on Latin), and the Oberrealschule (modern language and science). The sore point with the modernists was the blocking of science education by the entrenched classicists and the discrimination as among the graduates of the three types of schools. Only graduates of the Gymnasium were admitted to the study of the

29. For details see E. C. Helmreich, *Religious Education in German Schools* (Cambridge, Mass., 1959), 53–100.

professions—law, medicine, theology. Students completing the program in the Oberrealschule were admitted only to the technical and scientific courses of the higher institutions. At a conference of educators convened in Berlin in 1890, William II had criticized the narrowness of the Gymnasium program and stressed the need for a national and scientific basis in secondary education. "It is our duty," he said, "to educate young men to become young Germans, and not young Greeks and Romans."[30] However, equality among the types of secondary schools and their curricula was not achieved until 1900, when basic reforms were instituted. Thereafter in Prussia—other German states followed Prussia's lead—graduates of the nine-year course of the three types of secondary schools enjoyed virtually equal privileges in admission to the universities and choice of programs.[31] Gradually in Europe, and in the United States as well, science, modern languages, and history gained equal status with classical languages and literature.

The argument between those who read Euripides and those who built steel and concrete bridges—to borrow a figure from one authority—was by no means terminated in 1914. In Germany, France, and England, the upper and professional classes continued to show a preference for the full classical curriculum of the Gymnasium, the lycée, and the "public school" over the semiclassical or nonclassical programs of secondary education.

The objective of European higher education was not self-realization for the individual but the selection and preparation of an adequate number of qualified persons to meet cultural, professional, and governmental needs. Only state-approved degrees or certified success in state examinations opened the door to the learned professions, the highest technical posts, and the higher branches of the public service. European universities and technical schools were at the peak of their reputations before 1914. German higher education especially enjoyed world renown; and universities staffed by such figures as Wundt, Helmholtz, Ostwald, Schmoller, Lamprecht, Virchow, and Paulsen attracted students from all countries and continents. Altogether there

30. Quoted in James E. Russell, *German Higher Schools,* 2d ed. (New York, 1905), p. 392.

31. Specifically, six years of Latin but no Greek was required for the study of medicine; neither Greek nor Latin was required for the study of law, pedagogy, or technical courses. Russell, *German Higher Schools,* pp. 423 ff.

were twenty-one universities and higher technical schools in Germany with an enrollment exceeding 60,000. Especially favored by foreign students were Berlin, Leipzig, Munich, Heidelberg, Göttingen, and Freiburg.[32] It is estimated that 10,000 Americans attended German institutions of higher education in the course of the nineteenth century, but the number had declined to 287 in 1913. However, the American cultural debt to Germany was heavy: the graduate school, the Ph.D. degree, the seminar, the research laboratory and institute, the scholarly and the scientific journal—all were German imports, as were such subjects of instruction as formal pedagogy, psychology, sociology, and the various branches of chemistry.[33]

French university faculties were probably more careful than the German in awarding degrees, but French scholarship was regarded as inferior, just as the general opinion of the time held that France was a country in decline.[34]

Russia, like the United States, was heavily indebted to Germany. Russians constituted the largest foreign group in German universities and technical schools, and at home secondary and higher education followed German models. In Russia, however, by 1914 there were about 100 universities and technical colleges enrolling 150,000 students, the number of institutions and student enrollment having doubled between 1905 and 1914. This impressive growth was not exactly welcomed by the ministry of public instruction, which regarded higher education with considerable distrust. The drive to expand came mainly from the ministries of commerce and agriculture, under whose jurisdiction the technical and commercial colleges were founded and operated.

32. In 1908 approximately 4,000 foreign students matriculated in German higher institutions. By nationality they were: Russians, 1,578; Austro-Hungarian, 674; Swiss, 306; United States, 298; English, 155; Bulgarian, 154; Rumanian, 102; Asiatic, 175. The largest number was registered in medicine—944—and approximately a fourth of all foreign students were enrolled at Berlin. *Journal of Philosophy*, VI (1909), 476.

33. The basic treatise on German universities is the *Geschichte des gelehrten Unterrichts*, 2 vols. (Leipzig, 1896–97), by Friedrich Paulsen, an educational liberal and the inspired teacher of many American students enrolled in the University of Berlin. His book *German Education, Past and Present* (New York, 1908), is a small classic in the field.

34. Halvdan Koht, *Education of an Historian* (New York, 1957), pp. 114 ff. Koht makes some interesting comparisons of graduate work at Leipzig (1897–98) and at Paris (1898–99). Of his isolation at Paris he says that he never became acquainted with one of his professors, nor was he ever spoken to by a French student in the lecture hall or seminar.

It was the tragedy of Russian higher education that it became in these years the battleground for a reactionary government and a revolutionary movement bent upon the government's destruction. Political and social extremists chose the universities and polytechnic schools as preferred arenas of political agitation and action. For politically motivated students action became more important than education. The government responded with the most primitive police remedies, which provoked further student demonstrations, strikes, and riots. This became an established pattern in Russian institutions, and one has the impression that neither contestant cared basically for higher education.[35]

During the 1905 revolution a kind of "extraterritorial" position was granted the Russian institutions of higher learning, including the boon of student immunity from police interference. Soon it was charged by conservatives and nationalists that the lecture rooms were turned over to subversive meetings and the laboratories to the production of bombs, while the professors danced like marionettes as revolutionary student organizations pulled the strings. One after another, concessions made to students and faculties were withdrawn or aborted. Each repressive act of the authorities was met by student strikes and demonstrations. Dismissals, transfers, and invalidation of new faculty appointments by the minister of public instruction degraded higher education and alienated the faculties of colleges and universities.[36]

Significant for the history of Russian education at all levels is the fact that between 1898 and 1914 there were eight ministers of public instruction. One was assassinated, but most resigned after a year or two in office, usually in frustration and despair over the rejection or postponement of needed reforms at all levels of the educational system.

4. LITERATURE AND THE COMMON READER

Literature has been defined as "the way a society talks to itself about itself." Of the principal forms of imaginative literature—poetry, drama,

35. A typical personal history of a Marxist student revolutionary is W. S. Woytinsky, *Stormy Passage* (New York, 1961). Political activities and divisions among Russian students abroad are vividly portrayed in Fedor Stepun, *Das Antlitz Russlands*, pp. 78–148, 183–227.

36. Ignatiev, *Russian Schools and Universities*, pp. 33, 140–51; Johnson, *Russia's Educational Heritage*, pp. 180–83; Nicholas A. Hans, *History of Russian Educational Policy* (New York, 1964), pp. 165–222.

the novel—the novel by 1900 held a position of marked preeminence. In the course of the previous century it had grown in stature and favor through the development of the newspaper and periodical press and with the organization of public opinion. As practiced by the masters— Stendhal, Balzac, Dickens, Tolstoy, Zola, and James—it was a form of imaginary reporting, projecting a social philosophy or yielding a psychological revelation. By 1900 the range of themes had greatly increased and the tone and spirit was more subtle than that of the thesis novels of the nineteenth century. The best were highly analytical, imaginative, and sometimes scholarly.[37]

Novels of sociological and psychological significance predominated. Besides the family chronicle there were novels dealing with emigration, land hunger, and pioneering; also abundant were novels of provincial life, of regionalism, and of revolt from town and village. There were novels about the professions and those who practiced them. The social thesis novel—now more artful than its muckraking predecessor— sought to arouse the callous and complacent. Feminism and the changing status of women was a new theme in numerous works portraying with great insight the young woman's psychological experiences in liberating herself and adjusting to the social order. Similarly the psychology of childhood and youth, the conflict of generations, and love, marriage, and alienation were themes that received fresh and constant treatment. The novel was also used to project an antiwar ideology. Tolstoy was among the first to dramatize the idea that war might be ghastly as well as glorious and that men can become its pawns as well as its captains.

European literature—especially the drama and the novel—were enormously enriched during this period by the contributions of the Russians and the Scandinavians. Beginning in the last quarter of the preceding century, the stream of translation from both sources flowed unceasingly. England, France, and Germany were hospitable to the works of Turgenev, Dostoevsky, and Tolstoy and to those of Ibsen, Björnson, and Strindberg.[38]

In all this outpouring of creative literature there was no single direction, only a great many diverse and divergent trends. Much was

---

37. R. M. Albérès, *Histoire du roman moderne* (Paris, 1962), pp. 79–80.
38. Some translations of Russian masterpieces reached western Europe in the nineties, but the major work of translation in England was accomplished between 1900 and 1914. Amy Cruse, *After the Victorians* (London, 1938), pp. 100–10.

written by critics about decadence and the *fin de siècle* mood, but, objectively examined, these years do not appear to have been either sterile or decadent. Bourgeois writers dominated the scene, and as writers they were more numerous and more stimulating than the writers produced by the aristocratic societies and cultures of the past. But literature at the turn of the century was not the source of orientations, postures, life-styles, and positions. Literary intellectuals did not presume to replace the theologian, the moralist, and the social scientist.

It is surprising, since contemporary writers were overwhelmingly bourgeois in origin, that they should have devoted so much time and talent to attacking the social, moral, and economic values of the class from which they sprang. Ibsen, creator of the modern social drama and problem play, launched the attack upon the bourgeoisie—its culture, conventions, and values. In his twelve social dramas—from *Pillars of Society* to *When We Dead Awaken*—Ibsen maintained a heavy bombardment of bourgeois culture, values, and behavior. Ibsen's gospel of individualism was akin to Nietzsche's superman and Bergson's vitalism. The problems he exposed and analyzed have today been solved or forgotten, and his plays are performed as period pieces rather than relevant dramas; however, he established the playwright as a critic of society, a dramatist of ideas and causes. After his death in 1906 the targets he had defined continued to attract the fire of lesser literary aspirants. Many followed his lead—Shaw, Hauptmann, Sudermann, Brieux, and Galsworthy, to mention only some of the important figures. There was scarcely a writer of note before 1914 who did not produce at least one antibourgeois play or novel. Even the peasant-worshipers and regionalists, such as Knut Hamsun (*Growth of the Soil*), Gustav Frenssen (*Jörn Uhl*), and Wladislaw Reymont (*The Peasants*), denigrated the city and urban culture and exalted blood and soil.

Edwardian England's leading playwrights were James Barrie, G. B. Shaw, Arthur Pinero, and John Galsworthy. Barrie was the most superficial and enjoyable, and received the most popular acclaim. Galsworthy's plays—*Strife, Justice,* and *The Silver Box*—were too depressing to be popular. When he turned to the novel and published, in 1906, *The Man of Property*—the first volume in his *Forsyte Saga*—he met with greater success, although reviewers complained of the book's pessimism and harshness. G. B. Shaw, an active Fabian socialist and the century's greatest literary self-advertiser, enjoyed for many years the reputation of a brilliant but eccentric writer. In one year, 1904–1905, he became the most conspicuous if not the most popular English dramatist. At the Royal Court Theatre, where *Man and Superman* was presented to a select and discriminating audience in 1905, there was offered henceforth almost continuously a new Shaw play or a revival of an earlier unsuccessful work. Shaw's stage plays became fashionable, and they were presented in Paris, Berlin, and New York, but not for long runs. In theme and content many of his plays seem like dramatized political tracts, but the originality, wit, and vitality of his drama have kept his works marvelously alive for more than sixty years; and some of them find a reincarnation in captivating musical comedy—*My Fair Lady,* for example.

The writers of serious novels reached a much wider audience than the dramatists. In England the most popular late-Victorian authors were Hall Caine, Marie Corelli, and Mrs. Humphrey Ward, the latter a niece of Matthew Arnold. After 1900 all three were superseded in popularity and critical esteem by H. G. Wells, Arnold Bennett, Henry James, Joseph Conrad, and John Galsworthy. Bennett, who like Wells was heavily committed to journalism, wrote solid observant fiction, his strongest and most successful novel being *The Old Wives' Tale,* published in 1908. The Anglo-American Henry James never achieved the popular success that came to Shaw, Wells, and Bennett, but his reputation as a creative writer and technician stands higher today than that of any of his contemporaries except Shaw and perhaps Conrad. A recurrent theme in James' works was the encounter between American and European cultures, which he treated as a confrontation of American innocence and European sophistication—*The Wings of the Dove, The American,* and *The Ambassadors.* In their composition and texture James' works were slow-paced novels of sensibility in which the psychological reactions of his characters to one another and to events are endlessly explored without Freudian assistance. James was denied the popular esteem that his works merited, but to a rising generation of serious writers he was "the master."

H. G. Wells was condescending and patronizing to Henry James, whose works failed of the popular success that his own achieved. Wells had enjoyed a high reputation as a writer of science fiction when he embraced the ideology of the Fabian society and placed his skill as a writer in the service of the problems of the day and the reorganization of society. Beginning with *Anticipations* (1901), Wells' works became increasingly topical and didactic. It is the fate of such literature that it loses its interest and vitality as soon as the ideas and problems cease to be live issues or options. Relevance often equates with the ephemeral. This was the fate of most of Wells' prewar fiction.[39]

A popular French Poet, René Sully-Prudhomme, was awarded the first Nobel prize for literature in 1901, but no French writer was so honored again—except for the joint award to the Provençal poet Frédéric Mistral—until 1915, when the honor went to Romain Rolland. Although much was germinating and growing in French literature and drama that would later blossom, the decade and a half before the war was a relatively barren period. The Dreyfus Affair was a traumatic experience for French writers and intellectuals, dividing them into hostile camps. Such was the pressure that no man of letters could avoid taking a stand. The supporters of human rights and republican ideals rallied around Zola and his collaborator Anatole France. The latter emerged from the affair as almost the official man of letters of the Third Republic. Converted to socialism during the "affair," he became a friend of Jaurès and an active member of the socialist party. His political convictions were not much reflected in his principal works— *The Crime of Sylvester Bonnard, Penguin Island,* and *The Revolt of the Angels.* His barbed wit was frequently used against two objects: historic Christianity and the social system. The sum of his works and his reputation brought him a Nobel prize before his death in 1924, but since he was obviously not one of the "exciting moderns" his reputation suffered a sudden collapse and today his work is almost completely neglected.

Some of the French literary figures who dominated the postwar period were only emerging into view before 1914, although some of their number had begun to publish works of recognized promise. Of those who achieved international recognition we may note Charles Péguy, editor of the significant *Cahiers de la Quinzaine;* André Gide, who published *L'Immoraliste* in 1902 and *La Porte étroite,* the first of his works to reach a large public, in 1909; Marcel Proust, who gave the psychological novel a new status when he published *Swann's Way* in

39. Bernard Bergonzi, *The Early H. G. Wells* (Manchester, 1961), pp. 1–10, 21, 165, 170–73; Wells' *Experiment in Autobiography* (New York, 1934) is a personal document of rare value.

1913, the first volume in his *Remembrance of Things Past;* and Roger Martin du Gard, who published his *Jean Barois* in 1913.

Germany and Austria were more predisposed to literary and dramatic innovations from abroad than was France, England, or Italy. Germany especially had been warmly receptive to the Scandinavians and the Russians. Translations of foreign novels and adaptations of plays appeared with less delay in Germany than in any other country. About 1900 the German novel experienced a renaissance as new talent began to emerge. Thomas Mann published *Buddenbrooks* (1901); Jakob Wassermann contributed *The Jews of Zirndorf;* and Ricarda Huch, Germany's most distinguished woman writer of the century, published *Aus der Triumphgasse* (Told Round the Triumphal Arch) in 1901 and *Michael Unger* in the following year. Thomas Mann's *Buddenbrooks* immediately became a popular favorite, a sort of warm introduction of a great artist to an appreciative audience. The German novel also developed as a regional art and gathered strength with the emergence of provincial schools reflecting the history and characteristics of the Silesians, Saxons, Swabians, Bavarians, and Austrians. Vienna was also full of talent between 1900 and 1914—Hermann Bahr, Arthur Schnitzler, Hugo von Hofmannsthal, who had a world-wide audience as Strauss' librettist, and just on the horizon, Rainer Maria Rilke and Arnold and Stefan Zweig.

In the state and private theaters of central Europe the educated classes were offered an extensive program of the classical drama—German, French, and English. Ibsen, Shaw, and Strindberg were popular, as were the plays of Anton Chekhov. Gerhart Hauptmann, Frank Wedekind, and the Austrian Arthur Schnitzler were the leading German playwrights, who, working in the realistic manner of Ibsen, maintained an uninterrupted flow of joyless problem plays and topical pieces dealing with family life, exploited workers, and the awakening of sex.[40]

With the close of the nineteenth century, Russia's commanding position in world literature came to an end. Anton Chekhov died in 1904, Tolstoy in 1910. Most of Chekhov's work and all of Tolstoy's belong to the nineteenth century. Abroad they were regarded as the last representatives of the Russian tradition. Tolstoy had turned his back on art, repudiating even his own works, to propagate a personal philosophy which condemned civil authority, orthodox Christianity, the sanctions

40. On the German literary and dramatic scene at the turn of the century, the best survey is Arthur Eloesser, *Modern German Literature* (New York, 1933).

of war, the taking of life, and the use of violence. Education he held to be nothing, science created no values, and art was an evil insofar as it contributed to the propagation of conventional ethical and religious teachings. Tolstoy's writings in this period were not creative but didactic and propagandistic. The literary figures that followed the disappearance of the giants were only epigones. Maxim Gorky (A. M. Peshkov), the most publicized of Russian writers in our period, enjoyed an international reputation. Gorky gained fame by participating in the 1905 revolution and by making a world tour to collect funds for his fellow militants. He then went into exile while those who remained in Russia produced works that reflected the pessimism and intellectual disorganization that followed the failure of the revolution.[41]

As the world war approached, other notable writers of the twentieth century were emerging—Rilke, Gide, Proust, Joyce, D. H. Lawrence, Thomas Mann, and Hermann Hesse—but there were still no great movements or clear directions in literature.

If sales of a million copies in a brief period is taken as the test of a "best seller," none of the works of the aforementioned writers achieved that status. The reading public that accepted the canons of literary critics was comparatively limited, composed as it was of those with a good secondary education and some higher education. The middle class, which means the "common reader," read mainly entertainment fiction which did not qualify as serious literature. An early work to achieve mass circulation was the romance of ancient Rome *Quo Vadis* (1896), by the Polish author Henry Sienkiewicz. Hall Caine's *The Christian* and *The Woman Thou Gavest Me,* both full of pious sentimentality, won great popular acclaim. In the period 1900 to 1914 these books topped the list of best sellers: Victoria Cross, *Anna Lombard* (1901), Jack London, *The Call of the Wild* (1903), Baroness Orczy, *The Scarlet Pimpernel* (1905), Elinor Glyn, *Three Weeks* (1907), Jeffrey Farnol, *The Broad Highway* (1910), Ethel M. Dell, *The Way of an Eagle* (1912), and Edgar Rice Burroughs, *Tarzan of the Apes* (1914).[42] In the German-speaking world the travel and adventure stories of Karl May (1842-1912) were perennial best sellers. Without

41. Marc Slonim, *Modern Russian Literature* (New York, 1953), pp. 55-61, 184; "Russian Literature," by E. J. Simmons, in Columbia *Dictionary of Modern European Literature* (New York, 1947), pp. 695-708.

42. Desmond Flower, *A Century of Best Sellers, 1830-1930* (London, 1934), pp. 16-20.

having seen the American West or the Near and Middle East he wrote vivid and suspenseful tales of these romantically conceived lands peopled with simulated native characters. His productivity was immense, and the Karl May foundation in Fulda is still mining his vast literary legacy.[43]

Other types of reading matter favored by the middle class were the popular "libraries" and reprint series, such as Bohn's classics, Home University Library, the German Tauchnitz editions of English and American authors, the Albert Langen publications for workers, and Everyman's Library, which began publication in 1906. The number of periodicals and reviews also doubled, and in some countries tripled, between 1890 and 1914, although Spain, Portugal, and Russia were exceptions. The popular family-type weeklies, like the American *Saturday Evening Post,* which mirrored middle-class culture, achieved their highest level of prosperity and appreciation. In France, *Les lectures pour tous* (1898), *Femina* (1901), and *Je sais tout* (1905), and in Germany, *Die Gartenlaube,* were enormously popular. From the latter developed the German illustrated weeklies whose circulations today extend into the millions. The "Sunday papers," popular in England, the United States, and Germany, with their supplements on literature, sports, travel, and nature, supplied the family with a variety of reading matter for the entire week.

5. THE MASS CIRCULATION PRESS

As the democratization of reading became a reality through primary education, the market for printed matter was vastly expanded. The demand was met by books, periodicals, and cheap newspapers. Quantity rather than quality seemed uppermost in the minds and intentions of the new breed of publisher. Mass literacy fed on the popular press and the popular magazine as well as on cheap fiction. Basic economic factors conditioned the publication of newspapers and periodicals. The quantity of newsprint that cost three dollars in 1880 could be purchased for one dollar in 1900. The telephone and telegraph, and the mechanization of printing and distribution, which further reduced costs of production, made the mass circulation newspaper a commercial and technical possibility. It only remained to adapt the content to the needs and taste of the new reading public. This engendered a revolution in

43. Adolf Hitler's adult literary preferences were a strange combination: Karl May's American Indian tales and G. B. Shaw's satiric assaults on the bourgeoisie. Otto Dietrich, *Hitler* (Chicago, 1955), p. 149.

daily journalism which substantially transformed the press between the turn of the century and the outbreak of the war.

American newspaper styles and methods were familiar to European publishers, but the mass circulation press that developed in England and on the Continent was in a sense a "home-grown" product. The cheapest and most widely circulated serials in the 1890's were George Newnes' *Tit-Bits,* Cyril Pearson's *Pearson's Weekly,* and Alfred Harmsworth's *Answers.* Filled with anecdotes, scraps of information, riddles, and contributions from subscribers, they made little demand upon the intelligence of the reader. Often smugly described as "unwholesome," they were entertaining and helped to make reading an addiction among the newly literate. Harmsworth applied the experience gained in this kind of journalism to the task of revitalizing a derelict London evening paper, and after having achieved this, he invaded the field of morning journalism with the *Daily Mail,* which appeared in 1896. Homeliness, variety, and sensation were the conscious objectives of the editors. An entirely new scale of news values was introduced. What Kennedy Jones, Harmsworth's associate, called "a good meaty crime" topped the list, followed by sports, wars, and natural disasters. Politics—the staple of the established press—came far down on the list. The *Daily Mail* was an immediate success. Circulation rose to one million during the Boer War, then declined to 700,000, holding at that level until 1914. It was rumored that profits exceeded a million pounds annually.[44]

The astonishing success of the *Daily Mail* encouraged imitation. In 1900 C. Arthur Pearson launched the *Daily Express* as a competitor in the mass circulation field. Selling their papers for a halfpenny instead of the regular one or two pence, Harmsworth and Pearson put the newspaper within reach of the urban workingman and changed the conditions of newspaper publishing in London. The class papers did not lose readers, but they lost advertisers and advertising revenue. By 1900 the pressure was felt in the business offices, and by 1908 it was acute. Some old established journals ceased publication; others consolidated with more aggressive competitors; others, like the Cadbury's *Daily News,* were popularized and, with price reduced to a halfpenny,

44. Hamilton Fyfe, *Northcliffe: An Intimate Biography* (London, 1930), pp. 72–87; Georges Weill, *Le Journal* (Paris, 1934), pp. 248–54; Kennedy Jones, *Fleet Street and Downing Street* (London, 1920), pp. 130–49; Richard D. Altick, *The English Common Reader* (Chicago, 1957), pp. 363–64.

entered successfully the competition for mass circulation. Some of the older newspapers, such as the *Manchester Guardian*, held their position by improving news services and giving better value for a penny, without cheapening the spirit of the paper. But all, without exception, were forced to redefine news, to offer greater variety to the reader, to reduce editorial space, to provide features for women, and to modernize makeup and typography. In 1908, Harmsworth's purchase of the *Times* symbolized the complete conquest of the old journalism by the new.[45]

An observer surveying the French press at the turn of the century commented that there was still a substantial segment of the population which was not exposed to the influence of the newspaper press.[46] Between 1900 and 1914 this was changed, owing to the transformation of the Paris press and the development of provincial papers. French journals according to their main emphasis were divided into journals of political opinion and journals of information, the latter mainly news organs. While there was no decrease in the number of political journals, the greatest expansion occurred in the ranks of the journals of information. American methods were adopted, the price was reduced, politics were deemphasized, news was sensationalized, circulation sales and display advertising were aggressively promoted. The result of these efforts was a spectacular rise in sales and subscriptions. In Paris total newspaper circulation by 1913 reached 6 million copies daily. Of this number 5 million were divided among five popular papers—*Le Journal, Le Petit Journal, Le Matin, Le Petit Parisien,* and *L'Echo de Paris*. The French provincial press had lagged noticeably behind the Paris press. That was largely overcome between 1900 and 1914 through the modernization of methods, broadening the content of the paper, and the multiplication of regional and local editions. Bordeaux, Toulouse, Marseilles, and Lyons became centers of strong and influential provincial journalism. Thus by 1914 the French press had enrolled millions of new readers, especially workers, but the competition was fierce, single-issue sales generally exceeded subscription sales, and to meet the competition of aggressive rivals the solicitation of advertisers and readers was a critical and continuous concern.[47]

45. On the commercialization of the British press the best work is Max Grünbeck, *Die Presse Grossbritanniens,* 2 vols. (Leipzig, 1936), I, 45–50.

46. Weill, *Le Journal,* p. 264.

47. *Ibid.,* pp. 264–67.

The newspaper press in Germany was decentralized to a much greater extent than in France or Great Britain. The *Hamburger Fremdenblatt,* the *Kölnische Zeitung,* the *Frankfurter Zeitung,* and the *Münchner Neueste Nachrichten* were just as likely to be quoted abroad as authoritative voices in the German press as any Berlin journal. With a high rate of literacy, Germany supported a large number of papers—in round numbers about 3,000, of which a large number were rural weeklies or biweeklies. As in England and France, the German newspaper press was experiencing a technical and financial revolution, the end result of which was a popular mass-circulation press. The thrust of this revolution came from the development of the nonpolitical commercialized journal, or *Generalanzeiger.* The old historic name-papers were basically political; the *Generalanzeiger* was nonpolitical, emphasizing local news, and fat with classified and display advertising. Every feature of the *Generalanzeiger* was designed to reach and exploit a new reading public. Commercial competition and economic pressure forced the publishers of the old political press to modernize along the lines of the *Generalanzeiger* or to establish a popular local paper teamed with their old established journal. Thus the Rudolf Mosse firm in Berlin published besides the well-known *Berliner Tageblatt* the popular *Volks-Zeitung* and *B. Z. am Mittag;* the Ullstein concern published the historic *Vossische Zeitung* together with their mass-circulation *Morgenpost;* and August Scherl teamed the *Lokal-Anzeiger* with a popular evening paper. Similar pairing of political journals with popular papers occurred in Cologne, Leipzig, Munich, and Stuttgart.

Newspaper circulations in Germany never achieved the million mark of the London and Paris press, but the increase in total sales and circulation attest to the growth of the new reading public. Between 1885 and 1913, total newspaper circulation rose from approximately 8 million to 16 million.[48]

The scope and importance of the press in other European countries was closely related to the level of education, the density and distribution of population, and the state of economic development. Austria-

---

48. Otto Groth, *Die Zeitung,* 4 vols. (Mannheim, 1928–30), I, 205, 251–59, summarizing the principal statistical studies of the German press. On the *Generalanzeiger* press see Groth, I, 222 ff., 926; II, 536–41. Emil Dovifat, *Die Zeitungen* (Gotha, 1925), is a brief but reliable survey.

Hungary supported more than 500 daily and weekly newspapers; Switzerland, Belgium, and Holland had about 300 local and national papers each; and Sweden, Denmark, and Norway, predominantly rural, supported together fewer than 500 daily and weekly journals. Italy had approximately 120 daily newspapers in 1914, but they were chiefly of local importance. Only the *Corriere della Sera* of Milan and *La Stampa* of Turin enjoyed national circulation. The newspapers of Spain and Portugal were inferior by European standards, and the level of literacy could not support mass-circulation papers. The same was true of Russia, where there were fewer than seventy daily papers in the entire country before 1914. There were sixteen dailies in St. Petersburg, eight in Moscow, and approximately a hundred papers in the rest of Russia, of which only one-third were dailies.[49] The political restraints imposed by the czarist government did not encourage the expansion of the press.

The great flood of cheap reading materials for the masses—books, serials, and newspapers—was often deplored by the educated, who described the product as "cheap and nasty." Here was a consequence of the compulsory education laws that had not been foreseen. The reading habit was not raising the cultural level of the masses. To many contemporaries it seemed that more people were reading than ever before, but "they were reading the wrong things, for the wrong reasons, and in the wrong way."[50] Perspective gives us a better understanding of the value of this early reading matter for the masses. The role of the cheap serial and the mass press in their inception was not enlightenment but entertainment, and circulations were built on this knowledge and judgment. At this stage compulsory education was producing millions of boys and girls who "just wanted something to read." The reviews and newspapers produced for the educated classes did not interest them. They wanted printed matter that was simple and sufficiently interesting to hold their attention. When life and labor for common people were dull, drab, and monotonous, the cheap book, serial, and newspaper meant a little more color in the life of the masses, a little more brightness, and a little more entertainment.

49. *Encyclopaedia Britannica*, 11th ed., XIX, 580. A Soviet source in 1932 gave the number of newspapers in 1913 as 859 with a circulation of 3.5 million. Weill, *Le Journal*, p. 357.
50. Altick, *The English Common Reader*, p. 368.

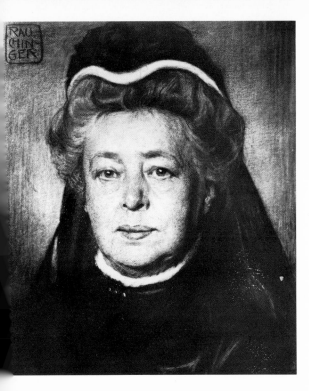

1. Bertha von Suttner. Leader of the international peace movement and holder of the Nobel Peace Prize. From a sepia pastel by Heinrich Rauchinger. (*Bildarchiv d. Öst. National-bibliothek*)

2. The Peace Palace at The Hague. The gift of Andrew Carnegie, it was completed in 1913. It has been the seat of the Permanent Court of Arbitration, the Academy of International Law, and the Permanent Court of International Justice. (From *History of the Carnegie Foundation and the Peace Palace at The Hague,* by A. Lysen)

Kaiser William II observing the Swiss army maneuvers of 1912, with Generals Sprecher (left) and Wille.

4. Test model of a light armored gun—a Swiss weapon—before World War I. (*Schweiz. Landesbibliothek*)

5. Krupp naval gun factory—1912. The giant lathes were used to mill the large gun turrets.

6. H.M.S. *Dreadnought* (1906). The first battleship to use turbine propulsion, it carried ten twelve-inch guns and made all other battleships immediately obsolete. (*Office of Chief of Naval Information, U.S. Navy Dept.*)

7. Louis Blériot arriving at Dover after his flight across the English Channel, July 25, 1909. He won the *Daily Mail* prize of 1,000 pounds and gave impetus to aircraft development. (*Radio Times Hulton Picture Library*)

8. Peasants in a Russian village. (From *Siberia and Central Asia*, by John W. Bookwalter)

9. A Siberian emigrant train. (From *Siberia and Central Asia*, by John W. Bookwalter)

10. A celebrated "spouter" in the Baku oil fields. (From *Siberia and Central Asia*, by John W. Bookwalter)

11. A station on the Berlin elevated railway (note the design and ornamentation).

12. Rudolf Diesel, inventor of the diesel engine, and Thomas A. Edison in Orange, New Jersey, May, 1912. (From *Diesel: Der Mensch, das Werk, das Schicksal,* by Eugen Diesel)

13. Test model of the diesel engine (1897). (*Deutsches Museum, Munich*)

14. Soapmakers were already large advertisers. (Permission of *Punch*)

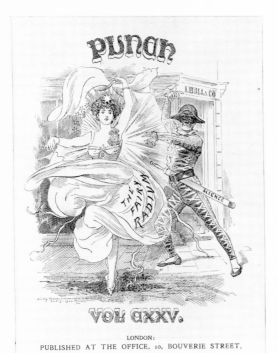

15. *Punch* celebrates the birth of "The Fairy Radium." (Permission of *Punch*)

16. Five Nobel prizewinners in physics and physical chemistry. Left to right: Walther Nernst, Albert Einstein, Max Planck, Robert A. Millikan, and Max von Laue. (*Courtesy of Mrs. R. W. Ladenburg, Princeton, N.J.*)

17. Raymond Poincaré, President of the French Republic.

18. P. A. Stolypin, Russian prime minister, 1906–1911.

19. Count S. Y. Witte, Russian minister of finance, 1892–1903, and prime minister, 1905–1906.

20. Czar Nicholas II (left) and King George V. The two monarchs were cousins, but the striking resemblance suggests twin brothers. (*Library of Congress*)

21. Kaiser William II, his uncle King Edward VII, and the Kaiser's sisters in Bad Homburg. Edward's luxurious Daimler motorcar was a sensation in Germany. (*Zeitgeschichtliches Bildarchiv*)

22. Arrest of a Catholic priest, 1906. Pursuant to the Separation Law, authorities in France began taking inventory of Church property. Riots and disturbances accompanied the action. (*Bibliothèque Nationale*)

23. Student riots. German national students drive non-German students from the ramp in front of the university. Vienna, 1905(?). (*Bildarchiv d. Öst. Nationalbibliothek*)

24. German universities began to open their doors to women in 1900. Here three Berlin "coeds" in traditional birettas and sashes march to a university convocation. (*Ullstein Bilderdienst*)

25. A lecture hall at the Sorbonne. At the professor's left is the *appariteur*, who assists the lecturer with books or apparatus and maintains order.

26. Henri Poincaré (1854–1912), mathematician, physicist, astronomer.

27. Professor Max Weber (1864–1920), Germany's most influential social scientist.

Scotson-Clark.

28. George Bernard Shaw. Pencil sketch by Scotson-Clark, *circa* 1912. (*Library of Congress*)

29. Scene from the London play *Votes for Women*, by Elizabeth Robins (1907). (*Courtesy Victoria and Albert Museum*)

30. A strike meeting of women workers at Millwall, England, 1914. (*Radio Times Hulton Picture Library*)

31. Amsterdam congress of the Second International, 1904. (*International Institute for Social History, Amsterdam*)

32. Jean Jaurès speaking at a socialist rally near Stuttgart. At the table, left: Karl Kautsky; right, Paul Singer. (*International Institute for Social History, Amsterdam*)

33. Social Democratic deputies in the first Russian Duma—intellectuals rather than proletarians predominate. (*Photograph by Bulla, St. Petersburg*)

34. Suffrage demonstration before the Austrian parliament building—Vienna, November, 1905. (*Bildarchiv d. Öst. Nationalbibliothek*)

35. The Young Czech party demonstrating in the Austrian parliament—
June 8, 1900. (*Bildarchiv d. Öst. Nationalbibliothek*)

36. Dust jacket for Knut Hamsun's novel
Hunger; an example of the Munich
Jugendstil. (*Staatliche Graphische Samm-
lung Munich*)

37. Entrance to the Paris Metro. Design by Hector Guimard (1867–1942); applied Art Nouveau.

38. The Fagus factory near Hanover, designed by Walter Gropius in 1911. It was the first completely "modern" steel and glass building erected in Europe before 1914.

39. *Nude Descending a Staircase*, by Marcel Duchamp. This was the most controversial work in the New York Armory Show of 1913. (*Courtesy Philadelphia Museum of Art, A. J. Wyatt, photographer*)

40. Scene from *Le Sacre du Printemps*—London, 1913. (*Mander and Mitchenson Theatre Collection*)

41. *The Table*, painting by Georges Braque (1882–1963), one of the originators of the Cubist style. (*Courtesy National Gallery of Art, Washington, D.C.*)

42. *Der Dorfgeiger* (Village Fiddler), sculpture by Ernst Barlach (1914). (*Courtesy of Mrs. Lisa Arnhold, New York City*)

43. *Over Vitebsk,* painting by Marc Chagall (1914). A vision of Vitebsk with a typical Chagall figure floating through the air. (*Ayala and Sam Zacks Collection, Toronto, Canada*)

44. The Japanese getting money out of John Bull—Russian cartoon from the Russo-Japanese War.

45. President Émile Loubet's visit to London, 1903. (Permission of *Punch*)

PUNCH, OR THE LONDON CHARIVARI.—July 8, 1903.

FRIENDS!

His Majesty the King. "SEE, M. LOUBET, HE OFFERS YOU HIS PAW!"

46. Winston Churchill and Admiral Sir John Fisher leaving the admiralty. (*Radio Times Hulton Picture Library*)

47. Chancellor Bernhard von Bülow—1905.

48. Baron Friedrich von Holstein.

49. Anglo-German "Naval Holiday"—"We could do a lot of damage with these things!" (*Simplicissimus*, April 14, 1913)

50. "The Embarrassed Trainer" —Nicholas II and his Balkan canines. (*Simplicissimus*, July 21, 1913)

51. Archduke Franz Ferdinand, his wife and children—September, 1913. (*Bildarchiv d. Öst. Nationalbibliothek*)

52. Colonel Dragutin Dimitrievich, chief of intelligence, Serbian Army General Staff, and head of the terrorist "Black Hand" organization, with his aides.

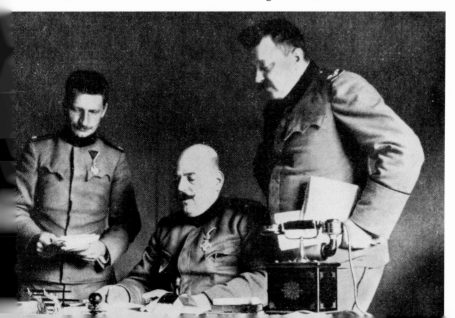

53. The Sarajevo conspirators in a Belgrade park, May, 1914. Left to right: Trifko Grabezh, Djuro Sarac, and Gavrilo Princip.

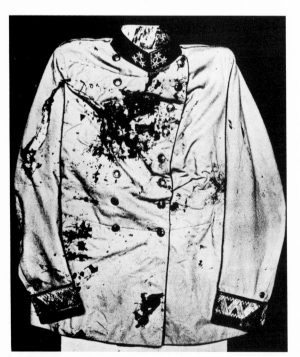

54. Archduke Franz Ferdinand's military tunic, showing the place of entry of the fatal bullet and the bloodstains. (*Bildarchiv d. Öst. Nationalbibliothek*)

55. "A Chain of Friendship"—"If Austria attacks Serbia, Russia will fall upon Austria, Germany upon Russia, and France and England upon Germany." (Brooklyn *Eagle,* July, 1914)

56. French cuirassiers passing through Paris, 1914. (*Bibliothèque Nationale*)

57. *The Cannoneer*, painting by Otto Dix (1914). (*Courtesy of Mrs. Martha Dix, Hemmenhofen, Bavaria*)

Chapter Six

THE BREAKTHROUGH TO MODERN ART

I. OFFICIAL ART AND REBELLIOUS ARTISTS

CONCURRENTLY with revolutionary developments in science new styles and forms in the arts made their appearance and clamored for contemporary recognition. Doubtless there was some interreaction between the revolutionary developments in art and those in science. Wassily Kandinsky, the first twentieth-century painter to plunge into abstractionism, has recorded how the discovery that there were bodies smaller than atoms caused him to rethink the whole problem of reality in nature and art. Franz Marc, an associate of Kandinsky's, declared: "The art of tomorrow will give form to our scientific convictions." Guillaume Apollinaire, poet and press agent for Cubism, related the mutliple perspective style of the Cubist artists to the newest mathematics and introduced the term "fourth-dimensional" into the vocabulary of modern aesthetics. The principal styles in painting of the prewar period—Fauvism, Cubism, Abstraction, and Futurism—paralleled on the time scale the momentous achievements of Röntgen, Curie, Planck, Einstein, Rutherford, Correns, De Vries, and Morgan. However, the assumption of cross-fertilization should not be pushed too far.[1] No cultural group was more isolated and estranged from science than the avant-garde artists. At most, through popular media of communication, they were made aware of the revolutionary changes in the scientists' conception of nature. We must also assume that changes in the concept of "reality," which the scientist developed and the philosopher sensed, also affected the artist. Artist, scientist, philosopher, all experienced a sharp displacement of their conceptions of "reality." "Modern art," writes Werner Haftmann, "began with a revolutionary change in the artist's attitude toward reality."[2]

Change was in the air, and the sensitive artist felt the pulse of the

1. Werner Haftmann, *Painting in the Twentieth Century,* 2 vols. (New York, 1960), II, 12–14, 17.
2. *Ibid.,* II, 49.

new century. In the 1890's, and increasingly as we approach 1900, the word "new" appears so frequently and in so many connections as to attract the historian's attention—the "new humor," the "new realism," the "new woman," the "new drama," and the "new art." It crept into title pages and appeared on mastheads—*The New Review, New Ages, New Statesman,* and *Nouvelle Revue.* Furthermore, technology with its geometric patterns and the optical effects that came with speed—the train, the motorcar, the airplane—were not without suggestive influence on the artists. More directly, the camera was taking out of the artist's hand the actual task of making records and providing "visual aids," thus requiring reconsideration of his social and intellectual function. From published remarks and writings we know that young artists felt that a new age required a new art. The generation of avant-garde artists that now began to gain attention wanted to escape from bondage to the nineteenth century; they felt that traditional modes and canons were antiquated if not hypocritical; they were skeptical and sometimes scornful of the standards of the state art schools; they wanted to arouse strong feeling in their audience, to destroy lethargy, to participate in a cultural revolution.

One of the roots of the revolutionary stirrings in the arts is clearly to be found in the reaction of the free artistic temperament to the institutionalization and rigidities that had developed in the fine arts during the preceding century. The great bastions in the system of "official art" were the museums and academies. The "museum movement" was rooted in the romanticism and historicism of the nineteenth century. By conquest and looting, by expropriation of religious establishments, by inheritance from princely houses, by gift and purchase, the great art museums of Europe had been established and filled with collections primarily classical, medieval, Renaissance, and eighteenth and nineteenth century. The taxonomy of periods and styles had been fully developed by a large corps of diligent *Kunsthistoriker.* Usually under the ministry of public instruction, these institutions were administered by directors trained in art history. Arrangement of the collections for public viewing and for study by students, the staging of special exhibits, and the preparation of catalogs and monographs were the principal duties of the museum director and his staff.[3] It is not possible to calculate the attendance at art museums and exhibitions, but the

3. Alma S. Wittlin, *The Museum: Its History and Its Tasks in Education* (London, 1949), pp. 94–184, *passim.*

annual total would run into the millions, especially after the practice of opening the museums on Sundays became general. In Britain, France, Germany, and Austria admission was generally free or else there were a minimum of "pay days." In Italy, where the national monuments and art treasures were exploited as an important source of revenue, "pay days" were more common than "free days." Indeed the fees for entrance to the Italian museums kept the poorer people from seeing their own national art treasures. Noted for their collections of old masters and the richness of their eighteenth- and nineteenth-century holdings were of course the state museums in Paris, Amsterdam, Berlin, Dresden, Munich, Vienna, Florence, Rome, Naples, Madrid, and St. Petersburg. The municipal museums usually contained the local gleanings, which were supplemented by borrowing from national collections and by traveling exhibitions. In Russia Western art was to be found only in Moscow and St. Petersburg.

Museum holdings represented a vast national and municipal investment in the traditional periods and categories of the arts. To round out these collections was the established acquisitions policy. In both the national and the municipal museums the directors had a fund for new acquisitions, but the "sticky wicket" for the director was the acquisition by purchase or bequest of works by contemporary painters, sculptors, and designers. The policy followed was the product of several forces— the attitude of the director, the pressure of the ministry, and considerations of public taste and acceptance. What this usually meant was that everything was loaded on the side of tradition and against the innovator and experimenter. One example will suffice: Hugo von Tschudi, a Swiss national, was a distinguished art historian and director of the National Gallery in Berlin from 1896 to 1907. A mild modernist, he carried the day against the expressed views of William II and exhibited and acquired works by non-German artists, including the modern Impressionists. It was a Pyrrhic victory, for his position in the state system was seriously undermined. In 1907 he left Berlin to assume the directorship of the state galleries in Munich. But Von Tschudi won the battle for inclusion of modern art in state collections in Germany. Less courageous directors now followed his lead, and it is owing to his stand that German galleries acquired representative collections of late nineteenth-century and early twentieth-century art.[4]

4. E. Schwedeler-Meyer (ed.), *H. Von Tschudis Gesammelte Schriften zur neueren Kunst* (Munich, 1912), *passim*.

The other stronghold of convention and conservatism was the art
academy. Academies of fine arts, with faculties in painting, sculpture,
architecture, design, and art history were maintained by almost every
European state, and by some municipalities. Foremost were the École
des Beaux-Arts in Paris, the Royal Academy of Arts in London, and
the Akademie der Bildenden Künste in Munich. Similar academies
with variant names but the same functions existed in Dresden, Vienna,
Florence, Rome, Barcelona, and other centers and capitals of Europe.
The École des Beaux-Arts was organized in three faculties—painting,
sculpture, and architecture—and enjoyed a quasi-monopoly in the
training of artists and architects, and, so some charged, exercised a rigid
dictatorship over national taste and style. All of these schools and their
faculties were perforce conservative and traditional in their outlook.
The Royal Academy of Arts in London is perhaps an extreme case.
Organized in 1768 under a charter granted by George III, it was a self-
perpetuating society limited to forty "academicians" chosen from the
roll of "associates," a group likewise limited originally to forty. Its
principal function was the operation of a school of fine arts with a full
array of professors and courses in all branches. How could this institution be anything but a bastion of tradition when its classrooms and
galleries at Burlington House were held from the Crown on a "999
years' lease at a peppercorn rent?" For more than a century, until the
Slade school of fine arts was established in London University, the
Academy dictated public taste and enjoyed a monopoly of art education and instruction. The art event of the year was the annual
Academy exhibit of the works of members together with selected
works by associates. Understandably the crushing authority of the jury
of selection and awards generated ill will and revolt in the ranks of
independent artists.

To form a secessionist group and exhibit independently of the parent
academy or national association became the established technique of
artistic revolution and the introduction of new styles. This dialectic in
the arts operated with greater public clamor and dissonance in France
than in any other country. In 1881 the state abandoned its control over
the Société des Artistes Français, which staged the annual Salon Exhibition, but art was scarcely less "official" and constricted as a result.
In 1884 the Salon des Indépendants was organized as a secessionist
group from the parent society. In 1903 the Salon d'Automne was estab-

lished for the exhibition of the avant-garde works of Post-Impression-ists, Fauvists, and later the Cubists. In Berlin a secessionist group was formed in 1899 by those who painted in the Impressionist style, and this was followed in 1906 by the formation of a "New Secession" group sponsoring even more radical departures from established canons. In Vienna the first split occurred in 1897. Munich was more receptive to new trends but did not escape schism in the quasi-official organization that sponsored the annual art show in the Glaspalast. Munich already had its secessionist organization when the Neue Künstlervereinigung was formed in 1909, which split again in 1911 when Kandinsky orga-nized his Blue Rider group.

Public patronage and sales became influential factors at the end of the century. Royalty and aristocracy had long ago abdicated as patrons and connoisseurs, being interested chiefly in paintings of record, family portraiture, and funeral art. Supporters of innovation came principally from the cultivated upper middle class. Official commissions went almost as a matter of course to the conventional artist with a popular reputation, and his private sales and commissions were facilitated by showings at the salons and exhibitions. The nonconformist, the modern-ist, was at a great disadvantage. His prospects improved, however, as independent critics made their influence felt through the newspaper and periodical press. Their judgments competed with those of the conservative exhibition juries. The private sales galleries, which became available for individual and group showings, also helped to educate the public and develop a market for experimental art. Thus a number of forces operated to free art from the strait-jacket of the state academies and the inflexible exhibition juries. The younger artists who invaded the field around the turn of the century were unwilling to continue in the groove of historicism, following the rules and precepts of the schools and academies, imitating their popular but banal elders, pro-ducing story pictures from mythology and history, and painting por-traits that pleased. Every national center of the arts produced its group of rebels against academic standards; they kept in touch with Paris and considered themselves the bearers of a new art and a new aesthetic attuned to their own times and destined to create a new art worthy of a new century. These were the groups that made the breakthrough to modern art between 1900 and 1914.

2. FROM IMPRESSIONISM TO ABSTRACTION

By 1900 Impressionism in painting had run its course, although some of its greatest figures—Renoir, Monet, and Degas—continued to work well into the twentieth century. Impressionism with all its pleasing qualities and visual delights had gained public acceptance in France and influenced a great many artists abroad. Scarcely was their position assured than critical voices were raised in their own ranks. The burden of this criticism was that Impressionist art was lacking in intellectual content, that the reality it portrayed was fleeting and superficial. Deviating from the mainstream of Impressionism were four notable artists—Paul Cézanne, Georges Seurat, Paul Gauguin, and Vincent van Gogh—who together with their imitators were described as Post-Impressionists, although chronologically they belonged to the Impressionist generation. Post-Impressionism was a collective term and not a description of their art. The career of Paul Cézanne, one of the important sources of twentieth-century painting, illustrates the course of development. Born in 1839, Cézanne had painted as an Impressionist but gained no recognition. A man of some means, he retired to Aix-en-Provence, where he lived and worked almost as a recluse. Cézanne died in 1906, and an impressive retrospective showing was held in Paris in 1907. For Picasso, Braque, and Léger, who were experimenting freely, the Cézanne exhibition was a revelation. The retrospective showing was not the capstone of a long career but the exposure of new concepts in painting which became points of departure for the development of twentieth-century art. As an innovating force his work influenced European painting for the next two decades. Cézanne's originality consisted of these elements: In structuring his works he started from the laws of geometry and attempted to reduce all forms to the simplest terms—the sphere, the cone, the cylinder. In thus re-creating nature he disregarded the conventional laws of representation, resorting to distortion in order to convey his own subjective view of reality. This is of course the substance and the hallmark of modern art.[5]

The works of Van Gogh, like those of Cézanne, met with no acclaim during his lifetime, and his canvases remained largely in the hands of

5. The facts and judgments presented in this section are drawn principally from two important works: John E. Canaday, *Mainstreams of Modern Art* (New York, 1959), and Werner Haftmann, *Painting in the Twentieth Century*.

his family. His message was not for his contemporaries—he died in 1890—but for the younger artists and critics when his works began to be shown posthumously around 1900. For Van Gogh painting was a passionate personal experience, which found expression in his flaring colors and leaping lines. His was a reality inspired by emotion. What made Seurat one of the "fathers of modern art" was his single-minded endeavor to find rules and principles for painting similar to those for music—counterpoint, phrasing, orchestration. Combined with a pointillist technique, this gave his pictures, such as *La Grande Jatte,* a "static sternness" which contrasted sharply with the light and airy works of the principal Impressionists. Gauguin, another deviationist searching for an individual style, finally found it in the elements of ancient Egyptian art, Roman frescoes, and Tahitian myths. Using about six primary and intermediate colors, and abandoning conventional perspective, he painted large flat pictures devoid of all modulation and more like frescoes than conventional paintings.

Whatever their individual styles, and they were highly original and divergent, the Post-Impressionists had this in common: they repudiated the natural look of the world of objects and distorted their images in any way they felt it necessary to convey their subjective impressions. Never again in our century, except on the canvases of "Sunday painters," would tree trunks be brown, leaves green, and shadows black. The Impressionists freed French painting from the dictatorship of the national Salon and the Beaux-Arts tradition; the Post-Impressionists provided the inspiration and point of departure for avant-garde movements which established modern art in the twentieth century.

Significantly, around 1900, artists whose works had been previously ignored began to win public acclaim. Memorial exhibitions were held for Seurat in 1900, Van Gogh in 1903, and Cézanne in 1907. At the World Exhibition in Paris in 1900, the works of Impressionists and Post-Impressionists were admitted in strength. Concurrently the new generation of artists, all of whom were born around 1880, made contact with Paris. Some like Rouault, Delaunay, Derain, and Vlaminck were Paris-born, and some moved in from the provinces—Dufy, Braque, Léger, Marcel Duchamp. From eastern Europe came Brancusi, Archipenko, and Chagall. Picasso settled permanently in Paris in 1904, while Kandinsky, Marc, Nolde, and Klee made extended visits to the French capital between 1900 and 1907. The leader of Italian Futurism, Boccioni, established contact in 1902 and Modigliani in 1906. Admittedly, modern art had important roots in Germany and Italy, but Paris was the principal source of ideas, experiments, and critical appreciation.

Henri Matisse and Pablo Picasso were unquestionably the most adventuresome artists working in Paris between 1900 and 1914. Matisse was the center of the group known as Fauvists—"wild animals"—a nickname affixed at the exhibition of their works at the Salon d'Automne in 1905. One of the group, André Derain, recalled: "It was the era of photography. That may have influenced us and contributed to our reaction against anything that resembled a photographic plate taken from life."[6] The Fauvists were not working on new principles but pushing to extremes features of the work of Van Gogh, Gauguin, and to a lesser extent Cézanne.

With Cubism, developed by Picasso and Braque around 1907, painting moved another step away from the imitation of objects and images toward the abstract. While Fauvism was a synthesis—some might say, a paroxysm—of Post-Impressionist painting, Cubism presented a new conception. In its influence on architecture, sculpture, and the applied arts, it has been a continuing force in Western art. Cubism had three sources of inspiration: the method and principles of Cézanne, primitive art—especially Negro sculpture—and the example of "primitive" painters, expecially Henri Rousseau.[7] The distinctive feature of Cubism was the division of the canvas into a large number of planes or facets, like a cut gem, and the representation of each part of the object as though it were a reflection in one of the facets or a view from a different angle. In the organization of their pictures the Cubists followed Cézanne's injunction to reduce everything to spheres, cones, and cylinders. The subject matter was unimportant; painters portrayed whatever was familiar and convenient—a wine or brandy bottle, a jug, a violin or guitar, a chair, a table, the title page of a Parisian newspaper. Enthusiastically publicized by Guillaume Apollinaire, Cubism became an established style that was absorbed into the mainstream of the advanced art movement. More than any other experimental style it lent itself to practical application in poster and advertising art. Who has not seen the poster showing a wheel of a railway coach, a siphon

6. Quoted in Haftmann, *Painting in the Twentieth Century*, I, 71.
7. John Golding, *Cubism: A History and an Analysis* (New York, 1959), pp. 15–18, and *passim*.

bottle, and a glass, all in overlapping planes and held together by complementary colors, with the caption: "Travel by *Wagon-lits* with Cook's"? Cubism was an important ingredient of modern art and a noteworthy step toward abstraction.

The abandonment of recognizable objects in painting and the resort to abstract forms came by way of Expressionism, the German counterpart of Fauvism. The German Expressionists were attuned to the spirit of Van Gogh, the Norwegian Edvard Munch, and the Belgian James Ensor. Even more than their French contemporaries, they sought to express emotions and feelings by a violent distortion of forms and the use of explosive colors. They borrowed much from Edvard Munch, whose works were dark and murky, full of symbols, and infused with a kind of *Weltangst*. One suspects also that they had read and absorbed Nietzsche. Dresden was a principal center of Expressionism, where in 1905 three young architectural students—Ernst Kirchner, Erich Heckel, and Karl Schmidt-Rottluff—organized Die Brücke (The Bridge), in a group effort to develop, perfect, and exhibit their revolutionary ideas in art. As others joined them and their work achieved recognition, the Brücke group became the vanguard of Expressionism.

Munich rivaled Paris as an abode of experimental art. An important center of the arts and crafts, especially lithography, Munich supported a large artists' colony, some of Europe's best museums, and a sophisticated public. The state academy of fine arts attracted many students from north Germany, Switzerland, Russia, and eastern Europe. Historicism, realism, a kind of supernaturalism, and a confident imitation of the "old masters" could all be seen in the official annual exhibition of art held in the Glaspalast. Munich was the home of the Jugendstil— German counterpart of Art Nouveau—which developed in the arts and crafts around the turn of the century. While concerned especially with architecture, furniture design, and decoration it was also an art style that contributed substantially to the movement of Expressionism.[8] Munich was alert and receptive to new trends and developments in the

---

8. One of its founders, August Endell, expressed it thus:

> Ich baute mir aus leichten Wolken
> seltsam ein kindlich kühnes Schloss,
> vergass die Erde, ihre Schmerzen,
> der Traum allein mein seliger Genoss.

Quoted in *München, 1869–1958: Aufbruch zur Modernen Kunst* (Munich, 1958), p. 150.

arts. Courbet had been lionized at the International Art Exhibition of 1869, and Munich's independent realist painter, Wilhelm Leibl, created a local scandal by painting a Munich matron, Frau Gedon, in all her finery, which did not conceal her pregnant condition. Munich had an active Künstlerverein, which in 1904 sponsored the first German exhibition of the works of Cézanne, Gauguin, and Van Gogh. In 1896 Wassily Kandinsky arrived in Munich, studied for a time at the Academy, and then traveled extensively in France and Italy. When he returned to Munich he took the lead in organizing the Neue Künstlervereinigung, representing the modernist element in Munich art circles. While this group wanted to consolidate the ground that had been gained, Kandinsky and a few close associates—Franz Marc, August Macke, Paul Klee, and Gabrielle Münter—seceded to form the Blaue Reiter (Blue Rider) group, which held its first Munich exhibition in 1911. A broad panorama of achievements in modern art was presented in Cologne in the 1912 Sonderbund Exhibition. The works exhibited were a *Who's Who* of advanced art in Europe: Van Gogh was featured, and there were separate rooms for Cézanne, Munch, and the Post-Impressionists. The Blue Rider, the Bridge group, and the Berlin Secession also exhibited. Significantly, the anteroom showed works of El Greco, whom the modernists were now claiming as an artistic ancestor.

Futurism was Italy's contribution to the modern art movement. The Venice Exhibition of 1895, presenting contemporary French, German, and Austrian art, was the first showing in Italy of the Impressionist schools. The industrial exhibition in Turin in 1902 introduced the Jugendstil of Munich in the fields of industrial art and design. In 1909 the first large exhibition of Impressionist and Post-Impressionist art, showing a wide selection of the French moderns, was organized in Italy. The generation of 1900 thought it was their task to awaken the nation artistically and bring Italy abreast of the other countries in the field of the arts.

Futurism began as a literary movement with strong political overtones. Art was one means of expressing the new ideology preached so aggressively by Gabriele d'Annunzio, Giovanni Papini, and their associates. The first Futurist manifesto, issued by Filippo Marinetti, in February, 1909, demanded that poets and artists free Italy from "its rotten cancerous tumor of professors, archaeologists, cicerones, and antique dealers."[9] In the same manifesto Marinetti rendered this artistic judgment: "A racing motor car, its frame adorned with great pipes, like snakes with explosive breath, a roaring motor car which seems to be running on shrapnel—is more beautiful than the Victory of Samothrace."[10] Futurism, unlike the modern art movement generally, was ultranationalistic and disturbingly aggressive.

Machines suggesting speed and power occupied a prominent place in the works of the Futurists—the railway train, motorcar, and steamship. To portray speed, which fascinated them, they used the "multiple exposure" technique on the principle that a running horse has not four legs but twenty. Their designs and techniques echoed the French Cubists. In 1912 a Futurist exhibition toured Europe and met with considerable interest and acclaim. Futurism, which leaves the impression of something contrived, endeavored to represent the dynamism of a new century, but as a significant development in the arts it did not survive the realities of war.

Cubism, Expressionism, and Futurism reveal clearly the movement away from likeness in painting toward pure abstraction, which emerged simultaneously and independently in several places between 1910 and 1914. The trend toward the abandonment of visible reality in painting had a philosophical as well as an artistic impulse. Also some sense of the new world of invisible nature discovered by the scientist came through to the artist, isolated though he usually was from scientific developments. A landmark in art theory and aesthetics was a small treatise published in Munich in 1908 by Wilhelm Worringer. Entitled *Abstraktion und Einfühlung,* it had been submitted as a doctoral dissertation in philosophy. Between 1908, when it was published, and 1951, it went through eleven editions—doubtless a record for a doctoral dissertation.[11] The most arresting thought in the book was the flat statement "that the work of art is an independent organism apart from nature, to which it is equal in rank and essentially unrelated." From Post-Impressionism onward, artists had been moving in this direction, but they had not dared to say it in print or demonstrate it fully in their painting.

9. Haftmann, *Painting in the Twentieth Century,* I, 106.

10. Quoted in Francis B. Blanshard, *Retreat from Likeness in the Theory of Painting* (New York, 1949), p. 108.

11. An English translation, entitled *Abstraction and Empathy,* was published in London in 1953.

In 1910 Kandinsky produced his first abstract watercolor and two years later published his treatise *Concerning the Spiritual in Art,* which was received as a statement of principles by the modernist schools. Kandinsky is regarded as the originator of abstract painting, but this development, as we have noted, had long been maturing. In 1911 the leader of the Russian "Suprematists," Kazimir Malevich, painted as a kind of group manifesto his *Black Square on a White Background.* In Paris, Robert Delaunay and Frank Kupka, working independently, advanced from Cubism to abstraction in 1912. Well before the war the breakthrough to modern art was an accomplished fact.

Werner Haftmann describes modern art before 1914 as "a dialogue" among three countries: France, Germany, and Italy. England and the United States did not participate, but they felt the shocks. England had its own tradition in art and a citadel of conservatism in the Royal Academy. These made English art almost impervious to outside influences. At the Academy exhibitions, presentation portraits of prominent persons, story pictures—*Vanity and Sanctity, Return from the Ball, Building the Rick, The First Communion*—and descriptive landscapes breathing poetic sentiment continued to predominate. A Toulouse-Lautrec exhibition in London in 1898 was a sad failure, and an Impressionist showing in 1905 aroused only mild interest. What seriously jolted London art circles was the second Post-Impressionist exhibition staged by Roger Fry at the Grafton Galleries in 1912. Cézanne was the central figure in the show, but Fauvism and Cubism were well represented. What could be seen there was especially unsettling to the students at the Royal Academy and the Slade School. Now "all of the cats were out of the bag." Paul Nash, who was attending the Slade School, tells how the director called the students together and told them he could not forbid their attendance but he would be greatly pleased if they did not contaminate their education by visiting the exhibition. The Royal Academicians and established art critics were acutely affected. Sir Claude Phillips of the *Daily Telegraph,* "the most honest and uncompromising of them all, threw down his catalogue upon the threshold of the Grafton Galleries and stamped on it."[12] After 1910 English art exhibited signs of a rapprochement with Continental rebel art, but the war interrupted this interchange. Only after

12. Paul Nash, *Outline: An Autobiography and Other Writings* (London, 1949), pp. 92–93.

World War I did English art come to terms with modern art in what John Canaday has aptly described as a "tepid compromise."

America's confrontation with modern art occurred in 1913 at the famous New York Armory Show, whose fiftieth anniversary was fittingly celebrated in 1963 with an exhibition containing many of the items that caused an explosion of criticism at the original exhibition. Conceived as a protest of American "realists"—the "Ash Can School"—at their exclusion from the established galleries, the Armory Show created a greater sensation than the organizers had anticipated. Indeed American art was never the same after this introduction to Europe's sophisticated innovators. French artists cooperated generously, and among the showings were examples of Picasso, Matisse, Gauguin, Van Gogh, and Rousseau. The "shocker" and storm center of the exhibit was Marcel Duchamp's *Nude Descending a Staircase,* the first Futurist work to be exhibited in the United States. One newspaper reporter described it as "an explosion in a shingle factory," which was more perceptive than derogatory, as the artist had broken the descending figure into "a cascade of shingle-like kinetic planes." A cartoonist lampooned the work by sketching a scene in the New York subway which he entitled *Rude Descending a Staircase!* "Phony," "degenerate," and "immoral" were some of the descriptive terms employed to describe this subversive invasion. Former President Theodore Roosevelt, agreeing with his friend William II on modern art, expressed strong disapproval in published comment. In Chicago the exhibition likewise excited public hostility, and in Boston it was politely snubbed.

The public was informed if not educated by the publicity that surrounded the Armory Show. But public hostility notwithstanding, from this point of confrontation onward American art and art appreciation moved on a new course toward absorption into avant-garde international movements. While modern painting after fifty years still shocks and puzzles a good part of the public, nevertheless reproductions of Cézanne, Picasso, Matisse, Marc, and Mondrian have replaced *The Blue Boy, Whistler's Mother,* and *The Sower* as decorative art in sophisticated middle-class homes.[13]

13. The Armory Show is treated in detail in Milton W. Brown, *The Story of the Armory Show* (New York, 1963); and in Canaday, *Mainstreams of Modern Art,* pp. 468–71.

3. ARCHITECTURE AND DESIGN

Modern architecture and design were fully prefigured in individual achievements before 1914. Nineteenth-century builders and decorators had imitated the classical, the gothic, the renaissance, and the baroque. They did everything but produce a style of their own. Something like a canon developed that required a classical façade for banks and financial institutions, gothic or romanesque for churches, and baroque, frequently mixed with classical, for large public structures. Visual opulence seemed to be the goal of popular architects, decorators, and stylists. Otto Wagner and Josef Hoffmann in Vienna, Frank Lloyd Wright in the United States, and Peter Behrens in Germany were in the vanguard of the revolt against the historical pageantry, style mimicry, elaborate ornamentation, and classical clichés of the schools and academies.

Functional building was not entirely absent from the nineteenth century. Steam and sailing vessels, bridges, trains, docks, and lighthouses were clearly functional. These could not be built in imitation of period styles. New materials, especially iron and sheet glass, found application in exhibition halls and in mammoth glass and iron vaulted railway stations, such as King's Cross in London, Gare du Nord in Paris, and the railway station in Frankfurt. These were the works of engineers and industrial designers, not of academic architects. The engineer, who kept function and materials in the forefront of his work, was one of the sources of the twentieth-century style.

Some important voices outside the technical field were also raised in criticism of period styles and ornamentation. William Morris had inveighed against artists who "wrap themselves up in dreams of Greece and Rome," and in demanding art for everyone he was a progenitor of the modern movement. But in rejecting machine production and advocating a revival of handicrafts he was clearly looking in the wrong direction. Morris was much read and pondered on the Continent. Among the first to advocate functionalism, denounce ornamentation, and accept the machine was the Belgian Henri van de Velde, who delivered a notable series of lectures to a group of Belgian architects and designers between 1896 and 1900. One of the originators of the Art Nouveau style in decorative design, he praised the machine and the engineer and prophesied a great future for the new materials—iron, steel, cement, linoleum, and celluloid. Otto Wagner, Vienna's foremost architect, was another convert to simplicity in design. In 1896 he published his *Moderne Architektur,* which had gone through four editions by 1914. The theme of his book was that the requirements of the modern age should be the starting point and guiding principle for the architect, designer, and builder. Wagner's most functional structure was the Vienna Postal Savings Building, which was completed in 1906. Fifteen of Austria-Hungary's leading architects were trained by Wagner, and he and his pupils kept Austrian architecture in the forefront of European styles for more than a decade. Another Austrian, Adolf Loos, was trained in Dresden and worked for a time in the United States before returning to Vienna in 1896 to practice his profession. Loos was a fiery critic of ornamentation as taught in the schools of architecture and design. In his book *Ornamentation and Crime* (Ornament und Verbrechen), published in 1907, he delivered this dictum: "The lower the standard of a people, the more lavish are its ornaments. To find beauty in form instead of making it depend on ornament is the goal towards which humanity is aspiring."[14] And since 1903 Frank Lloyd Wright had been pleading with designers to refrain from "petty structural deceit and end this wearisome struggle to make things seem what they are not and never can be."[15] Wright's voice carried further in Europe than in the United States. As early as 1910 Wasmuth in Berlin published the great folio edition of Wright's plans and drawings and followed it the next year with a large volume of plates and photographs.

Partially in response to these challenges was the creation of a new style in architectural and interior design which was variously called Art Nouveau, the English style, the Belgian style, or in Germany, the Jugendstil. These variants prevailed as advanced design from about 1895 to 1910. However, it was not basically organic, nor did its integrity depend upon new materials. It was essentially a new kind of mask, an attempt to found a style or develop a formula. "Curved is the line of beauty" was the message intoned in Art Nouveau. Pillars and columns were tortured into curves, and building fronts bulged at appropriate or

14. Quoted in N. Pevsner, *Pioneers of the Modern Movement: From William Morris to Walter Gropius* (London, 1936), p. 32.

15. From "The Art and Craft of the Machine," reprinted in Frank Lloyd Wright, *Modern Architecture* (Princeton, 1931), p. 20.

inappropriate points. Expensive to execute, the style was much favored by the wealthy bourgeoisie whose fortunes derived from modern industry and business.[16] Art Nouveau and Jugendstil were an improvement over the Victorian horrors of the nineteenth century, but the style was too artistically contrived, and when machine production was attempted the effects were cheap and shoddy and this killed it with the public.[17]

More significant, and in the long run more enduring, was the work of the Deutscher Werkbund (German Crafts Association), founded in Munich in 1907. The leading members were architects and designers, but the organization enjoyed the support of progressive industrialists, scientists, and social politicians—Rudolf Diesel, Robert Bosch, Wilhelm Ostwald, Friedrich Naumann. Through publications, regional meetings, and exhibitions the Werkbund exerted a positive influence on the design and production of household utensils and appliances, furniture, fabrics, and interior decoration. An Austrian Werkbund was organized in 1912 and a Swiss association in 1913. In 1914, the impressive Werkbund Exhibition, held in Cologne, was cut short by the outbreak of war.[18]

Although public buildings and monuments continued to be built in imitative styles, the requirements of modern industry, technology, and business encouraged experimentation and the development of utilitarian designs. Buildings were now constructed which in their functional design, absence of ornamentation, and use of new materials were visibly forerunners of the modern international style. Among these, department stores, built in increasing numbers, presented special problems in space arrangements and construction. In 1896, Alfred Messel ventured to design a façade for the Wertheim store in Berlin which revealed honestly what was behind it. The Tietz department store in Düsseldorf (1908) was even more functional in design. In France two builders, A. G. Perret and Tony Garnier, were the first to use reinforced concrete outside and inside their buildings without disguise or

16. When Rudolf Diesel, inventor of the diesel engine, built his mansion in the Bogenhausen district of Munich in 1901, it was designed and furnished in the Jugendstil at a cost of 700,000 marks. Eugen Diesel, *Diesel: Der Mensch, das Werk, das Schicksal* (Hamburg, 1937), pp. 370–73.

17. Pevsner, *Pioneers of the Modern Movement,* pp. 99–117. See also S. T. Madsen, *Sources of the Art Nouveau* (New York, 1955).

18. Pevsner, *Pioneers of the Modern Movement,* pp. 37–43.

period ornamentation. The first all-concrete building was designed and built by Perret in 1903.

Josef Hoffmann was Austria's leading architect, designer, and city planner. His earlier designs were adaptations, but he moved steadily toward the functional and nonornamental. Between 1907 and 1911 he designed and built the first completely modern mansion for the Belgian coal magnate Stoclet in Brussels. Although it echoed the Jugendstil in interior design, it displayed all the principal features of the modern style which became established in Europe during the next twenty years.

Among the German architects and designers, Peter Behrens was the most important influence in developing the modern style. After teaching in several arts and crafts schools, Behrens became architectural consultant to the German General Electric Company (AEG) in 1907, and designed the first major functional factory building—the AEG Turbine Building in Berlin, which has been called "the most beautiful industrial building ever erected up to that time." Behrens also designed the German embassy in St. Petersburg and supervised the design of AEG fixtures, appliances, and machines. Significantly, both Walter Gropius and Mies van der Rohe were employed in Behrens' studio and workshop before they began their independent careers.

Frank Lloyd Wright, apostle of functionalism and relentless critic of period styles, continued to exert a powerful influence on modern architecture in northern Europe. Through the publication of his plans and drawings covering the years from 1895 to 1910, European architects and designers were familiar with his "prairie houses" and such nondomestic structures as the Larkin Building (1904) and the Unity Church (1906). Still ignored in the United States, Wright's work met with interest and approval in Europe.[19]

Walter Gropius consolidated the innovations and precepts developed by the Vienna School, Frank Lloyd Wright, and Peter Behrens. After working with Behrens for three years, Gropius received an independent commission for the Fagus factory at Alfeld am Leine, which was completed in 1911. In this structure he used a steel frame, a complete glass façade, unsupported corners, flat roof, and no ornamentation. The composition was expressive of the cube with emphasis on the hori-

19. J. J. P. Oud, "The Influence of Frank Lloyd Wright on the Architecture of Europe," in Hendricus T. Wijdeveld (ed.), *The Life-Work of the American Architect Frank Lloyd Wright* (Santpoort, Holland, 1925).

zontal. The embodiment of the new message—form follows function—was fully expressed in the striking building designed by Gropius for the Werkbund Exhibition in Cologne in 1914. Even before Gropius organized the Bauhaus School at the end of the war, the distinctive features of organic architecture and design, expressive of the industrial age and emancipated from the past, had been made fully manifest.

4. MODERN MUSIC AND THE THEATER

And what of music, the most romantic of all the arts? Previously limited in its serious forms to church and court it became in the nineteenth century the proud possession of the rising bourgeoisie. Any middle-class family with a pretense to culture included music in the children's education, encouraged talent, if any appeared, and made attendance at musical performances a part of family recreation. Public concerts for paying customers or season subscribers began in the nineteenth century, and by its end the public concert and opera were conspicuous features of Europe's cultural life.

Composers of the late nineteenth century, especially Wagner, had pushed romanticism in music to its turgid limits. Nothing more could be achieved along this line. Unless all development ceased and music became monotonously derivative, a change in forms and styles was essential. The "Los von Wagner" movement at the turn of the century was part of the general and final break with romanticism. Significantly, Bach and Mozart now began to appear with greater frequency on instrumental and operatic programs, from which they had been conspicuously absent for two generations. Also, as in the visual arts, a period of experimentation in musical forms began around 1900. The leaders in this movement—Strauss, Debussy, Stravinsky, Schönberg, Bartók, and Webern—had first to assert their independence from their great predecessors and cast off the romantic heritage.

Richard Strauss (1864–1949), a transitional figure in the development of modern music, was the most newsworthy composer and orchestra director from the turn of the cenutry to 1914. Strauss has been described as "a fascinating red herring" in the German musical scene. Working at first within the tradition of Wagner, he won popular acclaim as well as grudging respect even from the musical iconoclasts. He was the master of his required technique, and he introduced enough of the novel into his work to convey the impression that he was being progressive and contemporary without repudiating the European musical tradition. After achieving success with his symphonic poems, he turned to opera, producing *Salomé* in 1905 and *Elektra* in 1909. The sustained violence of the action and the music of these operas both fascinated and repelled the musical world. But Strauss went no further along this road, and in *Der Rosenkavalier* (1911) he returned to harmony, color, and countesses. Strauss was modern in another respect in that he combined music and money. He received the highest fees as a conductor and the royalties on his creative works made him a sizable fortune. Strauss looked like a successful banker, worked banker's hours, and knew how to limit the risks in his art and still make a profit.[20]

The repudiation of romanticism in music and the arts was more abrupt and decisive in France than elsewhere. By 1900 the position that Wagner's music had won in the 1880's was rapidly eroding. In this there was an element of nationalism, which is revealed in the recorded remark of Erik Satie to Claude Debussy: "We ought to have our own music—if possible without sauerkraut."[21] In 1903 the *Mercure de France* conducted an inquiry "On the Influence of German Music in France." The respondent musicians and critics, with a few exceptions, agreed that Wagner's influence had greatly declined and that his art did not satisfy the requirements of a new epoch.[22]

Claude Debussy and Maurice Ravel represent not only a break with the tradition of Beethoven and Wagner but also a new departure in musical technique and style, their work being often compared to Symbolist poetry and Impressionist painting. The impressionist musical idiom which they developed became an international style.

Vienna was the custodian of the German musical tradition. Brahms died in 1897, Bruckner in 1896, Mahler left Vienna in 1907 and died in 1911. As manager of the Imperial Opera, Gustav Mahler's contemporary impact was greater as a director and conductor than as a com-

20. Criticized for commercialism when he conducted two concerts in the John Wanamaker department store in New York in 1904, he made a dignified defense: "True art ennobles any hall. And earning money in a decent way for wife and child is no disgrace—even for an artist." Quoted in Joseph Machlis, *Introduction to Contemporary Music* (New York, 1961), pp. 84–85.

21. Quoted in Machlis, *Introduction to Contemporary Music,* p. 210.

22. *Mercure de France,* XLIX (Jan.–Mar., 1903), 89–110.

poser. The last of the great Viennese symphonists, his music today is experiencing a justified revival.

Mahler was in a position to encourage Arnold Schönberg, although he insisted that he did not understand his music. Mainly self-taught, Schönberg began to compose around 1900. Significantly, he formed a close friendship with Wassily Kandinsky, absorbed his theories of art, and even attempted painting in the Expressionist style. Schönberg and his two most gifted pupils, Alban Berg and Anton Webern, began to compose "atonal" music about 1908. In 1911 Schönberg published his *Theory of Harmony,* which became the gospel of the atonal school. This kind of modern music became as cerebral as abstract art—music from the laboratory, as one critic described it.[23]

Anything as revolutionary as Schönberg's music was certain to excite the hostility of critics and public, but he forced every serious composer who was not blindly wedded to the past to reevaluate the teaching and principles of his art. The task set by the groundbreakers in modern music—Debussy, Schönberg, Stravinsky, Bartók, and Webern—was the restoration of logic and order in what had become a grand chromatic chaos under the great romanticists. By 1912 the Wagner cult had become a subject for caricature, and after 1914 no important musical drama was composed in the Wagnerian style.[24]

Whether Igor Stravinsky is the greatest composer of the twentieth century, as many critics unhesitatingly proclaim him to be, is a debatable judgment, but of his significant influence on musical development there is no question. Trained in the school of Rimsky-Korsakov, he came to prominence as a composer for the Imperial Russian Ballet, which dazzled Paris in 1910, and annually thereafter, with its original music and superb dancers—Pavlova, Karsavina, and Nijinsky. For the

23. Walter and Alexander Goehr, "Arnold Schönberg's Development toward the Twelve-tone System," in Howard Hartog, *European Music in the Twentieth Century* (London, 1957), pp. 76–93; and Karl H. Wörner, *Neue Musik in der Entscheidung,* 2d ed. (Mainz, 1956), pp. 56–67. According to one reporter, a concert of works by Schönberg, Webern, and Berg, given on March 31, 1913, occasioned "the greatest uproar which has occurred in a Vienna concert hall in the memory of the oldest critics." Nicolas Slonimsky, *Music Since 1900,* 3d ed. (New York, 1949), p. 135.

24. Marcel Proust in *Swann's Way,* the first volume of *Remembrance of Things Past,* has one of his minor figures caricatured as a Wagner enthusiast. Her pose is such devotion to Wagner that she cannot bear to listen to the outmoded music of Chopin; it makes her actively ill!

impresario Serge Diaghilev, Stravinsky composed *The Firebird* in 1910, *Petrouchka* in 1911, and *The Rite of Spring* in 1913. The latter touched off a riot in the Théâtre des Champs-Élysées and made Stravinsky famous overnight. To an audience accustomed to pastoral, antique, or Christian themes in the ballet, the motif was shocking—the rites of prehistoric man in propitiation of spring culminating in a human sacrifice. It could have come directly from the then popular Frazer's *Golden Bough*. If, at the opening performance, some were offended by the theme, more were offended by the music. Unperturbed by murmurs and hisses, Pierre Monteux led the orchestra through the new work with its dissonances and irregular rhythms. Catcalls greeted its conclusion, followed by arguments, and then by blows exchanged between partisans and opponents. Ladies struck out with their opera bags and bearded gentlemen exchanged punches in the aisles. It was what music critics in the Edwardian era politely described as a *succès de scandale*. Fifty years later in London, on the anniversary of its presentation, *Le Sacre* was again performed with Monteux as conductor and Stravinsky in the composer's box. Composer and conductor were feted as lions—old lions to be sure.[25]

Nationalism receded as a force in music in the twentieth century. Wealth, ease of travel, and publication facilities created a large international public. However, composers and performers who drew their inspiration from folk music and poetry continued to flourish in their homelands and to gain recognition. England, known to many Europeans during the nineteenth century as the "land without music," experienced a rebirth of musical interest and productivity. Three trends combined to produce the revival—the abandonment of the German forms and models, the recovery of England's musical past and tradition, and the assimilation of contemporary developments in Europe. Gustav Holst and Ralph Vaughan Williams were outstanding in inspiring the revival. Both composed works that were novel in style but expressive of the English tradition. Much music was heard in England. Provincial towns held "festivals" during which choral and instrumental works were performed, and London supported three symphony orchestras. Much appreciated were the Sunday concerts, which as one

---

25. *New York Times* (May 31, 1963), p. 30; see also Eric White, *Stravinsky: A Critical Survey* (London, 1947), pp. 42–43; and Slonimsky, *Music Since 1900*, pp. 137–38.

reviewer noted "do much to make pleasurable and interesting the dullness of our winter Sunday afternoons."[26]

Other national schools flourished. In Denmark and Norway Edvard Grieg dominated the musical scene and fixed the style of all local composers. Jan Sibelius occupied a similar position in Finland. In Bohemia, Anton Dvořák and Zdenek Fibich advanced the Czech tradition established by Bedřich Smetana. In Russia two schools of music flourished impressively. The nationalistic school centered in St. Petersburg with Rimsky-Korsakov as its leader and with Liadov, Glazunov, and Stravinsky as outstanding representatives. While St. Petersburg represented the Russian national tradition, the Moscow conservatory was classical and Western in its orientation.[27]

In Italy, opera filled the whole musical field. It was the supremely popular art, and it cast orchestral music in the shade. Italy had few philharmonic orchestras performing serious instrumental music. As a reaction against melodramatic opera, a revival of orchestral music began about 1900. Vivaldi, Monteverdi, and Gesualdo provided the models for Italy's neoclassical revival. From the Italian Futurists also came a new program for music, as well as for painting. In the place of traditional music they proposed an "art of noises" which would orchestrate the basic sounds of modern living, such as "the sounds of water, air, or gas in metal pipes, the purring of motors . . . the pounding of pistons, the screeching of gears, the clatter of streetcars on their rails. . . . the slamming of doors, the bustle and shuffle of crowds, and the uproar of railroad stations. . . ."[28] Fortunately the war prevented the realization of this program, but something similar was attempted in the experimental *musique concrète* in the 1920's.

Next to music, the drama and the serious theater occupied positions of prestige in the cultural life of Europe. Valued for educational purposes as well as entertainment, much talent and wealth were channeled into the theater arts. Here royal and princely patronage still played a role, but direct support by state and municipal authorities was also a distinctive feature of theater life. In the larger centers, theater societies,

26. *The Stage Yearbook—1909* (London), p. 23.
27. Hartog, *European Music in the Twentieth Century,* pp. 118–31, 204, 296–98, 310–12.
28. Issued in 1913 by Luigi Russolo, the manifesto is reprinted in Slonimsky, *Music Since 1900,* p. 538.

entrepreneurs, and venturesome capitalists had greatly increased the number of theaters and the volume of plays and dramas which the public might patronize. The theater was a cultural showcase, and a country's standing in the cultivation of the drama was thought to be a measure of its civilization.

In France the government subsidized and controlled four theaters— the Grand Opéra, the Opéra Comique, the Comédie-Française, and the Odéon. There were approximately fifteen major and ten minor theaters in Paris that operated as private enterprises. In St. Petersburg in 1908 there were twenty-three theaters, of which three—reputedly the best— were supported by the state. Moscow had eighteen theaters, of which two were state-supported. There was a popular saying in Moscow that "neither a school, a newspaper, nor a theater can be founded without a rich merchant." Such a merchant had made possible the founding of the Moscow Art Theater, the most experimental and perfectionist of all Russian, indeed of European, theaters. Besides the classical drama it offered the moderns—Chekhov, Ibsen, Tolstoy, Hauptmann, and Hamsun. The reputation of the Moscow Art Theater owed much to its experimental director, Constantin Stanislavsky. An English critic thought that the Russian theater was more advanced than the British and American, being more on a level with the French.[29]

Support of music and the drama was a well-established tradition in the Hapsburg Empire. The Imperial Opera and the Hof-Burgtheater in Vienna were state institutions, the Opera being one of the best in Europe. Eight private theaters, worthy of listing in the Vienna guide-books, offered light opera, drama, popular plays, and comedies. A royal opera and a national theater in Budapest were state-supported, and Prague had its Bohemian National Theater and its German Theater.

The cultural rivalry of the petty German principalities and towns had studded central Europe with opera houses, concert halls, and theaters. Public authorities played a significant role in encouraging and supporting the performing arts. There were six royal Prussian the-aters—three in Berlin and one each in Kassel, Hanover, and Wies-baden. Each German state supported one or more theaters, and usually an opera company. Municipal authorities also supported drama and opera. In Bavaria, for example, there were thirty municipal theaters which were either subventioned or operated by city authorities. To

29. *The Stage Yearbook—1909*, pp. 131–35, report on the Russian stage.

justify the expenditure of public funds for cultural ends, performances at reduced prices were offered regularly with all seats reserved for low-income groups, schoolchildren, and workers. What state and municipal institutions presented on these occasions was not experimental music and modern plays but the national classics of music and the stage.

Superficial entertainment and production of contemporary works were the province of the private enterprise theater. The range of productions extended from light opera to the problem plays of Ibsen, Shaw, Galsworthy, Hauptmann, Wedekind, and Brieux. Success was measured by public patronage, and few works survived more than a single season. Max Reinhardt, who became director of the Deutsches Theater in Berlin in 1905, was the most publicized producer in the European theater. While much of his fame resulted from massive "spectaculars" such as *Oedipus* and *The Miracle,* which he took to London and eventually to New York, he also organized and directed an intimate theater, the Kammerspiele, in which serious plays were presented with the best acting and staging procurable. Reinhardt pressed for dramatic effect in everything he presented, a quality in his work that was sometimes overdone. An English critic thought that in his staging of *Oedipus* in London in 1912, he had "destroyed the dignity of the tragedy," and that it was "a veritable hocus-pocus of stage art."[30] Although judgments clashed over Reinhardt's work, he modernized the German stage and his influence on the theater arts was vital and invigorating.

Music hall and variety shows provided entertainment for the urban masses. By 1914 the motion picture was seriously invading this field. Writers on the theater, who at first viewed the cinema as a transitory novelty, began to admit that as popular entertainment it would probably compete with the music hall and the variety theater. This appraisal was supported by the financial report of the city of Hanover for 1913, which showed that income from the amusement tax on the cinema now exceeded the combined receipts from the theater and the variety halls.

The turn of the century was a cultural watershed. In music the great romanticists began to tarnish; an experimental music, unorthodox as modern art, competed with traditional works for public attention. Strauss won acclaim if not complete acceptance, and the music of

30. *The Stage Year Book—1913,* p. 11.

Debussy, Stravinsky, Schönberg, and Bartók was recognized as belonging uniquely to the twentieth century. No musical nation repudiated its historical past, which still provided inspiration, but the new music was perceptibly supranational in its composition and appeal. The trend toward international sophistication in the theater was likewise striking. Ibsen's plays were performed everywhere, and Shaw found more understanding in Germany and the United States than in Britain. In France he received a respectful hearing but was held to be a kind of English Ibsen. In historical drama the sudden vogue of Shakespeare is astonishing. In 1910 there were 1,220 performances of his plays in Berlin and seven other German cities. Although the cultured middle classes provided the composers, playwrights, directors, actors, and musicians for the flourishing theaters and concert halls, elements of the working class, especially on the Continent, benefited and participated in the cultural life of the time to a greater extent than is ordinarily realized. The establishment of People's Theaters in Vienna, Berlin, and other populous cities in central and western Europe was also a significant development. Of art, architecture, music, and the theater it can be said, in conclusion, that they marched together, conscious of the past, oftentimes extravagantly experimental, seeking their identity in the new century.

Chapter Seven

THE SCIENTIFIC REVOLUTION

I. MEN, MEANS, AND IDEAS

KARL PEARSON, a twentieth-century English herald of science, noted "a wonderful restlessness" in the generation that came of age at the turn of the century. This can be verified in the biographical and memoir literature of the time. The recruitment of young men for scientific careers benefited from this spirit. By 1900 more good minds with their ripest powers were attacking unsolved problems of science and mathematics than ever before. The size of the attacking forces, a distinguishing feature of the twentieth century, had not a little to do with the spectacular advances made in the sciences after 1900.

Most of the recruits entered through Europe's universities. The amateur scientist possessed of sufficient means to pursue scientific interests as an avocation was fading from the scene. The new army of science was supported by institutions of higher learning, industry, or research foundations. An outstanding example of how a great research school in physics came into being is seen in the Cavendish Laboratory at Cambridge. In 1895, under the direction of J. J. Thomson, the status of advanced or graduate student, with suitable stipends, was established to bring the brightest graduates of other institutions to Cambridge for research in physics. Within a few years most of the important chairs of physics in the British Empire were occupied by men who had worked at Cambridge under Thomson.[1]

Most of the leading Continental universities made research an integral part of instruction in science. Achievement in research, as well as teaching and lecturing, was a required qualification for university appointment and promotion. Well equipped laboratories for physics and biology were essential to the kind of instruction given to students. The German professor of science, especially, was commended for his constant concern for advanced students. He instructed them in funda-

---

1. Edmund Whittaker, *A History of the Theories of Aether and Electricity,* 2 vols. (New York, 1951), I, 366.

mentals, supervised their research, examined them for their degrees, and frequently promoted publication of their work. Understandably, German scientific education was held in high regard, and Germany's universities were much frequented by students from other countries of the old and the new world. Science instruction in the German universities became a model for other countries.

Europe's accumulated wealth also made possible generous support of scientific research, an undertaking that began to assume the virtual image of a great national task. Such was the inspiration for the founding, in 1910, of the Kaiser Wilhelm Society for the Advancement of Science. The initial step was taken by Adolf von Harnack, who prepared a memorandum on the state of scientific research in Germany, with recommendations to William II that a great national effort be made to preserve Germany's leading position. That Germany might lose her preeminence in science he described as "a national political danger." Today, more than ever, he wrote, scientific discoveries are given a national label and in the daily press one reads of French, English, American, and German discoveries. Scientific advances instead of having an ideal value have acquired national and political values, and a kind of national competition has developed. "Our leading position in the natural sciences is not only threatened," he declared, "but in certain important sectors we have already fallen behind our foreign rivals." Harnack attributed this to Germany's failure to establish needed research institutes, independent of the universities and free from instructional obligations appertaining to the latter. To reinforce his thesis he pointed to the Pasteur Institute and its branches in France, the Carnegie and Rockefeller institutes in the United States, the Royal Institution and Lister Institute in Britain, and the Nobel Institute in Sweden.

The Kaiser adopted Harnack's proposal enthusiastically, and on the centenary of the founding of the University of Berlin, in 1910, he announced the creation of the Kaiser Wilhelm Society for the Advancement of Science. Initially 15 million marks were collected from industrialists and business concerns in return for decorations and titles. The first list of senators and donors reads like a *Who's Who* of the German economy. Between 1910 and 1914, seven research institutes were established in fields not sufficiently taken care of by the universities and where research required more funds, space, and time than were normally available in these institutions. Outstanding were the institutes in chemistry, electrochemistry, physics, serology, and experimental biology, which were staffed with such luminaries of science as Planck, Einstein, Nernst, Haber, Hahn, and Meitner in the physical sciences, and Correns, Spemann, Wassermann, Warburg, and Goldschmidt in the biological sciences.[2]

With private and public funds channeled in substantial amounts to research in science, with a sharply increasing number of recruits entering the technical colleges and universities, and with feelings of national rivalry and competition operating in the field, a great forward surge of science in the twentieth century was manifestly in prospect.

What inspired young men to pursue scientific careers? How did they acquaint themselves with unsolved problems and changing views in their respective fields? What serious books on science did members of this new generation read which helped them to orient themselves in their life's pursuit? While they influenced the climate of opinion and were avidly read, we may dismiss the popularizers of science and the fantasts, of whom there were not a few. We know from recorded recollections that many who entered the life sciences were inspired by Darwin's epochal work on evolution and the origin of species. In the mathematical and physical sciences, the works of Ernst Mach, Henri Poincaré, and Karl Pearson—to name but three—dealt seriously with the subjects of science, bore the stamp of originality, and opened new perspectives to twentieth-century minds. They spoke uniquely about science to the younger generation.

Ernst Mach (1838–1916), an Austrian physicist and philosopher of science, taught at Graz and Prague before being called to Vienna in 1895, where he held the chair of inductive philosophy. His books were numerous and his fame considerable. His foremost work was *The Science of Mechanics* (Die Mechanik in ihrer Entwicklung), first published in 1883, many times revised and reissued, and translated into English, French, Russian, and Italian. Mach was a thoroughgoing positivist devoted to the task of eliminating from science all latent metaphysical concepts. No statement, in his view, was admissible in science unless it could be verified by empirical data derived from experimentation and observation. This led him to oppose even the

2. Max Planck, *25 Jahre Kaiser Wilhelm-Gesellschaft zur Förderung der Wissenschaften*, 2 vols. (Berlin, 1936), I, 1–21; Harnack's memo (Nov. 21, 1909), pp. 30–44.

introduction of atoms and molecules into physical theory. But what attracted great attention to Mach's theoretical views was his criticism of Newtonian concepts of time and space and the classical laws of motion. The general laws of physics, according to Mach, are only simple economical summaries of sense perceptions; such terms as "absolute time" and "absolute space" are metaphysical creations and should be eliminated from the vocabulary of science. Mach's philosophical position, and his challenge to classical concepts in physics, engaged the attention of Albert Einstein while still a student at the Polytechnic College in Zurich, and he later credited Mach with orienting his thinking about science.[3]

Another critic of nineteenth-century physics was the French mathematician Henri Poincaré, cousin of Raymond Poincaré, wartime president of France. Eric T. Bell calls him the "Last Universalist," because he was "the last man to take practically all mathematics, both pure and applied, as his province."[4] Poincaré's contributions extended beyond mathematics and embraced astronomy and mathematical physics. A teacher of mathematics at the University of Caen, he was called to Paris at the age of twenty-seven, promoted to professor shortly thereafter, and elected to the Academy of Sciences when he was thirty-two. In 1906 he achieved the highest distinction in French science when he was chosen president of the Academy. A man of extraordinary mental powers and productivity, he published almost five hundred mathematical papers and notices, more than thirty books on mathematical astronomy and theoretical physics, and after 1902, when his scientific preeminence was established, a number of popular works on the method and philosophy of science. His *Science and Hypothesis* (1903) and *Science and Method* (1908) still sparkle and inform the reader. Less dogmatic and fusty than Mach, Poincaré too was sharply critical of classical physics. In his stated views the general propositions of science, such as the law of inertia, of the conservation of energy, and similar laws, are not statements about reality but "free creations of the human mind" and the only proper question to ask is whether, as general propositions, they have served their purpose or not. In his *Science and Hypothesis* he

---

3. For Mach's critique of Newtonian mechanics, see *Die Mechanik,* 9th ed. (Leipzig, 1933), pp. 179–96, 216–52. The English translation was entitled *The Science of Mechanics: A Critical and Historical Account of Its Development* (Chicago, 1902).
4. Eric T. Bell, *Men of Mathematics* (New York, 1937), pp. 527, 528–55.

sharply criticized classical mechanics and elaborated his views on "Relative and Absolute Motion." Indeed there are historians of science who insist that the special theory of relativity is more properly attributable to Poincaré than to Einstein.[5]

Poincaré certainly saw the new period developing in theoretical physics, and he busied himself with its mathematical statements but he could not usher it in. However, together with Max Planck he was among the first scientists of high standing to call attention to Einstein's work and to realize its full implications. He was still active and productive when he died in 1912 at the age of fifty-nine.

Serious students of science also read and acclaimed Karl Pearson's *The Grammar of Science,* which sold 4,000 copies in the first edition published in 1892. Substantially revised and enlarged by three chapters on biology, the work was reissued in 1900 and translated into several languages. The young Einstein and his circle of friends in Berne read and discussed it; Russian students of science found it provocative and illuminating; and a Harvard professor used it in his physics seminar.

Karl Pearson had studied mathematics and science at Cambridge and, like his father, prepared for a career in the law. He was diverted from this goal by a period of study in Germany, a false start in historical studies, and a period of free-lance writing for the London reviews. In 1884 he was appointed professor of applied mathematics in University College, London, and lecturer on the ancient Gresham College foundation. From his semipopular lecture series on "The Scope and Concepts of Modern Science" came his *Grammar of Science,* one of the most influential general books on science published at the turn of the century. Pearson became a major innovator in the development of statistics, but he otherwise scattered his talent and efforts and it is difficult to point to any singular discoveries and achievements. An enthusiast for modern science, possessed of a sharp wit and a ready pen, he often seemed to interpret his mission to be a writer of "polemics against the ignorance of the world." This is more or less the tone of his *Grammar.*

Much that was provocative and challenging in Pearson's book in 1900 has become commonplace. Employing a vigorous vocabulary, he roundly denounced all metaphysicians and "system-mongers" as hopelessly inadequate or hopelessly prejudiced, and hailed the scientific method as "the sole gateway to the whole region of knowledge." How-

5. Whittaker, *History of the Theories of Aether and Electricity,* II, 40–43.

ever, he did not think metaphysical dogmas—including religion—would now check scientific research, as Hegelian philosophy had once threatened to "strangle infant science in Germany." Pearson's philosophical position was that of Mach—only through sense perceptions do we attain to knowledge, and "knowledge beyond the sphere of perception [is] only another name for unreasoning faith." In his chapter on the "Laws of Motion" he critically examined Newton's mechanics and like Mach found that they abounded in "metaphysical obscurities." Of time and space, he declared, "we cannot assert a real existence. . . . Space and time are not realities of the phenomenal world, but the modes under which we perceive things apart." In insisting upon "the pure relativity of all phenomena," Pearson sounded a distinctly twentieth-century note. The last three chapters of the *Grammar* dealt with the biological sciences, which he saw being transformed from a descriptive to an exact division of science. Other motifs in Pearson's book were the insistence upon rigor in scientific reasoning and statement, and reiteration of the view that the task of science was to answer the question "How?" rather than the question "Why?"[6]

The list of serious writers about science might be extended beyond Mach, Pearson, and Poincaré to include Pierre Duhem, Wilhelm Ostwald, H. A. Lorentz, and J. J. Thomson. It is sufficient to note, however, that at the turn of the century there was a great ferment in the whole field of the physical as well as the biological sciences. Students entering these fields were aware that old landmarks were disappearing, established canons brought into question, and problems raised that would challenge the best minds of an entire generation of scientists. Advances in all branches of science were characteristic of the new century, but achievements in three fields impress the observer as uniquely revolutionary. Notably in physics, biology, and chemistry pioneer scientists pushed forward into unoccupied and difficult territory.

2. RAYS, RADIOACTIVITY, AND THE ATOM

By the end of the nineteenth century science was fully structured and compartmentalized—the observational sciences of astronomy, geology, and systematic biology, on the one hand, and the experimental fields of physics, chemistry, and experimental biology on the other. For nearly

6. *Grammar of Science* (London, 1889), pp. 24, 17–18, 537, 184, 191, and *passim.*

fifty years the great debate provoked by Darwin and his successors had focused public attention on the life sciences rather than the physical sciences. The waves of controversy had not entirely receded by 1900, but on the part of the scientists there was a slackening of interest as they left the field to the parsons, the popularizers, and the playwrights. Whether man descended from monkey, or whether they were simian brethren, whether man was the product of evolution or of a "special creation," whether natural selection through survival of the fittest had been the ordering principle of all life in nature—these were residues of the great debate. Most educated people doubtless accepted the view that man had biological ancestors, probably arboreal.

At the turn of the century the center of public and scientific interest began to shift from biology to physics and chemistry. Radioactive substances and atomic physics became the wonder and the nightmare of the twentieth century. The educated public shortly began to react to new formulations in physics as it had reacted previously to new formulations in biology.

Physics compared to biology had been in the doldrums for two decades following the death of James Clerk Maxwell (1831–1879), who had broadly formulated the problems that occupied the attention of physicists, both experimental and theoretical, for the next generation. There was still much to be done, it was believed, but it was not pressing work—merely filling in here and there until everything in the world would be explained in terms of atoms and energy. The technical literature, the journals and proceedings of societies, institutes, and academies did not lack for significant reports and papers, but there was nothing of a revolutionary character producing an impact upon the public. Christmas week, 1895, when Wilhelm Röntgen announced his discovery of the X rays, marks the beginning of a "new physics" and a new era in the history of science and human society. James B. Conant has commented perceptively on the stimulus that comes from the discovery of a new technique or the impact of a major discovery: "It is as though a group of prospectors were hunting in barren ground and suddenly struck a rich vein of ore. All at once everyone works feverishly and the gold begins to flow."[7] Stemming directly from Röntgen's achievement came the discovery of the radioactive property of uranium by Henri Becquerel in 1896, and the identification of the electron by

7. James B. Conant, *On Understanding Science* (New Haven, 1947), p. 74.

J. J. Thomson in 1897. The statement of the quantum concept by Max Planck in 1900, the special theory of relativity by Einstein in 1905, and the first model of the atom by Rutherford in 1911 were all closely interrelated, and together they established the foundations of the new physics.

It is a truism that science advances step by step and every scientist depends on the work of his predecessors. But Röntgen's discovery seems to come as close to a great accidental or intuitive breakthrough as recent science records. Professor of physics in the University of Würzburg, Röntgen was experimenting in his laboratory with electrical conduction using a cathode ray tube. A common piece of apparatus, it consisted of a simple glass bulb, with negative and positive electrodes sealed through the glass wall, and the bulb pumped down to a good vacuum. When high-voltage current was applied through the electrodes a fluorescent glow was produced on the surface of the bulb, and it was in this glow that the X rays were produced. Other experimenters had noted the manifestations of rays from this phenomenon, but Röntgen, who was an inquiring and painstaking scientist, investigated them. He discovered that they would penetrate many opaque objects and cast an image upon a photographic plate. His wife's hand showing the bone structure and her wedding ring was one of the first photographs made with his X-ray apparatus. Following the established practice of publishing the results of experimentation in order to establish priority and receive credit, Röntgen published his paper on the X rays in the proceedings of the local scientific society and mailed reprints to a number of Europe's leading physicists. The report of his discovery was carried first to the public by a Viennese newspaper which announced that Professor Röntgen of Würzburg had discovered a means of photographing "hidden things," especially the bones in a human body. The value of the discovery to medical science was immediately appreciated and rapidly appropriated. The first medical X-ray photographs were made in physics laboratories. Röntgen might have patented his photographic process but stoutly rejected suggestions that he do so. He was a scientist, and credit for the discovery and a professorship at the University of Munich were, for him, ample reward.[8]

8. Beyond fame as the discoverer, Röntgen reaped no benefit from the photographic X ray. Medical scientists have not honored his achievement in any appropriate way, and in 1952 his only survivor—an adopted daughter, his wife's niece—was living in near-poverty in Würzburg.

One of Röntgen's reprints was sent to the distinguished French scientist Henri Poincaré, a member of the Paris Academy of Sciences, whose members still met on Mondays for the reading of papers and reports, which were then published in its proceedings. At Poincaré's suggestion, two medical scientists, duplicating Röntgen's technique, showed the first French X-ray photographs at their scheduled meeting on January 20, 1896. Poincaré led the discussion that followed. One of the members who listened was Henri Becquerel, professor of physics at the Paris Museum of Natural History. What excited his interest was the source of the X rays. If they were produced in the fluorescence of the cathode ray tube, might they not also be found in emanations from other fluorescent substances? In his laboratory Becquerel wrapped a photographic plate in heavy black paper to exclude normal light, placed various fluorescent compounds and substances on the black paper, and exposed the packet to the direct rays of the sun to see if any rays penetrated to the photographic plate. He had no success until he used crystals of a compound containing uranium salts, which he knew would glow under ultraviolet light. Exposed to the sun's rays to induce fluorescence, the rays penetrated the black paper and produced a silhouette on the photographic plate. But further tests showed that the same result could be produced without exposure to the sun. Even in a dark room, as long as uranium was present, the effect on the plate was constant. Becquerel did not find the source of Röntgen's X rays, but more important he found that refined uranium had the power to emit rays from some unexplained source of inherent energy.

How graduate students find their dissertation topics, or rather how the topic finds the student, is an interesting phenomenon of the academic life. Marie Curie, born Marja Sklodowska in Warsaw, was a graduate student in chemistry at the Sorbonne when she married Pierre Curie, a teacher of physics at the School for Industrial Physics and Chemistry, an institution supported by the city of Paris. When it came to choosing a subject for her doctoral dissertation she elected to work in the field which Becquerel had opened up. Her original project was to measure the intensity of the mysterious rays given off by uranium and its compounds. Instead of using a photographic plate she proposed to measure, with an improved electrometer, the electrical properties which the rays possessed. (This had been discovered by Becquerel.) After developing the technique of measurement, she turned to a search for other ores, metals, and compounds that might have the ray-giving quality in intensity different from that of uranium. She tested refined metals, raw minerals, and purified compounds with no success. Only pitchblende ore, from which uranium was extracted, yielded results. Some of the pitchblende ores produced measurably greater activity than the same weight of pure uranium, indicating that there was something in the raw ore more active than uranium. Joined now by her husband, an intensive search for the unknown substance was undertaken, which finally resulted in the discovery of a new element to which they gave the name polonium, honoring Madame Curie's native country. The work on polonium put the Curies on the track of another active substance in the pitchblende residues, which they finally identified and named radium, because of the intensity of its emissions. The Curies had discovered two new elements in one year. Concentrating on radium, they analyzed and described its properties, Pierre Curie doing the physical analysis, Madame Curie the chemical. In 1903 her dissertation was completed and presented to the Faculty of Sciences of the Sorbonne.[9] In the same year, the Curies, jointly with Henri Becquerel, were awarded the Nobel prize for physics. The importance of the Curies' achievement lay not solely in the discovery of two new elements, but also in the hypothesis advanced that the "radioactivity" of these elements was an atomic rather than a chemical phenomenon.

Science before 1914 was like a game, and not a deadly competition; any number could play it, assuming possession of the requisite knowledge, access to facilities, and imaginative curiosity. Röntgen's X rays and the Curies' discoveries attracted not only public interest but also brought new workers to the field. As soon as Röntgen's discovery came to the attention of J. J. Thomson, director of the Cavendish laboratory at Cambridge, he had a copy of the apparatus built and employed it in current experimentation. Thomson had been occupied for some time with experiments in the electrical conductivity of gasses—a line of research that stemmed from one of the areas of interest of James Clerk Maxwell, the first director of the Cavendish laboratory. In one of his experiments Thomson applied the rays to a gas to see if they affected its electrical properties. To his great delight he found that the conductivity of the gas was greatly increased, even though the electric

9. A classic in the literature of science, it was entitled *Recherches sur les substances radioactives* (Paris, 1903), 142 pp.

charge applied was exceedingly small. Writing later in his memoirs, he recalled: "Until the rays were discovered the only ways of making electricity pass through a gas were either to apply very great electric forces to it, or else to use very hot gases such as flames. In either case it was exceedingly difficult to get anything like accurate measurements. . . . To have come upon a method of producing conductivity in the gas so controllable and so convenient as that of the X-rays was like coming into smooth water after long buffeting by heavy seas."[10]

From Thomson's imaginative experiments in the ionization of gases came the discovery of the electron, a major advance toward the determination of the reality and structure of the atom. What Thomson and his brilliant young assistant, Ernest Rutherford, observed was that a beam of X rays passed through air, or any gas, ripped from some of the gas molecules tiny particles charged with negative electricity. These particles could be collected on charged plates in an ionization chamber. But what were these particles? In 1897, after a year and a half of experimentation and reflection, Thomson reported his findings and conclusions. These were original and challenging, for he asserted, in opposition to the classical theory of the indivisible atom, that the "corpuscles" detected in his experimental gases were identical in their mass and electrical charge, and must therefore be constituent parts of atoms.

It is a happy fallacy that originality is always assured a cordial welcome in science and mathematics. But the experience of Darwin, Mendel, Planck, Thomson, and many others who might be named testifies strongly to the contrary. Skepticism and dissent greeted Thomson's published papers and reports. "I was not surprised at this," he wrote later, "as I had myself come to this explanation of my experiments with great reluctance, and it was only after I was convinced that the experiment left no escape from it that I published my belief in the existence of bodies smaller than atoms."[11] Thomson's conclusions, however, were amply confirmed by other experimenters who, in considerable numbers, were following his lead or working along parallel lines. The electron as a subatomic particle became an

10. J. J. Thomson, *Recollections and Reflections* (New York, 1937), pp. 325–26.
11. Thomson, *Recollections*, p. 341; Whittaker, *History of the Theories of Aether and Electricity*, I, 364–65.

accepted fact in science, and with its discovery the physicists had taken the first major step in investigating the private life of the atom.

Thomson was an ingenious experimenter and a bold thinker; he was also an organizer of scientific forces. Under his direction the Cavendish laboratory became the most productive center of experimental physics in the world. Seven Nobel prizes were awarded to men trained by Thomson in his laboratory at Cambridge. Outstanding among Thomson's students was Ernest Rutherford. Born and educated in New Zealand, he won an appointment to Cambridge in 1895 and became Thomson's assistant in the experimental work on ionization. He continued his research in this field when he accepted, in 1898, an appointment in experimental physics at McGill University in Montreal, where, as he wrote his fiancée, he was expected "to form a research school in order to knock the shine out of the Yankees." In Montreal, Rutherford began to experiment with thorium, another radioactive substance. His ionization experiments with thorium led to speculation on the nature of the processes observed. What was "radioactivity," as the Curies were now calling it, and what produced it in the substances of radium, uranium, and thorium? Chemical problems of great complexity were involved in Rutherford's work with thorium, so he joined forces with a gifted young chemist, Frederick Soddy. Together they published in 1902 a historic paper on "The Cause and Nature of Radioactivity."[12] What Rutherford propounded was the disintegration theory of radioactive substances as an explanation of the phenomenon of radiation. The elements of radium, thorium, and uranium are experiencing spontaneous transformation into new kinds of matter, which are themselves, in turn, radioactive. Thus thorium produces thorium X and so on. These changes are atomic and not chemical, and the rays emitted are the accompaniment of atomic change. What stood in the way of this explanation was the generally accepted principle of the conservation of energy. Here there was no visible input but measurable amounts of energy coming from a source which no one could detect. Rutherford's broad disintegration theory, based on his thorium experiments, was a gamble, but it subsequently received the fullest experimental confirmation. When in 1913 he published one of his major works, *Radioactive Substances and Their Radiations,* he could confi-

12. Sir James Chadwick (ed.), *Collected Papers of Lord Rutherford* (New York, 1962), I, 472–508.

dently assert: "It is safe to say that the rapidity of the growth of accurate knowledge of radio-active phenomena has been largely due to the influence of the disintegration theory."[13]

While Rutherford was basically an experimental physicist, he was fully aware of the larger implications of the atomic process of disintegration and transmutation. In 1903, speculating on the energy locked up in the atom, he wrote: "The energy latent in the atom must be enormous compared with that rendered free in ordinary chemical change." Speaking at a meeting of astronomers on the implications of radioactive substances in relation to the age of the earth, he said: "The discovery of radio-active elements, which in their disintegration liberate enormous amounts of energy, thus increases the possible limit of the duration of life on this planet, and allows the time claimed by the geologist and biologist for the process of evolution." He also speculated that if the heat and light emitted by the sun were the products of radioactivity, then scientists could extend the predicted duration of these processes by billions of years.[14]

In 1907 Rutherford accepted a call to the University of Manchester, where he remained until he succeeded J. J. Thomson as director of the Cavendish laboratory in 1919. Among his assistants and associates in Manchester, at various times, were Hans Geiger, Otto Hahn, and Niels Bohr. The great scientific event of the Manchester period was the development of the nuclear theory of the atom. In 1906 Rutherford began an intensive investigation of the alpha particles given off by radioactive elements. In the scattering phenomena of these particles he found the evidence upon which he based his theory of the structure of the atom. In May, 1911, he published the most theoretical paper of his career, in which he described the kind of atom that would scatter his alpha particles. It was a theoretical model which he unveiled, but it checked out mathematically and became the foundation of all later work in the atomic field.[15] The brilliant Niels Bohr picked up the threads at this point and in 1914, concurrently with the outbreak of

13. *Radioactive Substances and Their Radiations* (Cambridge, 1913), p. 5.

14. *Collected Papers*, I, 608, 657. In 1905 Rutherford delivered the Silliman lectures at Yale University and received an invitation to head the new physics research laboratory. His final thought on the proposal was confided to one of his assistants: "Why should I go there? They act as though the University was made for the students." *Collected Papers*, I, 163.

15. Whittaker, *History of the Theories of Aether and Electricity*, II, 22–25.

war, published his paper on the structure of the atom. It was a simple hydrogen atom with a heavy nucleus and one electron circling around it. By now it was evident that radioactivity was centered in the atom's nucleus. At this point atomic physics as a special branch of science became the business of the postwar generation of scientists.

3. PLANCK AND EINSTEIN—THE QUANTUM OF ENERGY AND RELATIVITY

As a dedicated experimental physicist, Rutherford was inclined to denigrate the work of speculative or purely mathematical physicists: "They play games with their symbols," he said, "but we in the Cavendish turn out the real solid facts of Nature."[16] Long before this statement was made the experimentalists were sorely in need of assistance from their mathematical and theoretical colleagues. The physical laws formulated by Galileo, Newton, and their successors satisfied the requirements of utility and observation and gave a conceptual framework to physics, astronomy, and engineering. But by the end of the nineteenth century more sophisticated probes into the secrets of nature produced results that could not be harmonized with the principles of classical physics. Some of the contradictions and discrepancies simply remained unresolved in the reports of research. The reality of this conflict was often revealed in the discussion periods of scientific societies after the members had listened to an unusually original research paper ending in unorthodox conclusions. Here one could see how binding the Newtonian canon was on those who pondered heaven and earth.

As signs of doubt and unsettlement multiplied toward the end of the century, a critical attitude toward the mechanistic interpretation of physical phenomena became increasingly evident. This general spirit of criticism was manifested in three areas: first, in connection with important experimental results that could not be reconciled with classical laws; second, in the general challenge implicit in positivist philosophy, which had a rebirth at the end of the century; and third, in direct criticism of mechanistic dogmatism by scientists of the caliber of Duhem, Poincaré, Ostwald, Mach, and Pearson.[17]

Although science was becoming increasingly a cumulative and col-

16. *Dictionary of National Biography, 1931–1940,* p. 773.
17. A brilliant analysis of this crisis in scientific thought is Charles C. Gillispie, *The Edge of Objectivity* (Princeton, 1960), pp. 492–520.

lective activity, we may single out two theoretical physicists—Max Planck and Albert Einstein—as outstanding in resolving disharmonies and in providing a theoretical container for twentieth-century physics. In justice one should also mention the Dutchman H. A. Lorentz and the French mathematician Henri Poincaré. While Einstein's relativity theory excited the world's imagination, it could be argued that Planck's quantum theory was more fundamental in effecting a conceptual revolution in physical science. Son of a German jurist, Max Planck was born in Kiel in 1858 and died in Göttingen in 1947. His long career as a scientist spanned the transition from classical physics to the physics of the quantum and relativity. After completing his doctorate in 1879, he spent five years at the University of Munich as a *Privatdozent* waiting for an opening in theoretical physics. In 1885 he received an appointment at Kiel and four years later replaced Gustav Kirchoff in the chair of theoretical physics at Berlin. Even here he found that the experimental physicists regarded the theoretician as "rather superfluous." At Berlin he concentrated on a problem that had engaged his attention and imagination for twenty years—the search for the principle governing the distribution of energy in the normal spectrum of radiant heat. Planck's attempt to find the principle in accord with traditional physical laws was unavailing. His solution was finally developed by introducing an entirely new concept—the elementary "quantum of action"—now called Planck's constant h, and accepted as a true constant of nature. Planck's formula, which displaced all other suggested laws of radiation, was presented in a paper—"On the Distribution of Energy in a Normal Spectrum"—read before the German Physical Society on December 14, 1900. The novelty of Planck's thesis was contained in the conclusion that radiant energy did not proceed in a continuous flow but was emitted and absorbed in integral quantities, or packets, not in fractions, and was therefore discontinuous.

Planck's revolutionary formulation, which became the basis of a new branch of physics, was limited to the field of thermodynamics, and its implications were not immediately appreciated even by Planck himself. Nor were his conclusions readily accepted, because the idea of discontinuity in energy radiation was contrary to the principle of continuity in all causal relationships in nature, a view that had prevailed since Newton and Leibnitz. Although Planck was not awarded the Nobel prize until 1918, it became increasingly evident that he had discovered something more than the secret of the spectrum of radiant heat. In 1905 Einstein applied the quantum theory to explain the constitution of light, showing that light rays follow the same process as energy radiation and are emitted too in packets or quanta. In other fields "Quantizing" clarified many problems—the specific heat of solids, the photochemical effect of light, the frequency of X rays, the movement of gas molecules, and finally through the work of Niels Bohr, the orbits of electrons in the atom. It is not surprising that Max Planck was held in high regard for his scientific achievements, but he was also appreciated for "his moral earnestness and his good will towards men of all creeds, races and nations."[18]

The image of Albert Einstein as a beloved eccentric, an intellectual sage, and the pride of Princeton belongs to his later years. But his most impressive contributions to science were made as a young man before and during the First World War. Born in Ulm, on the upper Danube, of middle-class Jewish parentage, he was educated in Munich and Zurich. With a passion for science and a strong mathematical bent, he entered the Polytechnic College in Zurich to prepare himself for a career as a teacher of science. He completed his course of study in 1901, but despite his recognized brilliance he could not secure an appointment as *Privatdozent*. After an unsatisfactory experience as a teacher in a secondary school, he sought and received appointment as an examiner in the federal patent office in Berne. This gave him a small but certain income, much time for his own interests, and the means to marry and found a family. Without the stimulus of a university connection, Einstein developed his interests and original ideas, concentrating on theoretical problems produced by experimental research during the preceding twenty years. In Berne he was a member of a small group of young men who frequently gathered to read and discuss books on science and philosophy. One of the group, Michele Besso, was an associate in the patent office who could often make pertinent critical remarks on Einstein's original and sometimes startling formulations.

18. A good biography is lacking. We have two brief autobiographical sketches: Max Planck, *Erinnerungen* (Berlin, 1948); and *Wissenschaftliche Selbstbiographie* (Leipzig, 1948); and a brief sketch by James Murphy in Max Planck, *Where Is Science Going?* (London, 1933). L. B. Loeb, *The Development of Physical Thought* (New York, 1933), pp. 527 ff., gives a good nontechnical explanation of the quantum theory.

"If they are roses, they will bloom," he frequently remarked. In 1905 the blossoms began to appear.[19]

Volume XVII of the German journal *Annals of Physics* (Annalen der Physik) for the year 1905 must be accounted one of the most notable of scientific publications, for it contained three original papers by Albert Einstein, including the famous article on the special theory of relativity. Of arresting originality and import, any one of the papers would have attracted attention to this minor official in the Swiss patent office. The first of the three papers dealt with the well-known but puzzling photoelectric effect—the discharge of electrons when a beam of ultraviolet light is thrown upon a metal plate. Here Einstein extended Planck's quantum theory into a new domain. Abandoning the wave theory of light and radiation, he assumed that all light was composed of individual particles of energy, which he described as photons, or light quanta. This was expressed in a fundamental formula —the photoelectric equation—which later received experimental confirmation. It was for this work nominally that Einstein was awarded the Nobel prize in 1921. Einstein's second paper, in this highly productive year, dealt with the "Brownian motion"—an old but unsolved problem in physics—and made a substantial contribution to the proof of the existence of molecules and of their motion in accord with the kinetic theory of matter.

Of Einstein's three papers, the one that attracted greatest attention dealt with the relativity theory, although the term did not occur in the title—"The Electrodynamics of Moving Bodies." Poincaré had coined the term "relativity theory," and H. A. Lorentz had contributed much of the basic mathematical work. Einstein's treatment of the problem amplified and synthesized the work of his predecessors and gave the theory more complete and satisfactory statement. Elaborated in subsequent papers it became the "special theory of relativity."

Clocks and rods, speeding trains, free-falling elevators, even "hot rods" and imaginary spaceships have been employed to explain the elements of Einstein's theory. In fact, most of its applications are beyond the reach of pictorial visualization. What special relativity con-

19. The intense intellectual life of Einstein's circle in Berne is vividly described by one of its members, Maurice Solovine, in his introduction to *Albert Einstein: Lettres à Maurice Solovine* (Paris, 1956). The best of several biographies is Philipp Frank, *Einstein: His Life and Times* (New York, 1947).

tributed to modern theoretical physics may be summarized, if somewhat inadequately, as follows: It assumed the constancy of the velocity of light regardless of the motion of its source or of its receiver, and therefore required the abandonment of the concept of space-filling ether; for conventional concepts of absolute space and time was substituted the idea of relativity in a space-time continuum; and the theory illuminated the relationship between mass and energy, which were represented as convertible. The latter concept eventually gave rise to the most important practical results, as well as the most famous equation in modern history: $E = mc^2$. What was suggested theoretically in this equation became a reality with the first atomic explosion in 1945.

The statement of the special theory of relativity impressed physicists such as Planck, Thomson, Poincaré, and Lorentz, but it produced no immediate public reaction or philosophical unsettlement, such as accompanied the publication of the general theory in 1916. Einstein's papers brought him an appointment in physics at the University of Zurich and shortly thereafter a call to the German University in Prague. Writing on Einstein's behalf to the faculty committee of selection, Max Planck made a prophetic statement: "If Einstein's theory should prove to be correct, as I expect it will, he will be considered the Copernicus of the twentieth century."[20] Einstein's sojourn in Prague was pleasant but brief; in 1912 he returned to Zurich as professor of theoretical physics at the Polytechnic College. In the following year, through the efforts of Max Planck, Einstein was invited to Berlin to fill a joint appointment in the Kaiser Wilhelm Institute and the Prussian Academy. Marital difficulties and his dislike of routine lectures probably influenced his decision to accept. Arnold Sommerfeld, a friend and colleague, has noted that "He never had any orderly lecture-manuscripts. By the time a certain lecture came around again, he had lost his former notes."[21] In Berlin he could devote full time to advanced students and his own problems.

The Berlin appointment and election to the Prussian Academy at age thirty-four was signal recognition of Einstein's standing as a theoretical physicist. He was also given a place on the program of the first Solvay Congress of physicists, held in Brussels in 1911. Ernest Solvay, a

20. Frank, *Einstein*, p. 101.
21. Paul A. Schilpp (ed.), *Albert Einstein: Philosopher-Scientist* (New York, 1949), p. 102; Frank, *Einstein*, pp. 106–9.

pioneer in industrial chemistry and a wealthy philanthropist, had developed a theory of the material universe which he wished to propagate among scientists. Walter Nernst, whose students in Berlin had dubbed him "Herr Kommerzienrat" because of his rare business acumen, suggested to Solvay that he convene a group of physicists to consider not only Solvay's schema but all other current theories and problems that were producing a crisis in modern physics and scientific thought. Twenty-five leading physicists, mathematicians, and physical chemists were invited to participate in the congress which convened in Brussels from October 30 to November 3, 1911. The distinguished Dutch physicist and mathematician H. A. Lorentz served as chairman, and the invited participants included Nernst, Planck, and Sommerfeld from Germany, Einstein and Hasenöhrl from Austria; Poincaré, Langevin, and Curie from France; Rutherford and J. H. Jeans from England; Onnes from Holland, and Knudsen from Denmark. The conference had as its theme "The Theory of Radiation and the Quantum of Energy."

In his opening remarks, Lorentz highlighted the current disarray in physical theory occasioned by the contradictions between classical principles and the striking experimental discoveries of the preceding twenty years. It was almost a lamentation: "We now have the feeling of finding ourselves in an impasse; the old theories have shown themselves more and more incapable of penetrating the obscurities that we encounter on all sides." The principal task of the congress, he said, was to examine the quantum theory advanced by Planck, and fruitfully applied by Einstein, as an avenue of escape from their dilemma. Through the papers and the recorded discussions we can see modern physics in the making. The first Solvay congress has historical significance immeasurably greater for the twentieth century than the second Moroccan crisis which reached its peak while the conference was in session.[22]

The success of the 1911 meeting led to the foundation of the Solvay International Institute of Physics, endowed by Ernest Solvay, with headquarters in Brussels. The Institute sponsored a second conference in 1913, which had as its theme "The Structure of Matter." A number

---

22. Maurice de Broglie, *Les Premiers Congrès de physique Solvay et l'orientation de la physique depuis 1911* (Paris, 1951); the papers and discussions are reproduced in P. Langevin and M. de Broglie, *La Théorie du Rayonnement et les Quanta* (Paris, 1912).

of younger physicists besides Einstein were on the invitational list—F. A. Lindeman, Max von Laue, and Maurice de Broglie. R. W. Wood of Johns Hopkins, who delivered a paper, was the first American to be invited. These two prewar congresses set the course for the postwar meetings, which were resumed in 1921. While the conference themes varied, they were always related to the composition of matter, the structure of elementary particles, the mechanics of radiation, or the stubborn enigmas of the atom.

While Einstein participated in the work of the Solvay Institute, his current interest focused on the extension of the special theory of relativity toward a new theory of gravitation. In 1913 he had publicly expressed the view that Newtonian celestial mechanics needed revision in light of the advances in physics during the preceding century. Late in 1915 he presented a report to the Prussian Academy outlining his theory of general relativity as it applied to astronomy, and in 1916 he published in the *Annals of Physics* the complete exposition of the theory with suggestions as to how it might be experimentally tested.[23]

Newton's celestial mechanics, positing gravitational forces operating on a linear basis in stellar space, impressed many scientists besides Einstein as too simple in view of the complexities that had been recently uncovered in ordinary mechanics. The electromagnetic field forces of Maxwell also suggested a more complex universe than Newton's laws envisaged. For Newton's linear gravitational forces Einstein substituted "curvature of space" and electromagnetic fields surrounding stellar bodies. In his theory the inertia of bodies is not produced, as Newton assumed, by the force of their motion in absolute space, but rather by the influence of the fields about them.

One test of Einstein's exciting mathematical-philosophical construction was immediately available. It had long been remarked by scientists that using Newton's formulas to calculate the orbit of the planet Mercury around the sun produced a discrepancy. Einstein showed that when his formulas were applied the discrepancy was eliminated. But the test that confirmed Einstein's theory and catapulted him to world

23. "Grundlage der allgemeinen Relativitätstheorie," *Annalen der Physik*, ser. 4, Vol. 49, pp. 769–822. Summaries and explanations of the theory are found in Lincoln Barnett, *The Universe and Dr. Einstein* (New York, 1948), pp. 88–91; Frank, *Einstein*, pp. 127–42; and Einstein's own treatise, *Relativity—The Special and the General Theory*, pp. 93–104.

fame was performed by British scientists in 1919. Einstein had suggested that a conclusive test could be performed by determining the curvature of light when it passed through the gravitational field of a massive body such as the sun. Since light has mass it would be deflected when passing near or through a gravitational field. Such proof was provided by a solar eclipse photographic expedition carried out by the Royal Astronomical Society in May, 1919. There was a good deal of publicity in this, considerable scientific interest, and some national feeling. Newton—England's pride—had been boldly challenged. In a widely advertised combined session of the Astronomical Society and the Royal Society on November 6, 1919, it was dramatically announced that the astronomical observations confirmed the prediction that rays of light are deflected in the sun's gravitational field to exactly the degree required by Einstein's theory.

When this news was carried by the press throughout the world there began the "relativity rumpus" that agitated the public during the 1920's. This debate, to use Pascal's words, "filled the ears but not the mind." In Germany it assumed political and anti-Semitic overtones because Einstein was an avowed republican, a Jew, a pacifist, and an internationalist. These repulsive developments had their sad denouement in 1933 with Hitler's advent to power and Einstein's departure from Berlin.

Well before 1919 a more meaningful and serious discussion had begun among philosophers of science. From 1900 onward, Einstein, Planck, Poincaré, Lorentz, and later Niels Bohr had sensed the epistemological implications of the new physics. Planck's quantum and Einstein's relativity excited speculation in those philosophical circles that kept in touch with scientific method. Einstein during these years firmly insisted that relativity and quantum physics had nothing to do with human problems such as determinism and free will, or with religion either, as he once assured the Archbishop of Canterbury. But this position could not be maintained. The analysis of knowledge has always been a major concern of Western philosophy. When such basic alterations are produced by physics in the concepts of time, space, energy, and the atom—the basic processes of nature—they will inescapably involve the whole of philosophy. This thoughtful dialogue which began in Europe before 1914 has been continuous to the present and has infused an older concept of "natural philosophy" with new meaning.

4. FROM EVOLUTION TO GENETICS

Any account, however brief, of the life sciences in the first decade of the twentieth century must take the heritage of Charles Darwin as a point of departure. Darwin's theory of evolution was a masterful synthesis which emphasized the unity of all living things, gave a rational explanation of how life forms had developed, and highlighted the relationship between such forms and the environment to which they had adapted. The theory of evolution produced a great ferment among men of science and attracted many recruits to the field, but as a guide and stimulus to new lines of research it does not appear to have had great effect. The young English naturalist William Bateson wrote his sister Anna in 1888: "My brain boils with Evolution. It is becoming a perfect nightmare to me."[24] However, to many young men of science evolution was not a "nightmare" but a squirrel cage. To Bateson's generation was committed the task of testing or proving the Darwinian generalizations.

Nineteenth-century biologists, like Darwin, concentrated their efforts on field work—observing, collecting, classifying, filling the great museums of natural history with rare collections, and describing the life cycle of living things. At the turn of the century a new contingent of recruits, with interests concentrated in the laboratory rather than the field, entered the domain of biology. They spent a good part of their lives bent over the microscope, the breeding cage, the seed dish, and the culture bottle. These scientists concentrated on the fundamental problem in evolution which Darwin had not convincingly solved: the problem of heredity. Lacking in the Darwinian system was a clear and convincing explanation of the causes of variation, and how the characteristics of parent organisms were implanted and transmitted to the offspring. August Weismann phrased it more vividly—"how a single cell can reproduce the *toute ensemble* of the parent with all the faithfulness of a portrait."

Darwin believed, as did most of his contemporaries, that inheritance resulted in blending, that the offspring of cross-breeding would always

24. Beatrice Bateson, *William Bateson: Naturalist* (Cambridge, Eng., 1928), p. 38.

show characteristics intermediate between the parents, and that parental characteristics would not normally continue to reappear in unaltered form in future generations. If an equal number of black and white cattle were isolated in a herd—so runs the usual example—after some generations the herd would be predominantly gray in appearance. This blending hypothesis was challenged in 1900 by the rediscovery of Gregor Mendel's researches in plant hybridization and his statement of the laws of heredity which derived from his experiments.

The solution to the problem of heredity, which was the missing link in the chain of evolutionary theory, was Gregor Mendel's gift to the twentieth century. The singular circumstances of the rediscovery and verification of Mendel's findings by three scientists in the same year working independently are recounted in every history of science. Mendel's experiments with garden peas were carried out between 1856 and 1863, and his principal findings were reported in a major monograph, "Experiments in Plant Hybridization," published in 1866 in the proceedings of the Brünn Society for the Study of Natural Science. Member of a Catholic teaching order, Mendel had studied in the University of Vienna, held a teaching post in science in Brünn, and was an active promoter of scientific studies in the province of Moravia. It would be more accurate to say that Mendel's publications were ignored rather than "lost" or "buried." His findings were ignored because they seemed almost foolishly to contradict the Lamarckian principle of the inheritance of acquired characteristics as well as Darwin's hypothesis of blending inheritance. Karl Nägeli, of the University of Munich, a leading botanist and authority on hybridization, with whom Mendel corresponded and exchanged reprints, failed throughout to appreciate the significance of his correspondent's revolutionary scientific discoveries.

Mendel's hybridization experiments, which he carried on for seven years, were rigorously executed. The characteristics of the materials which he chose for observation were sharply contrasting—tall and short plants, yellow and green pods, round and wrinkled seeds. Carefully he enumerated and recorded the production of each parent plant and each cross through a minimum of four generations. In the course of his work he had 10,000 hybrid plants under observation. It was the employment of accurate record keeping and the quantification of results that yielded the classic ratios of the Mendelian laws of inheritance.

Mendel's findings are known to every beginning student of biology, and even the uninitiated attach some significance to the terms *dominant* and *recessive* and to the ratio of "three green peas and one yellow." With great insight and power of discrimination Mendel drew the conclusions from his controlled data: that inheritance was determined by factors independent of each other (particulate inheritance); that characteristics passed unaltered from one generation to the next in constant ratios; and that the observed characteristics could also appear in various combinations, but always singular and never blended.[25]

By 1900, when Mendel's work was "rediscovered," the climate of interest and opinion was more favorable than in the 1860's. Significant advances in the biological sciences, especially in cytology and embryology, and the force of August Weismann's theory of heredity, set forth in his well-timed book *Das Keimplasma*,[26] created among scientists a climate favorable to the acceptance of Mendel's principles of heredity. By this time the cellular mechanism of heredity was under close and continuous investigation; and paralleling this research was a deepening interest in hybridization and variation in plants and animals. William Bateson, in his *Materials for the Study of Variation* (1894), had already repudiated "blending inheritance," and propounded a theory of "discontinuous variation." Bateson was branded a heretic by the orthodox Darwinists—Francis Galton, Karl Pearson, and W. F. R. Weldon—but he was getting close to the area of Mendel's discoveries.

However, it was three Continental experimenters—Hugo De Vries of Holland, Carl Correns of Germany, and Ernst Tschermak of Austria—who within months of one another, in 1900, announced results of hybrid experiments corresponding to those of Mendel. De Vries, in reporting his discovery of new principles of heredity to the French Academy of Sciences, ignored Mendel's work, but Correns, who had derived similar results from his experimentation with grains, insisted that credit go to Mendel for his prior discovery. By a singular coincidence, three botanists working independently had carried on research that confirmed Mendel's results and, in reviewing the literature on hybridization prior to publishing their own findings, ascer-

25. Hugo Iltis, *Gregor Johann Mendel: Leben, Werk und Wirkung* (Berlin, 1924), pp. 117–40; Conway Zirkle, *The Beginnings of Plant Hybridization* (Philadelphia, 1935); Gillispie, *The Edge of Objectivity*, pp. 328–37. Mendel's monograph is reprinted in *Ostwalds Klassiker*, No. 121; the first English translation appeared in the *Journal of the Royal Horticultural Society*, Vol. 26 (1901).
26. *The Germ Plasma, a Theory of Heredity* (1893).

tained that the Abbot of Altbrünn monastery had anticipated them by thirty-five years. Such is sometimes the bittersweet of scientific research!

On the Continent, Carl Correns became the principal propagator of Mendel's discoveries and of the need for proper recognition. Shortly after his first report to the *Botanische Zeitung* he published a longer article summarizing Mendel's work and the confirmation of his results by the newest research. With this article, the terms "segregation," "dominant," "recessive," "particulate inheritance," and "Mendel's laws" entered the vocabulary of science.[27]

In England, William Bateson welcomed the discovery of Mendel's monographs because they gave strong support to his theory of "discontinuous variation." Forthwith he became the champion and propagator of Mendelian principles of heredity, never missing an opportunity to speak on the subject before breeders and horticulturists. He even developed a popular lecture entitled "Mendelism Without Tears." For some time Francis Galton and Karl Pearson had been propagating, in their journal *Biometrika,* a statistical theory of natural selection and inheritance. When the two schools clashed sharply, Bateson published, in 1902, a brief treatise entitled *Mendel's Principles of Heredity—A Defence.* In 1905 he coined the word "genetics" for the cumbersome "heredity and variation," and in 1909 he published an expanded edition of his *Principles* in which he marshaled all the experimental evidence supporting Mendelian heredity. Bateson was the first to make the bold generalization that "Mendelian inheritance is virtually universal and virtually exclusive."[28]

Mendelian principles and the progress of genetics encountered no serious opposition in America. As an authority on heredity and variation, Bateson was invited to deliver a principal paper at a scientific conference in the United States in 1902. Jubilantly he wrote his wife of his departure from New York: "At the train yesterday, many of the party arrived with their *Mendel's Principles* in their hands! It has been 'Mendel, Mendel all the way,' and I think a boom is beginning at last."[29] Bateson's prophecy was fulfilled. While the older branches of biology suffered no loss of students or popularity, the keenest research interest and activity centered henceforth in the new field of genetics.

27. "Gregor Mendel's *Experiments in Plant Hybridization* and the Confirmation of Their Results by the Newest Researches," *Botanische Zeitung,* 38 (1900), 229–35.
28. L. C. Dunn (ed.), *Genetics in the Twentieth Century* (New York, 1951), p. 111.
29. Bateson, *William Bateson,* p. 81.

In Germany too, Mendel's principles were quickly integrated in biological thought and teaching. Young scientists, especially, were attracted to the new field of research. The career of Richard Goldschmidt, who entered this field at the turn of the century, provides an instructive case history. The gifted son of a respected Jewish family in Frankfurt, he enrolled at Heidelberg, where he studied premedical subjects for two years and, in his own words, "splashed in the pleasant ocean of life." Besides attending his premedical courses, he heard lectures by Max Weber, Kuno Fischer, and Dietrich Schäfer, who propagated an aggressive Prussianism in an unreceptive atmosphere. In 1898 he transferred to Munich for his medical work, but like Charles Darwin he could not bear the sight of sickness, disease, and suffering to which he was exposed in the clinics. Abandoning medicine, he fulfilled his personal inclinations, almost his passion, by enrolling for the doctorate in biology with a view to a life of teaching and research. He attended the International Zoological Congress held in Berlin in 1901, where he listened to the papers delivered by the great figures in the biological sciences. The lavish hospitality extended to the international guests on this occasion led Goldschmidt to comment that while "not everything was ideal in Imperial Germany . . . certainly science and its makers were ranked near the top of society." Goldschmidt qualified as *Privatdozent* in Munich in 1903 and was appointed first assistant to Professor Richard Hertwig, a famous zoologist. At Munich Goldschmidt's research interest shifted from life-cycle zoology to genetics and evolution. In 1910 he offered the first course in genetics given in a German university and in the following year published the first textbook in the field.[30]

Possessed of enormous energy and rare intelligence, Goldschmidt concentrated in his research upon problems of sex determination and geographical adaptation, using the gypsy moth as research material. His achievements and reputation were such that when the Institute for Experimental Biology of the Kaiser Wilhelm Society was established under the direction of Carl Correns, Goldschmidt was appointed professor of genetics. Before he could occupy the post, he traveled to Japan in search of new strains of the gypsy moth. The outbreak of war found him stranded in New York, where he continued his work as a private researcher until the United States became a belligerent and he was

30. A pioneer work, his *Einführung in die Vererbungswissenschaft* (Leipzig, 1911) was in its fifth edition when it was suppressed by the Nazis.

interned as an enemy alien. Not until 1919 was he able to return by way of Holland to Berlin. In the United States he made valuable contacts, and when his position in Germany became untenable under the Hitler regime, he accepted an appointment at the University of California in Berkeley, where he completed his distinguished career. Goldschmidt's professional life spanned the years from the rediscovery of Mendel to the highly complex researches in the genetic code; his was an odyssey through the golden years before 1914, through the trials of the war and postwar periods, expatriation under the Nazis, and finally a safe haven in the country where he was once interned as an enemy alien. Through it all he never lost his sense of humor, his devotion to science, his concern for culture, and his great humanity.[31]

For Goldschmidt and the scientists of his generation, Mendel's work served as a point of departure, a focus for experimentation, and a system of principles to be supplemented, interpreted, or altered. The first considerable augmentation came from Hugo De Vries' theory of mutation. After years of research with varieties of the primrose, De Vries concluded that species arose not by continuous and gradual adaptation but through sudden large changes, or mutations. Although his experimental results were later challenged, his views were widely accepted at the time and the principle of mutation was incorporated into biological science.[32] Probably more significant were the contributions of the Danish botanist Wilhelm Johannsen, who first made clear through experimentation the unequivocal separation of hereditary and nonhereditary changes in organisms and coined the terms "genotype," "phenotype," and "gene." Mendelian principles, mutation, and the chromosome and gene theories gave solid foundation to the new science of genetics, even though Karl Pearson might disparagingly describe them as "theoretical bridges of snow built across crevasses of ignorance."

Experimental evidence continued to accumulate. Great impetus was given to research in heredity in 1906 when Drosophila (fruit flies), which reproduce at the rate of thirty generations in a year, were introduced as new experimental material for genetic studies. In 1909 success-

---

31. Goldschmidt's most productive years were 1910–1920; he wrote popular works on science besides many technical papers. His autobiography, *In and Out of the Ivory Tower* (Seattle, 1960), is a work of great warmth and distinction.

32. De Vries' principal work, *Die Mutationstheorie*, was published in 1900–1903, in two volumes.

ful ovarian transplantation in the albino guinea pig gave indisputable proof that the hereditary pattern was transmitted independent of environmental factors. Other experimentation showed in 1911 that blood types were inherited in accord with Mendelian principles. In the same year, the gene theory received important confirmation through the brilliant work of T. H. Morgan and his associates in mutation experiments with Drosophila. Finally, in 1915, Morgan and other members of the "Columbia School" published their epochal book, *The Mechanism of Mendelian Heredity,* which organized the whole subject of genetics around the gene and chromosome theories.

It was now possible for geneticists to take stock and relate their achievements to the larger issues of natural selection, origin of species and evolution. The new synthesis of genetics and evolution confirmed by and large the Darwinian hypotheses of variation, natural selection, and adaptation. Genetic research also had shown Mendelian principles to be generally valid but the mechanism of heredity extremely complex. Confirmed also was the Darwinian theory that many forms of adaptation, but by no means all, could be accounted for in terms of survival value, but that natural selection also operated as much to stabilize species as to change them.[33]

By 1914 a field of interest which at the beginning of the century existed on the fringe of the life sciences had moved to the center of the stage. Genetics had become the principal unifying force in the biological sciences, bringing together zoology and botany just as atomic physics had united physics and chemistry. The gene was established as the fundamental unit of the life sciences; the atom had become the fundamental unit of the physical sciences. And in both there was discovered a high degree of randomness in action that Niels Bohr found disturbing in the atom and Harold Blum in the interactions of the gene. This was disturbing also to Einstein, who insisted that the deity did not play dice with nature. But the Christian Abbot of Altbrünn monastery quietly affirmed "the eternal game of dice that decides the fate of the next generation."

---

33. Important works setting forth the new synthesis—frequently described as neo-Darwinism—are Julian Huxley, *Evolution—The Modern Synthesis* (London, 1942); T. Dobzhansky, *Genetics and the Origin of Species,* 3d ed. (New York, 1951); and Dunn, *Genetics in the Twentieth Century.* Harold F. Blum's *Time's Arrow and Evolution,* 2d ed. (Princeton, 1955), is especially original and stimulating.

Chapter Eight

REFORMISM AND SOCIALISM

I. TOWARD A DEMOCRATIC FRANCHISE

POLITICALLY, from 1900 to 1914, Europe moved on a course little changed since 1870. The course was clearly toward parliamentary democracy through the perfecting of political parties, expanding the franchise, increasing civic involvement, and the forging of closer ties between legislatures and bureaucracies. Representation of the urban masses and landless agricultural workers became a pressing political issue in most European states. The right of the individual citizen to vote had its arresting mystique, and enthusiastic radicals and socialists endowed the ballot with power that it could never possess—the power to usher in the millennium. On the other hand, conservatives were quite as sure that political democracy would in the end overthrow the established political, economic, and social order. It was these exaggerated hopes and fears, clustering around the issues of electoral reform, that provided much fuel for controversial fires.

France and England were more advanced toward universal manhood suffrage than other European states. Under the electoral laws of 1871 and 1875, about 10 million adult male Frenchmen exercised the franchise, and in England the electorate numbered about 5 million. Although a fourth of the adult male population of England and Ireland was still voteless, the principle of universal male suffrage was established beyond dispute. In France the issue of female suffrage scarcely rippled the political waters; but in England, beginning in 1910, the picturesque "suffragettes" and their cry of "Votes for Women" were an embarrassment and a reproach to the Liberal cabinet.

Elsewhere in Europe "electoral reform" dealt with a checkerwork of historic practices, of strident demands and reactionary objections. However, the logic of history seemed inescapable—an age that had adopted universal taxation, universal military service, and universal compulsory education could scarcely in justice refuse universal suffrage. Most western and central European states followed the French and

English examples. With Bismarck's endorsement the German Reichstag was elected by universal male suffrage; Switzerland adopted manhood suffrage in 1874, Spain in 1890, Norway in 1898, Sweden in 1907, and Portugal in 1911. In 1913, voting rights in Denmark were conferred upon all citizens aged twenty-five, both male and female. The franchise was extended in the Netherlands in 1886 and 1896, but liberals and socialists were still petitioning and demonstrating for the unrestricted vote in 1911.

Despite appearances, manhood suffrage was thwarted or restricted in a number of ways. In Belgium, for example, the liberal franchise achieved in 1893 was actually nullified by a system of plural voting which kept the conservative-clerical party in power for twenty-eight years. Those with double votes regularly submerged the single votes of the workers in towns and cities. "One man, one vote" was a slogan with special significance in Belgium.[1]

There were other devices that nullified a democratic franchise—indirect elections, conservative second chambers elected on a restricted franchise, official candidates and managed elections. In Spain and Portugal provincial governors regularly employed "agents" to instruct the electors in the choice of representatives. In consequence, a legislature, such as the Spanish Cortes, represented the coterie in power rather than the nation.

In Germany, although a uniform franchise operated in Reich elections, voting requirements in the federal states were often as anomalous as they were anachronistic. Only in south Germany was the general European pattern followed. There Baden adopted universal male suffrage in 1904, Bavaria and Württemberg in 1906. In Bremen and Hamburg, and in the states of Prussia and Saxony, a class system of voting based on property and tax qualifications considerably limited the representation of urban workers. Saxony, which had a liberal franchise in 1900, reverted to class voting in order to eliminate socialist influence at state and local levels. Hamburg instituted a two-class system in 1906. The two grand duchies of Mecklenburg were still

1. In 1912 it was thought that a coalition of liberals and socialists, united on a moderate reform program, would prevail over their clerical opponents. Plural voting, however, again gave the clericals a majority in the new chamber. The election campaign attracted wide attention, and the outcome was a great disappointment to liberals everywhere. *Neue Zürcher Zeitung,* No. 319 (Nov. 18, 1910); and No. 154 (June 4, 1912).

governed through medieval estates. All the land was held by the grand duke and the provincial nobles. The estate owners and the appointed mayors of the forty-nine towns governed as little absolutists, assembling annually as noble and burgher estates to pass laws and vote taxes. "Hie hett Bismarck nix tau seggen," boasted the old grand duke, as he continued to repulse all efforts to penetrate and modernize his domains.[2] The old *Herrnrecht* stood unaltered.

Notorious for its inequities, the Prussian three-class system of voting was for years a principal target of socialist and radical agitation. Under this system all adult males twenty-five or older were divided into three classes, according to the amount at which they were assessed for taxation. The voters in each class then elected indirectly one-third of the deputies allocated to the city or district. A Class I vote therefore could be worth one hundred times as much as a Class III vote. In the Prussian Landtag 300,000 Socialist voters were unrepresented while the same number of Conservative voters returned 143 members! In Berlin, in the 1903 elections, the Social Democrats elected all but one of the city's Reichstag delegation but could not elect a single candidate to the Prussian Landtag. Similarly, in Saxony the Reichstag delegation was solidly Socialist but in the state legislature the party was barely represented.

Understandably, the disadvantaged political parties made electoral reform at the state level a major objective in their political programs. To this end the Social Democrats often collaborated with the Progressive and Catholic Center parties. After the Reichstag election of 1903, when the Socialists gained nearly a million in popular vote, the party leadership began a sustained campaign for electoral reform. The demand was broadly for direct and equal suffrage, a secret ballot, and reapportionment of seats. In Prussia, Bavaria, and Saxony there were great popular demonstrations in the spring of 1906 and in Hamburg serious riots, violence, and destruction of property. Nationwide demonstrations took place in January, 1908, which resulted in Berlin in serious clashes with the police. Such demonstrations, sponsored by the Socialists and supported by the trade unions, became annual occurrences in Prussia until the war brought a moratorium on political demonstrations.

2. A graphic description of these conditions is given in the *Neue Zürcher Zeitung*, No. 134 (May 14, 1908).

Electoral reform with all its several facets was still a popular issue in Europe, one for which radicals would demonstrate, workers would strike, and militants would battle in the streets. It was the culmination of an age that was easily and periodically stirred by the possibilities of political reform. "Suffrage riots," as they were labeled by the political journalists, were widespread. Such demonstrations accompanied by strikes and violence occurred in Belgium in 1902. At Louvain eight persons were killed and twenty-five severely injured. In the same year, demonstrations sponsored by the Liberal party and the trade unions in Sweden turned into serious riots, threats of a general strike, and bloody clashes with the police. Budapest in 1912 was the scene of suffrage demonstrations and riots in which streetlamps were smashed, tramcars wrecked or burned, and severe injuries caused to persons. Exasperation at the outcome of the Belgian general elections of 1912 inspired violent demonstrations in Brussels, Liège, and other centers.

Two notable victories for electoral reform were registered between 1900 and 1914. Manhood suffrage was established in Austria, the most aristocratic state in Europe, in 1907, and in Italy in 1912.

Electoral reform in Austria was a measure of modernization sponsored by the government. The new franchise law, enacted in 1906 and applied in 1907, abolished the system of class representation and indirect election. Henceforth every male citizen twenty-four years of age was entitled to register and vote.[3] The Emperor and his ministers hoped that manhood suffrage would produce a Reichsrat working for the interests of the people directly and not wasting its time squabbling over the naming of public buildings and railroad stations. Alas, the bitter strife continued, and by 1913 the parliamentary machine was working more irregularly than ever—the conflicts between Czechs and Germans, and Poles and Ruthenians, deadlocked the legislature and rendered parliamentary government inoperative.

In Italy the results of franchise reform were more positively favorable. The electoral reform bill introduced by the Giolitti government in 1911 extended the franchise to all literate males aged twenty-one

3. Seats in the Reichsrat were also reallocated on the basis of nationality, and in such a way as to favor the Germans and the Czechs. It gave the Germans 233 seats, the Czechs 107, and the Poles 82, out of a total of 516, leaving 94 for all the rest—Ruthenians, Serbs, Croats, Slovenes, Italians, and Rumanians. William A. Jenks, *The Austrian Electoral Reform of 1907* (New York, 1950), pp. 164–65.

or over, without tax or property qualifications. The vote was with-held only from those between ages twenty-one and thirty who had not performed military service or learned to read and write. The electorate was thereby increased from 3 million to 8.5 million. The law was popular and provided Giolitti and his associates with a fresh political triumph.

The first general election under the new franchise law was held in October and November, 1913. It was a picturesque campaign, especially in the south, where a Neapolitan carnival atmosphere prevailed. Since many illiterates would cast ballots, visual devices were developed, in-cluding "pictograms" to represent the names and platforms of the candidates. The motion picture and the phonograph were also em-ployed. Approximately 4 million ballots were cast by an electorate of 8.5 million. Although the parties of the Left made appreciable gains, the distribution of political power was not radically affected.[4]

Parliamentary democracy proved to be an adequate vehicle for need-ful social and economic reforms, as the legislative record in England, Germany, Italy, and other states plainly demonstrates. But where parliamentary democracy produced no solutions, promoted no com-promises, and brought no peace to the land was in those states where national and cultural rivalries were acutely prevalent. In Austria, in Russia, in Turkey the adoption of a constitutional regime and a broadened franchise proved quite ineffectual in mitigating such antag-onisms. Indeed, the spread of liberal ideas and institutions seemed to intensify the feeling of nationality as parliaments provided a forum, hitherto lacking, for the staging of acrimonious debates and demon-strations of national jealousy and ill will.

II. SOCIAL REFORM AND TAXATION

With what issues did pre-1914 legislatures especially concern them-selves? What would a concordance of published debates reveal as to the principal subjects of discussion and action? First place was as-suredly held by the government's annual budget of income and ex-penditure. The deference and the ritual with which the budget was handled reflected two generations of liberal indoctrination. Not far behind the budget came national defense, constitutional and electoral

4. Thomas Okey, "The General Elections in Italy," *The Contemporary Review*, 104 (1913), 773–83; *Annual Register—1911*, pp. 304–6.

reform, development and utilization of natural resources, education, local government, church and state relationships, and customs and tariffs. These were all fairly traditional. More recently legislatures were confronted with urban industrial problems—labor legislation, social insurance, public health and welfare. In labor legislation, including factory acts, workmen's compensation, and trade union regulation, England had the greatest experience and found most of the broadly applicable solutions.

By 1900 every European country except Russia and the Balkan states had enacted, or begun to enact, industrial codes that regulated the employment of women and children, prescribed the length of the working day in selected industries, and in all instances specified the measures of protection and sanitation that must be afforded the workers in factory, mill, or mine. Still leading in this field, the British parliament in 1909 passed legislation to remedy conditions in certain "sweated trades," and two years later entered the field of retail employment with the Shops Act. When the Liberal party came to power in 1906 it was deeply pledged to enact an effective program of social legislation. Old age pensions in 1908 and the National Insurance Act of 1911, which provided medical insurance for most wage earners and unemployment insurance for some, were sponsored by the Liberal government but enacted as nonpartisan measures. Two points deserve emphasis about the English reform movement down to 1914: First, Liberal and Conservative parties alternated in sponsoring and passing significant legislation; second, the principle of contributory insurance made it easier for laissez-faire liberals to accept state action in ameliorating the hardships of the working classes.[5]

In Germany, the problems arising out of modern industrial employment were met on two main fronts: the one municipal, where all manner of services and benefits were developed for the urban workers; the other national, under which insurance was provided for the most common adversities encountered by the worker and his family—sickness, death, disablement, and old age. The original Bismarckian enactments applied to a narrow range of industrial workers, but over the years the program was extended to include agricultural laborers,

5. E. P. Cheyney, *Modern English Reform* (Philadelphia, 1931), pp. 193–96; C. W. Pipkin, *Social Politics and Modern Democracies,* 2 vols. (New York, 1931), I, 8–41, 111–13, 220–44.

commercial employees, and domestic servants. Consolidated in the social insurance code of 1911, the system made the German worker the best-protected laborer in the world. And no one could say in 1914 that he had "nothing to lose but his chains."

By 1900 most industrialized countries had copied the British factory acts and the system of workmen's compensation for industrial accidents and diseases; further, by 1914 the German system of social insurance had found application, in whole or in part, not only in England but also in Austria, Italy, Switzerland, Belgium, and Denmark.

Parliamentary democracy, however, did not always ensure an adequate program of labor legislation and social insurance. France, for example, experienced a slower movement toward industrialization and urbanization; consequently the extent and intensity of her social problems were less than those of Britain and Germany. The French bureaucracy rather than parliament took the initiative in regulating conditions of employment in shops, factories, and mines. The results were not impressive—a ten-hour day and a six-day week, limited accident insurance, employment exchanges, and contributory old age pensions for persons whose incomes were below 3,000 francs. Labor councils to mediate disputes were authorized in 1899, and a ministry of labor was established in 1906. What one notes in the French scene is that many of the basic measures of industrial organization and social reform were placed on the statute book, but they were so limited in the number of persons covered as to be largely ineffectual.

French liberals had their opportunity in 1906 when the parties of the Left won a signal victory in the elections to the chamber and the senate. The triumphant Left promised a thorough renovation—social, political, economic. But beyond the anticlerical laws and the purging of the officer corps, they did little but hold power, maintain their majorities, and repress all manifestations of labor discontent. The Clemenceau ministry, formed in 1906, had a seventeen-point program that included a graduated income tax and important measures of social reform. But instead of an era of fruitful legislation, such as England experienced, France entered upon a long period of unsettled labor relations, which culminated in an attempted general strike in 1909. The seventeen-point program evaporated like water poured on desert sands. In consequence, the working-class movement drifted away from parliamentary democracy" toward inflexible Marxism or revolutionary syndicalism.

Closely linked with social reform was municipal reform. The opening years of the century found Europe midway in a comprehensive renovation and expansion of its municipal institutions. The municipal reform movement began in the 1880's with basic legislation and charter revisions endowing municipal corporations with broad powers to meet the urgent demands of city growth and urban living. Joseph Chamberlain made his reputation as a radical reforming mayor of the city of Birmingham by sponsoring municipal ownership of the city's public services. Parks, playgrounds, schools, water supply, sanitation, and slum clearing were other achievements of the municipal reform movement.

Although British town councils exercised extensive charter powers, German municipal authorities held almost a "blank check" to do whatever seemed advisable in the interest of their localities. Restrictive zoning of property developed in Germany, for example. Düsseldorf, which was a pacemaker for municipal administrations, besides providing police and fire protection, schools and public assistance programs, also operated the gas, water, and electricity services, the street railways, the slaughterhouses, public markets, public baths, and hospitals. Likewise owned and operated were lodging houses for workers, a mortgage bank, a savings bank, a pawnshop, and a cemetery. The city also supported libraries and museums, an art gallery, a theater, and a concert orchestra. Such an array of services and benefits went considerably beyond the concept of "gas and water socialism."[6]

Other countries besides England and Germany were caught up in the municipal reform movement. The reputation and political career of Karl Lueger, mayor of Vienna (1897–1910), was based on his vigorous and successful rehabilitation of the municipal life and institutions of the old Hapsburg capital. In centralized France, Italy, and Belgium the authority of the departmental prefects over the municipal councils and mayors was somewhat relaxed and the range and authority of local government substantially expanded. However, results comparable to

6. F. C. Howe, *European Cities at Work* (New York, 1913), Chap. III, "Düsseldorf and Municipal Socialism." Howe was a crusader for municipal reform in the United States. Although propagandistic, his book is a firsthand account of municipal administration in Britain and Germany.

those in England and Germany were not always obtained. Contemporary observers were inclined to rate the French cities high for their imposing boulevards, public architecture, squares, and museums, but to find them deficient in sanitary science and social services.[7]

Town planning and zoning for development were important features of the municipal movement. The most advanced aspect of town and city planning was the "garden city" movement for the development of planned self-sustaining towns in rural surroundings. Ebenezer Howard's *Garden Cities of Tomorrow,* published in 1898, was not taken seriously at first, but in the decade before 1914 some thirty to forty suburban developments and communities were built incorporating some of Howard's ideas. Widely publicized were Letchworth, the first "garden city"; Port Sunlight, sponsored by the Lever Brothers near Liverpool; Bournville, developed by the Cadburys near Birmingham; Hellerau colony near Dresden, and similar suburban projects in Munich, Nürnberg, Karlsruhe, and Frankfurt.[8]

The growing expenditure for social reform, social services, and local improvements had to be met from taxes extracted from the citizenry. It is a wonder of the age that parliamentary democracies could impose a tax burden which if levied by an absolute monarch in an earlier time would have provoked revolt in every corner of his kingdom.

Of new revenue devices the income tax was the one most in favor. Originally an English development, it was adopted in the late eighties and early nineties in Austria, Prussia, and the German states, and in Italy, Spain, Denmark, Norway, Switzerland, the Netherlands, and Japan. Indeed by 1914 only France, the United States, Hungary, and Belgium had not enthroned this "queen of taxes," as its enthusiastic proponents liked to call it. Also developed and widely adopted in the same decades were inheritance and estate taxes, transaction taxes on stock and bond transfers, and a variety of business and turnover taxes. Although advanced fiscal authorities and policy makers favored direct taxes over indirect, as a matter of justice, the older consumption and excise levies were not only retained but greatly augmented. On items

7. Percy Ashley, *Local and Central Government* (New York, 1906), pp. 103–4; William B. Munro, *The Government of European Cities* (New York, 1927), *passim.*

8. Howard's book was first published under the title *Tomorrow: A Peaceful Path to Real Reform.* See also Dugald Macfadyen, *Sir Ebenezer Howard and the Town Planning Movement* (Manchester, 1933), Chap. XVII, for the international aspects of the movement.

still regarded as luxuries—tobacco, tea, coffee, sugar, distilled spirits, and beer—the assessment and collection were rationalized and the rates periodically increased. Britain had the highest rates on spirits and the French on tobacco, and by 1914 a full quarter of the Russian state revenue was derived from the vodka monopoly.

Modernization of the tax structure in the various states was not effected without serious discord. Lloyd George's budget of 1909, from the standpoint of tax and fiscal precedents, was a revolutionary measure, and the House of Lords had considerable justification for insisting that it be submitted to the electorate for approval.[9] A two-year political Donnybrook ended with the passage of the Parliament Act of 1911, which affirmed the tax sovereignty of the Commons and left the Lords with only a suspensory veto over ordinary legislation. In France, which had the most antiquated fiscal system, the progressive income tax was a policy objective of the Left coalition that governed from 1905 to 1914, but the political parties were so divided and timorous that the income tax law was not enacted until the eve of the war. In Italy the Giolitti government was overthrown when it attempted, in 1909, to modernize the antiquated income tax. To Continental conservatives, endorsing a progressive income tax was equivalent to endorsing the views of Karl Marx, but to socialists and radicals income and inheritance taxes represented the principle of equality of burdens while serving also to redistribute wealth.

All modern states in this period saw their expenditures doubled and tripled, taxes increased in proportion, and the national debt mushrooming. Armaments accounted for much of the increase, especially as technological renovation and expansion of armies and navies became highly competitive. Expenditures for other state activities, however, increased in proportion to the outlay for armaments. Education, public health, social insurance, and social services were costly. Educational budgets in England, France, and Germany, for example, increased fivefold between 1870 and 1914. In this connection it might be noted also that Germany—reputedly the most militaristic of the powers—

9. Embodying the most advanced tax policies and devices, it increased the tax on tobacco and liquor, sharply increased estate and inheritance taxes, imposed a "supertax" on income over 5,000 pounds, a tax on unearned increment in land values, and a special tax on undeveloped land and mineral resources. E. R. A. Seligman, *Essays in Taxation,* 8th ed. (New York, 1913), pp. 482–96; Chap. XVII, "Recent Reforms in Taxation," covers the years prior to the war.

spent more per capita on nonmilitary services than any other major state.[10]

3. SOCIAL DEMOCRACY AND THE SECOND INTERNATIONAL

The portrayal of socialism displacing a played-out liberalism in the twenty years before the war is a distorted representation of the facts. The results of most elections show liberals as well as socialists gaining at the expense of conservatives and moderates. Where proportional representation and run-off elections were employed, socialists and liberals usually joined forces after the first ballot against conservative candidates. Rather than standing face to face, socialists and liberals more often stood side by side—on voting rights, on parliamentary supremacy, on separation of church and state, on public education and secular schools, and on the social responsibility of the state.

Socialism was an intellectual as well as a political force, for it included such diverse figures as August Bebel, Bernard Shaw, V. I. Lenin, H. G. Wells, Rosa Luxemburg, Anatole France, Jean Jaurès, Annie Besant, and Benito Mussolini. Middle-class intellectuals, and workers who had gained a formal education, predominated in the leadership of the socialist parties, while trade union organizers and officials were ordinarily recruited from the working class.

Membership in a socialist party was comparable to active membership in a church. The workers' movement was more than a political activity—for the dedicated it was a way of life, an existence in isolation from conventional society. Joseph Buttinger has described his total involvement in the Austrian labor movement:

Spurred on by the Socialist press, he furiously participated in the "cultural endeavors of the working class" by attending every evening lecture, never missing a rehearsal of the Socialist glee club, partaking in every excursion of the party's "Friends of Nature" and even becoming a Socialist folk dancer and amateur actor. . . . As a "matter of principle" he now changed his shirt once a week.[11]

10. The comparative expenditure per capita for nonmilitary purposes in 1908 was: Germany, 25 M.; France, 14.6 M.; Austria-Hungary, 13.9 M.; Italy, 7.8 M.; Britain, 5.7 M. The figure for Britain is low because she did not maintain a large bureaucracy. *Handwörterbuch der Staatswissenschaften*, 4th ed. (1927), IV, 71.

11. Joseph Buttinger, *In the Twilight of Socialism* (New York, 1953), p. 404. On the socialist labor movement as a subculture in isolation from the rest of society see the sociological treatise by Guenther Roth, *The Social Democrats in Imperial Germany* (Totowa, N.J., 1963).

Julius Deutsch, another Austrian socialist, also recalls their devotion and isolation: "The socialists constituted a self-conscious community, that bore almost the character of a religious sect. With my whole heart I entered into this closed circle. It was my world; I scarcely knew any other, and I felt no need to learn about any other."[12] It was to the labor movement and the party that members looked for enrichment of their lives and for social recognition, which was generally denied them in the dominant culture.

The First International, organized to promote socialist doctrine and working class solidarity, collapsed from internal dissension. The Second International was founded in Paris in 1889 during the centennial celebration of the French Revolution. Like its predecessor, it was much troubled by disruptive anarchists during the first decade of its existence, but by 1900 it was broadly and safely Marxist. A French delegate plaintively expressed the wish that their congress hall might be decorated with pictures of Blanqui, Fourier, and Saint-Simon, as well as those of Marx and Engels. But this was not to be. However, the invitation to the Paris congress of 1900, while it pointedly excluded anarchists, was addressed to "all organizations which seek to substitute socialist property and production for capitalist property and production, and which consider legislative and parliamentary action as one of the necessary means of attaining that end." This was broad enough to cover a variety of working-class organizations from conservative trade unions, which frequently sent "fraternal delegates," to revolutionary Marxists. After the meeting in Paris in 1900, the Second International held congresses at Amsterdam in 1904, Stuttgart in 1907, Copenhagen in 1910, and Basel in 1912. The congress scheduled for Vienna in 1914 became a casualty of the war.

Structurally a loose federation of autonomous organizations, the International was mainly a forum in which the intellectual leaders of the working classes by debating and passing resolutions gave a certain degree of unity and direction to the socialist movement. This objective was furthered by the establishment in 1900 of a permanent secretariat and an executive committee, which could represent the International in the intervals between congresses. Brussels was chosen as the site of the Bureau headquarters because of its convenient location, the freedom of speech permitted in Belgium, and the great facility in languages of the

---

12. Julius Deutsch, *Ein Weiter Weg* (Zurich, 1960), p. 38. See also Wilhelm Hoegner, *Der schwierige Aussenseiter* (Munich, 1959), pp. 11–43.

two distinguished Belgians chosen to head the Bureau—Émile Vander-velde, president, and Camille Huysmans, permanent secretary.

Whom did the International represent? By 1900 the distinguishing features of individual socialist parties were fairly well established. Their characteristics were determined by historical development and the goals and tactics prescribed by the national leadership.

The British Labor party, whose strength derived from the trade unions and the cooperative societies, stood aloof from the Continental socialist movement, although some of its constituent organizations were affiliated with the Second International. The Social Democratic Federation, headed by the eccentric and wealthy Etonian H. M. Hyndman, was professedly Marxist; the Independent Labor Party, in which Keir Hardie and Ramsay MacDonald were prominent leaders, strove for political leadership of the British labor movement; and the Fabian Society, with its galaxy of intellectuals and eccentrics, rejected Marxian tenets and espoused a program of gradual reform. (Justice Oliver Wendell Holmes described them as "fangless socialists.") In 1900 the three socialist organizations, together with the cooperators and trade unionists, united to form the Labor Representation Committee, to promote the participation of labor in parliamentary elections. The Taff Vale decision, which struck at the foundations of the trade union movement, brought organized labor belligerently and massively into the political arena, and in the elections of 1906 the new Labor party and the trade unions elected fifty-three representatives to parliament.

In the Scandinavian countries socialists had to direct their propaganda to agricultural laborers and small landowners as well as to urban workers. Franchise reform was still the major issue, and on matters concerning the workers the socialist parties advocated a modest program of social reform. Socialist gains in parliamentary strength were not spectacular—twenty-four seats in the Danish parliament in 1906, and eleven in the Norwegian parliament in 1909. Under a radically reformed franchise socialists won seventy-three seats in the Swedish elections of 1914.

Holland and Belgium were quite unlike in the history of their labor movements. The principal Dutch parties were based on confessional attachments and the labor movement was split into warring factions. In consequence, a socialist party was late in forming (1894), and its parliamentary representation did not rise above twenty before 1914. At that time labor had yet to gain a democratic franchise.

It is not surprising that in Belgium, which was industrial and highly urbanized, a strong trade union movement should have preceded the formation of a workers' political party. Such a party, organized in 1885, was designated the Belgian Labor Party rather than Socialist party. Of the members of the Second International the Belgian party was furthest removed from German Marxism; it was less centralized and authoritarian, and basically rejected the state as the instrument for building a socialist society. One of Émile Vandervelde's best-known books was entitled *Socialism Against the State*. The plural voting system—the "Law of the Four Infamies"—prevented the party from realizing its full political power. Catholic leaders and agencies also intensively combated socialist activity among Catholic workers. On the eve of the war the Belgian Labor party appeared to be losing rather than gaining ground.

Founded in the early nineties, the Italian socialist party mirrored all the difficulties that beset proletarian organizations operating in a liberal parliamentary state. Milan, Genoa, Turin, with developing industries, gave scope for normal trade union and socialist development, but in the south, especially in Naples, a great *Lumpenproletariat* was a natural target for the anarchists. Repression and violence marked the development of the Italian labor movement until Giolitti became minister of interior in 1901 and reversed the government policy of using troops against rioting strikers.[13]

Because of the literacy and property qualifications for voting, the political leadership of the Italian socialist party was composed almost entirely of lawyers, journalists, and professors, a fact that gave rise to deep suspicion in labor's ranks.[14] In practice the Italian socialist party was reformist and democratic rather than revolutionary. While its leaders declined cabinet posts in 1903 and 1911, they played the parliamentary game and collaborated in general elections with the liberals. The party split in 1911 when Leonida Bissolati and Ivanoe Bonomi supported the Libyan war and, in consequence, were expelled from the party. Manhood suffrage, adopted in 1912, worked strongly to the advantage of the socialists in the elections of 1913, when the three

13. D. L. Horowitz, *The Italian Labor Movement* (Cambridge, Mass., 1963), pp. 48–94.

14. In 1903, for example, the parliamentary delegation numbered thirty-three, of which two were workers, three were petit bourgeois, and twenty-eight were university graduates of bourgeois origin.

factions elected 78 representatives to parliament. Socialist gains were one of the surprises of the election, but this could not obscure the fact that Italy remained the country which was most subject to all the conflicting forces operating in the socialist movement.

The Austrian socialist party boasted distinguished leadership—Victor Adler, Karl Renner, Otto Bauer—but in many ways it was an offshoot or satellite of its sister party in Germany. Czechs, Poles, Slovaks, and Slovenes were organized in national sections so that the party had the qualities of a "little international." When the party concentrated on electoral reform and an equal vote for the laborer, all elements in the surging movement—trade unions, national sections, and central party— held firmly together. They reaped their reward in the general election of 1907 when socialist representation in the Reichsrat soared from ten to ninety. In consequence, the Social Democrats became more of a conventional political party, with parliamentary and nationality problems similar to those of other parties. Indeed success at the polls encouraged splintering, and soon nationalistic discords—keenest between Germans and Czechs—split the party into bickering factions and largely nullified its mission of social and economic reform.[15]

Every socialist party had its unique divisions arising from local and national conditions, but all were affected by two basic issues: the problem of reform versus revolution, and the question of collaboration with bourgeois parties.

4. REFORMISM AND OPPORTUNISM—FRANCE AND GERMANY

In prominence, tradition, and prestige the socialist parties in France and Germany stood in the front rank of the European labor movement. Germany became the scene of the ideological dispute over Eduard Bernstein's revisionism; and France became the source of the controversy over "opportunism," when Alexandre Millerand accepted appointment in the cabinet of Waldeck-Rousseau in 1899. "Opportunism" and "revisionism" encouraged heresy and schism in every

15. This survey of organized socialism is based on the standard works: G. D. H. Cole, *A History of Socialist Thought*, Vol. III, *The Second International, 1889–1914* (London, 1956); Carl Landauer, *European Socialism*, 2 vols. (Berkeley, 1959), Vol. I; James Joll, *The Second International, 1889–1914* (London, 1955); Henry Pelling, *A Short History of the Labour Party* (London, 1961); A. M. McBriar, *Fabian Socialism and English Politics, 1884–1918* (London, 1962); and the election statistics from the relevant volumes of the *Annual Register*.

socialist party. Naturally, the tumult was greatest where the infidelities arose, but in a brief time all organizations were affected, even the Second International.

In 1900 the Germans were running the most successful socialist movement in Europe, although only ten years had elapsed since the repressive Bismarckian laws had been rescinded. The party's growth and its success at the polls were arresting. There were about 400,000 enrolled members in 1904, more than a half-million in 1907, and a round million in 1914. Voting strength was always greater than registered membership: the popular vote was nearly 2 million in 1893, 3 million in 1903, and more than 4 million in 1912, when, with 110 seats, it became the largest party in the Reichstag. One German elector in every three was now voting socialist. Success in local elections gave the party more than 12,000 elected representatives at all levels of government. In 1914 the party published or sponsored ninety-one daily papers with 1.5 million subscribers. Party assets and income flourished. Between 1890 and 1914 socialism was transformed from a sect to a mass political party.[16]

Through the years the party leaders had maintained ideologically the Marxian posture prescribed in the Erfurt program of 1891, although the party had become increasingly reformist and parliamentary. Eduard Bernstein, a party theorist, was first to explore the contradictions that had arisen and to propose a revision of Marxist doctrine to bring it into alignment with reality. Bernstein, who possessed a subtle mind, an observant eye, and years of experience in England, published his first articles in 1896, in *Die Neue Zeit,* the leading socialist journal of theory and discussion, edited by Karl Kautsky, the dean of orthodox Marxism. His articles achieved wider circulation in book form when published in 1899 under the title *The Postulates of Socialism and the Tasks of Social Democracy.*[17] Bernstein was the chief but not the sole figure in the movement to revise Marxian doctrine at the turn of the century.

Bernstein pointed out that Marx's predictions had mostly proved

---

16. Douglas A. Chalmers, *The Social Democratic Party of Germany* (New Haven, Conn., 1964), pp. 1–20; Carl E. Schorske, *German Social Democracy, 1905–1917* (Cambridge, Mass., 1955), pp. 1–28; K. S. Pinson, *Modern Germany* (New York, 1954), pp. 208–18; *Annual Register,* 1903, 1907, 1912.

17. An English translation, *Evolutionary Socialism,* was published in 1909.

untrue, which raised critical doubts as to the validity of his basic assumptions and major conclusions. Concepts and prophecies in need of revision were the labor theory of value, the materialist interpretation of society, the growing impoverishment of the proletariat, and the extinction of the middle class. He even cast doubt on the class struggle as the prime mover in social change. From his economic studies Bernstein could show that capitalism was not digging its own grave, that the worker's standard of living had risen, and that social mobility made less rigid the divisions between classes. Socialism was still their objective, he insisted, but it could best be achieved through the development of trade unions and cooperatives, social reforms, and democratization of the state.[18]

To the orthodox, Bernstein's views were pure heresy. Critics and detractors sprang up all around. Karl Kautsky, since Engels' death the principal interpreter and guardian of the Marxian canon, was ponderously critical and eventually produced the official refutation of Bernstein's heresy (*Bernstein and the Social Democratic Program,* Stuttgart, 1899). Revisionism was hotly debated at the annual party congresses from 1898 to 1903. The most intemperate attacks upon Bernstein came from two young writers, Rosa Luxemburg ("Red Rosa") and Alexander Helphand (Parvus). Both were middle-class intellectuals from eastern Europe; both had taken doctorates in economics at Swiss universities, and both supported themselves as writers, lecturers, and journalists in the German socialist party. Bernstein was an honored leader, even though a deviationist, and his old comrades resented the vitriolic attacks upon him by young upstarts. At the Lübeck congress in 1901 they were denounced as "literary ruffians" and ridiculed as the "male and female arrivals from the East."[19] Finally, after the party's electoral success in 1903, Bebel and Kautsky at the Dresden congress forced the passage of resolutions reaffirming the party's loyalty to the orthodox Marxist position on the class struggle, the revolution, and the party and state.

However, this did not keep the socialists in Bavaria and Baden from

18. A closer analysis and more detailed statement is Peter Gay, *The Dilemma of Democratic Socialism—Eduard Bernstein's Challenge to Marx* (New York, 1952), pp. 131–244, *passim.*
19. J. P. Nettl, *Rosa Luxemburg,* 2 vols. (London, 1966), I, 165–69; Z. A. B. Zeman, *The Merchant of Revolution: The Life of Alexander Israel Helphand (Parvus), 1867–1924* (London, 1965), pp. 37–49.

collaborating with bourgeois parties, voting for the state budget, and supporting government-sponsored reform measures beneficial to the working class. As Ignaz Auer, the shrewd old Bavarian party leader, wrote to Bernstein: "One doesn't say it, one *does* it." Peter Gay has neatly summarized the situation: "The SPD continued to behave as a Revisionist party and, at the same time, to condemn Revisionism; it continued to preach revolution and to practice reform."[20] This would have had no effect beyond inspiring a certain cynicism had not the German socialist leaders, after advertising their doctrinal purity, gone on to impose this through the Second International upon the other socialist parties, notably the French.

France next to Germany had the most successful socialist movement, although it was divided ideologically and historically into four or five contending factions. Scriptural Marxism was espoused by Jules Guesde and his associates, while the independents, led by Jean Jaurès, and such rising politicians as René Viviani, Alexandre Millerand, and Aristide Briand, were politically the most sophisticated and potent. In Germany reformism presented itself as a doctrinal dispute; in France the socialist politicians faced problems of immediate action arising out of the Dreyfus Affair. Jaurès prodded the socialist factions into active collaboration with the republican parties in support of Dreyfus. Human rights and the preservation of the republic were compelling arguments, but, asked the proponents of orthodoxy, "What happens to the class struggle when socialists ally themselves with Clemenceau, a political figure still tainted by the Panama scandal?"

Even greater was the embarrassment when Alexandre Millerand joined the ministry of Waldeck-Rousseau in June, 1899—the first socialist to hold a cabinet post in France since Louis Blanc in 1848. It is difficult now to imagine the tumult this event produced in the socialist world.

Collaboration with bourgeois parties—or "Millerandism"—was dealt with by the congress of the International held in Paris in 1900. Since sharp disagreement persisted, the resolution proposed by Karl Kautsky was an expedient compromise. In substance, it left the decision on whether to collaborate to each national section, while condemning Millerand for acting without the approval of his party.[21]

20. Gay, *Dilemma of Democratic Socialism,* p. 266.
21. Joll, *The Second International,* pp. 95–97.

At the Amsterdam congress held in 1904, revisionism and collaboration were the principal issues on the agenda. Full of confidence and pride after the electoral triumph of 1903 the German delegation came to Amsterdam determined to establish the Dresden decisions as the party line for all members of the International. The heated debate lasted four days—three in committee and one in the plenary. Compromise resolutions proposed by Victor Adler and Vandervelde failed of adoption, and the resolution proposed by Jules Guesde, repeating the Dresden pronouncement textually, was rammed through. Tactics that allowed participation in bourgeois coalitions were sharply condemned, as were "all measures calculated to keep the ruling classes in power." Reformism, revisionism, and opportunism were broadly denounced and execrated.

Jaurès spoke brilliantly in defense of French socialist collaboration in the Dreyfus Affair—they had saved the Republic and it was worth saving. With unprecedented sharpness he attacked the German Social Democrats, declaring that even if they won a majority in the Reichstag they would still be impotent because the Reichstag itself was without decisive power.[22] Despite Jaurès' telling thrusts, the Dresden formulation carried by twenty-five votes to four with twelve abstentions. Another resolution, which was accepted unanimously, imposed unity on the contending French factions by stating that only one socialist party from each member country could be recognized by the International.

So far as French socialism was concerned, Amsterdam was a victory for the orthodoxy of Jules Guesde, a defeat for Jaurès. In 1905, comforming to the Amsterdam resolutions, the French socialists merged to found the United Socialist Party and the Jaurès group withdrew from the parliamentary Left bloc. Because of this prohibition some of the ablest socialists did not enter the new party—Millerand, Viviani, Briand. In the elections of 1910 the socialists polled more than a million votes and increased their representation from fifty-four seats to seventy-six. This, however, could not conceal the fact that the French socialists were now condemned almost to the same impotence as their German comrades, as indeed were all socialists who, like Jaurès, virtuously observed the Amsterdam ban on opportunistic collaboration.

22. *Ibid.*, p. 103; also Harvey Goldberg, *The Life of Jean Jaurès* (Madison, Wis., 1962), pp. 324–28.

Up to 1912 socialist successes in national elections ranged from modest to impressive. In France, Italy, Belgium, Sweden, and Austria the socialist parties registered gains but they were, on the whole, modest. It did not appear probable that in the immediate future socialism would be established in any major country either by revolution or by parliamentary majority. The performance of the Social Democrats in Germany in 1912 was a bright beacon, although in fact it meant no greater leverage for the party on the policies and actions of the government. In fact, the inability of the Social Democrats to use effectively the 110-man Reichstag delegation produced disillusionment and doubt in the socialist movement. In Germany for the first time since repeal of the antisocialist laws, the party membership ceased to grow, subscriptions to the socialist press dropped alarmingly, and party members began to encounter reverses in local and state elections.[23] The frustration and doldrums in the German socialist party were matched in the history of almost every other socialist organization in Europe. In the two years before the war, the indications that the socialist tide was receding are about as strong as the indications that it was rising. Indeed it appeared that by 1912 the movement had reached a plateau; it was not at all evident that the proletarian parties would inherit the political kingdom.

5. SOCIALISM AND NATIONALISM

Between 1900 and 1914 the socialist parties, with the exception of the Russian, were thoroughly penetrated by middle-class pacifist ideas, which were basically un-Marxist if not anti-Marxist. Neither Marx nor Engels, nor any of the Marxist "church fathers," had aligned themselves with the European peace movement. The shift in socialism to a near-pacifist position resulted from a growing concern that a major war could not be kept within bounds and that the working class would be the greatest sufferer. This conviction inspired the Second International to support the international peace movement and to use its power to check militarism and prevent war.

When the International convened at Amsterdam in 1904 the Russians and Japanese had been at war for six months. It was the first conflict involving major powers since the Russo-Turkish war of 1877.

23. Schorske, *German Social Democracy*, pp. 267 ff. The SPD enrolled only 12,000 new members in 1912–13, compared to 140,000 in the previous year.

Increasing international tensions posed two grave questions for socialists: What attitude should the party assume toward its own government's defense policies and arrangements? What concerted action should or could socialists take to prevent war? The answers were not self-evident. On the Continent every able worker had served two years or more in the army. Responsibility for defense of the homeland was deeply implanted. Despite Marx's dictum that the proletarian has no fatherland, workers were usually patriotic and under some circumstances stubbornly chauvinistic. The socialist propaganda position was that wars were capitalist inspired and that workers would have to pay for them and possibly give up their lives as well. Early in its parliamentary existence the German socialist party established the precedents usually followed by the other socialist parties: They voted as a bloc against the annual military budget and criticized at such times excessive expenditure, mistreatment of recruits, duelling in the officer corps, and the inordinate social privileges accorded the military caste. In 1900 the Paris congress of the International recommended that all socialist parties follow the German practice of voting against military appropriations; in a situation threatening war the International would coordinate the efforts of all socialist parties for the preservation of peace.

But what did the socialists propose to substitute for national armies and navies, since even the most pacific agreed that some kind of defense force was necessary? They proposed to substitute a locally trained national guard, a popular militia after the Swiss model, a solution based as much on myth as on fact—the myths of 1793 and 1813 when patriotic peoples defeated tyrants! The German Social Democrats placed the popular militia on their official program, and Jean Jaurès gave the idea its most extensive examination and exposition in his book *L'Armée nouvelle* (1910). The program of the popular militia in the twentieth century was unrealistic. As one critic commented: "You can't put a cannon in the bed of every former gunner and give each old sea dog a little warship to put in his farmyard trough or wash tub."[24]

A new direction was given to socialist policy on war by the Russian revolution of 1905, which also influenced socialist attitudes on other

24. Quoted in Joll, *The Second International*, p. 111. For a detailed analysis of Jaurès' book see Goldberg, *Life of Jean Jaurès*, pp. 385-89.

important issues. It revived confidence in direct revolutionary action, reminding socialists that violent revolutions were still a possibility and that they need not wait for the slow-acting forces of history. It also focused attention on the mass political strike—the general strike—as a tactical weapon. Socialists were now encouraged to believe that a general strike would be the best way for workers to prevent or stop a capitalist war. This possible use of the general strike was explored at the German party congresses of 1905 and 1906, but Bebel and the trade union leaders were adamant in opposing a commitment to strike or to lead an insurrection.

Action against war was a principal topic on the agenda of the International congress that met in Stuttgart in 1907. This was forced upon the socialist movement by pressure from the pacifist French schoolmaster Gustave Hervé, who formally proposed to the International that any declaration of war be met by a workers' insurrection or a general strike. When Bebel marshaled all the German objections, Hervé denounced the German Social Democratic party as just "a machine for counting votes and cash."[25] An innocuous resolution placed before the congress was given some substance by an amendment offered by Rosa Luxemburg and V. I. Lenin. Prophetically, their amendment called upon socialist parties, in the event of war, "to intercede for its speedy end, and to strive with all their power to make use of the violent economic and political crisis brought about by the war to rouse the people, and thereby to hasten the abolition of capitalist class rule."[26] The amended resolution was received with enthusiasm— Gustave Hervé jumped on the table, holding up both hands in a victory gesture, as it was adopted unanimously. Much the same ground was covered at the Copenhagen congress of 1910—same arguments, same doubts, same equivocal conclusions. The only new departure was the responsibility placed directly on the International Bureau to co-ordinate the peace efforts of the member parties in any major crisis that might threaten the general peace.

Exercising this authority, the International Bureau called a special meeting at Basel in November, 1912, to demand peace in the Balkans. Attended by 500 delegates from twenty-three socialist parties, the Basel congress was a notable demonstration by international socialism of its

25. Joll, *The Second International*, p. 134.
26. *Ibid.*, p. 139; and Nettl, *Rosa Luxemburg*, I, 396–404.

sincere concern for peace. Demanding peace in the Balkans and the abandonment of alliances and secret diplomacy, the congress undoubtedly contributed to the belief entertained by people in many parts of Europe that the socialist parties could prevent war by international action.

However high-minded, cosmopolitan, and warmly humanitarian the debates in the Second International, the trend in the socialist movement lay in the direction of nationalism. The death of August Bebel in 1913 signaled the passing of older traditions in German Social Democracy. Ebert, Scheidemann, Hermann Müller, Otto Braun, Gustav Noske, and a large section of the parliamentary delegation belonged to a younger generation. For them support of national defense was not inconsistent with socialist tradition and principles. The limits of the party's antimilitarism were revealed in 1913 with the government's introduction of a military expansion bill to be financed by a Reich property tax and a one-time capital defense levy. The support of the Social Democrats was not required to pass the military bill, but the tax measure would be defeated without their support, and the Conservatives would be the beneficiaries. By a narrow margin the socialist delegation in the Reichstag agreed to support the government's tax bill. This led one dissenting party leader to comment wryly that "the bourgeois parties voted the soldiers and the Social Democrats voted the funds."[27]

In France, Jaurès and the socialists were no more effective in opposing the three-year service law. In light of these facts the coming and going of fraternal delegations between France and Germany during the last years of peace have about them an air of pathetic unreality. In all the discussions it was admitted that French socialists would be justified in resisting a German attack upon France, and the German socialists made it clear that they would march if Russia attacked Germany.

Despite the official position of workers' solidarity, the socialist movement revealed the cleavages of nationalism. With the outbreak of war in 1914 not only the German Social Democratic party but all members of the International had to resolve the issue of the relations of the party to the state within the framework of the capitalist order. With the exception of the socialists in the Russian Duma, the socialist parties

27. Schorske, *German Social Democracy*, p. 266.

rallied to the national cause and voted the war credits, although at the Copenhagen congress they had pledged themselves not to do this. Likewise the trade unions abjured all ideological commitments to organize general strikes and sabotage the war. In the world crisis, socialists in both belligerent and neutral countries generally accepted responsibility by joining bourgeois coalition governments, and the trade unions contributed to the war effort by keeping the workers on the job and supporting their morale.

6. THE FIRST STORM—THE RUSSIAN REVOLUTION OF 1905

Marxian socialists talked, wrote, prophesied, and sometimes conspired to bring about revolution. But when a real revolution began in 1905 it came for Marxists in the wrong country, at the wrong stage of development, and was carried forward by the wrong social and political elements. For the Russian revolution of 1905 was more liberal and populist than socialistic in its inspiration, more the work of an exasperated nation than of a class-conscious proletariat, more the work of spontaneous masses than of professional revolutionaries. Claiming to be experts in the history and workings of revolutions, European socialists were surprised by the violent turmoil that began in January, 1905.

Theorizing about revolution—its aims, means, and tactics—was a principal preoccupation of the Russian intelligentsia which, inspired by collectivist ideas, aspired to indoctrinate and lead the masses. By 1900 two schools of socialism—Socialist Revolutionary and Social Democratic—had emerged to propagate conflicting theories of revolution and to point to divergent roads to socialism. The Socialist Revolutionaries opposed the introduction of Western capitalism into Russia and based their hopes for socialism on Russian agrarian society and the communal village. They appealed to all classes, but especially to the peasants. With a theory and practice indigenous to Russia, the Socialist Revolutionaries reached larger numbers than the rival Social Democrats with their imported Marxian revelations. The Socialist Revolutionaries also practiced terrorism and violence as a means of promoting their cause. The terrorist section of the party was formed in 1901, and the first party congress convened in Finland in December, 1905. At this meeting a statement of policies and goals was drafted and a central committee elected.

The rival Social Democrats professed Marxian principles and a socialism based on the power of an industrial proletariat, a class that was visibly weak in Russia. George Plekhanov (1857–1918) was the most active propagator of Marxian doctrine. For nearly forty years he lived abroad, devoting his time to translating and interpreting the writings of Marx and Engels. Isolated groups espousing Marxism developed in Russia, and to bring them together a Social Democratic congress was held clandestinely in 1898. However, there was not much party organization until Lenin returned from his Siberian exile in 1900.

Lenin soon joined Plekhanov in Switzerland and is credited with taking the lead in reorganizing the party, giving it a central organ— *Iskra*, the Spark—and in calling the second party congress, which met in Brussels and then moved to London. A revised party program, drafted by Lenin and Plekhanov, was accepted by the congress with little discussion or dissent. What divided the leadership and eventually split the party—Bolsheviks and Mensheviks—were the issues of membership, party structure, discipline, and tactics. Lenin stood obstinately for a screened and disciplined membership of dedicated revolutionaries. "We must train people who will dedicate to the revolution not a free evening but the whole of their lives," he declared.[28]

The Menshevik faction envisaged a mass political party, modeled on the German socialist party, which would include workers, intellectuals, and party professionals. The Mensheviks would also cooperate with bourgeois reformists. There was no compromising these fundamental disagreements, and the congress broke up with the Bolsheviks in control of the party central committee, the Mensheviks in control of the party organ, *Iskra*. Neither could prevail over the other, and the history of Russian socialism down to 1914 was one of continuous factional strife and rancor.

Born of the Czar's routed battalions and sunken warships, the revolution of 1905 was a direct result of the failure of the Russian government in the Russo-Japanese War. The Japanese attack on Port Arthur took the Russians utterly by surprise; further disasters followed on sea and land. The sanguinary campaign in Manchuria ended in March, 1905, with the defeat at Mukden; and on May 14 Russia

28. Leopold H. Haimson, *The Russian Marxists and the Origins of Bolshevism* (Cambridge, Mass., 1955), pp. 119–20; Landauer, *European Socialism*, I, 43.

suffered her greatest naval disaster at Tsushima Strait with the loss of the entire Baltic fleet. Hostilities were formally ended with the conclusion of the Treaty of Portsmouth in September, 1905.

Stunned and discredited by these military disasters, the autocracy was overwhelmed by the demands of various groups for a radical reconstruction of the government. What socialists, radicals, and liberals could all agree on—although they agreed on nothing else—was that autocratic government must be radically modified or ended, that Russian affairs could not continue in the same channels as heretofore. Only the most conservative landlords, the bureaucracy, and the higher Orthodox clergy were unwavering in their support of the autocratic regime.

Under the impression created by a floundering government that was becoming every day more alienated from the people, a zemstvo congress met in St. Petersburg in November, 1904, and demanded the election of a legislative assembly and the granting of civil liberties. But it was the massacre of peaceful petitioners before the Winter Palace on Sunday, January 22, 1905, that sparked the violent phase of the revolution. The events of Bloody Sunday stunned the nation and evoked bitter criticism in the world press. The brutal use of force crystallized dissent and for a time united all factions in a single program of resistance. Massive strikes of sympathy and protest followed. Liberals rather than socialists and revolutionaries provided the program and effective leadership. The liberal program, and especially that of the Constitutional Democrats, was fully developed and in tune with the country's economic and political situation. As a result the liberal demand for civil liberties and a representative assembly was supported by workers, factory owners, and socialists alike. There was one popular cause against autocracy.[29]

From their exile tenements in western Europe the socialist leaders followed closely the strikes and demonstrations that swept the country after Bloody Sunday. But only Rosa Luxemburg, Leon Trotsky, Alexander Helphand (Parvus), and Leo Deutsch, among the leaders, returned immediately to throw themselves into the revolutionary

29. Sidney Harcave, *First Blood: The Russian Revolution of 1905* (New York, 1964), pp. 116–17; Jacob Walkin, *The Rise of Democracy in Pre-Revolutionary Russia* (New York, 1962), Chap. VIII, "The Revolution of 1905 and the Emergence of Constitutional Government"; Valentin Gitermann, *Geschichte Russlands,* 3 vols. (Zurich, 1944–49), III, 387–91.

movement. In the spring of 1905 Bolsheviks and Mensheviks held rival party congresses in London and Geneva, where they debated the meaning of events transpiring in the homeland and their relation to Marxist theory. Engrossed in factional quarrels, Lenin and other socialist leaders did not return to Russia until the autumn, when the October Manifesto, promising civil liberties and amnesty, made it safe to do so. The time when they might have exerted a directing influence had passed.[30] The socialists resident in Russia—Bolsheviks, Mensheviks, Socialist Revolutionaries—concentrated on pushing the revolution forward rather than on propagating a socialist program. Recognizing the strike as the most effective instrument of agitation, they concentrated on organizing and activating militant groups in factories, in universities, and in the armed forces.

The Czar's first declarations and assurances of magnanimity did not satisfy a disturbed nation, and during the spring and summer signs of discontent multiplied. Zemstvos, municipal councils, university faculties, learned societies, trade and professional organizations, all adopted resolutions demanding that the regime be liberalized and a constitutional assembly convened. The national minorities in Poland, the Baltic provinces, Transcaucasia, Ukraine, and Finland—all hating Russification—began also to petition for restoration of former rights and privileges. When an official plan for a national Duma was finally produced it was so restricted and shadowy as to be an affront to every opposition group in Russia. The resulting confrontation set the stage for the October general strike.

Unplanned and unanticipated, the "Great October Strike" began in Moscow when the printers struck for more pay. It spread to other trades and soon turned into a mass political strike. From Moscow the general strike spread to Kharkov, to St. Petersburg, and eventually, as a common pattern developed, to all the principal cities of European Russia. Newspapers ceased to publish, streetcars were at a standstill, no mail was received or delivered, the cities were isolated by the halting of all trains. Water, gas, and electrical services failed, while milk, meat,

---

30. Lenin did not attempt to play a leading role; he moved about a good deal, concentrating on party organization. He left Russia in 1907 as the reaction intensified. Louis Fischer, *The Life of Lenin* (New York, 1964), pp. 51–53. For a graphic account of an active participant in the revolution—a young university student—see Wladimir S. Woytinsky, *Der erste Sturm: Erinnerungen aus der russische Revolution 1905* (Berlin, 1931).

and bread grew scarce and prices skyrocketed. Schools were closed and the streets filled with strikers who went from plant to plant and shop to shop, forcing the closing of those that were still open.[31] The strike council in St. Petersburg, because it identified itself with the capital city, attempted to play a national role as the St. Petersburg Soviet. The chairman, Khrustalëv, was a liberal, Trotsky became vice-chairman, and Helphand (Parvus) was a prominent member. Representing mainly the militant unions, the St. Petersburg Soviet pushed its authority to the limit as a rival or competitor of the central government.

The civil authority lacked the power to suppress the revolution. How then were the strikes to be ended and order restored? After consulting the military authorities Nicholas II appointed Count S. Y. Witte chairman of the council of ministers with a mandate for reform, and simultaneously issued his famous October Manifesto promising civil liberties and a representative assembly for the Russian people. The brevity and ambiguous wording of the proclamation raised doubts in many minds as to the Czar's good faith. Nevertheless, the proclamation achieved its main purpose: the end of the general strike and the appeasement of the liberals.

Turmoil in the cities was accompanied by peasant disorders, although the two were not coordinated. Especially affected were the Baltic provinces, Poland, and south central Russia. The rural disorders reached a peak of destructive violence in October and November. In December the government began forceful pacification of the disturbed areas. At a critical juncture the St. Petersburg Soviet issued an appeal to resume the general strike, but it went unheeded except in Moscow, where soon detachments of armed workers clashed with troops in the streets. Order was not restored until the Czar sent the Semyonov regiment from St. Petersburg to suppress the insurrection. Failure of the Moscow rebellion was the turning point; thereafter the government had the initiative. Fires of resistance continued to burn and flicker, but the Czar was determined to make no more concessions and to use all necessary force, treating his subjects as though they were a conquered people.

The first Duma met on May 10, 1906, in the throne room of the Winter Palace to hear the Czar's dignified but uninspiring speech. Its

31. For greater detail see W. H. Crook, *The General Strike* (Chapel Hill, N.C., 1931), pp. 154–77.

members listened in stony silence to the Emperor's words and withdrew to their own hall to frame a reply; it was critical and negative. Neither the first nor the second Duma would accept the settlement of 1905 and collaborate in the government's reactionary program. Finally, a change in the electoral law, put through by the new premier, P. A. Stolypin, so favored the nobles and property owners at the expense of the workers and peasants that the next two Dumas were as cooperative and amenable as the first two had been recalcitrant and uncompromising. The third Duma served its full five-year term, and the fourth continued until the revolution of 1917.

In 1905 neither the government nor the people gained a clear-cut victory or suffered an unqualified defeat. Russian society was clearly moving into the modern age. The government ceased to be wholly autocratic, although it could not be called a pure constitutional monarchy. In the *Almanach de Gotha* it was described after 1906 as "a constitutional monarchy under an autocratic Czar." The Duma shared prominently in the legislative process, although conservative bureaucrats unfavorable to change still controlled the machinery of government.[32]

A number of significant "firsts" were registered in Russian history by the revolution of 1905: the first soviets, the first political strikes, the first stirrings of nationalism among some of the minorities, and the first introduction of the peasants to politics. In western Europe liberals viewed Russian developments as proof of her progress toward modernity, freedom, and constitutional government. Socialists, trade unionists, and radicals interpreted the upheaval as a workers' victory over the same forces with which they were contending—class rule and capitalist exploitation. The awakening of the Muslim peoples in Russia also had repercussions beyond the frontiers. A Russian-type revolution occurred in Persia in 1906, resulting in the grant of a constitution by the Shah. In Turkey, Russian developments served as a warning to Abdul Hamid and a stimulus to the Young Turks and the constitutional party. Political unrest in India also received direct inspiration from events in Russia.

---

32. The third Duma was not a subservient do-nothing assembly, as often alleged. It passed 2,340 projects of law submitted by the administration; 106 were withdrawn; 79 were rejected by the Duma and 31 by the Council of State; of 205 bills proposed by Duma members 81 were enacted. *Annual Register—1912*, pp. 342–43.

Whether the settlement of 1905 afforded a foundation for Russia's development on Western liberal lines, or whether it was just a stage on the "road to disaster," is still debated by scholars with considerable warmth. Those inclined to the latter view stress the alienation of government and people, the anachronistic character of czarism and its incapacity for leadership in the twentieth century, the hostile and isolated intelligentsia, and the ethnic minorities alienated by anti-Semitism and Russification. They also insist that a more representative body than the Duma would have provided only a forum, like the Austrian Reichsrat, for the wrangling of antagonistic groups.[33]

Much can be cited to support the opposing view. A measure of popular control through fundamental laws and the Duma was achieved in 1905. A modernization of the land system and of agrarian society was also one of the consequences of the revolution. Russia's economic progress up to the war was impressive. A long period without war and unsettling crises would have afforded an opportunity for further peaceful change and consolidation. But the government with the greatest need of tranquillity was in 1914 one of the most reckless in gambling on war—and, as has been observed, the most unlucky.

33. Theodore H. von Laue, "Of the Crisis in the Russian Polity," in John S. Curtiss, *Essays in Russian and Soviet History* (New York, 1963), pp. 303–23.

Chapter Nine

THE DIPLOMATIC REVOLUTION

I. MAKERS OF GERMAN FOREIGN POLICY

In consequence of Europe's expansion in the nineteenth century and the development of her power, international relations had become, like Europe's economy, a system of worldwide relationships. The rise of states like the United States and Japan further complicated international relations and affected the balance of power. France, Britain, Russia, the United States, and Japan were expansionist, while Germany in the Bismarckian era, owing to the circumstances under which unification was achieved, was more vitally concerned with security and power in Europe. Bismarck's Three Emperors' League, the Austro-German alliance of 1879, the Triple Alliance of 1882, the adherence of Rumania to that grouping in 1883, and the Reinsurance Treaty with Russia in 1887—all had as their rationale the stabilization of great-power relationships and the security of Germany in central Europe. Britain's policy, determined by her insular position and imperial interests, was described as "splendid isolation," but in fact she collaborated closely with the Triple Alliance in matters of mutual interest; and in her imperialist clashes with France and Russia she could generally depend on diplomatic support, or at least benevolent neutrality, from the Bismarckian grouping. Observing Bismarck as he manipulated the balance and kept on good terms with Russia and Britain at the same time was to witness the diplomatic juggling act of the age.

The epigones who succeeded Bismarck inherited neither his chart nor his compass. In a matter of weeks they scuttled the Russian Reinsurance Treaty, and in a matter of months the Franco-Russian alliance became a reality. Further, after 1895, Britain became estranged from Germany and, finding her position of isolation perilous, concluded first an alliance with Japan in 1902, an entente with France in 1904, and a similar arrangement with Russia in 1907. This was nothing less than a diplomatic revolution, a realignment of the major powers that divided Europe into two armed camps—Triple Alliance and

Triple Entente—and set the stage for the First World War. How the estrangement of England and Germany developed and how this fateful alignment of the powers came into being must now be considered in this and subsequent chapters.

The estrangement of England and Germany, which was the source of the diplomatic revolution, resulted from four disruptive developments: the personality factors of those who shaped German policy; the presumed economic and commercial rivalry; the carping press campaign that accompanied the Boer War; and the security fears engendered in Britain by the German naval program.

William II was a catastrophe for Germany. The Emperor's constitutional powers in foreign policy were similar to those of the President of the United States. When his grandfather left the conduct of affairs to Bismarck, the mechanism functioned satisfactorily. When Bismarck disappeared and a personal regime was established, the faults and fissures of William II's character became critically significant. As a private individual he would have been accounted a brilliant man, but as a responsible statesman he resembled, as one associate put it, a branch that bore many blossoms but little fruit. A man of talent, charm, and warmth, he was also self-willed, capricious, and full of rooted preconceptions; not deficient in intelligence, he mainly lacked judgment and stability. The Kaiser's "hurrah moods" were often followed by blackest gloom and depression. His political indiscretions and oratorical derailments were numerous—some were amusing, some serious. Bülow's memoirs are replete with these incidents, which the former chancellor narrates to discredit his sovereign and in so doing often discredits himself.[1]

Given the Emperor's deficiencies, the qualities of his highest officials and advisers became of the greatest importance. Between 1890 and 1914 he was served by four chancellors: Caprivi, Hohenlohe, Bülow, and Bethmann Hollweg. As new sources become available and historians appraise and reappraise their records in office, the stock of these men rises and falls. Caprivi was an able soldier and administrator but unschooled in politics and foreign affairs. Notwithstanding, his reputa-

1. The most recent appraisal of William II is Michael Balfour, *The Kaiser and His Times* (London, 1964). Starkly revealing are the published diaries of the chief of the Kaiser's naval cabinet: Walter Görlitz (ed.), *Der Kaiser: Aufzeichnungen des Chefs des Marinekabinetts Georg Alexander von Müller* (Göttingen, 1965), Chap. VI, for the period 1904–14.

tion seems to be rising. Prince Hohenlohe, a Bavarian, was an experienced diplomat aged seventy-five when he was appointed to the office. As a diplomat his idea of governing was to smooth over difficulties rather than solve problems. The advice he gave a young diplomat—always wear a good black coat and keep your mouth shut—was quite in character.

Hohenlohe's successor, Bernhard von Bülow, also made his reputation in the diplomatic service. From the embassy in Rome, he moved to the Wilhelmstrasse as foreign secretary, succeeding Adolf Marschall von Bieberstein in 1897. Bülow was already a marked man. The Kaiser is reported to have said: "Bülow is to be my Bismarck." His appointment as chancellor, when Hohenlohe retired in 1900, was no surprise in government circles. Bülow was a clever and witty speaker, ever ready with an apt quotation, a skillful debater, and an adroit politician. He had charming manners and a highly cultivated mind. However, he was not a creative statesman like Bismarck, nor was he entirely at home in domestic politics. While he had his political successes he was never able to build a strong party coalition or impose his will, like Bismarck, upon the Reichstag. Bülow prided himself on being able "to handle" the Kaiser, and affairs proceeded more smoothly under his direction than under his predecessors'. But mainly he employed flattery and made no attempt to curb or educate his impressionable master. Bülow has been aptly described as more courtier than diplomat, more diplomat than statesman. The most that one can say on his behalf is that for nine years he kept the cart from going into the ditch. Had he not been in the driver's seat worse might have happened. This was recognized and acknowledged by contemporaries when he retired. But his memoirs, published in 1930, made a very bad impression and seriously tarnished his historical image.[2]

Bethmann Hollweg, who succeeded Bülow in 1909, came from the higher bureaucracy. He was not as clever or brilliant as his predecessor, but he was steadier, more reliable, serious, and thoughtful. A considerable fault was his timidity and indecision. He could not greatly alter the course of German or world politics, but he was regarded generally as more trustworthy than Bülow. In his relations to the Kaiser he

2. F. Hiller von Gaertringen, *Fürst Bülows Denkwürdigkeiten* (Tübingen, 1956); Oron J. Hale, "Prince von Bülow: His Memoirs and His German Critics," *Journal of Modern History*, IV (1932), 261–78.

could not escape the constitutional reality of ultimate dependence upon the sovereign rather than upon the Reichstag.

William II once described Friedrich von Holstein, senior councillor in the foreign office, and a pivotal figure in the shaping of foreign policy, as "an old man for whom I have broken many a lance; full of intellect—and of hallucinations, who occasionally makes the Wilhelm-strasse even more lunatical than it is already."[3] Holstein rose in the foreign service under Bismarck until he became one of the great man's principal assistants. From 1890 to 1900 his influence on foreign and domestic politics was at its zenith. Under Bülow his independence was somewhat curbed, but he was the chancellor's principal adviser on foreign policy and the most influential of the experts in its execution. Because of his avoidance of high office and his solitary personal life, Holstein, until recently, was regarded as a mystery man, a devious intriguer exerting an insidious influence on German foreign and domestic policy. Since the publication of his private papers and a full-length biography the mystery is pretty thoroughly dispelled.[4]

Since Holstein worked literally a seven-day week, his influence was continuous, but it is sufficient to note his role in shaping the most important decisions taken by the makers of foreign policy during the years of his greatest influence. In 1890 the experts were divided, but Holstein advised against renewal of Bismarck's Reinsurance Treaty with Russia—a fateful mistake because it drove Russia immediately into the arms of France. In the matter of the Kruger telegram, which has been described as "one of the greatest blunders in the history of modern diplomacy," Holstein locked his desk and took a holiday while the frivolous message was being concocted and dispatched. He was opposed basically to the naval policy of the Kaiser and Tirpitz but was unable to modify it in any important way. In his opinion, colonies and concessions were not worth the trouble they caused. With regard to Anglo-German relations and the Chamberlain alliance proposals, Holstein was proved clearly wrong in the assumption that Britain would never come to an understanding with France and Russia and that

---

3. Johannes Haller, *Philipp Eulenburg: The Kaiser's Friend*, 2 vols. (New York, 1930), II, 11.

4. Norman Rich, *Friedrich von Holstein*, 2 vols. (Cambridge, Eng., 1965), II, 835–49; also Norman Rich and M. H. Fisher, *The Holstein Papers*, 4 vols. (Cambridge, Eng., 1955–63).

Germany could continue her profitable business of selling support at a good price. Holstein's masterpiece was the Moroccan policy, which instead of rupturing the Anglo-French understanding only solidified it. The Algeciras conference revealed Germany's isolation and the bankruptcy of Holstein's policy. Throughout, however, Holstein insisted that he did not direct policy, but only worked to see that affairs moved as smoothly and expeditiously as possible. "So it has been since 1885, since Hatzfeldt ceased to be Secretary of State and was replaced by Herbert Bismarck."[5]

These were the men who together with the Kaiser made the major and sometimes fateful decisions in the conduct of German foreign policy. Returning now to the course of events that led to Anglo-German estrangement and the revolution in the diplomatic alignments, we have to consider briefly economic and commercial rivalry, the public rancor resulting from the Boer War, and the gravity of German *Weltpoltik* and the naval program.

2. THE ESTRANGEMENT OF ENGLAND AND GERMANY

The upsurge of German competition in industry, trade, and shipping figured prominently in the public relations of England and Germany in the eighties and nineties. German methods, materials, and practices were much discussed in the public press, where the German trade bogey was regularly exhibited. As Continental countries industrialized and became both self-suppliers and competitors, England lost Continental markets, it is true, but she easily found replacement markets overseas and in her empire. What spotlighted trade rivalry and foreign competition was the imperial preference and tariff campaign launched by Joseph Chamberlain at the turn of the century. Germany was the competitor most frequently cited in the tariff versus free trade controversy. Repudiated in two elections (1906 and 1910), the trade bogey receded into the background as the security issue, resulting from Germany's naval policy, came to the center of the stage. Protectionist propaganda was not the equivalent of public opinion. This was the conclusion of the studious German ambassador Count Paul Metternich, who wrote in 1909: "Germany's trade and industry no longer

5. H. Rogge (ed.), *Friedrich von Holstein, Lebensbekenntnis in Briefen an eine Frau* (Berlin, 1932), p. 222. During Christmas week 1895, a constabulary force under the command of Dr. Leander Starr Jameson invaded the Transvaal and was ignominiously defeated and captured. The Kaiser was roundly berated in the British press for sending a congratulatory telegram to President Paul Kruger.

stand in the foreground of British fears. Both would serve rather as a bond between the two nations if the disturbed political atmosphere itself did not throw an unfavorable light upon the mutually beneficial commercial relations."[6] Manipulation of the German bogey on an economic level by tariff reformers never engaged the emotions and attitudes of the British electorate. On the other hand, it was quite simple to sweep the press and arouse the public, irrespective of party, to the national danger inherent in Germany's bid for sea power. The maintenance of British predominance at sea was a credo held without regard to party or class lines.

Germany's *Weltpolitik* combined colonial aspirations with naval ambitions. It was natural that Germany should seek to expand her markets and develop her navy in a degree commensurate with her great industrial growth and worldwide trade. But it was also inevitable that this activated world policy should engender friction and tension with the other great powers, especially Great Britain.

Proclaimed as a New Course, *Weltpolitik* was the goal set for the nation by William II and his associates. Bismarck and William I had made Germany a great European power—they must make her a great world power. A world empire of commercial, political, and cultural interests, floating on a big navy, was the dream that William II, Bülow, and Tirpitz set out to make a reality. In Tirpitz's blueprint for the future, the role played by the German army in the nineteenth century would pass to the navy in the twentieth. Primacy of the navy over the army would result from Germany's growing industrial, maritime, and colonial interests. Tirpitz, of course, emphasized the defensive role of a navy. Without sea power, he said, Germany was "like a mollusc without a shell." Even Britain, the mightiest naval power, would not risk an attack on a strong though smaller German navy. William II accepted and repeated the standard navalist theses, but he was also greatly attracted by the glamor of the sea and the idea of a bright and shining navy. Bülow, who became secretary of state for foreign affairs within a month after Tirpitz's appointment to the naval post, wanted a navy because the Kaiser passionately wanted it, because it became popular with the German people, and because it symbolized

---

6. Metternich to Bülow (Jan. 1, 1909); *Die Grosse Politik*, 40 vols. (Berlin, 1922–26), XXVIII, 47. The case for commercial rivalry is stated by R. J. S. Hoffman, *Great Britain and the German Trade Rivalry, 1875–1914* (Philadelphia, 1933). See also Pauline Anderson, *The Background of anti-English Feeling in Germany* (Washington, 1939).

Germany's status as a world power. A strong undercurrent of support for a big navy came from the commercial classes, the shipping companies, and especially from the large industrialists who would profit by supplying guns, engines, armor plate, and communications systems. Only the agrarian conservatives and the socialists opposed the program.

Alfred Tirpitz (he was later ennobled) was not yet fifty years of age when he was appointed state secretary for the navy in 1897, but his luxuriant beard and great bald dome made him appear much older. He already knew exactly what he wanted. This had been set forth in his Service Memorandum No. IX, composed in 1894, three years before he became head of the naval establishment. His genius for organization, clarity of exposition, and great political talent enabled him to carry his naval program with the Reichstag and the German people.

Tirpitz's plan, set forth in the navy laws of 1898 and 1900, embodied two novel principles. The first provided that the number and type of ships should be fixed by statute for a stipulated period of years (six in the first law) with the Reichstag committed to vote the necessary funds; also, old ships would be retired and replaced on schedule at specified intervals. By these means the annual wrangle with the Reichstag over appropriations and the size of the naval establishment would be avoided. Thus the naval program resembled the septennial military laws, which fixed the size of the German army for seven years. Probably no one foresaw the technological advances that were impending, which would make the navy program an exceedingly costly one. The statutory replacement ships, for example, were far larger and more expensive than the retired, obsolete vessels. A 4,000-ton ship, for instance, was later replaced by an enormously costly 26,000-ton dreadnought!

The second important principle which was built into the Tirpitz program provided for construction of a "battle fleet" composed of capital ships designed for high-seas duty. Under the law of 1898 this fleet would be composed of two squadrons of eight ships each, with an additional vessel to serve as the flagship of the commanding admiral. Thus the decision in the German navy fell in favor of Admiral Alfred Mahan's theory of a large striking force that would bid for control of the seas rather than a navy concentrating on cruiser warfare, commerce destruction, and coastal defense. Such a fleet in Tirpitz's view could fulfill all the missions of a conventional navy and be so strong that not even the greatest naval power, Great Britain for example, would dare risk an attack upon it. To be an effective deterrent it was not necessary that the German navy be as large as that of Britain, which normally would be dispersed over the globe and unable to concentrate against them. Tirpitz recognized that until the fleet was built, they would pass through a "danger zone" during which the uncompleted force might be attacked and destroyed. It was the task of German diplomacy to bring them through this "danger zone."[7]

The great fallacy of the "risk fleet" and the "danger zone" lay in the estimate of the British response, which was totally misjudged by the German leaders. Actually Germany never emerged from the danger zone. The British, vitally dependent upon sea power for the protection of the empire and their overseas supply, showed bulldog determination to maintain a safe margin of superiority over any rival, and when strategic circumstances required it, to take the political measures necessary to concentrate a preponderance of power in home waters and the North Sea.

The navy law of 1898 fixed the size and character of the German navy and launched a six-year building program. But within two years Tirpitz was asking the Reichstag for a new law, or an amending act, that would double the size of the navy and increase the cost several times. To promote the naval program Tirpitz had organized in the ministry the first effective press and public relations bureau to function in a German government department. A Navy League was sponsored on the British model, a semiofficial yearbook, *Nauticus,* was established, journalists and publicists were supplied with literature, and a mighty propaganda campaign was launched in the country.[8] Meanwhile, since 1898, the public had observed several object lessons in the value of sea power—Fashoda, the Spanish-American War, the dispute over Samoa, and now the Boer War. When the German mail steamer

7. Alfred von Tirpitz, *My Memoirs,* 2 vols. (New York, 1919), I, 63–90, 118–65; H. Hallmann, *Der Weg zum deutschen Schlachtflottenbau* (Stuttgart, 1933), pp. 123–25, 173–76; William L. Langer, *The Diplomacy of Imperialism,* 2 vols. (New York, 1935), II, 427–42.

8. Oron J. Hale, *Publicity and Diplomacy* (New York, 1940), pp. 217–26; Jonathan Steinberg, *Yesterday's Deterrent; Tirpitz and the Birth of the German Battle Fleet* (New York, 1966); A. J. Marder, *From the Dreadnought to Scapa Flow,* Vol. I, *The Road to War, 1904–1914* (New York, 1961), pp. 105–25. On the politics of the German navy laws, see the masterly treatment by Eckart Kehr, *Schlachtflottenbau und Parteipolitik, 1894–1901* (Berlin, 1930).

Bundesrath was stopped and held by the British navy on suspicion of transporting contraband to South Africa, the incident was so exploited politically that the navy bill passed the Reichstag with scarcely more than token opposition from the socialists. The law of 1900 doubled the size of the battle fleet (two flagships and four squadrons of eight ships each), including the necessary complements of cruisers and destroyers. Instead of the six-year program of 1898, the law optimistically extended to 1917 the statutory period for the completion of Germany's naval establishment.

When William II agitated for a larger navy he was merely following international fashion, for all the powers were renovating and expanding their navies in response to revolutionary technological and engineering advances. However, building a major battle fleet in the North Sea was certain to be taken as a deadly threat to Britain's security. As the German navy progressed and paper ships became realities of iron and steel, the naval issue and the question of security became the main cause of Anglo-German antagonism and threw them into a continuous arms race. Henceforth, to 1914, the navy dominated Germany's international relations. Although the security issue was not always acknowledged publicly, it was one of the reasons for Britain's concluding an entente with France in 1904 and with Russia in 1907. It thus contributed significantly to the diplomatic revolution and the division of Europe into two armed camps, with fatal consequences in 1914.

However, before the naval arms race became the dominant issue in Anglo-German relations, the two nations were completely alienated over issues arising out of the Boer War. Here journalists and publicists played a paramount role, and the Germans were by no means solely to blame.

When the South African war began in October, 1899, Britain was not only diplomatically isolated but her cause in South Africa was universally condemned by world opinion. False news reporting and atrocity stories flourished from the beginning. No country ever had a worse press. British publicists and statesmen expected this in France and Russia, and in New York and Boston, but the virulence of "Boeritis" in Germany was an unpleasant surprise, and it was deeply resented. The German press was not so scurrilous and vulgar as the French press in attacking Britain and lampooning the royal family, but the unrelieved vehemence of the journalistic assaults was almost frightening. Demonstrating enthusiasm for the Boers by abusing the English became standard practice in all but the semiofficial press in Germany.

At the outset a deep division arose between the official directors of German policy and the angry critics of British action in South Africa. Any show of friendliness, support, or understanding for the British nation was the signal for attacks upon the government by Boer sympathizers and Pan-German chauvinists. There were public demonstrations against the Kaiser's visit to his English relatives in November, 1899; and Chamberlain's warm words about a possible Anglo-German alliance encountered embarrassed silence or evoked blasts of Anglophobia. Bülow spoke so coolly in response in the Reichstag that his words were interpreted as a rude rebuff. However, at the same time Bülow rendered Britain a considerable service by derailing a Russian proposal for concerted diplomatic intervention on behalf of the plucky Boers. Later, when Paul Kruger, president of the Transvaal, toured the European capitals seeking support for a lost cause, he was intercepted at Cologne and told that he could not be received officially in Berlin. This inspired the bitter quip that "the Kaiser fears only God and his grandmother." Without openly repudiating or rebuking the Anglophobic extremists, Bülow and the press bureau in the foreign office did what they could to moderate the tone of the press and to publicize Bülow's foreign policy prescription—*Realpolitik nicht Gefühlspolitik* —a policy of interest rather than a policy of sentiment.[9]

While the barometer indicated foul weather in the public relations of the two countries, diplomatically the governments continued to pursue a policy of mutual accommodation and support. This had yielded agreements on the Portuguese colonies, on Samoa, and in October, 1900, on China. The latter—the so-called Yangtze Agreement—announced a common policy in dealing with the Chinese puzzle, which was greatly complicated by the Boxer War in the summer of 1900 and the international occupation of Peking. Stated baldly, Britain was isolated and heavily engaged in South Africa; she was subjected to severe pressure at every vulnerable point by France and Russia; and she needed support especially in the Far East. The agreement with Germany was greeted in both countries as a measure of relief and insurance. In London, on every hand, reported the correspondent of the

9. Hale, *Publicity and Diplomacy*, pp. 193–217.

Berliner Tageblatt (Oct. 29, 1900), one heard the comment: "Well, in China we are all right."

But from the beginning a misunderstanding prevailed as to whether the German government was obligated to support Britain diplomatically in opposing Russian interference in Manchuria. When the first test came with a series of Russian demands on Peking, in January, 1901, Bülow publicly repudiated the British interpretation of the accord. Speaking in the Reichstag, he said: "As regards the future of Manchuria, really, gentlemen, I can imagine nothing which we regard with more indifference." Questions were asked in the British Parliament, and in August a blue book was published on China, giving the correspondence between the two governments. From this it was crystal clear that Germany would not cooperate with any power in China against the Czar's government. The influential elite which really determined British foreign policy was woefully disillusioned. They had taken their bucket to an empty well! The *Times'* editor, reviewing the Far Eastern transactions in light of the blue-book revelations, drew the conclusion that "in no circumstances whatever, where our interests and those of Russia come into conflict, can we expect the slightest real support from the 'honest brokers' of Berlin." Finding the Germans a broken reed so far as British interests in the Far East were concerned, British statesmen turned to the Japanese and with remarkable dispatch concluded the Anglo-Japanese alliance of January, 1902. This was Britain's first political-military alliance of fixed duration; it marked her initial step in abandoning splendid isolation; and it set a bear trap into which the Russians blundered two years later.

The several stages through which the misunderstanding over the Yangtze Agreement passed cannot obscure its importance for Anglo-German relations. It marked unmistakably the point at which British authorities turned away from Berlin. It signaled the end of the policy of understanding and parallel action that had prevailed during the 1890's. When, toward the close of the next year (1902), the two governments sought to revive that policy in dealing with Venezuela, the violent reaction in press and parliament was such as to threaten the existence of the Balfour government.

Scarcely had the public relations between Great Britain and Germany righted themselves, as the Boer War passed into history, than they were again agitated by Joseph Chamberlain's defense of the

British army's conduct of the war in South Africa, especially the measures taken to deal with the insurgent bands which prolonged the hopeless struggle for nearly two years. Chamberlain, who could find the right words for British hearers, could always be depended upon to find the wrong word for a foreign audience. When he said that British methods were no more "barbarous" than those employed by the Germans in the war of 1870, he touched off an explosion of patriotic hysteria over an alleged "insult" to the German army that convulsed the veterans' societies, university students, patriotic groups, and the press. Chamberlain was reviled beyond all measure, and so strong was the tide of emotions that Bülow felt constrained to repudiate before the Reichstag the implied insult to the German army. "Let the man alone," he said, quoting Frederick the Great, "he is biting on granite."[10]

The Chamberlain episode appeared to work as a sort of catharsis on the German public, but it did irreparable damage in England, where anti-German feeling was now deeply implanted in all classes of the population. This was noted with alarm by German diplomats and press correspondents resident in Britain. As the Germans began to recover from their severe case of "Boeritis" the British public became thoroughly indoctrinated with Germanophobia, and under the impact of the German naval threat and under the tutelage of the periodical and newspaper press remained in that condition henceforth until the eve of the war.

The real depth of English hostility toward Germany became evident when the governments undertook to renew the policy of cooperation in matters involving mutual or parallel interests. When Balfour's government joined Germany in a debt-collecting sortie in Venezuela in the autumn of 1902, they ran head-on into a stone wall of political opposition. At first the action provoked no outcry, but when the cooperating authorities instituted vigorous action—blockade, seizures, and bombardment—the American press took alarm and began to raise the issue of the Monroe Doctrine. At this point the English journalists turned on the government, castigating the ministers for embarking on an ill-considered adventure which was leading them on to a collision with the United States. Without regard to party lines the editors labeled the affair the "Venezuelan Mess," caviled at the "alliance" with Germany, and decried the stupidity of their diplomats who were repeating the

10. *Ibid.*, pp. 241–51.

folly of the Yangtze Agreement. Solemnly the editors warned the government that Germany was a "fatal partner," and a "deadly rival," who "will embroil us with the United States"; Germany was out to grab territory, and protestations to the contrary were worthless.

In time of stress and crisis the British were accustomed to look to their national poets for expression of their deepest feelings. Obviously moved, Rudyard Kipling published in the *Times* (Dec. 22, 1902) a poetic commentary under the none too apt title "The Rowers." In Kipling's imagination the victorious "Rowers" are returning from South Africa, when they are told that they must now change course to South America.

> Last night ye swore our voyage was done,
>   But seaward still we go;
> And ye tell us now of a secret vow
>   Ye have made with an open foe!
>
> The dead they mocked are scarcely cold,
>   Our wounded are bleeding yet—
> And ye tell us now that our strength is sold
>   To help them press for a debt!
>
> In sight of peace—from the Narrow Seas
>   O'er half the world to run—
> With a cheated crew, to league anew
>   With the Goth and the Shameless Hun!

This "frenzied poet of great talent," as Bülow referred to Kipling in the Reichstag, was publicly rebuked by Lord Lansdowne, the foreign secretary, but Kipling unquestionably expressed a sentiment that was widely prevalent in the nation. The government withdrew from the enterprise with embarrassed excuses to its own parliamentary majority.[11]

Understandably, this episode made the cabinet nervous and timid about any kind of cooperation with Germany. It was unfortunate, therefore, that the question of British participation in the Baghdad Railroad should have been raised so soon after the "Venezuelan Mess." When the first concession was granted to the Deutsche Bank, in

11. *Ibid.*, pp. 258–60.

EUROPE—1914

RUSSIA

SIBERIA

FINLAND

Petrograd
(St. Petersburg)

ESTONIA

LIVONIA

KURLAND

LITHUANIA

Minsk •

POLAND

Kiev •

Dnieper

Vistula R.

UKRAINE

GARY

RUMANIA

Bucharest •

Sofia •

BULGARIA

Constan-
tinople

BLACK   SEA

Sea of Azov

CASPIAN SEA

ASIA   MINOR

GREECE

BIA

Athens •

Crete

Cyprus

Results of the
**Balkan Wars:
1912-13**

To Serbia

To Montenegro

To Rumania

To Bulgaria

To Greece

November, 1899, the enterprise drew favorable comment from the London press. It was obvious that such a road would promote the economic development of the vast territory of Anatolia and the Tigris-Euphrates Valley. Lacking the capital for such a massive project, the German bankers invited French and British participation on the basis of parity in promoting and controlling the enterprise. The structure of the company they proposed to organize did not exactly ensure equality in corporate control, but this was subject to further negotiation.

Early in 1903, when the Germans approached a group of London capitalists, the government indicated its approval and willingness to examine sympathetically the political concessions essential to the co-operation of British capital. A statement to this effect was made by Balfour in response to a question in the House of Commons on April 7, 1903. But such a publicity storm blew up in political and press circles that the government beat a hasty retreat, and on April 21 announced that the government could not give the assurances desired by the British capitalists. The French government, like the British, was at first favorable but then changed its position and refused the listing of shares on the French market. Since Russia was opposed from the beginning, a promising international project was effectively blocked. With available German capital and the Turkish government's kilometric guarantee— the means by which most of the Turkish lines were constructed—the first 200 kilometers of the line from Konia to Eregli were built and opened with joyous acclaim on October 25, 1904. But there the line stopped with the rail ends sticking out into space. The next 200-kilo-meter section carried into the Taurus Mountains, where construction costs were beyond the resources of the Deutsche Bank and its associates. It was British and French policy that had brought construction to a standstill, and there was no good prospect of continuing. Thus a valuable opportunity for international cooperation in a vast and bene-ficial enterprise was turned into a source of resentment and ill will. Since Germany had been unwilling to concede to the other powers equality in control of the enterprise, there was plenty of blame to be shared by all the participants in this regrettable affair. The effect on Anglo-German relations was discordant and productive of resentment. Except for abortive naval conversations, no negotiations for cooperation or collaboration were again undertaken by the two governments until the Portuguese colonies and Baghdad Railroad accords were concluded shortly before the outbreak of war in 1914.[12]

The excesses of the press during the Boer War played a large role in the alienation of the British and German governments. On the whole the impact was more damaging and lasting in Britain than in Germany. The unfavorable image created by these events dominated the public relations of the two countries for a decade. It was believed that attempts at cooperation in the Far East had shown the unreliability and double-crossing tendencies of German diplomacy; the German press had revealed the true feelings of the German nation toward Britain during the Boer War; Pan-Germanic preachments proved that the objectives of German policy could be achieved only by destroying the British Empire; and Germany was forging the instrument of that policy by building a big navy. Thus formulated, the "German menace" became a driving force in Britain's rapprochement to France and Russia.

3. THE ANGLO-FRENCH ENTENTE AND THE FIRST MOROCCAN CRISIS

While the Anglo-Japanese alliance was being forged, discussion of colonial problems with France began in a casual way in London between Lord Lansdowne, British foreign minister, and the French ambassador, Paul Cambon. Begun in 1902, the conversations continued intermittently until agreement was reached and the accords signed on April 8, 1904. Some of the soreness over Fashoda had disappeared, and French enthusiasm for the Boers had subsided. The atmosphere in which the negotiations took place was also improved by King Edward's visit to Paris in May, 1903, and President Loubet's return visit to London in July. Loubet was accompanied by Théophile Delcassé, French foreign minister, who was obviously eager to push ahead with the negotiations. With Egypt now clearly out of reach, French colonial aspirations were focused on Morocco. Delcassé indicated that if they could reach an agreement on Morocco all the other points of difference

---

12. On the Baghdad Railroad and rejection of the German proposals, see *Die Grosse Politik*, XVII, 438–39, 440, 448–49; *British Documents on the Origins of the War*, 11 vols. (London, 1926–38), II, 196; *Journals and Letters of Viscount Esher* (London, 1934), I, 396–97; Lord Newton, *Lord Lansdowne: A Biography* (London, 1929), p. 254; George Monger, *The End of Isolation* (London, 1963), pp. 118–23. Lansdowne favored collaboration despite the clamor in press and parliament, but he could not carry the cabinet. The opposition in the ministry was led by Chamberlain.

could be settled without difficulty. Lansdowne indicated that Egypt was as important to Britain as Morocco to France and should be included in the discussions. To this Delcassé readily assented. After six months of hard but friendly bargaining, evenly balanced compromises were reached on all points at issue and embodied in the formal agreements of April 8, 1904. Some of the conventions were public, others secret. A number of minor but long-standing colonial differences were settled. France abandoned her fishing rights on the Newfoundland shore for a money indemnity and territorial compensation in the border districts of Gambia and Nigeria; their respective spheres of influence in Siam were adjusted; Britain withdrew her objections to the French tariff in Madagascar; and a joint commission was arranged to arbitrate differences in the New Hebrides.

But the important arrangements concerned north Africa. In this area France acknowledged the legitimacy of Britain's position in Egypt, while Britain recognized France's special interest in Morocco. Because of the coterminous frontier with Algeria, France, it was acknowledged, was concerned with the maintenance of order in Morocco and in providing assistance in such administrative, economic, and military reforms as the country might require. Equality of economic opportunity was guaranteed for a period of thirty years to the French in Egypt and to the British in Morocco. Both governments promised diplomatic support in the execution of their agreement—a provision that proved of immense value to the French, although inserted at the request of the British. These published accords, disclaiming any intention of altering the international position of Egypt and Morocco, were negated by secret articles providing for the future partition of Morocco into French and Spanish zones of control. The extent of the Spanish sphere was to be negotiated between France and Spain. By implication the rest of Morocco would become a French sphere of influence under French administration.

Thus long-standing and irritating causes of friction between Britain and France—the Newfoundland fisheries dispute derived from the Treaty of Utrecht—were cleared off, and the two governments now enjoyed what was soon called an *entente cordiale*. During the Moroccan crisis that followed, Britain and France drew closer together, military conversations and understandings followed, and in 1914 their relationship was one of alliance, although a formal treaty was lacking.

Lord Lansdowne prudently negotiated immediately with Berlin concerning Egypt; the Germans insisted on the same guarantees given to France. Delcassé, however, made the serious mistake of ignoring Germany, while he came to terms with Spain over their spheres of influence in Morocco. An agreement with Italy, in which France had recognized Italy's ambitions with regard to Tripoli, had been concluded in 1900. Now with much publicity a special French mission was dispatched to Fez, the Moroccan capital, bearing a list of desired reforms and a major loan proposal, which if adopted would have ended Moroccan independence. The French press began to speak of a "pacific penetration" of Morocco, implying that the country would soon be integrated into France's north African empire.

Announcement of the Anglo-French agreement was an unpleasant shock to the Kaiser, Bülow, and Holstein. It negated a major assumption upon which German policy had hitherto rested—that Britain would never pay the price of an understanding with France. The first appraisal was made by Holstein in a letter to his cousin Ida von Stülpnagel, his political confidante for many years.

Politically I am not happy. The perverse attitude during the Boer War now bears its fruit in the entente between France and England. . . . But the good Bülow would rather swim with than against the current. Now what a pickle we are in. England and France will hardly attack us, that is not what I fear, but we shall be unable to make any overseas acquisitions. I do not demand such acquisitions but a great mass of people cry out for them and wonder why none fall to us. Indeed, but how shall it be done? Against France and England an overseas policy is impossible. We could have gone along with England and could today have had the position which France has, that is, good friends with both England and Russia. But we missed the opportunity and Delcassé shows that he is the wiser.[13]

Holstein was correct in his judgment of the effect of the Anglo-French agreement on Germany's colonial ambitions. England's favor, which since Bismarck's years in office had enabled Germany to pursue a colonial policy, was now withdrawn and bestowed upon France. Henceforth, when Germany sought to expand her interests—in Africa, the Near East, the Orient—she encountered a stone wall of Entente opposition.

13. Rogge, *Friedrich von Holstein*, p. 231; Monger, *The End of Isolation*, pp. 164–66, 175–79.

What additional significance the Anglo-French agreement might have was not immediately apparent, although in the press of both countries it was endowed with uncommon importance. Bülow through the foreign office press bureau put a good face on a bad matter. It was not a serious check to Germany, as some British journals were saying, but a sign of the tendency to iron out international difficulties before they became acute. Germany was not being thrust into isolation, and even if she were Germany was strong enough to defend her own house single-handed. Publicly it was stated that Germany had commercial interests in Morocco—she stood third in trade after Britain and France—and these interests would be firmly upheld. Beyond the reaction of the semiofficial press, Berlin maintained a sphinxlike reserve toward developments in northwest Africa.

German foreign office officials and local representatives in Morocco agreed that some action should be taken to uphold Germany's great power position—her right to be consulted—and to protect her economic interests in Morocco. Since they had been ignored they could not approach France directly, and the Kaiser vetoed anything like a naval demonstration along the Moroccan coast. So from April to the end of the year there was much discussion but little action.

A principal reason for this inactivity was the alliance negotiations which the Germans were conducting with Russia, a move that also held out the prospect of a revision of their relations with France. Russia's involvement in war with Japan afforded opportunities for demonstrations of friendship and support by Emperor William and his government. (The coaling of the Russian Baltic fleet on its voyage to the Far East by the Hamburg-America Line was an example of such favors.) The alliance negotiations collapsed in December when the Russian foreign office insisted that their French ally be fully informed of the conversations.[14] Appeasing France no longer seemed necessary, so moves to block French penetration of Morocco were then initiated.

The action recommended by Holstein and adopted by Bülow required the countering of each French move in Morocco with a similar German move, the encouragement of the Sultan of Morocco to resist

14. These negotiations were reopened on William II's initiative at the dramatic meeting of Kaiser and Czar at Björkö on July 23–24, 1905, when the two sovereigns without consulting their ministers signed the defensive agreement which had been shelved the previous December. The treaty was scuttled a second time by the Czar's ministers, who convinced him that French adherence would be impossible to achieve. Sidney B. Fay, *The Origins of the World War*, 2 vols. (New York, 1928), I, 171–77.

French demands, and the rejection of any overtures for a settlement that might now come from Delcassé. The first round of the game of pressure and counterpressure took place in Fez with the arrival of a French mission headed by the diplomat Saint-René Taillandier. When he presented to the Sultan a comprehensive list of reforms, he was reported to have said that France had an international mandate to institute this program. The Germans immediately countered by assuring the Sultan that France had no mandate and urged him to resist French pressure and institute his own reform program.

The Kaiser's dramatic visit to Tangier, at the end of March, 1905, was a part of the Bülow-Holstein action designed to stiffen the Sultan's resistance and strengthen Germany's hand in the diplomatic tug-of-war at the Sultan's court. From beginning to end William II was unsympathetic to the Wilhelmstrasse's Moroccan policy, and he did not relish at all the "Lohengrin role" assigned in conjunction with his annual spring cruise to the Mediterranean. Indeed, whether he would land at Tangier was uncertain because of weather conditions, but Bülow briefed him by cable and kept him under heavy pressure to go through with the visit which had been officially announced in Berlin. The Kaiser's party was on land only about three hours—long enough to attend a reception at the German legation. There the Emperor made his formal statement to the Sultan's great-uncle, who headed the official receiving party. Replying to the words of official welcome, William II assured the Moroccan emissary that he regarded the Sultan as an independent sovereign, free from foreign control; he wished to see a prosperous Morocco and he would consult directly with the Sultan on the best means to achieve this end. He also advised caution in making reforms in order to avoid offending Moslem religious feelings. To the French representative at the reception he remarked rather brusquely that Germany had commercial rights in Morocco which must be upheld. Since no official report of the Kaiser's words was issued to the press, several versions were circulated in the newspapers. Regardless of the exact content it was now clear that France and Germany were moving on lines that threatened a collision.

All manner of interpretations were placed on the Kaiser's visit by European observers, but the Moors, high and low, were enormously pleased. So reported the American minister in Tangier. "They regard it as a check to the plans of the French government and openly declare that the Emperor is sent by God to deliver them from the French."[15] This view was encouraged by the dispatch of a German mission to Fez under the aggressive Count Tattenbach, who was instructed to encourage the Sultan to resist French pressure and to appeal for an international conference on Moroccan reforms. The legal basis of such a demand was the Madrid conference of 1880, at which all states with trade interests in Morocco signed a convention which guaranteed most favored nation treatment to the signatory powers. The French attempt to "Tunisify" Morocco threatened the rights of other states; if Morocco were in need of reforms they should be authorized and effected internationally. Hence the appeal by the Sultan, coached and backed by Germany, for an international conference. Bülow optimistically thought that on the issue of international rights and the "open door" Germany could count on the support of a majority of the Madrid signatories, including the United States, while the smaller states—Switzerland, Holland, Belgium—would rally to support the principle of economic equality when they found themselves in good company.

The Tangier demonstration and the deadlock in Fez forced Delcassé to undertake what he had stubbornly refused to do in the preceding twelve months—reach an understanding with Germany over Morocco. Through several channels he now endeavored to open discussions but in each instance encountered a closed door. Through intermediaries the German government let it be known that they would not deal with Delcassé and that they would insist on an international solution of the Moroccan question. Most of the signatories of the Madrid convention were reluctant or unwilling to accept a conference solution unless it was agreeable to France. Thus the matter became a test of strength, a drama of brinkmanship that caused nervous tension in Paris and concern throughout Europe.

Maurice Rouvier, who had replaced Émile Combes as premier, was a banker without experience in diplomacy, and he took German blustering at face value; Delcassé, an experienced diplomat with seven years' experience in the foreign office, was familiar with the art of bluffing.

15. S. R. Gummere to Secretary of State John Hay, April 1, 1905; Department of State, Morocco, I, No. 7. On the Kaiser's visit to Tangier, see E. N. Anderson, *The First Moroccan Crisis, 1904–1906* (Chicago, 1930), 159–96; French policy from 1904 to the convening of the Algeciras Conference is covered in *Documents diplomatiques français, 1871–1914*, 41 vols. (Paris, 1929–59), 2d ser., Vols. VI–VIII. Volume IX, in two parts, deals with the conference and its consequences.

He recommended to the premier that they reject a conference, put the Sultan under heavy pressure, and rely on their understanding with England for security and support. Rouvier, distrusting Britain and intimidated by communications from Berlin, practically offered Bülow Delcassé's head in return for an understanding and a relaxation of tension. Delcassé was ready to go to the brink; Rouvier was not. In the chamber of deputies, in the press, and in the ministerial council Rouvier's view prevailed, and Delcassé was forced to resign.

Was Germany bluffing? Who was right, Rouvier or Delcassé? Even today it is difficult to determine Germany's real intentions. Despite his emotional and vocal belligerency the Kaiser was a somewhat timid man; and he made it clear to his advisers on several occasions that he would not sanction a war over Morocco. Whether Baron Holstein in collaboration with Von Schlieffen, the chief of staff, was steering German policy toward a preventive war has been much discussed by scholars. But the most recent consideration of this thesis, based on Holstein's papers, has produced a negative answer.[16] As to Bülow's intentions, the distinction between a warning and a threat is often indeterminate. If he was threatening, then he was also bluffing and Delcassé was right in his evaluation. In other respects Delcassé was also right. For Rouvier, when he came to negotiate the conference agenda, soon found himself obliged to adopt his fallen minister's policy and maintain the closest association, short of a formal alliance, with Britain.

Delcassé's elimination did not end the Moroccan crisis. Germany appeared to have won a brilliant diplomatic victory and to have weakened if not ruptured the Anglo-French entente. Prime Minister Balfour wrote Edward VII on June 8 that Delcassé's fall under German pressure "displayed a weakness on the part of France which indicated that she could not at present be counted on as an effective force in international politics."[17] But the German statesmen profited little from their apparent success, and in the end their tactics produced results the opposite of what they desired.

Having eliminated Delcassé, Bülow and Holstein forced France to submit her Moroccan reform program to an international conference. In dealing with the French on the conference issue and the agenda for such a meeting, the Germans used the same cajoling and bullying

16. Rich, *Friedrich von Holstein*, II, 696–99, 742–45.
17. Sidney Lee, *King Edward VII*, 2 vols. (New York, 1927), II, 344.

tactics that had succeeded against Delcassé. This prolonged the crisis, with lessened intensity, through the summer and into the fall. By the time the conference convened at Algeciras in mid-January, 1906, Rouvier had swung around and adopted Delcassé's policy of resisting German pressure and working in close collaboration with the British foreign office. On the eve of the conference military conversations between the French and British general staffs were initiated, which continued over the years and resulted in detailed military plans envisaging joint action in the event of war. In consequence of German policy, national feeling in France was much aroused and fortified; measures to strengthen the military forces were taken and the conviction deeply implanted that it would be better to fight than yield again to German threats. German tactics also made a bad impression on the other governments, so that sympathy and understanding accrued to France rather than Germany. That Germany was upholding the principle of internationalization against French monopolistic aims did not carry much conviction, nor did it rally supporters to Germany's side. The German triumph over Delcassé turned out to be a Pyrrhic victory, and the Algeciras conference became a humiliating and irritating experience for German policy makers.

Algeciras, where the conference met from January 16 to April 7, 1906, was a small town in southern Spain across the bay from Gibraltar. It was quite unsuitable for such a meeting but had been selected because of its proximity to Tangier. Algeciras had two hotels and a lunatic asylum. One hotel was occupied by the delegates and their assistants, the other by more than fifty news-hungry journalists. The Algeciras conference was the first international congress to be exploited by the new journalism for the instruction and entertainment of the masses. After the first week the local color of Algeciras, and the three wives brought to the conference by the Moroccan delegate, El Mokri, had been exploited to the limit in countless background articles.[18] Thereafter the dearth of news of a sensational kind led to the fabrication of interviews, journalistic espionage, and general badgering of the delegates. Only the French deputation was prepared to deal with a large group of newspaper correspondents, and their handling of the press

18. The Paris *Figaro* (Jan. 31, 1906) published an amusing cartoon entitled "The Gaieties of Algeciras, or Three Wives for El Mokri."

corps was described by one observer as "a perfectly brilliant technical performance."

Organized as a committee of the whole, the conference delegates dealt first with matters on which there was substantial agreement—control of contraband arms, improvement of customs services, public works, better collection of taxes, and creation of new revenue. The most divisive items were the proposed state bank and the organization of police forces in the Moroccan ports. Whoever controlled the bank and commanded the police would eventually control Morocco—so it was thought.

The French desired and proposed a joint French-Spanish mandate for the police; on the state bank they were willing to compromise. The German government insisted on an international police force instead of an allocation of ports to the French and Spanish alone. Soon the police and bank issues deadlocked the conference. Formal votes in the committee of the whole had been avoided up to this point so that no state would be forced to take a public stand which might be embarrassing or which might tend to isolate this or that power. A turning point was reached with the "Vote of March 3," when the British delegate, Sir Arthur Nicolson, astutely forced a decision on an important procedural question in which Germany encountered a humiliating rebuff. Supported only by Austria-Hungary and Morocco, she was outvoted ten to three. Even her ally Italy defected and voted with the majority, as did the lesser states—Holland, Belgium, Sweden, and Portugal. After this mortifying exposure of Germany's isolation Bülow took the negotiations out of Holstein's hands and with the Kaiser's approval accepted several compromises on the police question which enabled the conference to conclude its work with a rush and to sign the Act of Algeciras on April 2. The conference had a copybook ending, recorded in the diary of the French delegate, M. Révoil, who gave an official *banquet d'adieu* for the bored and tired representatives: "Après le dîner les délégations prennent le café avec nous dans le salon des dames."[19]

The Act of Algeciras was not very durable and it was soon scrapped, but it marked the end of a severe international crisis and noticeably relaxed the tension in Europe. It gave the appearance of recognizing

19. *Documents diplomatiques français*, X, 966. Other accounts, Anderson, *The First Moroccan Crisis*, pp. 348–96; Harold Nicolson, *Lord Carnock* (London, 1930), pp. 170–99.

the principle of internationalization which Germany had advocated, although France and Spain reaped most of the tangible advantages for which they had contended. Despite the unfavorable power position of France, resulting from Russia's defeat in the Far East, the French gained recognition of their special position in Morocco; they owed this to unwavering British support—in fact Britain was the real victor at Algeciras, while German policy sustained a severe check with regard to the immediate issue as well as in the attempt to halt the formation of a power grouping designed to set limits to German expansion. Algeciras was also a testing ground for all the alliances, ententes, and special understandings that had developed in the preceding years; it highlighted the weakness of the Triple Alliance and revealed the increasing strength of the Entente system. In consequence of Germany's action in the Moroccan crisis France, England, and Russia had all drawn noticeably closer together.

Throughout the crisis Germany's military position was much stronger than her diplomatic position. With Russia's military power at lowest ebb France could not have resisted a policy of force; had she done so she would have been crushed. At no stage in the prolonged crisis did the directors of German policy seriously consider a military solution. On the contrary they went to extreme lengths to avoid war. But since Germany's attitude was consistently intransigent she was branded a disturber of the peace.

Finally, the future alignment of the powers was made clear at Algeciras. On crucial issues only Austria stood by Germany; opposed were France, Britain, and Russia, with Italy neutral, and the United States seeking to play a mediatory role. This was the grouping of the powers as they were drawn into war in 1914.

4. THE ANGLO-RUSSIAN AGREEMENT OF 1907

The diplomatic revolution, which found England abandoning isolation by concluding an alliance with Japan and an entente with France, was completed in 1907 by a broad understanding with France's ally Russia. Thus was born the Triple Entente. The directors of British policy had made the first overtures to Russia in 1903, when the negotiations with France were in train. The initiative was at all times in British hands. However, anti-British sentiment was strong in Russian circles and in the press during the Russo-Japanese War, and this precluded any effective moves toward a rapprochement. After Russia was sharply checked in Asia by the Japanese, after the Björkö treaty, which would have made Russia an ally of Germany, was repudiated, and after France and England had concluded their understanding in colonial matters, the atmosphere in St. Petersburg was more favorable to an agreement with Britain. The two governments also collaborated to support France at the Algeciras conference, and British financiers were helpful in the matter of Russian loans, which were critically needed to shore up the government against the forces of domestic revolt. Sir Edward Grey, like his predecessor Lord Lansdowne, was convinced of the necessity of an agreement with Russia to form a triple bloc which could check Germany if occasion for such action should arise.[20] In May, 1906, Alexander Iswolski, a reputed liberal Anglophile who spoke flawless English, succeeded Count Lamsdorff as foreign minister. Iswolski was a man of some gifts, great ambition, and a considerable reputation, and his appointment signaled the redirection of Russian foreign policy from the Far East, where Russia had been unsuccessful, to the Near East, where her traditional interests lay.

Concurrently with Iswolski's appointment, Sir Arthur Nicolson, who won ecstatic praise for his success at Algeciras, succeeded Sir Charles Hardinge as ambassador in St. Petersburg. Nicolson, indubitably England's ablest diplomat, had precise instructions from the cabinet for negotiating an Asiatic agreement with Russia. Negotiations began with almost undiplomatic haste following Nicolson's arrival in the Russian capital. But the Russians were timid in their approach to the negotiations, and from time to time they were interrupted and put aside. It was a serious test of Nicolson's skill and finesse as a negotiator. The ambassador's instructions were simple and direct: to remove from Anglo-Russian relations three points of friction and rivalry in Asia represented by Tibet, Afghanistan, and Persia. The status of the Straits was brought into the discussion—the British indicated willingness to consider Russian proposals—but then was postponed to a later date. Negotiations began in June, 1906, and continued for fifteen months, the agreement being signed in August, 1907. The preamble to the instrument registered the traditional good intentions of the signatories and

20. *British Documents on the Origins of the War*, III, 266–67. The most recent treatment of the Anglo-Russian negotiations, based on hitherto unused sources—India Office, War Office, etc.—is Monger, *The End of Isolation*, pp. 281–95.

the desire "to settle by mutual consent the questions relating to their interests in the Asiatic continent." The document embodied three separate agreements. The first, and the most difficult to negotiate, concerned Persia. Pledging themselves to respect the integrity and independence of that country, they proceeded to mark out spheres of influence—a large Russian zone in the north, a smaller British zone in the southeast, and a middle intermediate zone in which the two parties were to enjoy equal rights and opportunities. The second part of the agreement concerned Afghanistan, which Russia, in deference to Britain's concern for the security of the Indian frontier, recognized as a British sphere of influence. Britain's concession in this matter was a pledge not to annex the mountainous native state. With regard to Tibet both powers recognized Chinese suzerainty over that Buddhist country and agreed not to interfere in its internal affairs. Thus Persia and Afghanistan were held in subjection by the two European powers while an unstable compromise governed their relations in the troubled area.

Iswolski was seriously concerned that the improvement of Russia's relations with England should not entail a corresponding deterioration of Russia's relations toward Germany. Therefore both British and Russian governments assured Berlin that the agreement was not directed against Germany. In diplomatic circles two interpretations were placed on the convention: one, that it was simply an Asiatic agreement without European significance; the other, that its sole purpose was the isolation and encirclement of Germany. In fact it was a combination of both. The immediate objective of the British government was the security of India, but there were also considerations of broader scope that involved the balance of power and security problems of the highest order. Germany was a major consideration, and the fear that she aimed at domination of the Continent was a motive in forging the agreement. However, it was probably not so much a matter of getting Russia to join England against Germany as it was a matter of preventing Russia from joining Germany and then drawing France into a German-dominated Continental bloc.[21] Although Bülow put a good face on the matter in the Reichstag and in the officially inspired press, the

21. Nicolson, Lord Carnock, pp. 234–35, 238, 257. The evidence indicates that the War Office and Foreign Office wanted an entente with Russia as a means of isolating and containing Germany. Monger, The End of Isolation, pp. 281–82.

Kaiser was of the opinion that "when it is taken all round it is aimed at us."

What created public alarm and perturbation in Germany and gave rise to fears of encirclement was the visit of King Edward VII to the Czar at the Baltic port of Reval on June 9–11, 1908. Coming soon after the visit of French President Fallières to London, it gave the public the impression that great political schemes were afoot. This was reinforced by the presence in King Edward's suite of the highest army and naval authorities and the permanent undersecretary for foreign affairs, Sir Charles Hardinge. The Czar was accompanied by Iswolski and the prime minister, Stolypin. This suggested that far-reaching military and naval conversations were being held. In fact, while there was an exchange of views there were no agreements concluded or negotiations set in train. The barren formalities of the Reval meeting, with nothing tangible to report except the usual toasts, left the field free for the workings of the journalistic imagination. The result in Germany was a near midsummer nightmare. Optimistic assurances fed to the public through the semiofficial press did not wholly banish anxiety and concern. There still remains, wrote the editor of the *Berliner Tageblatt,* the fear that through the net of agreements and alliances being drawn over Europe and Asia we are being increasingly restricted in our freedom of movement.[22]

As an Asiatic agreement the convention satisfied no one. It was not popular in Britain or in Russia, or in Persia, or in Afghanistan. In Persia it proved largely unworkable, the Russians simply using it as a new cover for their old designs, which were as devious as they were dastardly. The agreement on its own then was rather more divisive than uniting, and it did not create immediately an entente between St. Petersburg and London. What forged a close understanding between the two governments and made the Triple Entente a tangible combination was the Bosnian annexation crisis.

By 1907 a significant and fateful realignment of the powers was clearly in the making. Britain had moved from a position of detachment toward the Continental alignments to one of commitment to

22. Hale, *Publicity and Diplomacy,* pp. 309–11; Fay, *Origins of the World War,* I, 240–45; Sidney Lee, *King Edward VII,* II, 586–96; *Die Grosse Politik,* XXV, 441–94. On the state of Anglo-German relations in 1906–1907, and the conflicting currents in the British cabinet, see Monger, *The End of Isolation,* pp. 296–331.

France and Russia. The advent of the Liberal party and the occupation of the foreign office by Sir Edward Grey reinforced and solidified the entente policy initiated by the Conservative cabinet. Grey shared all the suspicions and animosities of the foreign office experts toward Germany, and he carried his policy in the cabinet. Extremely sensitive to any signs of cordiality toward Germany that might disturb the French, he opposed reciprocal visits by the sovereigns, the exchange and reception of various delegations, even the visit of the Coldstream Guards band, which had been promised and authorized by the Army Council. Grey's fear of Germany was at the center of British policy, and as long as this situation persisted the peace of Europe depended upon a precarious balance.[23]

23. Monger, *The End of Isolation*, pp. 325-31.

Chapter Ten

THE ARMED CAMPS, 1907–1914

I. THE BOSNIAN ANNEXATION CRISIS

The Bosnian crisis that kept nerves and tempers taut for six months began in October, 1908, and only subsided in April of the following year. The crisis illuminated existing tensions and distractions and left new deposits of ill will, resentment, and frustration. Of the crises in European international relations prior to 1914, it was perhaps the noisiest, as it was the most complicated, for it involved the foreign ministers of the great powers in continuous diplomatic wrangling over a prolonged period of time. In many ways it also served as a test run for the crisis of 1914, but without the latter's tragic end. The instigators of the crisis were the foreign ministers of Russia and Austria, Alexander Iswolski and Alois Aehrenthal. Both were recent appointees to their important and responsible posts; both were ambitious, somewhat reckless, and not above being devious. Both had specific foreign policy goals which if achieved would establish their reputations and forward their careers.

For the previous ten years, since 1897, Austrian-Russian relations in the Balkans had been marked by mutual understanding and attachment to the status quo. Such a passive foreign policy was not to the liking of either of the new foreign ministers. The initiative, which started the train of events, and eventually carried Europe to the brink of war, came from Iswolski. Begun in great secrecy, conversations about mutual aims and ambitions in the Balkans had revealed two elements of a possible horse trade. The Russians, after the experience of the Russo-Japanese War, greatly desired to open the Straits to Russian warships, while keeping them closed to other powers; Austria wished to consolidate her position in the western Balkans by annexing Bosnia-Herzegovina, which under Article 25 of the Berlin Treaty she had "occupied and administered" since 1878. Communications indicating that the two ministers were agreed in principle on such a bargain, without, however, specifying the method of procedure or the timetable, passed between them in July, 1908. These compromising documents Aehrenthal used later to blackmail Iswolski into silence.

The Young Turk revolution, which began in July, 1908, determined Aehrenthal and his associates to act quickly and unilaterally, without regard to the other signatories of the Berlin Treaty. Their concern was that a rejuvenated Turkey might insist upon the restoration of the provinces to Turkish sovereignty. Also since constitutional government was now reestablished in Turkey, Austria could not do less for the natives of Bosnia-Herzegovina; but it would be safer to integrate them fully into the Hapsburg Empire before introducing representative government.

Annexation was secretly considered and approved in two sessions of the Council of Joint Ministers. The case for immediate action seemed overrriding, and on September 16 Aehrenthal and Iswolski had their historic meeting at Buchlau castle in Bohemia. Their conversations gave rise to one of the most acrimonious diplomatic controversies of the prewar period. It is still not entirely clear what the one minister proposed to the other, what the other understood by the proposal, and what they finally agreed upon. It was indeed "a day of dupes." The memorandum of record that each prepared some days after the conference was less than frank, because once the public announcement was made and the violent reactions registered, each participant tried to justify his actions or disclaim responsibility before his sovereign, his countrymen, and the signatories of the Berlin Treaty. There is no doubt that at Buchlau the Russian foreign minister agreed to the formal annexation, but only on condition that Russia gain her objective at the Straits. But Iswolski failed to pin Aehrenthal down on the procedure for effecting the changes and the date for the formal annexation. That is why Iswolski went first on vacation and then began a leisurely journey around the capitals of Europe for the purpose of gaining the consent of the powers to the opening of the Straits and the revision of the Berlin Treaty. While he was thus engaged, the time bomb that had been set going at Buchlau suddenly exploded.

In advance of Austria's action Aehrenthal encouraged Bulgaria to seize this favorable moment to declare her independence and like Austria-Hungary to become a violator of the Berlin Treaty. On October 5, Prince Ferdinand proclaimed Bulgaria a sovereign state and assumed the medieval title of Czar. Francis Joseph's proclamation of annexation and his notification to the sovereigns and heads of state followed on the next day.

The concerted Austrian and Bulgarian action had a bad press in all the capitals except Berlin and Paris. British editors were aggrieved at the violation of the Berlin Treaty, the Italian press hinted at compensation, and Russian editors were incensed that more Slavic peoples were being brought under German rule. The Turkish political press showed more concern for Bulgaria's action than for the Austrian registration of a *fait accompli*. The most effective Turkish action was the popular boycott of Austrian firms and goods, which spread rapidly throughout the Ottoman Empire.

The most violent reaction was evoked in Serbia, where deep national feeling focused on Bosnia and Herzegovina. The dream of uniting Serbia, Bosnia, and Montenegro to form a large South Slav kingdom had been rudely dissipated. Blocked now from access to the Adriatic and frustrated in the hope of combining all the Balkan Serbs in a single state, national resentment rose to fever pitch. Crowds demonstrated in the streets of Belgrade, and excited patriots clamored for war. The government convened the parliament and ordered partial mobilization. Although not a party to the Berlin Treaty, the Serbian government sent a note of protest to the signatories demanding observation of Article 25 or "a corresponding compensation." Serb nationalism also found expression in these days in the organization of the society called "National Defense" (Narodna Odbrana) with the object of promoting and defending Serbian interests in the provinces. Although it later converted to cultural propaganda, Narodna Odbrana never entirely lost its original subversive and insurrectionary character. It was this organization which the Austro-Hungarian government charged with responsibility for the turmoil and ferment in Bosnia which provided the context for the Sarajevo assassinations in 1914.

After the first shock waves subsided, the Bosnian affair developed along two lines—an Austro-Serbian crisis that dangerously threatened peace in the Balkans, and the larger issue of regularizing or legitimating the Austrian and Bulgarian actions. England, France, and Russia favored a conference to alter the Berlin Treaty, but Austria objected if the annexation were to be subject to a decision by the powers. In her opposition Austria was loyally supported by her German ally.[1] Iswolski was still traveling in western Europe. In Paris, London, and Berlin, he received kind words and many smart luncheons but no encouragement in his aspirations with regard to the Straits. The British especially were averse to opening up this question at the moment, as they had just regained a preponderance of influence in Constantinople with the seizure of power by the Young Turks. This position they were disinclined to jeopardize. After his proposals with regard to the Straits had been vetoed in London and Paris, Iswolski stood with empty hands—an embarrassing position for any diplomat. More disconcerting and alarming was the criticism at home. The prime minister, Stolypin, demanded of the Czar that Iswolski be disavowed and an official statement issued that he had acted without the consent of the government. Russia, he insisted, should not consent to the annexation of a Slavonic land by a German state. The Czar, however, demurred as Iswolsky insisted that he had not made anything like a "Buchlau bargain" and that he was the victim of Aehrenthal's falseness and double dealing. This disavowal and the subsequent disagreement over the conference issue produced a personal breach between the two foreign ministers and a resort to press polemics that generated great friction and reflected little credit on either party.

It was owing mainly to Iswolski's determination to salvage something from the wreckage of his plans that the crisis dragged on through the winter. His proposal for a conference to consider the Bosnian question and compensation for Serbia and Montenegro gained diplomatic support in Paris and London but not in Berlin and Vienna. Meanwhile, the tension increased between Austria and Serbia until Aehrenthal and the chief of staff, Conrad von Hötzendorf, agreed that they would meet Serbian intransigence with force if necessary. Russian support of Serbia was not taken too seriously, since everyone knew that in this kind of Balkan poker game the Russians at the moment held paltry cards.

In the diplomatic entanglement, Aehrenthal skillfully used the artichoke technique, plucking one leaf after another. Decisive for the out-

1. William II's immediate response had been highly explosive: "The lying hypocrite Ferdinand, and the aged and venerable Emperor appear together on the stage amid Bengal lights as despoilers of Turkey." However, Bülow expressed fidelity to the alliance "without equivocation, restriction or recrimination." L. Albertini, *The Origins of the War of 1914*, 3 vols. (London, 1952–57), I, 228–29.

come of the crisis was the conclusion, first, of an Austrian agreement with Turkey on February 26, 1909. Austria-Hungary agreed to pay 2.5 million Turkish pounds as compensation for state domains within the provinces, and in return Turkey recognized the annexation. Bulgaria concluded a similar agreement with the Turkish government. The boycott of Austrian trade soon tapered off and relations with Turkey became normal again. The Austrian-Turkish agreement fed the fires of agitation in Serbia, but Aehrenthal could now demand recognition of the annexation by the remaining signatories of the Berlin Treaty. Serbia's claims for compensation were likewise weakened.

In the final phase of the crisis the conference plan was shelved and the Russians requested Germany to use her good offices in Vienna to devise a procedure that would be acceptable to the parties concerned. In agreement with Vienna, Berlin proposed that Article 25 of the Berlin Treaty be abrogated and Austria's annexation of the provinces regularized by an exchange of notes among the signatories. The German proposal was incorporated in a needlessly peremptory note drafted by the acting secretary of state, Kiderlen-Wächter, who fancied himself the heir of Bismarck's style and genius. Kiderlen, impatient with Russian equivocation, bluntly demanded that Iswolski answer yes or no. If this was not an ultimatum it bore the spirit of one. In a Russian ministerial council the alternative to acceptance—which would probably involve an armed clash—was considered. The Russian minister for war stated formally that while their chances of success against Austria were considerable, the same could not be said with regard to a war in which Austria was supported by Germany. Without consulting Paris and London the Russian government accepted the German formula. For Bülow and Kiderlen it was a diplomatic victory, but it was also a needless and senseless humiliation of Russia and its foreign minister, who admittedly had made a bad blunder. Although the text of the German communication was not immediately published, its tone and content were thoroughly aired in diplomatic circles. In Entente capitals it was a stimulus to closer cooperation in their confrontations with the Austro-German combination.

The Austro-Serbian dispute was mediated by Sir Edward Grey, who performed more diplomatically than Kiderlen. Austrian policy makers were determined to use force against Serbia if she persisted in a course of violent intransigence. When the Russian government accepted the German formula for legalizing the annexation it was apparent that

Serbia could expect no diplomatic or military support from this quarter. Now all the powers joined in a move to coerce the Serbs. The text of a note—its terms agreed to by Vienna—was formulated by the British and jointly presented in Belgrade. The joint presentation had an inescapable implication—that if Serbia rejected the advice of the mediators she would be left to her fate. In this instance the great powers were willing to coerce Serbia in the interests of peace, which they refused to do in 1914. The dictated pledge which Serbia then gave to the Austrian government recognized the annexation and renounced claims to compensation; Serbia further promised to cease propagandizing and agitating among the Austrian Serbs, to suppress all guerrilla bands on their common frontiers, and to conduct herself henceforth as a good neighbor. The subsequent violation of these commitments was the basis of Austria's indictment of Serbia in the ultimatum of 1914.

The crisis had consequences both immediate and far-ranging. The wrangling of the foreign ministers over a protracted period was productive of much irritation and suspicion. Aehrenthal and Iswolski, moreover, had destroyed the entente or balance which Austria and Russia had mainatained in the Balkans since 1897. Publicly the new Triple Entente did not prove to be an invincible combination diplomatically or militarily. France circumspectly held back throughout the crisis; and the British, who at first were firmer in supporting Russia, in the end shifted to a mediating position. However, Bülow's assertion that the diplomatic victory had rendered the Triple Entente and the encirclement policy ineffective was mistaken. In fact, the Germans had gained a Pyrrhic victory, for Russia was now irrevocably committed to France and Britain. And then there were the logical military consequences. Conversations between Helmuth von Moltke and Conrad von Hötzendorf over several months resulted in agreements for joint military operations in accordance with the Schlieffen plan. These understandings, together with Bülow's dogmatic interpretation of the Austro-German alliance, transformed Bismarck's defensive arrangement into a German obligation to bolster Austria's deteriorating position in southeastern Europe.

For Russia the Bosnian crisis was a significant turning point in that it marked the beginning of the rebuilding of Russian armed forces on a major scale. After the Russo-Japanese War there had been a reform flurry in the military and naval establishments. A National Defense Council was created with one of the grand dukes as president. This ensured its failure, and little was done to repair the damage of a disastrous war. Indeed, until 1909 the mission of the Russian army was mainly one of civil rather than national defense. The Bosnian humiliation changed this. The crown council, convened in March, 1909, heard the minister of war, General Rödiger, state that the Russian army was not prepared to take the offensive against a major power, or successfully to defend itself against such an enemy. In consequence of this grave admission the minister of war was replaced by the chief of the general staff, General Sukhomlinov. Sweeping reforms in army administration followed, and large sums were made available to rebuild Russia's military power. The diplomats, the court, the army leaders, and the publicists really brought about Rödiger's replacement, which was followed after a decent interval by that of Iswolski. And all united in demanding that the army become again an instrument of foreign policy appropriate to a great power.[2]

2. THE ANGLO-GERMAN TENSION

While Russia and Austria were playing with fire in the Balkans, the international scene in western Europe was dominated by the antagonism between England and Germany. The stereotype of the "German Menace" was deeply implanted in the British foreign service, in Parliament, and in a large part of the political press. Through her economic development and by unfair competition, Germany, it was held, sought to displace Britain as the leading industrial and trading nation; Germany was also striving for political hegemony on the Continent; and the Tirpitz naval program was a direct threat to Britain's security. The latter—the German naval challenge—eclipsed all other concerns in the relations of the two powers. This was the sober opinion of Count Metternich, German ambassador in London:

The uneasiness over economic rivalry, and the political embitterment engendered by various causes, have retreated before a new factor that has forced them far into the background. This new factor is the fear, not of our economic evolution but of our development in military-naval power. There is scarcely an Englishman of importance who does not see in the

2. W. A. Sukhomlinov, *Erinnerungen* (Berlin, 1924), pp. 207–24. This account of the Bosnian crisis and its significance is based on Albertini, *The Origins of the War of 1914*, I, 190–300; Bernadotte E. Schmitt, *The Annexation of Bosnia* (Cambridge, Eng., 1937), pp. 164–253; Sidney B. Fay, *The Origins of the World War*, 2 vols. (New York, 1928), I, 364–406; Hans Uebersberger, *Österreich zwischen Russland und Serbien* (Cologne and Graz, 1958), pp. 1–41.

German navy, in the dimensions prescribed by the navy law, and in the tempo of construction, a serious danger to his country.[3]

All the loyalties, traditions, and sentiments that clustered around Continental armies were concentrated in Britain on the navy. The British Naval Discipline Act summed it up in these words: "Upon the Navy, under the good providence of God, depends the wealth, safety, and strength of the United Kingdom." Thus any apparent threat to Britain's naval predominance was a national concern. In the beginning, the British attitude toward the German naval program had been one of vexed anxiety that another nation should contemplate challenging them at sea. As the German fleet became a reality and the building program more ambitious, opinion in Britain hardened, and in 1908–1909 a new outbreak of armament fever seized the public and generated new tensions and animosities.

Understanding of British anxiety over naval security must take into account the increasing popularity of a new type of literature dealing with imaginary wars, the armed invasion of neighboring states, and the shape and novelty of the war of the future. This innovating literature—*guerres imaginaires*—was born with the publication in 1871 of Lieutenant Colonel G. T. Chesney's *Battle of Dorking*. With emphasis on the "signal of alarm," "the cry of dismay," "the sound of gunfire," and "the shrieks of terrified villagers," Chesney's popular thriller was imitated henceforth by writers in France, Germany, Italy, and Austria. Stories of the "war to come" were an annual crop until a real war put an end to this type of literature.[4]

Written by military men, active or retired, and by civilian hacks, these tales usually portrayed the invasion of a country by the historic enemy, or a war that was to be expected next year or the year after. The French literature was revanchist against Germany and England, and the British always cast the French in the role of aggressor. This remained the custom until 1903, when the popular *Riddle of the Sands* for the first time put the Germans in the role of invader, a part that they played continuously thereafter. The German reply was Niemann's *Der Weltkrieg,* which was translated in 1904 as *The Coming Conquest of England.* In the "Wake up England" campaign, following the Boer War, these counterfeit tales supported Lord Roberts' agitation for

3. Metternich to Bülow, Jan. 1, 1909; *Die Grosse Politik,* XXVIII, 47.

4. I. F. Clarke, *Voices Prophesying War, 1763–1984* (London, 1966), p. 44, and especially Chap. IV, "Politics and the Pattern of the Next Great War, 1880–1914."

compulsory military service as well as Sir John Fisher's skyrocketing naval estimates.

In March, 1906, the *Daily Mail* began serialization of a commissioned work by William Le Queux. Entitled *The Invasion of 1910,* the naval chapters were written by the distinguished authority H. W. Wilson and the preface by Lord Roberts. To advertise the serial, Northcliffe had sandwich men dressed in blue uniforms with spiked helmets parading the streets of London advertising the revelations that were to be read in the *Daily Mail.*[5] In book form *The Invasion of 1910* sold more than a million copies and was translated into twenty-seven languages. Thus universal literacy, mass journalism, and popular fiction encouraged the unthinking and the gullible in England and Germany to see themselves as inevitable enemies.

Despite invasion and espionage scares, and the agitation of conscriptionists, the British public still put its trust in the navy. As long as the navy was supreme in the North Sea and the Channel they could, as Sir John Fisher assured them, "sleep safely in their beds." But when this supremacy was questioned on the highest authority, as it was in the spring of 1909, the mass feeling of insecurity built up by successive spy and invasion scares rose abruptly to panic proportions.

In Britain it was axiomatic that the only force standing between Germany and the accomplishment of her far-reaching designs was Britain's sea power. German naval advances, therefore, became the accepted means of reconciling the British electorate to rising naval expenditure. British naval estimates were in a sense "Made in Germany." It never failed, moreover, that in parliament and press the discussion went beyond the range of the technical and statistical and overflowed into the field of policy, aspiration, and purpose as symbolized by the German naval program.

Since the scare of 1909 was the culmination of preceding alarms, some attention must be given to naval developments antedating the great "Dreadnought, Fear-All" panic. With the appointment of Sir John Fisher as first sea lord in 1904, the British navy entered upon a period of venturesome reform and modernization without precedent. Assuming his position as technical chief for the navy, Fisher found a

5. *Ibid.*, pp. 144–45. Concurrently P. G. Wodehouse made his debut as a writer with an invasion tale entitled *The Swoop! or How Clarence Saved England.* It was a "spoof" but also a "flop"—readers were not amused by such folly!

barnacle-incrusted service; but at his retirement in 1910 he turned over to his successor a technically modern and highly trained fighting force. The publicist J. L. Garvin described Fisher as "the genius incarnate of technical change." His slogan throughout the reforming years was "The efficiency of the navy and its instant readiness for war."[6]

Fisher's name will always be linked with the launching of H.M.S. *Dreadnought* and the transition from the older capital ship to the new all-big-gun type which became standard in the world's navies. Fisher's dreadnought, completed in 1906, was larger, faster, and more heavily armed than any capital ship previously constructed. Not only were the specifications of the new vessel puffed to the skies, but the speed of construction—approximately eighteen months—was advertised as a demonstration of England's technical-engineering superiority. The whole procedure and its treatment in the press was a challenge to the other naval powers to enter the race if they thought they had a chance.

Whether it was wise to have taken the lead in a type of ship that made rapidly obsolete all current ships of the line, in which Britain possessed a three-to-one superiority, is arguable, although technologically Fisher was in the right. But the new model did not permanently paralyze or discourage the Germans, as Fisher boasted it would. Instead, Tirpitz and his staff went doggedly to work designing a German version of the dreadnought and widening the Kiel Canal to accommodate the larger vessels. In the long run this development was advantageous to Germany and the other naval powers, for it gave them the opportunity to start even with the British in this dominant type of capital ship.

The immediate advantage, however, rested with Britain. For eighteen months no capital ship was begun in the German yards. Two ships of the dreadnought type were authorized in 1906 but not begun until 1907. Three more were authorized in 1907 and their construction undertaken, while in 1908 the amended naval law provided for four ships annually for the next four years. The British in 1908 had ten ships of the new type in commission or under construction. With the reluctant approval of the admiralty, the cabinet provided for only two dreadnoughts in the 1908 estimates. But in that year under the new

6. On Fisher's reforms and administration see the study in depth by A. J. Marder, *From the Dreadnought to Scapa Flow*, Vol. I, *The Road to War, 1904-1914* (London, 1961), pp. 28-46, 151-211.

law, the Germans would increase their construction to four annually. The British, to maintain their two-to-one ratio in this all-important category, would have to expand their program in 1909 or persuade the Germans to contract theirs. Anxious to fulfill its pledge of "peace, retrenchment and reform," the Liberal cabinet sought during 1908 to effect an agreement with German authorities that would secure Britain's predominance without incurring large additional naval expenditures in 1909. When the overtures made by King Edward and Sir Charles Hardinge at Cronberg were rudely rejected by the Kaiser, everyone conversant with naval matters knew that at least four dreadnoughts would have to be undertaken in 1909 to give Britain a safe margin in 1912–1913.

When the admiralty asked for six ships in the 1909 budget, trouble developed immediately in the cabinet. Lloyd George and Winston Churchill took the lead, insisting that four would give them a safe margin in 1912. The admiralty held out for six, basing its case in part on unconfirmed reports that the Germans were accelerating their scheduled construction and increasing their building capacity. Five cabinet sessions during January and February failed to break the deadlock. At the last session Asquith, who favored six, brought forth the compromise that all accepted—four ships to be authorized, and four contingent vessels to be laid down if developments in the German program seemed to justify this action. This was the "curious and characteristic" solution to which Churchill subsequently referred: "The Admiralty had demanded six: the economists had offered four: and we finally compromised on eight."[7]

When Asquith presented the naval estimates to the Commons on March 16, he had to justify the increases to his Radical supporters, who demanded a budget for social reform rather than naval expansion. Asquith stated that the four certain and the four contingent ships were required by reports of German acceleration by six months of two of the dreadnoughts of the 1909 schedule and that by 1912 Germany might have thirteen or even seventeen of the new type of vessels. Balfour, leading the opposition, tried to show that the government instead of

7. *The World Crisis* (New York, 1923), I, 33. Fisher in a ragging letter to Churchill (March 4, 1909) suggested that the four contingent dreadnoughts be named *Winston, Churchill, Lloyd,* and *George.* "How they would fight! Uncircumventable!" R. H. Bacon, *The Life of Lord Fisher of Kilverstone,* 2 vols. (New York, 1929), II, 91.

doing too much was doing too little. He had information from private sources—British armaments manufacturers—that indicated the Germans would, or could, have seventeen or possibly twenty-one of these capital ships in 1912. Britain, he implied, was in grave danger of losing her supremacy in big ships within the next two years. As Balfour and Asquith compared notes on the German building rate from the front benches in the House of Commons, it reminded one reporter of a council of war. News of the government's admissions stunned the country and inspired a popular panic unprecedented in recent British history. In attempting to prove to his Radical followers that the cabinet's proposals were not excessive, Asquith laid himself open to the charge that they were not doing enough, and the gravity of his words spread alarm throughout the country.

Asquith's tactics were clearly at fault; he had moved the naval issue into the arena of party politics and mass agitation. For a week following the Commons debate, the publicity in the press was of a scare and panic nature. When the Conservatives proposed a motion of censure the naval estimates became the party issue of the hour. The "dreadnought gap" was the theme of every editorial writer, the subject of comment by every member of Parliament addressing his constituency, and the subject of every special meeting of service clubs and patriotic societies. The provincial leaders of the Conservative party encouraged the agitation, and the important armaments firms and shipbuilders issued public statements on how they were happily prepared to save the country by building more dreadnoughts.

The popular mass-circulation press cultivated the scare for its news appeal. Under an alarmist headline—"Britain's Danger: What the Crisis Has Revealed"—the *Daily Mail* repeated Balfour's prediction of twenty-one German dreadnoughts in 1912, while the government's proposal of four capital ships and four contingent vessels was denounced as "invertebrate trifling with the greatest emergency in our recent history." "There is only one way of safety: Four Dreadnoughts in June and four in November. Without that the Empire is on the knees of the Gods three years hence." The Tory political press took up the chant, "We want eight! And we won't wait!"

From the time the Conservatives proposed a vote of censure the dreadnought issue became an out-and-out party fight. Asquith speaking before the House on March 22 endeavored to abate the public alarm and throw responsibility for the scare upon the Conservatives. Liberal party journalists took their cue from Asquith's clever speech. "The plain truth is," wrote one London correspondent, "that the Tories are making a flagitious use of the Navy scare for party purposes. . . . If they cannot sail to power on Tariff Reform they mean to try to do so on Dreadnoughts." Many speakers and letter writers denounced the government for wasting money on social reform schemes that was needed for national defense. "We cannot afford to give away on social schemes of improvement what is wanted for national insurance," wrote one correspondent. And a letter writer in the *Times* roundly scolded the chancellor of the exchequer, "who seeks to rob hen roosts to pay for the Socialist eggs he has hatched."[8]

The Liberals easily defeated the Conservative motion of censure when it was debated in the House on March 29. Much of the shock at Asquith's revelations had abated, and public assurances from German authorities that they were not secretly building additional capital ships were not without some moderating effect. However, at the end of July, the first lord of the admiralty announced that the four contingent ships would be made a part of the 1909 program and would not be charged against the program for 1910. There were no secret German dreadnoughts; in fact the German schedule of capital ship construction was not fulfilled. There was also a delay of eight months on the 1910 ships as a result of another Fisher surprise—the 13.5 naval gun. In March, 1912, Germany had only nine dreadnoughts in commission instead of thirteen, while England had fifteen commissioned and four more ready for tests and trials. Not until the spring of 1914 did Germany have seventeen capital ships of the dreadnought class in commission. In retrospect it is difficult to dissent from the judgment expressed by Alan Bourgoyne, editor of the *Navy League Annual*, that the dreadnought panic was "one of the most portentous pieces of Parliamentary humbug ever practised on the electorate."[9]

In the publicity that emanated from the press and platform, demands for a preventive war were not lacking. These were duly reported in the German press, where they stimulated like-minded people to demand more armaments as insurance against attack. But the public reaction in

8. On the political and publicity aspects of the crisis see Oron J. Hale, *Publicity and Diplomacy*, pp. 350–63.
9. Quoted in Philip Noel-Baker, *The Private Manufacture of Armaments*, 2 vols. (New York, 1937), I, 497.

Germany was less vigorous than might have been expected. The peak of the scare coincided with the last phase of the Bosnian affair and the crisis in block politics which brought about Bülow's replacement by Bethmann Hollweg. It did point up, however, the case for reducing tension by some kind of agreement with the British on the naval question, and conversations with this in view were initiated by the new chancellor. As a basis for discussion the Germans proposed a slower tempo in fleet construction and concessions in the Baghdad Railway against a British promise of neutrality in the event of an armed clash between the Dual and Triple Alliances. The neutrality formula was wholly unacceptable to Grey and his professional advisers, while in Germany the Emperor and the navy department had no sincere desire to curtail by agreement their naval program. Bethmann Hollweg never gave up hope of reaching a political understanding with Britain as discussions continued intermittently for two years. A relaxation of tension and a substantial improvement in their public relations were about the only recorded gains. Then the negotiations were shelved as the Agadir crisis burst upon Europe.

3. THE AGADIR CRISIS

The crisis that carried Europe to the brink of war in the summer of 1911 had its origin in the clash of French and German imperialisms, but when the British government intervened in support of France it turned into a nasty public quarrel between Berlin and London, with injurious consequences both domestic and international. The Algeciras settlement had not worked well; Morocco was not pacified; the French had not abandoned their determination to add the country to their north African empire, and the Franco-German agreement of 1909 for economic cooperation in Morocco had yielded little of value to either party. Meanwhile, French control expanded in the port towns and in the adjacent territory. The spreading of French influence, like a drop of oil, gave Germany no convenient occasion for intervention until the summer of 1911, when rebellious tribesmen, resentful of French pressures on their weak sultan, revolted against the authority of their ruler. Finally, under the pretext that native unrest threatened European lives, a French military force was dispatched to the sultan's capital at Fez. Soon the Spanish followed the French example and occupied Larache. Thus page after page of the Act of Algeciras became mere scraps of paper. A salvage operation of major proportions would be necessary if

Germany realized anything from the claims asserted and defended at Algeciras.

Three alternatives were open to Berlin: first, to demand that France observe the letter and spirit of the Algeciras Act; second, to effect a partition of Morocco among France, Germany, and Spain; third, to acquiesce in a *fait accompli* and secure compensation for the surrender of German rights. The first possibility was unrealistic, as the Act of Algeciras was practically a dead letter; the second, while appealing to Berlin, seemed impossible of achievement in light of British support of France; the third, withdrawal and compensation, while less attractive than the second, seemed to involve the least danger in accomplishment. It was, therefore, on the basis of prospective colonial concessions in central Africa (the French Congo) that the Emperor authorized Bethmann and the foreign secretary, Kiderlen-Wächter, to open negotiations with the French. The latter had already indicated that they were willing to consider a reasonable horse trade when Kiderlen broached the subject in a meeting with the French ambassador, Jules Cambon—then en route to Paris—at Bad Kissingen on June 20. Although Kiderlen was not specific as to a *quid pro quo,* he said to Cambon as they parted: "Bring us back something from Paris."

As no French offer was immediately forthcoming, Kiderlen proceeded to the second step of his tactical plan—reinforcement of the demand for compensation. On July 1, the German gunboat *Panther,* returning from South Africa, was ordered to the Moroccan port of Agadir, ostensibly for the same purpose for which the French had occupied Fez—to protect German lives and property, although these were extremely scarce in southern Morocco. This move, described charitably by the mild and moderate De Bunsen, British ambassador at Madrid, as "high-handed and needlessly aggressive," had more than a single objective. Kiderlen wanted to put France under heavy pressure by holding Agadir as a pledge, and he wanted to be in a strategic position if circumstances should open the way for a tripartite division of Morocco. However, the "Panther's Spring" was a grave tactical mistake; for it gave rise immediately, in both press and diplomatic circles of the Entente countries, to the complaint that Germany always wanted to negotiate with a pistol on the table. While Kiderlen's "conversational opening" at Agadir had a bad press, it also misled some German interest groups as to the government's diplomatic priorities.

Especially was this true of the colonial, Pan-German, and industrial interests, from whence came immediately a clamorous demand for German acquisition of southern Morocco. In the press these elements campaigned vigorously against abandonment of territorial compensation in Morocco.

When Cambon and Kiderlen resumed their conversations the French ambassador had nothing specific to offer. Finally Kiderlen, pointing to a map of Africa, indicated that the Germans wanted all of the French Congo. The shock was great, although it was foreseen that the transfer to France of some German territory in the area might be considered as part of the deal. When the French, seeking support, communicated the German demand to London, and at the same time leaked it to the press, British officials were taken aback at the magnitude of the demands. Immediately they concluded that German claims were inadmissible and so far-reaching as to constitute aggression. The foreign office advisers insisted that if they did not line up with France the French might give in to Germany and the Entente would be devalued. Also if the German demands in the Congo were unacceptable, the conversations might turn back to southern Morocco as an object of compensation. Whether a German foothold on the west coast of Morocco would be tolerable to the world's leading sea power was an unanswered question in British official circles.[10]

On July 21 Grey invited the German ambassador to call at the foreign office. During their interview Grey expressed concern at the reports of German demands upon France, which amounted in his words to "a cession of the French Congo." He indicated also that he was disquieted by the reports of German activity at Agadir. Should Moroccan territory become an object of discussion, then the British government must become an active party to the negotiations. Before Kiderlen's reassuring reply could reach London from Berlin, Grey and Asquith sanctioned the setting off of a rhetorical rocket into the heavily charged atmosphere.

10. On the Agadir crisis the following are basic: *Die Grosse Politik,* XXIX, 142–293; *Documents diplomatiques français,* 41 vols. (Paris, 1929–59), 2d ser., XIII, 673, and Vol. XIV, *passim; British Documents on the Origins of the War,* 11 vols. (London, 1926–38), VII, 322–481; Ernst Jäckh, *Kiderlen-Wächter, der Staatsmann und Mensch,* 2 vols. (Berlin, 1924), II, 122–42; Ima C. Barlow, *The Agadir Crisis* (Chapel Hill, N.C., 1940), pp. 207–324; Hale, *Publicity and Diplomacy,* 381–419, on the press aspects, especially Lloyd George's Mansion House speech.

The nationalistic statement which Lloyd George interpolated in his speech to the bankers at the Mansion House was drafted by Asquith, Grey, and Lloyd George after a cabinet meeting at which Grey had expressed concern at the tension that was building up. Neither Grey's subsequent statement in Parliament nor the published *British Documents on the Origins of the War* clarifies the grounds for resorting to publicity before the German foreign office had time to reply to Metternich's report from London.

As to Lloyd George's statement, there was no clear indication in its wording that he was referring to the Moroccan issue. But striking a strong national note, the chancellor of the exchequer said that Britain would make great sacrifices in the interest of peace, but if a situation were to develop in which Britain was treated "as if she were of no account in the Cabinet of Nations, then I say emphatically that peace at that price would be a humiliation intolerable for a great country like ours to endure." This was a bit of spread-eagleism foreign to Lloyd George, who only a few years previously during the Boer War had been branded a "miserable pacifist." The significance of the statement was not immediately discernible, but the London press was apparently well briefed and on the next morning sent the message speeding on its way to its calculated destination—Berlin. With remarkable uniformity press headlines and editorials announced: "Britain Warns Germany— National Honour Is at Stake." Lloyd George's words were interpreted as a declaration of solidarity with France, a warning to Germany, and an assertion of Britain's right to a voice in the matter of compensations.[11]

In Germany the reaction was bitterly resentful. Kiderlen fired off an arrogant protest at the press interpretation of Lloyd George's statement. The delivery of this note caused Grey to warn the navy chiefs that the British fleet might be attacked at any moment without warning. In the moderate, liberal, and democratic press in Germany resentment was intense though restrained. To these journals it seemed that the British chancellor of the exchequer had interposed a provocative veto upon satisfactory compensation in central Africa, no less than in Morocco; Britain's policy of blocking legitimate German expansion at every turn was becoming a danger to world peace. The reaction in

11. Indeed it was all of these, but historically it was an instance of epic mistiming in view of the state of Franco-German negotiations. Hale, *Publicity and Diplomacy,* pp. 388–90.

National Liberal, Pan-German, and independent chauvinist papers was frenzied and venomous. On the threadbare pretext of her vital interests, England intervenes whenever Germany moves to secure a place in the sun, was the universal complaint. Britain had always drawn profit from the quarrels of Continental neighbors; that is why she seeks now to disrupt the negotiations between France and Germany. King Edward is gone, but his policy continues. Lloyd George's saber rattling shows the trend of British policy toward Germany since the turn of the century. But Agadir must not become Fashoda, they declared.

By July 26 the press agitation had reached war-scare proportions and all kinds of alarm signals were sounded in London—a special cabinet meeting was called, a British fleet visit to Norway was canceled, and there was a run on Lloyd's for war-risk insurance. An official statement released through Reuter's Agency and a statement by Asquith in the House of Commons (July 27) relaxed the tension somewhat. The prime minister denied that Britain wished to participate in the Franco-German negotiations and he hoped a solution acceptable to both parties would be reached. "The question of Morocco itself bristles with difficulties," he told the House, "but outside Morocco, in other parts of west Africa, we should not think of attempting to interfere with territorial arrangements considered reasonable by those who are more directly interested." Asquith's words had a moderating effect in Germany, but resentment did not disappear at once. A moderate liberal editor and an internationalist, Theodor Wolff, could not conceal a certain bitterness over the general direction of British policy. The term "British interests," he wrote, was a notoriously elastic concept. "The world is already divided, and England takes pains to see that nothing is traded or changed."[12]

After the polemics had abated, German-French negotiations were resumed in early August and continued through the fall. On November 4 the agreements were signed and placed on the docket for approval by the respective parliaments. Germany got much less than the whole of the French Congo, in fact about 100,000 square miles, or approximately half the area originally demanded by Kiderlen. To make the cession palatable to French public opinion Germany ceded a small area of the Cameroon territory in the neighborhood of Lake Chad. France, however, was the great gainer, for she was at last free to impose a protectorate on Morocco. With this addition to Tunis and

12. *Berliner Tageblatt*, No. 379 (July 28, 1911).

Algeria, France now possessed a handsome north African empire. In the German press and in the Reichstag the judgment on the accords was extremely unfavorable. The *Berliner Tageblatt* (Nov. 10, 1911) summarized the meaning of Bethmann Hollweg's speech recommending the agreements to the Reichstag: "We have secured what it was possible to secure without war, and we refuse to make war for Morocco."

Injected into every comment in the press and in the Reichstag was bitter criticism of the part played by England. Some complaints were dignified, some were outrageous diatribes, but all came to the same conclusion: The diplomatic defeat suffered by the government was in the final analysis a charge upon the English account. Britain was the real victor because she had asserted her pretension to be the world's arbiter and had vetoed Germany's legitimate claims. The debate in the country turned on Anglo-German relations rather than relations with France. The diplomatic exchanges between London and Berlin were made available in detail to the Reichstag committee dealing with the Moroccan accords, and this drew Bethmann and Kiderlen into an unpleasant exchange of public statements with Grey and Asquith. Tension and discord mounted with retrospective disclosures of military and naval preparations during the summer, and the close brush with war.

In the British cabinet, in Parliament, and in the press a sharp backlash was generated by the foreign policy revelations of the autumn. The dissatisfaction latent in Radical, Labor, and isolationist circles with regard to the direction of England's foreign policy now surfaced and found vigorous expression. Critics focused their complaints on Grey's entente policy, which consisted in "pandering to Russia and irritating Germany." An amazing current of retrospective criticism swept the country and Parliament in the winter of 1911–1912. The Cabinet's response to the expressed dissatisfaction over the dangerous disagreement with Germany was the Haldane mission to Berlin in February, 1912. Although this move was much misliked by the foreign office professionals and its consequences were not far-reaching, it does not altogether deserve the description "a pilgrimage of misunderstanding."

Given the desires of the two governments, the area of Haldane's conversations in Berlin fell naturally into three parts: a formula of neutrality, or "a political understanding," naval limitation, and colonial matters. Haldane returned from Germany in an optimistic mood, but the negotiations on a neutrality formula, which would have weakened Britain's position in the Triple Entente, were soon at an impasse, as were also the negotiations on naval limitation. Only the discussion of colonial problems bore fruit in the Portuguese colonies agreement and the Baghdad Railway accord, both being signed and awaiting ratification when war broke out in 1914.[13]

With regard to the critical naval issue Haldane's mission was a failure. In the German military minds the situation had its simple logic: They had received a box on the ears over Morocco—they must bring in an armaments bill to show the world that they would not take another. Tirpitz with the Kaiser's encouragement was pressing for a new navy law. During his visit, Haldane was given a copy of the draft *Novelle,* and it was immediately analyzed in the British admiralty. What was found to be alarming was not the building program but the measures and expenditures to keep a larger part of the German fleet fully manned and ready for action. After the negotiations on the neutrality formula had failed, the *Novelle* was published and in due time enacted. Basically the measure afforded Britain considerable relief from pressure, as the building rate dropped from four to two capital ships annually beginning in 1912, with three additional ships—they had now reached superdreadnought size—to be added to the program at unspecified future dates. The building ratio was now 16 to 10 in dreadnoughts, and while no formal agreement was signed and Winston Churchill, the new first lord of the admiralty, continued to speak of the need for a "naval building holiday," this ratio was tacitly accepted by the two governments.[14]

It is apparent that by 1912 a good deal of water had gone into the German naval wine. Even the most enthusiastic navalists were becoming aware of Germany's national limitations—her resources did not permit her to maintain the largest army establishment in Europe, the most costly system of social insurance and welfare, and at the same time compete with England for first place as a naval power. The change was noted by the British naval attaché in Berlin, who reported that he now frequently heard Germans say: "Of course you English have a very large navy compared to us; we must put our strength into

13. For the Haldane mission, see *British Documents,* VI, 666–761; Fay, *Origins of the World War,* I, 299 ff.; Hale, *Publicity and Diplomacy,* pp. 420–25.
14. For a more detailed treatment of the naval problem, see Marder, *From the Dreadnought to Scapa Flow,* I, 274–87, 311–27.

our army." The Balkan wars also shifted the emphasis to Germany's Continental position. In fact, all the major powers began to "beef up" their land forces. Germany led off with the army bill of 1913, which was financed by an unprecedented capital levy. In Russia large additions were made to the army and more capital was expended on strategic railroads. The point of all this arming—the fear that it expressed and the further apprehension that it induced—was that it necessitated a reconsideration of Germany's security requirements. The mirage of *Weltpolitik* based on a navy rivaling that of the leading world power began to fade before the reality of Germany's position as a Continental state dependent upon her land forces and alliances for national security and existence. As the pressure of the great German army bills was exerted on the Continent, the naval pressure on Britain was correspondingly relaxed.[15]

Although policy makers and circumstances moved toward a détente in Anglo-German relations, at the same time Britain's defense requirements dictated that she assume more specific obligations toward her associates in the Triple Entente, especially France. After the North Sea, the Mediterranean was of greatest concern to Britain. The Tripolitan war, the dreadnought construction programs of Italy and Austria-Hungary, as well as the growth of Germany's naval power, were components of Britain's Mediterranean difficulty. The problem was how to maintain superiority in the North Sea and the Channel while fully protecting their position in the Mediterranean. A greatly enlarged building program was one alternative, a political agreement with Germany was another, and still another was an agreement with France on the redisposition of their naval forces. This last was the solution chosen by the British cabinet. In September, 1912, Britain's Malta-based squadron was moved to Gibraltar and the Gibraltar fleet withdrawn to home waters. Concurrently the French forces based on the Channel and Atlantic ports were concentrated in the Mediterranean, which gave France a clear superiority over the combined fleets of Italy and Austria.

France could not leave her western coasts unguarded without a commitment from England for their defense in the event of war with

15. By 1912 it was obvious that Germany could hardly achieve more than third place in naval rank. The United States was destined to be the second-largest naval power and, with the completion of the Panama Canal, the predominant naval presence in the Pacific. Already in 1911–1912, in ships of the line, armored cruisers, personnel, and budgets Britain stood first, the United States second, and Germany third.

the Triple Alliance. Naval conversations of a technical nature began in August, 1912, with cabinet approval, and in November the historic exchange of notes between Grey and Cambon took place. The British being averse to a "tight agreement," the note stated that joint planning was contingent and did not commit the governments to participate in any war that might arise. Britain agreed to consult and consider joint measures in the event of an unprovoked attack by a third power, or in circumstances that might threaten the general peace. This interpretation also governed the joint plans developed by the French and British army staffs since 1906.

There is little to be added to judgments by other scholars and experts on the British commitment to France. Certainly a serious moral obligation was incurred, and this became a matter of deep concern in the 1914 crisis. Sir Arthur Nicolson put it succinctly when he said that it "committed the government to a guarantee which would involve England either in a breach of faith or a war with Germany."[16]

A signal result then of the second Moroccan crisis, like the crisis of 1905-1906, was to bind France and England more closely and to consolidate the Triple Entente. The Agadir affair also set off a chain reaction of severe crises and regional wars—the Tripolitan war and the first and second Balkan wars—that brought Europe to its final crisis in 1914.

4. TWO WARS AND THEIR DIPLOMATIC CONSEQUENCES

The Moroccan crisis precipitated action by Italy in respect to the Turkish dependencies of Tripoli and Cyrenaica. If France gained a protectorate over Morocco, then Italy must maintain a Mediterranean balance by foreclosing on Tripoli. Years of effort by Italian foreign ministers had gone into the preparation of the ground for the acquisition of Libya as an Italian colony. Beginning in 1887, pledges of support or benevolent neutrality in realizing her aspirations had been secured from Germany, Austria, England, France, and finally, Russia. In return Italy had given away very little because she had little to give. In 1912 the time arrived to realize on all the mortgages and clearances.

16. Marder, *From the Dreadnought to Scapa Flow,* I, 309. "Grey was only technically correct [writes Marder] when, in informing the House of Commons for the first time of the military and naval arrangements with France, 31 July 1914, he explained that the notes did not bind England to enter the war."

Circumstances favored action. Turkish hostility to Italy's expanding interests in Libya generated frequent clashes between Turkish and Italian officials. But in the calculations of the Italian premier, Giovanni Giolitti, it was plainly a matter of acting in Libya before it went the way of Tunis—into the hands of another power. French acquisition of Morocco was a spur to action. When the preliminary agreement between France and Germany was announced on September 23, 1911, Italy immediately delivered an ultimatum to Turkey followed by a declaration of war on the next day. Not even her allies were given advance notice of the ultimatum. To the powers Italy's action was a most unwelcome event, since it threatened wider complications, especially in the Balkans and the Aegean. However, since Italy was asserting previously validated claims, the powers could only work to localize the war and keep it from spreading to European Turkey.

The initial operations went well for Italian arms, and Tripoli and Tobruk were shortly in Italian hands, but the indigenous Arabs had no wish to change one overlord for another and soon put up a surprising resistance. In the end the invasion and pacification of the hinterland required large forces, and was not completed until 1916. Somewhat premature was a royal decree issued on November 4, 1911, proclaiming Italian sovereignty over the new colony. Once begun, peace negotiations with Turkey dragged on for almost a year after the Italian armies had occupied the principal areas of settlement in Libya. By threatening to extend military operations to European Turkey, Italy forced the powers to put pressure on the Turks to accept the inevitable and abandon Tripoli. Even then the Turks did not capitulate until events were moving swiftly toward war in the Balkans. Preliminary peace terms were signed on October 16; but as one war ended another began.[17]

With Italy's attack on Turkey and the danger of the war spreading to the Balkans, all the governments with interests in southeastern Europe were inspired to review and reassess their policies and positions. If the "sick man" of Europe should collapse utterly, how would his wealth be divided—the Straits, Macedonia, Thrace, Albania, and Novibazar? Would everything be up for grabs? It was also easily imaginable that the leaders of the Balkan states would strive to take advantage of the Tripolitan war to realize their "historical goals" in

17. William C. Askew, *Europe and Italy's Acquisition of Libya* (Durham, N.C., 1942); Albertini, *The Origins of the War of 1914*, I, 341–63.

European Turkey. In these months, Germany and Austria, with substantial interests in the Ottoman Empire, were curiously passive; Britain and France naïvely hoped that the status quo would not be disturbed; and only Russia and the Balkan states may be said to have had concerted plans for the achievement of desired goals or for the defense of their interests.

The Straits question stuck like a bone in Russia's throat, and the Turkish predicament seemed to afford an opportunity for action in Russia's interest. Special and exclusive rights of transit through the Straits for Russian war vessels was the objective, together with guarantees that Russian exports and imports would under no circumstances —belligerency or other condition—be denied passage through the waterway. Beset with difficulties, the Porte could hardly resist St. Petersburg's urgent demands. The first maneuver—to effect a rapprochement with Turkey—failed signally and resulted in the recall of the Russian ambassador. Meanwhile, with the encouragement and active participation of the Russian minister Hartwig in Belgrade and his colleague A. V. Nekliudov in Sofia, the Bulgarian and Serbian governments sought to establish a united front among the Balkan states to deal with any complications that might arise from the Italo-Turkish conflict. Once the negotiations were begun, St. Petersburg gave its blessing because it was mistakenly thought that a Bulgarian-Serbian alliance would be an element of stability in a volatile situation; a further mistake was to assume that it would be a defensive arrangement and that Russia's thumb would be on the button.

Negotiations at the cabinet level between Belgrade and Sofia began in the autumn of 1911, and the treaty, after months of Balkan haggling over Macedonia, was finally signed on March 13, 1912. Ostensibly a treaty of friendship and alliance, it contained secret annexes which made it an instrument of aggression against Turkey. The *casus belli* was so broadly stated that hostilities could begin almost at will, although Russia was accorded a vague veto over a resort to arms. The foundation of the alliance was the anticipated division of Macedonia between the two rival claimants. Bulgaria's "territorial rights" were defined in detail, Serbia's allotment was left unclear; and this became one of the roots of the second Balkan war. A military convention, apparently negotiated without Russian participation, supplemented the treaty of alliance. When Russian minister of foreign affairs Serge Sazonov—recuperating from a severe illness—was told of the progress of the negotiations, he is reported to have said: "Well . . . this is perfect if it could come off! Bulgaria closely allied to Serbia . . . five hundred thousand bayonets to guard the Balkans—but this would bar the road forever to German penetration and Austrian invasion."[18]

Scarcely was the Serbian-Bulgarian alliance concluded than the Russians lost control of their Balkan clients. When Bulgaria began to negotiate an alliance with Greece and the Russian government expressed disapproval, negotiations were suspended temporarily but taken up later and concluded without Russia's knowledge or blessing. In May, 1912, the Russians belatedly received a copy of the secret treaty. Likewise, against Russian advice a military convention was signed with Montenegro in mid-September, 1912. By this time war was decided upon; only its date—a matter of weeks—was uncertain.

Meanwhile, Sazonov seemed embarrassed before his allies. And well he might be, for he had misled the French as to the spirit and terms of the Balkan alliances, and the belief that the Balkan Slavs could be restrained was becoming daily more doubtful. When Poincaré was finally given a copy of the Serbo-Bulgarian treaty in August, 1912, he sharply protested the deception and characterized the document as "une convention de guerre," which contained "the germ not only of a war against Turkey, but a war against Austria." And later when hostilities had begun, Poincaré said movingly of Russia's role: "She is trying to put on the brakes, but it is she who started the motor."[19] However, this did not cause Poincaré to withhold France's support for Russia's Balkan gambles. From the other cabinets, except the British, Russia's role in the genesis of the Balkan *Plünderbund* remained concealed or obscured. As land mines were being planted all over the Balkans with Russian knowledge and concurrence, Sazonov played well the part of a worker for peace, a loyal member of the European concert, and a guardian of the status quo in southeastern Europe!

As the beat of drums became more audible in the Balkans, the

---

18. Quoted in Edward C. Thaden, *Russia and the Balkan Alliance of 1912* (University Park, Pa., 1965), p. 78. This study is based on Russian documents that have become available since the works of Fay, Schmitt, and Albertini were published. Still valuable are the studies by E. C. Helmreich, *The Diplomacy of the Balkan Wars* (Cambridge, Mass., 1938); and Philip E. Mosely, "Russian Policy in 1911–12," *Journal of Modern History*, XII (Mar., 1940), 69–86.

19. Fay, *Origins of the World War*, I, 433. More condemnatory of French and Russian policy on the eve of the Balkan wars is Albertini, *The Origins of the War of 1914*, I, 370–77.

Concert of Europe made its final appearance as an agent and instrument of peace. Reform and pacification of the Turkish provinces would deprive the Balkan states of their excuse for attacking, and a concerted warning by the powers might check the drive toward war. On the initiative of Raymond Poincaré, French premier since January, 1912, the powers authorized Russia and Austria jointly to warn the Balkan states that no change in the status quo by force of arms would be tolerated by the Concert. Platonic formulas availed little. When this declaration was finally agreed to by the foreign ministers, it was too late to stop the war.

In a land so full of violence and unhappiness the Albanians and Macedonians could be depended upon to revolt whenever such action was required. This they did with perfect timing. The Balkan states now demanded administrative autonomy for the inflamed provinces, which they knew Turkey would not grant. On October 8, shortly before the joint Austrian-Russian *démarche,* King Nicholas of Montenegro handed the Turkish envoy his passports and, on the next day, fired the first shot across the frontier into a Turkish military camp.[20] His allies of the Balkan League, already mobilizing, hastened to join the crusade to drive the Turk from Europe. Now the critical problem for the powers was to localize the war in the Balkans.

Most observers doubted that the military power of the Balkan nations was sufficient to give them the victory. However, by the first of November Turkey was defeated in the field and the League was everywhere victorious. The Bulgars drove the Turkish forces out of Thrace and besieged Adrianople; it seemed that they might even take Constantinople and plant the cross on Hagia Sophia. The Greek forces raced to Salonika and occupied the lower Vardar Valley; the Serbs drove the Turks out of Macedonia and the Sanjak, and reached the Adriatic after overrunning northern Albania; the Turks barely held out in a few isolated strongpoints and fortresses. It was the worst military performance by the Turks since they appeared in Europe. On December 4 the Porte appealed to the powers collectively to mediate in respect to an armistice. Talk of maintaining the status quo was now meaningless. As one commentator quipped, the "grandes puissances" had become the "grandes impuissances."

Events moved so rapidly that Austrian statesmen had little time to

20. E. Malcolm Carroll, *Germany and the Great Powers, 1866–1914* (New York, 1938), p. 717.

produce a policy to safeguard their Balkan interests. After much hesitation and uncertainty, Count Berchtold, who had succeeded Aehrenthal in February, 1912, formulated the demand, which was supported by Italy, for an independent Albania that would block Serbian expansion to the Adriatic. As Russia was supporting Serbia, tension between Vienna and St. Petersburg built up rapidly. Sir Edward Grey at this point proposed an ambassadorial conference to settle the Near Eastern conflict and maintain peace among the powers. Germany and France supported Grey's proposal, but Austria made her acceptance conditional upon the assent of the other governments to her demand for an independent Albania. Such was the birth certificate of this new "foundling state" of Europe.

The "conference policy," which henceforth tied Austria's hands, was not popular in all political circles; some would have preferred a showdown with Serbia and Montenegro—and with Russia too if that should eventuate. The Archduke Franz Ferdinand and Conrad von Hötzendorf, recently reappointed chief of the general staff, were "hawks" in this respect, but after an exposition of policies in a conference with the Emperor, the latter sided with his civilian ministers and rejected a solution by force.[21]

Following the cease-fire of December 3, Turkish and Balkan League plenipotentiaries assembled in London to negotiate peace. A deadlock developed, followed by a temporary resumption of hostilities, but fortune again favored the Balkan states, and peace, largely on their terms, was concluded with the signature of the Treaty of London on May 30, 1913. Turkey ceded all Balkan territory west of the Enos-Midia line, including Adrianople; she abandoned all claims to Crete, and left the status of Albania and the Aegean Islands to be decided by the great powers. Turkey was no longer an important political or territorial factor in European affairs.

The Ambassadors' Conference, which convened on December 17, concerned itself mainly with the problems of establishing an Albanian state, and especially the delimitation of its frontiers. Italy and Austria wanted an Albania of maximum size; Russia in the interest of her Balkan clients wanted a small Albania. In consequence every Albanian village, every silted-up Turkish port with a population of 2,000, became an object of angry contention. With the resumption of hostilities in

21. Hugo Hantsch, *Leopold Graf Berchtold,* 2 vols. (Graz, 1963), I, 359–64.

February, 1913, Serbs and Montenegrins occupied territories allocated to the new Albanian state. The conference was slow to react, and only under great pressure from Austria-Hungary were the intruders forced to withdraw from the disputed areas. A naval demonstration by the powers was necessary to get King Nicholas out of Durazzo. These tensions registered heavily on the scale of Austrian-Russian relations as the two powers played the game of *Machtpolitik,* with military preparations, partial mobilizations, and troop build-ups along their Galician frontier. A climate of extreme violence also prevailed in the Albanian areas occupied by Serb troops and along the Serbian-Austrian frontier. The Slav population of Bosnia was deeply stirred by these events, and nationalistic youth slipped across the frontier to serve in the guerrilla bands with the Serbian army.[22]

Berchtold was under heavy pressure from the military—especially Conrad and General Potiorek, governor of Bosnia—to abandon his conference policy and at the risk of Russian intervention take unilateral action against Serbia and Montenegro. The case for and against this course came before Francis Joseph in the crown council and in interviews with Conrad and Berchtold, but the Emperor emphatically rejected war. On different grounds the Archduke took a similar position, and a private letter from Bethmann Hollweg to Berchtold was practically a veto of the use of force in the current crisis.[23]

Tension between Vienna and St. Petersburg reached crisis level in April–May, 1913. Both monarchs and their ministers were under considerable pressure from aroused segments of their public opinion. The Czarist regime was sensitive to the clamor of the Pan-Slav press, while the Dual Monarchy was under pressure from the Austro-Imperialists. A direct exchange of conciliatory messages between Francis Joseph and Nicholas II had a calming effect on their cabinets and military chieftains. As proof of its pacific intentions, each government agreed to reduce in equal measure its troop concentrations in the Galician area. This relaxed the tension, and the Serbs, deprived of Russian support, were constrained to heed the decisions of the Ambassadors' Conference and withdraw from disputed Albanian territory. Montenegro, after

22. The impact of the Balkan wars and the activities of societies such as "Young Bosnians" can be followed in Vladimir Dedijer, *The Road to Sarajevo* (New York, 1966), pp. 175–284.

23. See the hitherto unpublished letters of Bethmann and the Archduke in Hantsch, *Leopold Graf Berchtold,* I, 387–88, 388–90; and on the crisis in general, pp. 358–83.

weeks of chicanery, likewise bowed to the will of the powers and evacuated Scutari. This removed the last obstacle to the conclusion of peace.

In this crisis, pregnant with danger, the principal decision makers opted for a peaceful settlement. Francis Joseph and the Archduke would not risk a general war in a doubtful attempt to cure the monarchy's South Slav ailments; Nicholas II preferred a diplomatic to a military solution, and Sazonov was no more inclined to war than Berchtold. Germany's desire for peace in the Balkans was genuine; their main task, as her diplomatists saw it, being "to guard Germany's roof from the flying sparks."[24] Both Kiderlen and Bethmann made it clear to Vienna that they wanted no Balkan adventures and that their alliance did not commit Germany to unconditional support of Austrian policy. No one among the principles would risk a general war. But a year later, in the crisis created by the Sarajevo assassinations, every one of these policy makers reversed his previous position and took the road that led to war.

The causes, course, and consequences of the second Balkan war require no detailed exposition. The short but decisive conflict arose over division of the spoils. Since Serbian aspirations in the west were thwarted by the powers, she entered a claim for compensation in Macedonian territory which had been promised to Bulgaria in the original alliance. Greece supported the Serbian demands, hoping herself to get a larger share of the disputed spoils. The situation was made more explosive with Rumania's demands for some gain for herself in the liquidation of European Turkey. Rejecting the mediation of the Czar, Bulgaria unwisely launched a surprise attack against both Serbia and Greece, who had already concluded an alliance directed against their former ally. Rumania then attacked Bulgaria, and even Turkey entered the fray. The outcome was never in doubt; hostilities lasted but a month (June 29–July 30), and the war ended with the Treaty of Bucharest. Bulgaria naturally paid the piper: Rumania received the southern Dobrudja; Turkey recovered Adrianople; Serbia took the Macedonian territory originally allocated to Bulgaria; and the latter lost to Greece her territory on the Aegean seaboard, including the best port, Kavalla, retaining only the coastal strip between the Mesta and Maritza rivers. This settlement in the eastern Balkans has remained fairly stable through two world wars, although even today when a Bulgarian publicist praises the aborted Treaty of San Stefano, which historically embodied the idea of Greater Bulgaria, he is certain to draw immediate fire from the official press in Belgrade and Athens.

The military events of 1912–1913 gave a new configuration to Balkan relationships and shifted some positions in the European alliance structure. Territorially Turkey ceased to be a European state although still an object of great power politics. Balkan irredentism was now concentrated on Austria-Hungary. For the Pan-Slav and Italian irredentists, Francis Joseph became, in the words of the frenzied poet D'Annunzio, "the angel of the everlasting gallows." Bulgaria was isolated and resentful, and therefore the object of Austrian diplomacy, which attempted to draw her into the orbit of the Triple Alliance. Rumania, courted by the Czar and his government, was perceptibly shifting her allegiance from the Triple Alliance to the Triple Entente. Serbia bitterly resented Austria's blocking of her Adriatic plans, and the Dual Monarchy rightly feared the subversive effect of Serb propaganda upon her South Slav subjects. The Sarajevo assassinations, coming within a year, had as background all the hostility and ill will that had developed between Austria and Serbia since the turn of the century.

As for great power relationships and the condition of the alliances after the Balkan wars, these can only be described as somewhat mutable and uncertain of direction. Both alliance systems were in some degree tightened up during the crisis and obligations more precisely defined. Representing an uncertain balance, the alliances gave some temporary assurance of peace and security to the members. Significantly the Ambassadors' Conference was able to find the compromises that kept peace among the powers. This was owing in large measure to the cooperation of England and Germany and the restraining influence exerted by the latter upon its ally Austria. Grey as chairman of the conference deserved great credit for his patient but determined conduct of its business. Notwithstanding, he was incredibly cautious about recommending any action that might be unacceptable to Russia and France. As her only certain ally, there were also limits to the pressure Berlin would put upon Vienna. As for the French, their leaders moved closer to a position of unconditional support of Russia and her Balkan interests. With regard to Italy's posture, the Triple Alliance was renewed in December, 1912, with considerable publicity, and Austria and Italy cooperated in the creation of an Albanian state. Soon, however, they became manifest rivals for influence over this ambiguous international creation.[25]

Enough of the spirit of a "concert of Europe" worked through the Ambassadors' Conference to prevent a general war in 1912–1913, but the fear of such a catastrophe was widespread, and this encouraged a new round of armament increases. Since the Balkan wars were a diplomatic setback for Germany and Austria, it was natural for their leaders to give the armament's screw another turn. Germany increased appreciably her permanent establishment and brought in a military budget so stiff that it necessitated a capital levy. While the one does not appear to have inspired the other, the French concurrently raised the military service obligation from two to three years. Large loans were also made by France to Russia on condition that they be used to improve communications and speed Russian mobilization. The Liman von Sanders affair, the Russo-German war scare in the spring of 1914, and the exhibitions of German militarism in Alsace-Lorraine added to the international tension. The European situation was described by Colonel House, President Wilson's personal envoy, as "militarism run stark mad."

However, the "road to disaster" pattern, with the course of events leading inexorably to the great smash-up in 1914, which is the theme of many general histories, is largely wisdom made manifest after the event. The coin has another side. In western Europe the current issues in the relations between England and Germany, France and Germany, and Italy and her neighbors were conciliable and not irreversibly dynamic. Anglo-German naval rivalry, Alsace-Lorraine, colonial aspirations, economic competition—these had become static and bearable conditions rather than acute problems. But in the Balkans and the eastern marchlands of Europe explosive conflicts between imprudent nationalism and multinational dynastic states could scarcely be avoided. In this respect the Balkan wars were both symptomatic and prophetic. In the rivalry of Austria and Russia in this area there was more than the clash of imperialisms; involved also in their relations was the necessity of maintaining the integrity of their multinational territories against the powerful forces of disruptive nationalism. The failure of statesmen to localize these convulsions and to prevent their linkage with the alliance systems made a general war possible if not probable in 1914.

25. Albertini, *The Origins of the War of 1914*, I, 518–27, 540–78.

Chapter Eleven

THE CRITICAL THIRTY-NINE DAYS—1914

I. THE MEN OF POWER AND DECISION

From doubtful beginning to dreadful end the crisis of 1914 unfolded through the judgment and decisions of men. Few of the central figures then in authority were of sufficient stature to deal with so grave a situation. Indeed one is inclined to say that the men who directed international affairs in 1914 were at the lowest level of competence and ability in several decades.

Three monarchs—Francis Joseph, Nicholas II, and William II— under their respective constitutional systems exercised authority in diplomatic relations comparable to that of the President of the United States. No major policies or actions could be initiated without their express authorization, no ultimatums issued, armies or fleets mobilized, wars declared or frontiers crossed without their constitutional assent. One could find in these three men all kinds of built-in deficiencies, but they were not mere puppets manipulated by advisers.

Francis Joseph was the oldest—a legendary figure among reigning monarchs. Generally motivated by dynastic considerations, he had shown remarkable flexibility during his long reign—adapting to a measure of constitutional government, democratization of the franchise, and the changing economic and social order, but always retaining in his own hands final decisions in the appointment of ministers, in the direction of foreign affairs, and in national defense. He recoiled from the prospect of war, but in 1914 he judged the circumstances to be so grave as to justify a resort to force at the risk of a general war.

Nicholas II exercised close supervision over the conduct of Russia's foreign relations. His judgments were not sharp or perceptive, and he was moved more often by prejudice and preconceptions than by informed opinion. He could be influenced, especially by the wrong people, and he could defend stubbornly a bad decision. His major concern was the preservation and strengthening of the dynasty and the czarist state, a concern that was constant and strongly motivating.

William II considered himself a peerless expert in diplomacy. No

285

significant actions or policies could be initiated without the Kaiser's concurrence. After the shock of the *Daily Telegraph* affair and the "November storm" that followed, William II never recaptured his former brash self-assurance. In consequence he suffered fewer rhetorical derailments, such as had punctuated his earlier career. In 1914 his statements and pronouncements—especially his marginalia on diplomatic dispatches—were such a mixture of sense and nonsense that they are difficult to sort out and evaluate as indications of German policy.[1]

Bethmann Hollweg, who succeeded Bülow as chancellor in 1909, was not a professional diplomat, which may account for his deference toward the Kaiser and the career officials in the foreign office. In contemporary news photos Bethmann always looked a little sad and vaguely overwhelmed. But he was a man of high intelligence and basic moderation. He was tenacious in pursuing his policy goals, although he could not always maintain his position against the Emperor and the military leaders. There were flaws and weaknesses in his makeup, and he woefully misjudged the situation in 1914. But fundamentally he was a man of honor, sensibility, and peace.[2]

Bethmann needed a strong and able secretary of state for foreign affairs. Kiderlen-Wächter, a somewhat controversial figure, occupied the key post after the retirement of Bülow and the death of Holstein, but Kiderlen died in December, 1912, and was replaced by Gottlieb von Jagow, German ambassador in Rome. When his appointment was announced, the *Neue Zürcher Zeitung* playfully headed its Berlin dispatch: "Gottlieb, who are you?" (*Gottlieb, wer bist du?*). And the 65 million inhabitants of the German Empire might well have asked the same question! Jagow may have looked like a supporting pillar, but in fact he was only a dubious ornament. A member of an old and noble family in Mark Brandenburg, he had entered the diplomatic service, where his experience was limited to the "inner circle"—that is, minor posts in the capitals of continental western Europe. His surprise ap-

---

1. Kiderlen-Wächter, famous for his sarcastic judgments, is reported to have said to a guest at a royal shooting party: "Take care that you do not shoot the Kaiser, for the Crown Prince is even worse." *Das politische Tagebuch Josef Redlichs,* ed. by Fritz Fellner, 2 vols. (Graz, 1954), I, 220.

2. I am aware that current research on German war aims has revealed a new Bethmann Hollweg, but it should be remembered that war leadership produces unique transformations; the Lloyd George of 1909, for example, was not identical with the Lloyd George of 1918.

pointment as ambassador in Rome suggested to some observers that Bülow, the outgoing chancellor, wanted a young client in Rome, where he intended to retire. However, Jagow preferred to make his mistakes unassisted by Bülow, one such mistake being his failure to penetrate Italian intentions and to inform his government that Italy would soon make war on Turkey. A man lacking originality, vision, and initiative, and not very intelligent, Jagow had numerous counterparts in the principal European embassies and foreign offices. No wonder Europe slid easily into war in 1914.

Count Berchtold belonged in the same pigeonhole. Moderately intelligent, wealthy, and cosmopolitan, he was recalled from semiretirement to the post of foreign minister after serving as ambassador in St. Petersburg. He accepted the appointment under pressure after two preferred candidates were vetoed by the Archduke Franz Ferdinand. Professor Fay describes Berchtold as "helpless and incompetent," and the British ambassador, Cartwright, thought he was "overburdened" by his office. He depended heavily on his staff and found it difficult to make decisions—in fact, he lacked force and understanding and he dithered. He gathered no laurels in his first test—the Balkan crisis of 1912-1913. What he proclaimed as Austria's "vital interests" in that area seemed to change every day, and he withdrew from so many positions that it was suggested he would soon even withdraw himself! Professor Bernadotte E. Schmitt notes that in 1912-1913 he resisted military and diplomatic pressure to engage Serbia in war but in 1914 he took the plunge. "Why?" asks Schmitt. "Simply because he thought no other course was open to Austria-Hungary if it were to survive as a Great Power."[3]

Sazonov, the Russian foreign minister, like Berchtold, completely misread the European situation in 1914 and contributed to the faulty decision making that produced a general war. A professional diplomat and a protégé of Stolypin, his brother-in-law, Sazonov became increasingly independent as he gained the esteem and confidence of the Czar. Stolypin's policy in broad outline had been to avoid conflict with Russia's western neighbors and to bring the Balkan states and Turkey closer to Russia and to each other. The Balkan wars and the Liman von Sanders affair—the appointment of a German general to a training

command in Constantinople—discredited this policy, and in consequence Russian chauvinists and Slavophiles gained ground in political
circles. "Peace at any price" was denounced as "ignominious and dangerous." Sazonov was not the person to ignore or resist such pressures.
Possessed of a mercurial temperament which sometimes led him to talk
wildly, he began to denounce Austria in threatening terms. His voice
became more agitated after Sarajevo as rumors of Austrian intentions
began to circulate. He was the first responsible official to accept the idea
of European war; and he bears heavy responsibility for Russian mobilization which triggered other rash decisions and made a general war
almost inevitable.

A moderating influence upon Russian policy might have been exercised by France if there had been a person of sufficient stature in
control of her foreign policy. France's strength and skill in this department were concentrated in the quality and experience of her ambassadors in London, Berlin, and Rome rather than in the foreign
ministry in Paris. Events showed that there was no salvation in the
ninety-day wonders who shuffled in and out of the Quai d'Orsay as one
cabinet succeeded another. Raymond Poincaré was elevated to the
presidency in 1913 and according to report had the cabinet in his pocket
in a short time. As premier and foreign minister when the Balkan war
broke out, he did not hesitate to invoke the concert and initiate mediation, endeavoring to calm the storm. Had he not been isolated from the
center of action during the most critical days of the July crisis in 1914
he might have taken the initiative in a saving act that conventional
diplomats and politicians shunned. The prestige of the French presidency, and of the man who occupied that office, was never brought to
bear, as it might have been, in the interest of peace in 1914.

While Poincaré was a thorough and tireless worker, and not at all
fearful of taking the lead in the international community, Sir Edward
Grey went weekending and fishing. Sir Edward had the prestige, the
potential power, and the strategic position for the exertion of tremendous leverage upon the situation in 1914. Britain as a world empire, the
paramount naval power, and less entangled on the Continent, had
more freedom of movement than any of the Continental states. Yet
Grey failed to use effectively his position and prestige to avert catastrophe. Sir Edward was a man of elegant and commanding appearance
and of pleasing but reserved presence. Asquith, his close friend and
colleague, described him as always "dolorous and despondent" and

lacking any "buoyancy." He was not at all acquainted with the world through study or travel, and he scarcely ever left the British Isles. His vision and foreign policy objectives never went beyond "England's security." Grey's policy of ententes was much criticized by the Radicals in Parliament and the press, but he made no effort to educate either the country or his party. In the 1914 crisis Grey failed to appreciate or accept the consequences of his own diplomacy—the 1912 commitment to France. He gave no real lead to the cabinet or the country, and he allowed events to dictate his policy.

This roster of men who formulated and executed the foreign policies of the major powers could be interminably extended, but that would not erase the general impression of mediocrity and insufficiency which in general they betray. All those immediately involved in the 1914 crisis responded conventionally and played their roles according to the script, but not one attempted the bold action or the unconventional move that might have saved Europe from disaster. Members or surrogates of a privileged aristocratic class, they represented an elite whose power, privilege, and distinctions were in decline and doomed to disappear by midcentury.

2. THE TEMPER OF EUROPE AND THE SARAJEVO CRIME

In 1914 prophets of war and prophets of peace abounded; the portents were both good and bad. The tensions produced by the Balkan wars had considerably relaxed; the treaty of Bucharest was not a perfect settlement but no one was likely to challenge it; the troubles in Albania were now mainly local; Greece and Turkey appeared to be moving toward a settlement of their difficulties in the Aegean; the Liman von Sanders mission had exacerbated German-Russian relations but the czarist government had accepted a compromise that saved everyone's *amour-propre;* the long-disputed Baghdad Railway question had been adjusted to the satisfaction of France, Britain, and Germany; and linked to this agreement was an understanding over the economic development of Anatolia and Mesopotamia by the interested powers.

In western Europe the signs were even more encouraging. There was an appreciable détente in Franco-German relations. Preparations were being made for the second conference on cooperation and understanding by French and German parliamentarians; and President Poincaré abandoned a tradition of forty years by dining officially at the German embassy. Great Britain and Germany had reached a de facto understanding on their naval building programs, and a new agreement on the disposition of the Portuguese colonies had been negotiated and only needed ratification; also there was less talk of economic rivalry as Britain concentrated more on trade within her empire and the Germans cultivated the markets and investment opportunities in eastern and southeastern Europe. On the whole, surface tensions seemed to be relaxing; to the optimistic observer Europe did not appear to be a City of Destruction.

It cannot be denied, however, that among publicists, diplomats, and statesmen the view was widely held that a general war could not long be postponed. When the crisis came, this spirit of fatalism weakened the will to peace. Among the military leaders the "coming world war" was a stereotyped theme.[4] Social Darwinism too strongly influenced the attitudes of many leaders. The letters, memoranda, and marginal notes of such people as William II, Conrad von Hötzendorf, Helmuth von Moltke, and spokesmen for the Pan-groups carry all the clichés of racial rivalry and conflict. William II especially liked to spout prophecy on "the imminent struggle for existence which the Germanic peoples of Europe . . . will have to fight out against the Slavs . . . and their Gallic supporters." In this, as in so much vaporing in high places, wind must not be mistaken for will. Generalized speculation on the political weather is a constant factor in international life, and it does not mean that Europeans were suffering a harrowing sense of strain and anxiety in 1914.

In the spring of that pregnant year the visible areas of conflict were northern Ireland, where armed rebellion threatened, and Mexico, where the United States had occupied Veracruz and was shortly to invade Mexican territory in pursuit of "bandits." It was another punitive act by a great power against a small transgressor state in the Balkans that produced a local war which shortly became a European war and eventually a world war.

After the upheaval of 1912–1913 and the extinction of Ottoman rule in Europe the thrust of Serb nationalism was directed against the multinational empire of the Hapsburgs. For Austria-Hungary the Balkan wars were like a mighty earth tremor—the structure still stood, but

4. Gerhard Ritter, *Staatskunst und Kriegshandwerk*, II, 134; Fritz Fischer, *Germany's Aims in the First World War*, pp. 32–33; F. von Bernhardi, *Germany and the Next War* (New York, 1914), pp. 18–20.

the initiated knew that it stood on volcanic ground. The most vulnerable part of the structure was the South Slav provinces, especially as Serbia under Russian patronage became the banner carrier for the idea of South Slav unity and independence. In this part of Europe the bomb, the gun, and the knife had been for centuries the means of "settling" political accounts. It was the tradition of violence against Turkish rule that inspired youthful Serb fanatics to deeds of terrorism against Hapsburg officials. Prior to the assassination of the Archduke Franz Ferdinand in June, 1914, there had been five attempts in four years against the lives of Hapsburg officeholders.

As to the central figure in the tragedy that set off a world war, there has been much speculative writing about the character, reputation, and political views of the heir to the Hapsburg throne. Since documents and records have become available, Franz Ferdinand's position, personality, and political views have been more sharply delineated. As the Archduke emerged from obscurity there was considerably less nonsensical prophecy about the realm disintegrating at the death of the old Emperor. Franz Ferdinand had been given more and more responsibility with regard to foreign policy and national defense, and it was believed that when he succeeded his uncle the impact would be forceful if not altogether agreeable. Some publicists predicted that after the stagnation of Francis Joseph's later reign the Archduke's role would be that of a modern Joseph II. Franz Ferdinand was not popular in Hungary. The Magyar magnates and politicians were fully aware of his partiality for the Rumanians, the Slovaks, and the Croats, and his distrust of the ruling Hungarian elite. They fully reciprocated this distrust because it was known that he was quite out of sympathy with the Ausgleich of 1867 and that he desired major constitutional changes. This political element scarcely tried to conceal its satisfaction when the Archduke was removed from the political scene by an assassin's bullet. Even in Vienna the Archduke was not popular; indeed there was considerable antipathy toward him because of his imperious manner, his bigotry, his meanness in money matters, and his pathological lust for killing, which went far beyond mere "hunting."[5] The duchess was no more popular than her spouse.

5. *Das politische Tagebuch Josef Redlichs*, I, 235. Also Rudolf Kiszling, *Erzherzog Franz Ferdinand von Österreich-Este* (Graz, 1953); Vladimir Dedijer, *The Road to Sarajevo* (New York, 1966), Chaps. VII and VIII, "Reorganization of the Empire" and "The Archduke Franz Ferdinand."

With respect to constitutional reform the Archduke's name was occasionally linked with the projected program of Trialism, which was really a Croat discovery looking toward the creation of a third state in the empire composed of Croatia, Bosnia, and Dalmatia. In fact, the Archduke seems to have been more favorable toward a type of Greater Austrian federalism than toward further experiments with dualism or trialism. As to the Archduke's foreign policy views, or better his prejudices, he was anti-Italian, anti-German, and pro-Russian; ironically, he would have welcomed a restoration of the Three Emperors' League. Most historians agree that Hapsburg state institutions were incompatible with the developing cultural and territorial imperatives that inspired the Balkan peoples and the nationalities of the Dual Monarchy. Whether the Archduke could have reformed the empire in a way to meet the demand for self-determination among the peoples became a mere speculative matter after the events of June 28 at Sarajevo.

Sarajevo was a place whose name was unknown to the average newspaper reader but which became the fate of Europe in 1914. The events that occurred there, on a bright Sunday morning in June, have often been described in sober fact as well as imaginative fiction. Only a brief recapitulation is here required. Three Bosnian youths—Gavrilo Princip, N. Chabrinovich, and Trifko Grabezh—all aged nineteen, were at the center of the conspiracy that took the lives of the Archduke Franz Ferdinand and his spouse. Fitful and unsuccessful students, these youths were active members of a nebulous nationalistic organization, the Young Bosnians. Their patriotic cup overflowed with the Serb successes in the Balkan wars, and they aspired to liberate Bosnia as the Serbs had liberated Macedonia. For them the historic enemy and oppressor was not the Turk but the Austrian. Excluded from service with the Bosnian guerrilla bands in the Balkan wars because of their age and poor physical condition, they aspired to win fame as patriots by striking a blow against the Hapsburg monarchy. Although residents of Sarajevo, they visited Belgrade regularly, where they came into contact with the Pan-Serb cultural society Narodna Odbrana and subsequently, as the plot to assassinate Franz Ferdinand began to form, with the political terrorist organization Union or Death, commonly called the Black Hand. The mastermind of the plot, it would appear, was Colonel Dragutin Dimitrievich, leader of the Black Hand and chief of the intelligence division of the Serbian army general staff. Dimitrievich, it might be noted, was one of the principal participants in the massacre of the royal family of Obrenovich in 1903. With his concurrence, two associates, Major Tankosich and Milan Ciganovich, supplied the three youths with Browning pistols and grenades from state arsenals and trained them in their use. They were also given a sum of money and a quantity of poison to be taken upon completion of their mission. Toward the end of May they left Belgrade and were assisted across the frontier into Bosnia and moved along one of the Black Hand's protected routes or "tunnels" to Sarajevo. There the weapons were delivered to Danilo Ilitch, a local revolutionary activist with Black Hand connections, who recruited three additional assassins, distributed the weapons, and posted the conspirators on the morning of the Archduke's official visit to Sarajevo.

Significantly none of the local recruits attempted to use his weapon when the opportunity presented itself on that fateful Sunday morning of June 28. But Chabrinovich threw his bomb at the Archduke's automobile as it passed along the main street on the way to a ceremonial reception at the city hall. The grenade exploded under the following automobile, wounding a number of bystanders and a member of the Archduke's suite. On the return from the city hall, by the merest chance the Archduke's automobile was misdirected and as the driver stopped to reverse the car, Princip, who had moved from his original location to this very corner, had a perfect target—two shots fired point-blank found vital marks and within half an hour both the Archduke and the Duchess were dead.

For shocking negligence in matters of security the Austrian officials incur severe blame. The responsible person was the military governor of the province, General Potiorek, who because the Archduke was visiting Bosnia to observe army maneuvers had insisted that all arrangements, including security, be made by the military. Even elementary precautions seem to have been neglected with results far from creditable for the army and the military governor.

Shock and sympathy were universally expressed at the news from Sarajevo, and the courts of Europe went formally into mourning. However, the hurried and shabby funeral, as well as the absence of sincere public mourning, was noted by diplomats and the foreign press. In commenting on the background and motivation of the deed, before any reports of police investigations in Sarajevo reached the press, the event was put into a context of the monarchy's South Slav problem, and especially Austria's relations with Serbia. The "mad racialism" of the Serbs had inspired another outrage, was the common interpretation.

Despite the detailed treatment of the Sarajevo crime by the Italian scholar Luigi Albertini, and more recently in the book by Vladimir Dedijer, *The Road to Sarajevo,* there are some important points that remain unclarified. But from the interrogations of the prisoners in Sarajevo—all but one being immediately apprehended—it was soon discovered that the threads of the conspiracy led to Belgrade, where the assassins procured the weapons and where they had co-conspirators— Tankosich and Ciganovich. How much the Serbian government knew about the plot and what steps they took to prevent the crime—either by closing the frontier or by warning the authorities in Vienna—are matters that remain in dispute. Certainly there was official culpability if not complicity. In summary it can be stated that the conspiracy was hatched by Bosnian students in Belgrade in cooperation with the Serbian Black Hand; that Serbian officers, members of the Black Hand, supplied the assassins with arms and taught them their use; that they gave them money and assisted them to cross the frontier into Bosnia; further, that the Serbian prime minister, M. Pashich, and other members of the government had knowledge of the conspiracy but did not warn the Austrian government directly of its existence; also, during the month that elapsed between the assassination and the ultimatum, the Serbian government took no steps to investigate the Belgrade ramifications of the plot or to apprehend the Serbian officials who had promoted it; finally, the government did nothing to moderate the press attacks upon Austria and the glorification of the deed as a patriotic act.[6]

The apppalling news from Sarajevo had a numbing effect on the leaders and peoples of the Dual Monarchy. Anger was cumulative, and it became difficult to refute those who said that now accounts must be settled with the Serbian irredentists or the monarchy would lose its South Slav provinces as it had previously lost its Italian territories.

6. For a searching examination of the evidence of fault and negligence on the part of Austrian and Serbian authorities, see Luigi Albertini, *The Origins of the War of 1914,* II, 89–115.

Josef Redlich, scholar, member of the Reichsrat, and a true cosmopolitan, wrote in his diary: "The impossibility of peaceful coexistence of this half-German and Germany-allied monarchy with the murderous nationalism of the Balkan peoples must now be clear to everyone." Pessimistic about the future, he concluded that "Only the sword can save Austria," ignoring the biblical prediction that he who takes the sword will perish by the sword.[7]

In decision-making circles in Vienna the Sarajevo tragedy tipped the scales decisively in favor of those who insisted that military rather than diplomatic action was now imperative. Conrad von Hötzendorf had written to Moltke in February: "What are we waiting for?" And when he heard the shocking news from Sarajevo, he exclaimed: "The hour has struck with shrill clangor."[8] Significantly Berchtold, who had shied away from war in 1912–1913, now aligned himself with the war party. In Hapsburg councils there was no one strong enough to stand up against the advocates of force. Berchtold was not that man; and Count Tisza, the Hungarian premier and most forceful figure among the political leaders, tried and failed. The Emperor's position too shifted. He certainly longed to end his reign peacefully, but he came to the conclusion that relations with Serbia could not continue on the present course. In 1914 Francis Joseph did not veto a punitive war against Serbia; he did not say as he had in 1913: "That would mean [a general] war and as such must be avoided."[9] In the court, in the councils, and in the chief ministries the view prevailed that if the Dual Monarchy was to survive, drastic surgery would be required. Public opinion and the press moved in the same direction.

3. A BLANK CHECK AND AN ULTIMATUM

Berchtold and Conrad could take no action except in agreement with the prime ministers of the two monarchies, and since Tisza was opposed to drastic action some means of bypassing or overcoming his opposition had to be devised. This was in part the object of the Hoyos mission to Berlin. Since action against Serbia might provoke Russia's intervention, any use of force must have the approval of the German ally. The mission of Alexander Hoyos, chief of the foreign office secre-

7. Das politische Tagebuch Josef Redlichs, I, 235, 198.
8. Albertini, The Origins of the War of 1914, II, 122.
9. Hugo Hantsch, Leopold Graf Berchtold, I, 394.

tariat, to Berlin on July 5–6 was designed to learn the attitude of their ally and to insure Austria of German support in the event of warlike complications arising out of their contemplated action against Serbia. The Austrian emissary carried two documents for delivery to the German Emperor. The one was a long memorandum, prepared in the foreign office before Sarajevo, setting forth proposals for improving the position of the Triple Alliance in the Balkans by drawing Bulgaria into the alliance and putting pressure on Rumania, who was clearly gravitating toward Russia and the Triple Entente. Approval and cooperation of the German government in implementing the plan was requested. The second document was a personal letter from Francis Joseph to William II, the most important part of which dealt with Austro-Serbian relations and the necessity of eliminating Serbia "as a factor of political power in the Balkans." Although the word "war" was not used, the implication was clear that force would be employed if necessary.

The documents which Hoyos brought from Vienna were presented to the Kaiser by the Austro-Hungarian ambassador, Count Szögyeny. William II, who had visited the Archduke only two weeks before the assassination, had been deeply moved by the tragedy. He scarcely hesitated in giving, subject to the concurrence of the chancellor, an unconditional promise of support for the proposed plans. He also urged immediate action and gave his offhand opinion that Russia would not intervene because she was unprepared and could be dealt with by Germany. While Szögyeny was lunching with the Kaiser, Hoyos was disclosing quite frankly to Zimmermann, the undersecretary of state, the nature and scope of the action advocated by Berchtold—military action against Serbia and her diminution or partition among Balkan neighbors. The following day, Bethmann Hollweg, after conferring with William II, confirmed in an interview with Hoyos and Szögyeny the commitment given previously by his sovereign. It remained for Austria-Hungary to decide what measures to take—they would find Germany unconditionally at their side in the event of complications. Again quick action was urged and the optimistic view with regard to the international situation was reiterated.

In the past fifty years much printer's ink and paper have been expended in the controversy over the "blank check" and the extent of German responsibility for what policy makers in Vienna now decided to do. In all this it must be kept in mind that Berlin could promise, encourage, and even prod, but the initiative had to be taken by Austria. But it was a foolhardy decision—giving Austria a free hand even though it might mean unleashing a European war. Words such as "reckless" and "irresponsible" are not too strong. It is almost unbelievable that a decision of such weight could be taken by William II and Bethmann, and confirmed by experts in the foreign office, without a meeting of either the Crown Council or the Federal Council. It is astounding also that an evaluation of the international situation, touching war and peace, should have been made so lightly and subjectively, without requesting situation reports from the ambassadors in London, Paris, and St. Petersburg.

Both Berlin and Vienna exaggerated the impact and the lasting impression made upon the governments by the bloody deed at Sarajevo. Their illusions were boundless—the Czar did not like the Serbs, abhorred regicides, and Russia's military program was two years from completion; moreover, a war on behalf of Serbia would not enlist much sympathy in Russia, or elsewhere in Europe. The Czar's government, it was thought, would bluff at first and then be "reined in" by England and France; likewise, France was not in the best position to wage war and would not do so over the Serbian issue. And to complete the record of mistaken judgments both Vienna and Berlin counted on England's neutrality.

The assurances that Hoyos elicited in Berlin brought a clarification of Austrian policy in the Council of Joint Ministers held in Vienna on July 7. Certain of German support, Berchtold became a "hard liner," carrying the other ministers with him, subject only to conditions imposed by Tisza. Resort to military action against Serbia immediately, without any diplomatic preliminaries, would have faced Russia and the Triple Entente with a *fait accompli* while Europe was still under the impression of the Sarajevo crime. But Tisza insisted upon diplomatic preparations, the presentation of stiff but not impossible demands, followed by armed intervention, and no annexation of Serbian territory by Austria-Hungary. It is clear from the protocol of the meeting that Tisza was wavering in his opposition to what Berchtold had described as war "to decapitate the Pan-Serb movement." By July 14 his conversion, as he confided to the German ambassador Tschirschky, was complete.

Influencing Tisza, the Emperor, and the joint ministers were Germany's unconditional promise of support, the facts revealed by the police investigation in Sarajevo, and the violent and provocative attitude of the Serbian press. Also by mid-July the political press in the Dual Monarchy had become a factor in public opinion. The most chauvinistic statements of the Serb press were paraded through the Austrian and Hungarian newspapers. Also the results of the judicial investigation were leaked to the journalists, and this reinforced the public demand that the government take forceful action.[10]

While the investigation continued in Sarajevo, the Austrian demands upon Serbia were formulated in the foreign office. Tisza had insisted on examining and approving the text of the note. This took place at a meeting of the joint council on July 19, after which the approval of the Emperor was secured. Presentation of the note was delayed until July 23, when President Poincaré and foreign minister Viviani, who were on a state visit to Russia, would be leaving St. Petersburg. About the middle of July rumors began to circulate in diplomatic circles that Austria was preparing severe demands to be presented in Belgrade. Efforts to elicit specific information were unavailing, but the feeling of anxiety and tension persisted.

The note, which was not formally an ultimatum, took as its point of departure the pledge which the Serbian government had given to the powers in 1909 promising to observe the rules of the international community in its relations with the Dual Monarchy. It then specified Serbian departures from this commitment, which had culminated in the Sarajevo assassinations. Then followed ten demands, the most important of which required Serbia to suppress all propaganda against the Hapsburg Empire—in the schools, the army, the press, and the bureaucracy—and to admit Austrian officials into Serbia to participate in the investigation and prosecution of those persons believed to have been implicated in the assassination of the Archduke. An ultimative character was given the note by the demand that the Serbian government return a satisfactory reply within forty-eight hours, that is, by 5 P.M., Saturday, July 25. At first glance there seemed no chance that Serbia could accept unconditionally many of the demands, but the reply, delivered just a few minutes before the deadline, was remarkably conciliatory and went far toward meeting the Austrian terms. In

10. Jonathan F. Scott, *Five Weeks* (New York, 1927), pp. 47–62.

European opinion the ultimatum was seen as "a clarion call to war," the Serbian reply as a moderate and responsible rejoinder. Notwithstanding, diplomatic relations were broken off, partial mobilization of the Austrian army was ordered, and three days later, on July 28, war was declared against Serbia.

German officials pretended to be shocked by the severity of the Austrian demands, insisting that they had not been advised in advance of the content of the note. The published documents show that this was considerably less than the truth. For already on July 21 the chancellor had sent a circular instruction to the ambassadors in Paris, London, and St. Petersburg indicating the role they were to play when the Austrian demands upon Serbia were published. This statement aligned Germany unequivocally with Austria and set forth the Wilhelmstrasse's formula of "localization"—that is, nonintervention by the other powers while Austria chastised Serbia. The semiofficial German press was briefed on the same lines so that the localization formula was aired and endorsed in almost all segments of the press: Austrian action is justified, it was said; Germany fully supports the Dual Monarchy; the dispute must remain localized; and if third powers intervene, Germany's alliance obligation becomes effective and she will make common cause with Austria. By this public affirmation of Germany's commitment the Wilhelmstrasse oracles thought that a Balkan dispute could be kept from becoming a Continental war. German policy makers accepted the risk of warlike complications. On July 18, Jagow wrote Lichnowsky, German ambassador in London, that Austria was going "to force a showdown with Serbia," but expressed optimism as to the possibility of localization. But if this were not achieved and Russia attacked Austria, the *casus foederis* would arise for Germany. "We could not throw Austria over then. . . . I desire no preventive war, but if war should come we cannot avoid the challenge."[11]

From July 19 on, the diplomats knew that a severe storm was blowing up in the southeast, one which would probably affect all the western capitals. With the delivery of the Austrian note the crisis became public through the medium of the newspaper press and the agencies of publicity. This was a new and potent ingredient in the crisis—it put the actors on the stage in full view of their clients; it inspired in some emotional attitudes of patriotic enthusiasm and in

11. Imanuel Geiss, *Julikrise und Kriegsausbruch 1914,* 2 vols. (Hanover, 1963), I, 208.

others abhorrence of violence; it became meshed in some instances with strong ideological and political forces; and it ushered in a period of great public excitement manifested in street crowds, newspaper extras and broadsides, as well as spontaneous and not so spontaneous parades and demonstrations. One can see this force operating in Austria, where after the break with Serbia crowds began to gather on the Ringstrasse to shout "Down with Serbia" and "Down with Russia." From every principal city and town in the next days came reports of demonstrations in favor of war. "This country," reported the British ambassador, "has gone wild with joy at the prospect of war with Serbia, and its postponement or prevention would undoubtedly be a great disappointment." It seems reasonable to conclude that Berchtold's intransigent rejection of all mediation proposals was a response to this aroused state of opinion and the war fever that now gripped the country. On July 29, following the declaration of war on Serbia, the respected *Pester Lloyd* of Budapest declared that Austria-Hungary had burned her bridges, and no power on earth could now change the course, "not even our own will."[12]

4. RUSSIAN INTERVENTION

Hasty in judgment, mercurial in temperament, and impulsive in action, Serge Sazonov was not especially suited to hold the helm when navigation became uncertain and dangerous. When he received news of the Austrian *démarche* in Belgrade, he exclaimed: "C'est la guerre européenne." To the ambassadors whom he received that day he spoke excitedly, as though war were a certainty. To the Austrian ambassador, who advanced the official arguments emphasizing "monarchical solidarity," he sharply protested: "The monarchic idea has got nothing to do with it. . . . The fact is you mean war and you have burnt your bridges. . . . One sees how peace loving you are, seeing that you set fire to Europe."[13] In conference with the French and British ambassadors Sazonov urged that their governments declare solidarity with Russia in respect of anticipated Austrian action against Serbia. A firm and united attitude was the best, perhaps the only, means of averting war, for it would serve to check Austria and warn Germany. The French ambassador urged firmness and gave the desired assurance that

12. Scott, *Five Weeks,* pp. 74, 98.
13. *Österreich-Ungarns Aussenpolitik,* VIII, No. 10619, p. 648.

France would fulfill all obligations imposed upon her by their alliance. Without being instructed to do so by his government, Paléologue, the French ambassador, renewed this pledge several times during the tense days that followed until it seemed, like Germany's blank check, almost an incitement to war.

Buchanan, the British ambassador, had a much cooler head than either Sazonov or Paléologue. He could hold out little hope that his government would proclaim its solidarity with France and Russia in this matter; for public opinion in England would never sanction a war on behalf of Serbia. However, he would recommend to his government that a friendly warning be given in Vienna and that they support a request for an extension of the time limit on the Austrian ultimatum while mediation was attempted. Buchanan's statement to Sazonov was confirmed by Grey on July 25 and communicated immediately to Sazonov. When in the course of their discussion the foreign minister said Russia might have to mobilize, Buchanan warned that "if Russia mobilized, Germany would not be content with mere mobilization or give Russia time to carry out hers, but would probably declare war at once."[14] This was of course exactly what happened. No caution or restraint, however, was recommended by the French ambassador.

Sazonov then proceeded with his plan to put heavy pressure on Austria and to register Russia's decision to stand by Serbia. After conferring with the chief of the general staff he called a meeting of the ministerial council to frame recommendations for presentation to the Czar at a council scheduled for the following morning. More as a diplomatic than a military measure Sazonov proposed that they recommend unconditional support of Serbia and mobilization against Austria. At the council of ministers the Czar authorized mobilization, at Sazonov's discretion, of forces in the five military districts of southwestern Russia, and immediate implementation of measures prescribed in their mobilization planning for the "period preparatory to war." The latter measures could not be concealed from foreign observers, and they had to be instituted uniformly throughout the country—that is, in the provinces adjacent to Germany as well as those bordering on Austria-Hungary. By taking this step at the outset Russia gained considerable time on her mobilization schedule, but it was these measures that alarmed the German general staff and led to pressure on

14. *British Documents on the Origins of the War*, XI, 94.

civilian authorities to hurry their diplomatic actions lest Germany be placed at a crucial disadvantage in the event of war with Russia. Among the military leaders in all affected countries, this grave concern for the timetable was universal in 1914. Since in their calculations there would be but one fling of the dice, a margin of one or two days might be the factor determining victory or defeat. All feared they might be caught without their swords drawn.

Close observers of Russian trends and developments agreed in 1914 that there had been a notable growth of Slav solidarity—something broader and deeper than conventional Pan-Slavism—among all classes of the Russian population in recent years. This was attested in many ways. When news of the fall of Adrianople reached St. Petersburg in March, 1913, the Duma organized spontaneously a thanksgiving celebration in which members acted as cantors and the speaker directed the choir of deputies.[15] Ambassadors of foreign powers with experience or knowledge of Russian developments commented on this strong trend —Delcassé, Buchanan, Jules Cambon, Paléologue, and Buissert, the Belgian minister in St. Petersburg—and when the crisis broke in 1914 foremost in the minds of participants and observers was the question: Will the Czar and his ministers be able to formulate a peaceful policy, which would be their desire, or will they be overwhelmed by public opinion and the feeling of Slav solidarity and thus forced into armed intervention on behalf of Serbia?

Russian opinion developed in two phases: the first, with the announcement of the ultimatum on July 24; the second, from the Austrian declaration of war until the Russian order for general mobilization. The ultimatum, in the first phase, aroused general indignation, and it was resented as an attack not only upon a Slav state but as a challenge to Russia as well. Patriotic street demonstrations were reported, and nearly all newspaper commentators agreed that Russia could not remain passive. Many urged the government to mobilize the frontier forces at once.[16] These manifestations notwithstanding, the

15. J. Stengers, "July 1914: Some Reflections," in *L'Annuaire de l'Institut de Philologie et d'Histoire Orientales et Slaves*, XVII (1963–65), 123. This is a suggestive examination in depth of the public opinion factor in Russian decision making in 1914. See also the older but still valuable study by Jonathan F. Scott, *Five Weeks*, Chap. VII, "The Psychotic Explosion in Russia."

16. Stengers, "July 1914," pp. 124–32. On July 25 and 27 the British ambassador Buchanan reported on the rising level of excitement in the press and in the streets. *British Documents*, XI, 136–37, 184.

country as a whole was calm. The German ambassador, Count Pour-talès, mistook this for indifference rather than a sign of quiet resolution. The French ambassador and correspondents of the French press reported the government in complete accord with public opinion and determined to preserve Serbia from any infringement upon her dignity or independence. This view was confirmed by an official communiqué, published on the morning of July 25, asserting that Russia was "intently following the development of the Austro-Serbian conflict," to which, indeed, she "could not remain indifferent."

Slavism and not Czarism was the moving slogan. The first secretary of the French embassy, Charles de Chambrun, wrote on July 27 that if Austria should violate Serbia she will provoke an explosion of Pan-Slavism that can be neither banished nor contained. At the court as well as in the streets the idea of Slav solidarity united the government and the public. This feeling even influenced the mass of workers who were striking at this time in St. Petersburg. Almost overnight the strikes collapsed as the workers returned to their jobs and hastened to participate in the patriotic demonstrations.

Austria's declaration of war, which became known in St. Petersburg through extra editions of the newspapers on the evening of July 28, opened the second phase. With this announcement the dam burst. Mass demonstrations occurred in the capital and all the large cities; thousands of excited people, singing and cheering, marched through the streets; enthusiastic crowds gathered around the French and British embassies. Reuter's correspondent wired on July 31 that the general sentiment of both men and women was that "We must and will fight for our Servian brothers and sisters." The order for general mobilization was eagerly obeyed, and on the day of its proclamation throughout the empire the American chargé d'affaires in St. Petersburg cabled tersely: "Whole country, all classes, unanimous for war."[17]

Since the Bosnian crisis, animosity toward Austria in Russian political and military circles was unquenchable. Whatever the personal inclinations of the Czar and his ministers, probably they did not dare leave Serbia in the lurch and retreat a second time before the threats of the Vienna government. Austrian assurance that they would not annex Serbian territory was not enough because, as Sazonov insisted, even with such a guarantee Serbia would inevitably become a vassal of

17. Quoted by Stengers, "July 1914," p. 133, from *Foreign Relations of the United States, 1914. Supplement: The World War* (Washington, D.C., 1928), p. 26.

Austria. "Were the Russian government to tolerate this, there would be a revolution in the country." Russia as a whole, he said, "would rise against us." Pourtalès, in a report to Berlin, quoted Sazonov as saying that "the life of the Czar" would be in danger. And Alexander Kerensky testified shortly thereafter that in his judgment, had the government yielded, the result might quickly have been its over-throw.[18] Two very keen observers, the St. Petersburg correspondent of the *Frankfurter Zeitung* and the British ambassador Buchanan, both reported on July 30 that the tension had now gone beyond the point where it would be possible for the Czar and his government to resist public pressure. There is much truth in the conclusion drawn by J. L. Stengers from his reexamination of these crucial hours—"that during the last phase of the drama, the Russian Government was practically the prisoner of its public opinion: it had no other way out than war."[19]

It was under pressure from these popular forces that Sazonov, the chief of staff, Yanushkevich, and the Czar took the fateful decisions with regard to mobilization during the last phase of the crisis. Sazonov had not abandoned hope of compromising the Austro-Serbian dispute when news of Austria's declaration of war on Serbia reached St. Petersburg late in the afternoon of July 28. The card that Sazonov now proceeded to play was that of partial mobilization against Austria, which had been approved previously by the ministerial council and the Czar. The Austrian general staff would think twice before proceeding with mobilization against Serbia, which would require twelve days, when Russian forces of more than one million were mobilizing on the Polish and Galician fronts. This was an obvious power move called for by the book. Prematurely, as it turned out, notice of this decision was sent to the Russian missions abroad while implementation became snarled in the bureaucratic mechanism in St. Petersburg. What happened was that Yanushkevich and the chiefs of the general staff sections were having painful second thoughts about an improvised partial mobilization against Austria and were beginning to urge, on technical grounds, that they switch to general mobilization, for which they had planned and prepared. On July 29 two ukases—providing for partial

18. Stengers, "July 1914," pp. 117–18, quoting Sazonov's statements to the British, French, and German ambassadors; also Scott, *Five Weeks,* pp. 177–78.

19. Stengers, "July 1914," p. 138. Possibly the same could be said for Austria-Hungary, but Germany, France, and Britain were not under such pressure and had far more freedom to exercise judgment and restraint.

and complete mobilization—were approved by the Czar, but neither was to be proclaimed until he had rendered a final decision.

The decision for general mobilization was taken on July 29 under the impact of the news of the bombardment of Belgrade—which was accorded more significance than it actually possessed—and the delivery of a sharp warning by the German ambassador, acting on instructions from Berlin, to the effect that further preparatory measures would compel Germany to mobilize, and then war could scarcely be avoided. Sazonov, it seems, joined the chief of staff in recommending final action to the Czar. Reluctantly Nicholas II gave his approval for general mobilization but later in the day rescinded the order as it was being transcribed in the central telegraph office. On the following morning Yanushkevich appealed to Sazonov, who in an interview lasting more than an hour finally persuaded Nicholas to reconsider and approve the order that made a European conflict inevitable. Neither the Czar nor Sazonov, even though they insisted Russia's mobilization did not mean war, was under any illusion as to the probable consequences of this act. The official notice was filed in the central telegraph office at 5 P.M., July 30, announcing general mobilization effective July 31. With this the landslide to disaster had begun.

In concluding our review of events in St. Petersburg during these historic hours it is appropriate to quote a short passage from Albertini: "Never, in tracing the history of the July crisis, can too much stress be placed on the point . . . that it was the political leaders' ignorance of what mobilization implied and the dangers it involved which led them light-heartedly to take the step of mobilizing and thus unleashing a European war."[20]

One aspect of the diplomatic situation that inclined Sazonov to push the mobilization button was the unyielding attitude of Austria with regard to her demands on Serbia and the absence of any visible inclination on the part of Berlin to restrain their Austrian ally. Grey's proposal of a conference to mediate on the basis of the conciliatory Serbian reply had received no support in Berlin and was answered in Vienna by the declaration of war on Serbia, undoubtedly a step taken to block further proposals for mediation. Meanwhile the Berlin au-

20. Albertini, *The Origins of the War of 1914*, II, 579. From Sir Edward Grey's numerous references to "mobilization" it is clear that he did not comprehend the significance of this act in the plans of Continental armies.

thorities continued to urge speedier action in Vienna and stood firm on the localization formula vis-à-vis the Entente powers. French logic inherent in the statement that "the best means of avoiding a general war was by preventing a local one" had been unwisely rejected in Berlin. Despite this discouraging record there was still a chance that diplomatic action might save Europe from a general war. That is why Russian mobilization was such a tragedy.

5. THE FAILURE OF DIPLOMACY—GERMANY, FRANCE, BRITAIN

When it was probably too late the German government began to modify its policy of unconditional support of Austria and localization of the Austro-Serbian conflict. Influencing the chancellor and the foreign office were the violent reaction in Russia, the virtual mobilization of the British fleet, and Grey's warning to the German ambassador Lichnowsky that if France were drawn into war Britain could probably not stand aside. The optimistic calculations of Bethmann and Jagow rapidly evaporated as the prospects of a general war and Germany's isolation became daily more visible. But it was the Kaiser who called for a turnabout as he perceived the dangerous course on which they were moving. He did not receive the text of the Serbian reply until July 28. In his opinion it represented a great moral victory which removed every reason for war. The unsettled points could be negotiated. As a pledge of fulfillment, and to satisfy the Austrian military, Belgrade could be occupied until the affair was settled. (A similar "Halt in Belgrade" proposal was made by Grey the next day, after the Austrian declaration of war.) The foreign office was instructed by the Emperor to communicate the proposal to Vienna, but Bethmann altered substantially the Kaiser's proposals and delayed transmission for some hours. When the communication was finally sent he instructed the ambassador to "avoid giving rise to the impression that we wish to hold Austria back." And then in a rather devious final sentence he said: "It is simply a matter of finding a way to realize Austria's desired aim, that of cutting the vital cord of the Greater Serbia propaganda, without at the same time precipitating a world war, and, if the latter cannot be avoided in the end, of improving, in so far as possible, the conditions under which we shall have to wage it."[21]

On the twenty-ninth the Wilhelmstrasse's illusion that Britain would

21. Geiss, *Julikrise und Kriegsausbruch 1914*, II, 184–85, 196–98.

remain neutral and Italy and Rumania would cooperate was finally dispelled. Russian partial mobilization was a certainty. A general conflagration under the most adverse conditions for Germany became a fearsome possibility unless Austria could be brought to accept the "pledge plan" and to resume direct conversations with St. Petersburg. Extremely heavy pressure was applied by Bethmann through sharp—almost threatening—communications to the Vienna authorities. Two urgent messages were dispatched on July 30, the second concluding somewhat heatedly: "We are prepared to fulfil our duty as allies, but must decline to let ourselves be dragged by Vienna, wantonly and without regard to our advice, into a world conflagration. . . . Pray speak to Count Berchtold at once with great emphasis and most seriously."[22] There was nothing insincere in these communications, although Bethmann was deeply concerned to make Russia appear the aggressor in the eyes of neutrals and the German people, and to ensure a united Germany in the event of war. Despite increased pressure in Vienna, Bethmann got neither frank nor definite answers. Determined to crush Serbia, Vienna would only repeat for Russia's benefit the pledge of disinterestedness. Meanwhile, developments in the military sector made diplomatic action almost irrelevant.

From the beginning of the crisis the German press, except for the Social Democratic papers, supported official policy in the spirit of *Niebelungentreue*. As a leading National Liberal journal put it, "There is no better way to localize the war and to preserve the peace of Europe than to show beyond the shadow of a doubt that the German army will mobilize at Russia's first move against Austria."[23] On the whole, the German press was remarkably free from chauvinism; editors did not demand war but gradually moved toward accepting it. Their attention was focused on Russia, and fact and rumor as they appeared in the press cast her in the role of aggressor. This ensured the loyalty of the Social Democrats and a united country. Although the socialists had organized peace demonstrations in the major cities, the vision of Cossack forces ravaging the fatherland proved stronger than proletarian solidarity. "The Social Democratic workers will not tolerate an attack by the Czar's Cossacks," declared the *Rheinische Zeitung,* an

22. Albertini, *The Origins of the War of 1914,* II, 525.
23. *Magdeburgische Zeitung,* quoted in E. Malcolm Carroll, *Germany and the Great Powers, 1870–1914* (New York, 1938), p. 793.

important socialist paper. And Kurt Eisner in Munich wrote that they were prepared to resist an attack upon the fatherland and reminded socialists that Bebel had once said that "against Russia he would shoulder a musket."[24] By August 1 the socialist policy line had shifted to a recognition of Russia's will to war and a readiness on their part to take the field against "Czarism." Socialist leaders had already given their word to Bethmann that there would be no strikes or sabotage if mobilization were ordered.

It is well to point out, as Albertini does, that general staffs were not, like diplomats, concerned with averting war but rather with winning victories. In consequence, as tensions increased, the military leaders put heavier pressure upon the civil authorities not to delay preparations to the point where the chances of military success might be jeopardized. Confirmation of Russian partial mobilization evoked urgent demands from Moltke that they proclaim the state of imminent danger of war preliminary to mobilization. Anticipating the advantage domestically that would result from Russian mobilization prior to their own, Bethmann resisted, but promised to act not later than noon on the following day (July 31). Russia's mobilization was confirmed shortly before the deadline. An ultimatum with a twelve-hour limit was dispatched to St. Petersburg, and when it was rejected the order for general mobilization and the declaration of war followed on the next day.

France played a secondary role in the 1914 crisis. She had no direct interest in Serbia, but if she did not support her ally the relationship might be ruptured and France left isolated as she had been before 1891. The French people had fallen into the habit of saying and presumably believing: "If war comes of course we have Russia." And in the popular imagination the Czar's army of 3 million men would flood across central Europe and meet the French at Strasbourg. Any critical analysis of this stereotype was unwelcome to the French government, the Russian embassy, and the French bankers. The middle classes knew they were financing the Russian government and especially its military establishment. It was an investment in national security, and besides it paid interest; they expected effective military support in

24. Quoted in E. Malcolm Carroll, *Germany and the Great Powers*, pp. 802–3; Philip Scheidemann, *Memoirs of a Social Democrat*, 2 vols. (London, 1929), I, 185–205; Georg Kotowski, *Friedrich Ebert, eine politische Biographie* (Wiesbaden, 1963), I, 222–28.

return. The alliance with Russia and the close association with England created a balance of power which best served the security and interests of France; even war would be justified in defense of this policy which was accepted in French political circles by all but the socialist and leftist elements. Revanche and Alsace-Lorraine played no significant role in convincing the French public that war was justified and necessary. French opinion was formed around the ideas that the maintenance of the balance of power was essential to peace, to France's security, and to her interests.

From the publication of the Austrian ultimatum, French public opinion, French political leadership, and the French press were in complete accord—expressing sympathy for Serbia, alleging German influence behind the ultimatum, and proclaiming that the balance of power was at stake. Therefore, they must support Russia without any reservations, maintain unity in the Triple Entente, and stand ready and united for the conflict.[25] Since the president of the Republic and the premier were isolated on shipboard at the height of the crisis (July 23–29), this practically precluded any French initiative or effective collaboration in attempts at mediation and compromise. The French authorities, supported by the press, proclaimed their solidarity with Russia and rejected all suggestions that they advise moderation in St. Petersburg.

Paléologue, the French ambassador, as we have seen, encouraged Sazonov's excitable intransigence and repeated at every opportunity assurances of unconditional French support. His provocative behavior and influence matched that of the German ambassador Tschirschky in Vienna. When Poincaré and Viviani returned to Paris they began to counsel caution in St. Petersburg with regard to mobilization and troop movements that might be provocative toward Germany. But like Bethmann's attempts to reverse German policy and restrain Austria, French action came too late to check Sazonov and the military leaders. In retrospect this seems a great pity because Russia, Austria, Germany, and France could have postponed mobilization by another day or two without untoward consequences, thus giving the diplomats a last chance to avoid the catastrophe which was now clearly impending.

Following the Russian example, the French general staff began

25. E. Malcolm Carroll, *French Public Opinion and Foreign Affairs, 1870–1914* (New York, 1931), pp. 285–310.

military preparations early in the crisis. When the German ultimatum was sent to St. Petersburg on July 31, Germany, through her ambassador in Paris, formally inquired if France would remain neutral. Instead of replying, as the Germans expected, that they would march with Russia, the French government said that they would consult France's own interests, and later, following Russia's lead, ordered mobilization on August 1. For the moment Germany took no further action, but on August 3, alleging wrongly a series of frontier violations, she declared war on France, so that France like Russia appeared to be the victim of German aggression. This was important to France in her relations with England, whom France desperately desired as a timely co-belligerent.

In Britain the crisis found the government facing the prospect of civil war in Ireland over the issue of Home Rule. During the month that elapsed between Sarajevo and the Austrian ultimatum public attention was concentrated on the domestic crisis. This nourished the illusion in Berlin that Britain would avoid involvement on the Continent at this time. The ultimatum was therefore a bombshell. Sazonov was nearly right when he complained to Buchanan that "with the exception of *The Times* nearly the whole of the English press was on the side of Austria. . . ." In fact, the reaction was somewhat mixed. The Tory *Morning Post* saw the Triple Entente already engaged with the Triple Alliance, while the Conservative *Standard* denounced Serbia as "a half-civilized and wholly waspish and disorderly little state, whose annals are a dreary record of incompetence, violence, and political crime. . . . Were Great Britain under similar affliction, our attitude would be that taken by Austria-Hungary." On the other hand, Sir Edward Grey described the ultimatum as "the most formidable document I had ever seen addressed by one State to another that was independent."[26] Between these positions were all shades of opinion, but the general consensus was that the ultimatum was harsh but justified.

We have seen that Britain was urged by Germany to support the policy of "localization" and by Russia and France to proclaim her solidarity with them as the only sure means of turning Austria and Germany from a course leading to war. Sensing correctly the disposi-

---

26. *British Documents on the Origins of the War*, XI, 73; Oron J. Hale, *Publicity and Diplomacy*, pp. 450–52; Scott, *Five Weeks*, pp. 206–15; E. Anrich, *Die englische Politik im Juli 1914* (Stuttgart, 1934), pp. 154–64.

tion of the cabinet, and probably of Parliament, Grey refused to commit the government to either course of action. He was quite frank in telling the Russians that British opinion would not sanction a war on behalf of Serbia or support Russia in a war with Austria over control of the Balkans. On the other hand, Grey's restraint toward the Germans encouraged Bethmann to gamble on British neutrality. However, with the Austrian declaration of war, to which Russia responded by ordering mobilization, the British cabinet had to face the prospect of a general war and chart the course that Britain would pursue. Although the cabinet was united in endorsing Grey's mediation efforts, it was hopelessly divided on the issue of neutrality or intervention. The Liberal Imperialists—Asquith, Grey, Churchill, and Haldane—favored supporting France, the balance of power, and the preservation of the Triple Entente. They would have understood Buchanan's appeal to Nicolson, the undersecretary: "I only pray that England will be true to herself and to her friends, as if she deserts them in their hour of need she will find herself isolated after the war; and the hours of our Empire will be numbered."[27]

Resolutely opposed to intervention were five Radical cabinet members led by Lord Morley. A numerous middle group, undecided but strongly pacific, looked to Lloyd George for leadership. It was clearly evident that an early commitment to France and Russia would produce multiple resignations and the fall of the government. In the daily cabinet meetings two issues were outstanding: first, the nature and extent of Britain's obligations to France should she be attacked; second, the anticipated violation of Belgium's neutrality. A long step toward a decision was taken when the leaders of the Conservative-Unionist party rallied to support the interventionists in the cabinet. On August 2 a letter was sent to Asquith over Bonar Law's signature stating that in their opinion "it would be fatal to the honour and security of the United Kingdom to hesitate in supporting France and Russia," and offering to back the government in any measures necessary to effect that policy. With this pledge from the opposition in hand, Asquith made his move, and on August 2 Grey was authorized by the cabinet to give the French ambassador the assurance he had been pressing for, namely, that the commitment in the Grey-Cambon letters of 1912 would be honored, and that the British navy would protect the French

27. *British Documents*, XI, 346.

coasts and shipping from German attack. With that the die was cast. The hesitating cabinet members followed Lloyd George when he quickly shifted to the interventionist side; in the end only four members retired and two of those subsequently withdrew their resignations.[28]

The action of the cabinet on August 2 was decisive, but it was the Belgian issue that determined the form and time of Britain's intervention. Germany's violation of Belgian neutrality united the country and convinced the cabinet, Parliament, and the nation of the necessity for entering the war. It brought unity if not unanimity. On the afternoon of August 3, Grey spoke to a tense and crowded House of Commons, presenting the decision of the cabinet to make the violation of Belgian neutrality the *casus belli*. The first part of his address dealt with their obligations to France, and he read the written assurance that had been given to Cambon the day before. The second part of his presentation was devoted to Belgian neutrality. Here was a vital interest and a treaty obligation of the highest order. If Belgium rejected the German ultimatum and appealed to the powers, then Britain really had no choice— "We must face it." Then as a general example of how little foresight the decision makers of 1914 possessed, Grey said: "For us, with a powerful Fleet, which we believe able to protect our shores, and to protect our interests, if we are engaged in war, we shall suffer but little more than we shall suffer even if we stand aside."[29] When the report of Germany's invasion of Belgium was confirmed, an ultimatum was presented in Berlin; as anticipated, it was rejected, and Britain and Germany were formally at war as of midnight August 4.

The Triple Alliance collapsed when Italy and Rumania proclaimed their neutrality at the beginning of hostilities. This was scarcely offset by Turkey's entrance into the war as an ally of the Central Powers. With Japan's declaration of war upon Germany at the end of August, the conflict spread from Europe to Asia; and since the colonies and commonwealths of the British Empire loyally supported the homeland, the war became in a formal sense a global affair.

28. Lord Newton, *Lord Lansdowne* (London, 1929), p. 440; Austen Chamberlain, *Down the Years* (London, 1935), pp. 92–106; Winston Churchill, *The World Crisis* (London, 1923), I, 228–30; Anrich, *Die englische Politik im Juli 1914, passim;* Hale, *Publicity and Diplomacy,* pp. 457–60.

29. *Parliamentary Debates,* 5th ser., Vol. 65, 1881; for Grey's speech in its entirety and the ensuing debate, *ibid.,* 1810–84.

6. THE GREAT ILLUSION IN AN ERA OF CONFIDENCE

Scarcely had the "guns of August" sounded when publicists and historians began to ask: Was this war willed by individuals or was it an inevitable product of historic forces that could not be contained? More than a half-century has elapsed and the *Kriegsschuldfrage* is no nearer resolution than it was in the 1920's when first bruited. The personal responsibility of the diplomats, military leaders, and statesmen is incontestable because only individuals can make decisions and act. And yet the men of 1914 did not act irresponsibly in violation of the powers and terms of their office. Only the French ambassador in St. Petersburg, Maurice Paléologue, has been charged with exceeding the limits of his instructions, pursuing a personal policy, and concealing from his superiors in Paris the critical decisions being taken by the Russian government in the matter of mobilization. Schooled diplomats and experienced statesmen made every move by the book—predictably, unimaginatively, without an original idea that might have broken the chain of decisions which was dragging them all to the brink. It is historically inconceivable that a Metternich, a Castlereagh, a Bismarck, or even a Salisbury would have acted so conventionally and with so little wisdom and vision. Furthermore, it is significant that in all the volumes of diplomatic dispatches, notes, and memoranda pertaining to the 1914 crisis, there is not to be found a recorded discussion of the crucial question: What will a civil war mean to Europe, and how will it affect the position of predominance that the European nations enjoy in the world? And it was not too much to expect of statesmanship that this question be raised; but statesmanship was lacking in large quantities in 1914.

The impersonal forces in play require somewhat more detailed consideration. In this connection, it cannot be argued convincingly that the First World War was predestined or prefigured in the arts and sciences, in economic relations, in the area of ideas, or even in the public relations of the peoples of Europe. In other areas—social and political—institutions and policies seemed adequate to accomplish the necessary adjustments and compromises. Europe before 1914 had an inner unity and a common ideology arising from its social institutions, its history, and its religions. The network of contacts and communications was very thick among the educated classes and businessmen, and there was a consciousness of sharing a common European culture. There was also a good deal of imitation and much borrowing from others' experiences. The number of international congresses, organizations, and commissions founded between 1900 and 1914 is both impressive and significant. All this reinforced the optimism and belief in progress which was dominant in popular thought during these years. Interpreters who must divine a *Zeitgeist* in every era have insisted that the end of the century was "decadent" and the period covered by this study the tag end of a heroic age. This judgment must be repudiated. As has been well said, the *fin de siècle* was really a beginning rather than an end; it was not the twilight of a golden age but the seedbed of our twentieth-century problems and concerns. Confident of the future and proud of the past, Europe welcomed the twentieth century.

This leads us to conclude that if there was a fatal flaw threaded through this era of confidence—and this was the great illusion—it was the humanitarian belief that a general war among Europeans was really unthinkable. But while this popular conviction was spreading among the enlightened, the European governments in their international relationships continued to wear the outmoded garments of the nineteenth century. Never were values associated with the nation state so grossly inflated—and this in a period when interdependence in all vital matters was weaving a girdle around the world. But this new reality was only faintly reflected in the relations of governments. Every country had its contingent of "jump-to-glory" militarists and navalists and second-rate statesmen engrossed in the mechanics of power. In the crisis of 1914 both the men and the mechanism failed. This brings us close to the view prevalent at the time: The war resulted from a series of fateful human decisions—mostly mistaken and erroneous—involving risks that decision makers would have avoided had they been endowed with a larger measure of foresight and prudence. Dawning light, rich in promise for a fair day, never became high noon because of the failures and miscalculations of Europe's political and military leaders.

BIBLIOGRAPHICAL ESSAY

In standard historical works the years 1900–1914 are customarily treated as an integral part of the conventional period extending from 1870 to the First World War. No sharp break is ordinarily associated with the transition from the nineteenth to the twentieth century, and most works of substantial scope span the full forty-five years. Such comprehensive studies are listed in the bibliographical essay of the preceding volume in this series: Carlton J. H. Hayes, *A Generation of Materialism, 1871–1900*. The bibliography of the Hayes volume has been updated to 1963, and the student is referred to the detailed listing of major comprehensive histories that is to be found there. As far as possible in this essay duplication will be avoided and the emphasis placed upon recent works and studies for the period 1900–1914.

GUIDES, GENERAL WORKS, AND NATIONAL HISTORIES

The following bibliographical guides will introduce the student to the specialized literature for most fields: The American Historical Association, *Guide to Historical Literature* (New York, 1961), ed. by George F. Howe and others, does not entirely supersede the 1931 edition, which still has value for some periods; the annual *International Bibliography of Historical Sciences* (Paris, 1930 ff.) is also comprehensive in its listings.

National historical guides include the old established Dahlmann-Waitz, *Quellenkunde der deutschen Geschichte* (Leipzig, 1931), of which a new edition in five volumes is now in progress; the *Jahresberichte für deutsche Geschichte* (Leipzig, 1927 ff.) affords interim coverage. The Richard Charmatz *Wegweiser* for Austrian history, published in 1912, is sadly dated; the Austrian section of the new Dahlmann-Waitz should help fill this void. For British history in the twentieth century the student will derive some help from the Historical Association's *Annual Bulletin of Historical Literature* (London, 1911 ff.) and the annual *Writings on British History* (London, 1935 ff.), published by the Royal Historical Society. The standard French guide, G. Brière and P. Caron, *Répertoire méthodique de l'histoire moderne et contemporaine de la France,* 11 vols. (Paris, 1899–1914), is inadequate but still useful. For Spain and Italy the following are indispensable though not entirely satisfactory: B. Sanchez Alonso, *Fuentes de la historia española e hispano-americana,* 3 vols. (Madrid, 1952); E. Rota, *Questioni di storia moderna,* 4 vols. (Milan, 1952–55). Robert J. Kerner's bibliography of *Slavic Europe* (Cambridge, Mass., 1918) may be supple-

315

mented by the extensive listings in the *Jahrbücher für Geschichte Osteuropas* (Breslau, 1936–41; Munich, 1953 ff.). On Russian history David Schapiro, *A Select Bibliography of Works in English on Russian History, 1801–1917* (Oxford, 1962), is useful; and although the emphasis is on the Soviet period, the two aids by Paul L. Horecky are recommended: *Basic Russian Publications* (Chicago, 1962), and *Russia and the Soviet Union: A Bibliographic Guide to Western Language Publications* (Chicago, 1965).

A number of specialized journals, some new and some now suspended, present articles and bibliographical information on particular topics: *Journal of World History* (Paris, 1953 ff.); *Revue d'histoire moderne et contemporaine* (Paris, 1954 ff.); *Journal of Economic History* (New York, 1941 ff.); *Journal of Contemporary History* (London, 1966 ff.); *Central European History* (Atlanta, 1968 ff.); *Journal of Central European Affairs* (Boulder, Colo., 1941–64); *Die Kriegsschuldfrage* (Berlin, 1923–28), continued as *Berliner Monatshefte für Internationale Aufklärung* (1928–41); *Austrian History Yearbook* (Houston, 1966 ff.); *Journal of the History of Ideas* (New York, 1940 ff.); *Isis* (Brussels and Baltimore, 1913 ff.) publishes regularly a bibliography covering all fields of the history of science.

Three multivolume series treat Europe as an entity rather than a conglomerate of national states. The volumes relevant to the pre-1914 scene are: *Propyläen Weltgeschichte*, ed. by Golo Mann, Vol. IX, *Das zwanzigste Jahrhundert* (1960); *New Cambridge Modern History*, Vol. XII, David Thomson (ed.), *The Era of Violence, 1898–1945;* and in the French series *Peuples et civilisations*, M. Baumont, *L'essor industriel et l'impérialisme coloniale, 1878–1904*, 3d ed. (Paris, 1965); P. Renouvin, *La crise européenne, 1904–1918*, 4th ed. (Paris, 1962). An interesting but uneven cooperative enterprise by international scholars is *L'Europe du XIXᵉ et du XXᵉ siècle, 1870–1914*, 2 vols. (Milan, 1962); briefer treatises of Europe as a unity are: R. Schnerb, *Le XIXᵉ siècle: l'apogée de l'expansion européenne, 1815–1914* (Paris, 1955), a volume in the *Histoire générale des civilisations;* and J. R. de Salis, *Weltgeschichte der neuesten Zeit*, 2d ed. (Zurich, 1962), covers the period since 1904.

Britain

The works of R. C. K. Ensor, G. M. Trevelyan, É. Halévy, D. C. Somervell, and Esmé Wingfield-Stratford are so well known that they need not be cited here. Although designed as a text for advanced students, Alfred E. Havighurst, *Twentieth-Century Britain*, 2d ed. (New York, 1966), is excellent on the Edwardian era. Other treatises and monographs of recent date are: Robert T. McKenzie, *British Political Parties,* 2d ed. (New York, 1963); W. L. Guttsman, *The British Political Elite, 1832–1935* (London, 1964); David Butler and Jennie Freeman, *British Political Facts, 1900–1960* (London, 1963); Brian R. Mitchell and Phyllis Deane, *Abstract of British Historical Statistics* (Cambridge, Eng., 1962). With these works available the student can now be very precise about the political structure of modern Britain. On cultural history nothing rivals Simon Nowell-Smith (ed.), *Edwardian England, 1901–1914* (London, 1964), for depth and completeness; on Edwardian thought and ideas Samuel Hynes, *The Edwardian Turn of Mind* (Princeton, 1968), is scintillating.

We are now in the second round of biographies of the Edwardian worthies, and this round is more critical than the first. Sir Sidney Lee, *King Edward VII,* 2 vols. (London, 1925–27); Philip Magnus, *King Edward the Seventh* (New York, 1964); Harold Nicolson, *King George the Fifth* (London, 1952), is outstanding; and James Pope-Hennessy, *Queen Mary, 1867–1953* (New York, 1960), is respectfully candid. Many of the political leaders are also receiving a "second round" appraisal: J. A. Spender, *Campbell-Bannerman,* 2 vols. (London, 1923); Blanche E. C. Dugdale, *Balfour,* 2 vols. (London, 1936), supplemented by the more critical work of Kenneth Young, *Arthur James Balfour, 1848–1930* (London, 1963); J. A. Spender and C. Asquith, *Asquith,* 2 vols. (London, 1932), contrasts sharply with Roy Jenkins, *Asquith: Portrait of a Man and an Era* (New York, 1964); J. L. Garvin's biography of Joseph Chamberlain has been continued by Julian Amery through Vol. IV, *At the Height of His Power, 1901–1903* (London, 1951); this is supplemented by Austen Chamberlain, *Politics from Inside* (London, 1936), a daily report on party politics for his invalided father. Recent biographies of political leaders are: Dudley Sommer, *Haldane of Cloan: His Life and Times, 1856–1928* (London, 1960); R. S. Churchill, *Winston S. Churchill,* Vol. II, *The Young Statesman, 1901–1914* (Boston, 1967); Frank Owen, *Tempestuous Journey: Lloyd George, His Life and Times* (New York, 1955), is the best of the numerous studies; unique in its frankness is Richard Lloyd George, *My Father, Lloyd George* (New York, 1961) ("My father was probably the greatest natural Don Juan in the history of British politics, and there seems to be living evidence to prove this"). Sir John E. Wrench, *Alfred Lord Milner* (London, 1958), is a sympathetic biography, while Alfred M. Gollin, *Proconsul in Politics: A Study of Lord Milner in Opposition and in Power* (New York, 1964), focuses on Milner at the height of his political career; the great influence wielded by the publicist J. L. Garvin in the Unionist party is revealed in Alfred M. Gollin, *"The Observer" and J. L. Garvin, 1908–1914* (London, 1960).

France

For an extended list of older works on the Third Republic the student should consult the preceding volume in this series: Hayes, *A Generation of Materialism*, pp. 348 ff. Gordon Wright, *France in Modern Times: 1760 to the Present* (Chicago, 1960), is a model text with valuable bibliographical essays; E. M. Earle (ed.), *Modern France: Problems of the Third and Fourth Republics* (Princeton, 1951), is a valuable symposium by American scholars; D. W. Brogan, *The Development of Modern France, 1870–1939*, 2 vols. (New York, 1966), treats mainly French politics. Jacques Chastenet attempts to integrate all aspects of French history in his *Histoire de la Troisième République*, 7 vols. (Paris, 1952–63), of which Vol. IV, *Jours inquiets et jours sanglants*, covers the years 1906–18; G. Bonnefous, *Histoire politique de la Troisième République*, Vol. I, *L'avant-guerre, 1906–1914* (Paris, 1956), is a kind of guide to French parliamentary history; the best study of Third Republic politics is F. Goguel, *La politique des partis sous la IIIᵉ République*, 2 vols. (Paris, 1946); a companion study by the same author is his *Histoire des institutions politiques de la France de 1870 à 1940* (Paris, 1952); D. Thomson, *Democracy in France Since 1870*, 4th ed. (Oxford, 1964), is a study of political and social dynamics; C. J. H. Hayes, *France: A Nation of Patriots* (New York, 1930), and Eugen Weber, *The Nationalist Revival in France, 1905–1914* (Berkeley, 1959), are two distinguished studies of French nationalism; the most recent review in depth of the Dreyfus Affair is Guy Chapman, *The Dreyfus Case* (London, 1955); and Malcolm O. Partin, *Waldeck-Rousseau, Combes, and the Church, 1899–1905* (Durham, N.C., 1969), reexamines the issue of anticlericalism.

Political biography is not honored in France as it is in England. In consequence there are few notable biographies of French statesmen for this period. Geoffrey Bruun, *Clemenceau* (Cambridge, Mass., 1943), and J. H. Jackson, *Clemenceau and the Third Republic* (New York, 1948), are good sketches; Jacques Chastenet, *Raymond Poincaré* (Paris, 1948), gives a balanced appraisal; the best treatment of a political figure is Harvey Goldberg, *The Life of Jean Jaurès* (Madison, 1962); Georges Suarez, *Briand*, 6 vols. (Paris, 1938–52), is based on the private papers; Rudolph Binion, *Defeated Leaders: The Political Fate of Caillaux, Jouvenel, and Tardieu* (New York, 1960), is both scholarly and original; three intellectual critics of the political regime are presented in Michael Curtis, *Three Against the Third Republic: Sorel, Barrès, and Maurras* (Princeton, 1959).

Marshal Pétain once remarked that he would not write his memoirs since he had nothing to hide! For French politicians of the pre-1914 era memoirs are more numerous than conventional biographies. A selection from the more prominent should include: Emile Combes, *Mon ministère, mémoires, 1902–1905* (Paris, 1956); A. Combarieu, *Sept ans à l'Élysée, 1899–1906* (Paris, 1932); J. Paul-Boncour, *Recollections of the Third Republic,* Vol. I (New York, 1957); Raymond Poincaré, *Au Service de la France,* Vols. I–IV (Paris, 1926 ff.); Joseph Caillaux, *Mes mémoires,* 3 vols. (Paris, 1942–47).

Italy

In the liberal tradition and emphasizing ideas, B. Croce's *History of Italy, 1871–1915* (Oxford, 1929) is a minor classic; the best-balanced treatment now available is Christopher Seton-Watson, *Italy from Liberalism to Fascism, 1870–1925* (London, 1967); G. Volpe, *Italia moderna,* 3 vols. (Florence, 1943–52), generally disparages the parliamentary system of the prewar period; Saverio Cilibrizzi, *Storia parlamentare, politica e diplomatica d'Italia, 1848–1918,* 5 vols. (Milan, 1925–40), is a well-documented political history; D. Mack Smith, *Italy: A Modern History* (Ann Arbor, 1959), concentrates on the post-Risorgimento period, stressing the negative aspects of Italy's national development; his critical treatment of Giolitti is balanced by A. W. Salomone, *Italian Democracy in the Making: The Political Scene in the Giolittian Era, 1900–1914* (Philadelphia, 1960); John A. Thayer, *Italy and the Great War: Politics and Culture, 1870–1914* (Madison, 1964), also argues that Giolitti was leading Italy toward effective democracy. Giolitti's *Memoirs of My Life* (London, 1923) is the autobiography of the statesman who dominated Italian politics from 1900 to 1914; his principal critic was Luigi Albertini, editor of the *Corriere della Sera,* who has published his memoirs in five volumes: *Venti Anni di Vita Politica* (Bologna, 1950–53).

Spain and Portugal

The period 1900–1914 is not much cultivated by Iberian historians; the dearth of monographs testifies to this. In English the standard surveys are William C. Atkinson, *History of Spain and Portugal* (Baltimore, 1960); Harold V. Livermore, *A New History of Portugal* (Cambridge, Eng., 1966); Gerald Brenan, *The Spanish Labyrinth* (Cambridge, Eng., 1950), valuable for the background of Spain's history since 1874. Two recent surveys are Rhea Marsh Smith, *Spain: A Modern History* (Ann Arbor, 1965), and Raymond Carr, *Spain, 1809–1939* (London, 1966), in the Oxford History of Modern Europe. Antonio Ballesteros y Beretta, *Historia de España y de su influencia en la historia universal,* 2d ed., 11 vols. (Barcelona, 1942–56), is the best comprehensive treatment of Spanish history to 1931; Vol. V of the collaborative work ed. by J. Vicens Vives, *Historia sociale e económica de España y América* (Barcelona, 1957 ff.), treats the nineteenth and twentieth centuries.

Germany

Of the surveys the best in English are K. S. Pinson, *Modern Germany,* 2d ed. (New York, 1966), and Hajo Holborn, *A History of Modern Germany,* Vol. III, *1840–1945* (New York, 1969); worthwhile German works emphasizing political developments are: Johannes Bühler, *Vom Bismarck-Reich zum geteilten Deutschland: Deutsche Geschichte seit 1870* (Berlin, 1960); Adalbert Wahl, *Deutsche Geschichte von der Reichsgründung bis zum Ausbruch des Weltkrieges, 1871–1914,* 4 vols. (Stuttgart, 1926–36), presents a conservative interpretation; Johannes Ziekursch, *Politische Geschichte des neuen deutschen Kaiserreiches,* 3 vols. (Frankfurt a.M., 1925–30), has a liberal viewpoint; and Arthur Rosenberg, *The Birth of the German Republic, 1871–1918* (New York, 1931), presents a socialist interpretation; Erich Eyck, *Das persönliche Regiment Wilhelms II* (Zurich, 1948), is an unqualified condemnation of William II; two additional surveys are Fritz Hartung, *Deutsche Geschichte, 1871–1919,* 6th ed. (Stuttgart, 1952), and Werner Frauendienst, *Das deutsche Reich von 1890–1914* (Constance, 1959). The most recent study of political parties is Helga Grebing, *Geschichte der deutschen Parteien* (Wiesbaden, 1962); it should be supplemented by Wolfgang Treue, *Deutsche Parteiprogramme, 1865–1956* (Göttingen, 1956). Some special studies are: Martin Göhring, *Bismarcks Erben* (Wiesbaden, 1959); J. C. G. Röhl, *Germany Without Bismarck, 1890–1900* (Berkeley, 1967), answering the important question: "Who ruled in Berlin?" N. von Preradovich, *Die Führungsschichten in Österreich und Preussen, 1804–1918* (Wiesbaden, 1955); Wolfgang J. Mommsen, *Max Weber und die deutsche Politik* (Tübingen, 1959).

Of the great number of biographies and memoirs the following are basically important: Michael Balfour, *The Kaiser and His Times* (Boston, 1964), the fairest account; Paul Herre, *Kronprinz Wilhelm: Seine Rolle in der deutschen Politik* (Munich, 1954); Klaus W. Jonas, *The Life of Crown Prince William* (Pittsburgh, 1961); J. Haller, *Philip Eulenburg, the Kaiser's Friend,* 2 vols. (New York, 1930), apologetic but contains important documentary material; *Memoirs of Prince von Bülow,* Eng. trans., 4 vols. (Boston, 1931–32), anecdotal and colored but naïvely revealing; also illuminating is W. Görlitz (ed.), *Der Kaiser: Aufzeichnungen des Chefs des Marinekabinetts Admiral Georg Alexander von Müller* (Berlin, 1965); Norman Rich, *Friedrich von Holstein,* 2 vols. (Cambridge, Eng., 1965), a scholarly biography of a key figure. Other recent biographical studies are: Theodor Heuss, *Friedrich Naumann: Der Mann, das Werk, die Zeit* (Stuttgart, 1949); Klaus Epstein, *Matthias Erzberger and the Dilemma of German Democracy* (Princeton, 1959); Lamar Cecil, *Albert Ballin: Busi-*

ness and Politics in Imperial Germany, 1888–1918 (Princeton, 1966); Annelise Thimme, *Hans Delbrück als Kritiker der Wilhelminischen Epoche* (Düsseldorf, 1955); James J. Sheehan, *The Career of Lujo Brentano: A Study of Liberalism and Social Reform in Imperial Germany* (Chicago, 1966). The old biographical dictionary *Allgemeine deutsche Biographie* is now being replaced by the *Neue deutsche Biographie,* 7 vols. to date (Berlin, 1955 ff.).

Austria-Hungary

The most recent comprehensive work is Hugo Hantsch, *Die Geschichte Österreichs,* Vol. II, *1648–1918,* 2d ed. (Graz, 1953); Arthur J. May, *The Hapsburg Monarchy, 1867–1918* (Cambridge, Mass., 1951), is the standard treatment in English; Oscar Jászi, *The Dissolution of the Hapsburg Monarchy, 1867–1914* (Chicago, 1929), emphasizes the Hungarian aspects of the monarchy's decline; Robert A. Kann, *The Multinational Empire, 1848–1918,* 2 vols. (New York, 1950), is the best treatment of the nationality problems; important for recent interpretations and scholarship is Vol. III of the *Austrian History Yearbook* (Houston, 1967), which includes papers given at an international conference on the Dual Monarchy held at Indiana University in 1966. Other works worthy of note by Austrian scholars are: Viktor Bibl, *Der Zerfall Österreichs,* 2 vols. (Vienna, 1922–24); on constitutional history, B. Weisz, *Die Verfassungen Österreichs seit 1848 und ihre unitarischen und föderalistischen Elemente* (Innsbrück, 1937).

Political biographies and memoirs are not numerous for this period. The following are among the more important works: Josef Redlich, *Emperor Francis Joseph of Austria* (New York, 1929); Rudolf Kiszling, *Erzherzog Franz Ferdinand von Österreich-Este* (Graz, 1963); H. Hantsch, *Leopold Graf Berchtold, Grandseigneur und Staatsmann,* 2 vols. (Graz, 1963); Fritz Fellner (ed.), *Das politische Tagebuch Josef Redlichs,* 2 vols. (Graz, 1954), is a veritable political *Who's Who* for the period 1908–1919; Joseph M. Baernreither, *Fragments of a Political Diary* (London, 1930), is important for the South Slav problem.

The best English language survey of Hungarian history is C. A. Macartney, *Hungary: A Short History* (Edinburgh, 1962); by the same author, *National States and National Minorities* (London, 1934), on the national movements in central and eastern Europe; J. Miskolozy, *Ungarn in der Habsburger-Monarchie* (Vienna, 1959), is a rare defense of the dualist solution; S. Harrison Thomson, *Czechoslovakia in European History* (Princeton, 1953), is a standard treatment; see also R. W. Seton-Watson, *A History of the Czechs and the Slovaks* (London, 1943).

Russia

For guidance in a burgeoning field of history the student can rely on the relevant section of the AHA *Guide to Historical Literature* (Section X, by Fritz T. Epstein); Charles Morley, *Guide to Research in Russian Historiography,* 2d ed. (Princeton, 1958). Among the survey works that emphasize, or treat adequately, the twentieth century may be cited: Karl Stählin, *Geschichte Russlands von den Anfängen bis zur Gegenwart,* 5 vols. (Berlin, 1923–39), of which Vol. V covers the reign of Nicholas II; P. Miliukov, Charles Seignobos, and L. Eisenmann, *Histoire de Russie,* 3 vols. (Paris, 1932–33), Vol. III, treating the period 1855–1917; Michael T. Florinsky, *Russia: A History and Interpretation,* 2 vols. (New York, 1953); Valentin Gitermann, *Geschichte Russlands,* Vol. III (Zurich, 1949); Hugh Seton-Watson, *Decline of Imperial Russia* (New York, 1952), and *The Russian Empire, 1801–1917* (London, 1967), in the Oxford History of Modern Europe; Donald W. Treadgold, *Twentieth Century Russia* (Chicago, 1964); a Marxist synthesis is offered in M. N. Pokrovsky, *Brief History of Russia,* Eng. trans., 2 vols. (London, 1933); of Bernard Pares' many works, the one most valuable for this period is *The Fall of the Russian Monarchy* (New York, 1939); Jacob Walkin, *The Rise of Democracy in Pre-Revolutionary Russia* (New York, 1962), treats objectively political and social development under the last three Czars.

There have been many superficial treatments of Nicholas II and the monarchy; the best study is probably S. S. Ol'denburg, *Tsarstvovanie Imperatora Nikolaia II,* 2 vols. (Belgrade, 1939–41); the letters and diaries of Nicholas II offer one approach: *Das Tagebuch des letzten Zaren von 1890 bis zum Fall* (Berlin 1923); *Letters of Tsar Nicholas and Empress Marie* (London, 1938); *The Letters of the Tsar to the Tsaritsa, 1914–1917* (London, 1929); A. Yarmolinsky (ed.), *The Memoirs of Count Witte* (New York, 1921), is an abridgment of the important *Vospominaniia,* 2 vols. (Berlin, 1922); M. P. Bock, *Vospominaniia o Moem Otse P. A. Stolypine* [Reminiscences of My Father, P. A. Stolypin] (New York, 1955); the memoirs of the finance minister and president of the council, Vladimir N. Kokovtsov, *Out of My Past* (Stanford, 1935), is a shortened version of *Iz moego proshlago: vospominaniia 1903–1919,* 2 vols. (Paris, 1933); of considerable importance are the memoirs of the Cadet and Socialist Revolutionary leaders: P. N. Miliukov, *Vospominaniia, 1859–1917,* 2 vols. (New York, 1955); and V. M. Chernov, *Pered burei; vospominaniia* (New York, 1953). Two exile memoirs of unusual interest are Fedor Stepun, *Das Antlitz Russlands und das Gesicht der Revolution, 1884–1922* (Munich, 1961); and W. S. Woytinsky, *Stormy Passage: A Personal History Through*

Two Russian Revolutions to Democracy and Freedom, 1905–1960 (New York, 1961).

Biographical studies of the Russian revolutionaries are numerous; only a few recent works can be noted here: Samuel H. Baron, *Plekhanov* (Stanford, 1963), portrays the father of Russian Marxism; Bertram D. Wolfe, *Three Who Made a Revolution*, 2d ed. (New York, 1956), is a standard work; Louis Fischer, *The Life of Lenin* (New York, 1964), is skimpy on the pre-1917 years; Isaac Deutscher portrays Trotsky the activist in the second volume of his trilogy, *The Prophet Armed, 1879–1921* (New York, 1954).

Two parts of the Russian Empire merit mention: J. H. Jackson, *Finland*, 2d ed. (New York, 1940), and John H. Wuorinen, *A History of Finland* (New York, 1965), are reliable political histories, the latter emphasizing the twentieth century; for Poland one should turn to the second volume of *The Cambridge History of Poland* (Cambridge, Eng., 1950), ed. by W. F. Reddaway; also the short histories by Oskar Halecki, *A History of Poland*, 2d ed. (London, 1956), and Hans Roos, *A History of Modern Poland* (New York, 1966), should be mentioned.

Ottoman Empire and the Balkans

The best survey with a good bibliography is L. S. Stavrianos, *The Balkans Since 1453* (New York, 1958), which emphasizes the Ottoman presence in Europe. Other surveys and specialized works are: Charles Jelavich (ed.), *The Balkans in Transition* (Berkeley, 1963); A. de La Jonquière, *Histoire de l'empire ottoman*, 2d ed., 2 vols. (Paris, 1914); Donald C. Blaisdell, *European Financial Control in the Ottoman Empire* (New York, 1929); Joan Haslip, *The Sultan: The Life of Abdul Hamid* (London, 1958), considerably improves the Sultan's image; scholarly treatment is given the revolutionary movement by Ernest E. Ramsaur, *The Young Turks: Prelude to the Revolution of 1908* (Princeton, 1957); for the intellectual background see S. Mardin, *The Genesis of Young Ottoman Thought* (Princeton, 1963). On individual Balkan countries scholarly works are not numerous. For Greece: William Miller, *A History of the Greek People, 1821–1921* (London, 1928), is outdated; barely adequate surveys are J. Campbell and P. Sherrard, *Modern Greece* (New York, 1968); and Christopher M. Woodhouse, *A Short History of Modern Greece* (New York, 1968); Douglas Dakin, *The Greek Struggle in Macedonia, 1897–1913* (Salonika, 1906); H. A. Gibbons, *Venizelos*, 2d ed. (Boston, 1923).

On Rumania: R. W. Seton-Watson, *A History of the Roumanians*

(Cambridge, Eng., 1934); Henry L. Roberts, *Rumania: Political Problems of an Agrarian State* (New Haven, 1951).
On Bulgaria: Stanley G. Evans, *A Short History of Bulgaria* (London, 1960); K. A. Khristov, *Bulgarische Geschichte* (Sofia, 1963); Hans R. Madol, *Ferdinand of Bulgaria* (London, 1933).
On Serbia: Emile Haumont, *La formation de la Yougoslavie, XVe-XXe siècles* (Paris, 1930); Robert J. Kerner (ed.), *Yugoslavia* (Berkeley, 1949); Jozo Tomasevich, *Peasants, Politics and Economic Change in Yugoslavia* (Stanford, 1955), emphasis on period since 1900; Vladko Macek, *In the Struggle for Freedom* (New York, 1957), memoirs of the Croat peasant leader.
On Albania: Joseph Swire, *Albania: The Rise of a Kingdom* (London, 1929); Stavro Skendi, *The Albanian National Awakening, 1878-1912* (Princeton, 1967).

Holland, Belgium, and Switzerland

Jan A. van Houtte (ed.), *Algemene Geschiedenis der Nederlanden*, Vol. XI, *1885-1914* (Utrecht, 1956); Adriaan Barnouw, *The Making of Modern Holland* (London, 1944); J. Deharveng (ed.), *Histoire de la Belgique contemporaine, 1830-1914,* 3 vols. (Brussels, 1928-30), contributions by specialists; Shepard B. Clough, *A History of the Flemish Movement in Belgium* (New York, 1930), treats the most divisive issue in modern Belgium. On Switzerland: Ernst Gagliardi, *Geschichte der Schweiz von den Anfängen bis auf die Gegenwart,* 3d ed., 3 vols. (Zurich, 1938); W. Oechsli, *History of Switzerland, 1499-1914* (Cambridge, Eng., 1922), concise history by a leading Swiss scholar; Edgar Bonjour and others, *A Short History of Switzerland* (Oxford, 1952).

Scandinavia

Folke A. Lindberg, *Scandinavia in Great Power Politics, 1905-1908* (Stockholm, 1958), and Raymond E. Lindgren, *Norway-Sweden: Union, Disunion, and Scandinavian Integration* (Princeton, 1959), treats relations in the Scandinavian community. Ingvar Andersson, *A History of Sweden* (London, 1956), and Stewart Oakley, *A Short History of Sweden* (New York, 1966), are adequate surveys; Douglas Verney, *Parliamentary Reform in Sweden, 1866-1921* (Oxford, 1957), and Arthur Montgomery, *The Rise of Modern Industry in Sweden* (London, 1939), treat important aspects of Sweden's recent history. On Norway: Karen Larsen, *A History of Norway* (Princeton, 1948); Knut Gjerset, *History of the Norwegian People,* 2d ed. (New York, 1932); Harry Eckstein, *Division and Cohesion in Democracy* (Princeton, 1966), is a case study of Norway as a stable political democracy. John H. S. Birch, *Denmark in History* (London, 1938), and John Danstrup, *A History of Denmark* (Copenhagen, 1949), are popular surveys; Johan Hvidtfeldt and others, *Danmarks historie,* 2 vols. (Copenhagen, 1951), a symposium emphasizing social and economic developments.

CHAPTER I: BEGINNING THE TWENTIETH CENTURY

The rationalistic attacks of the Zionist leader Max Nordau upon *fin de siècle* literature, philosophy, and art had a considerable vogue. His best known work, *Degeneration* (New York, 1895), was first published in German (*Entartung*) in 1892. G. B. Shaw's *The Sanity of Art* (London, 1908) was a spirited refutation of Nordau's thesis. The opposing optimistic view of the course of human history finds expression in Ludwig Stein, *An der Wende des Jahrhunderts: Versuch einer Kulturphilosophie* (Freiburg i.B., 1899). The climate of thought is perceptively delineated in Gerhard Masur, *Prophets of Yesterday* (New York, 1961), H. Stuart Hughes, *Consciousness and Society* (New York, 1958), and the preceding volume in this series, C. J. H. Hayes, *A Generation of Materialism.*

Because of the linkage of imperialism with political ideology we have almost an oversupply of works on colonialism and related topics. For the older literature the reader is referred to the extensive listings in Hayes, *A Generation of Materialism,* pp. 370–74. Only key works and recent reappraisals will be listed here. A reexamination of the subject in historical perspective will be found in the December, 1961, issue of the *Journal of Economic History,* which is devoted to the theme "Colonialism and Colonization in World History." Although he was not a Marxist, the starting point for the Marxist-Leninist interpretation of colonialism is J. A. Hobson, *Imperialism: A Study* (London, 1902); W. L. Langer, *The Diplomacy of Imperialism, 1890–1902,* 2d ed. (New York, 1951), treats in detail both the theoretical and diplomatic aspects; George W. Hallgarten, *Imperialismus vor 1914,* 2 vols. (Munich, 1963), is a sociological study of German imperialism; Earle M. Winslow, *The Pattern of Imperialism* (New York, 1948), is an illuminating examination of the theories of imperialism; Joseph Schumpeter, *Imperialism and Social Classes* (New York, 1955), offers a sociological rather than an economic interpretation. For a survey of the colonial scene, Mary E. Townsend, *European Colonial Expansion Since 1870* (Philadelphia, 1941), is useful; *Cambridge History of the British Empire,* Vol. III, and Paul Knaplund, *British Commonwealth and Empire, 1901–1955* (London, 1956), survey the most successful of the overseas empires. The following special studies are scholarly and important: Richard Koebner and H. D. Schmidt, *Imperialism: The Story and Significance of a*

Political Word, 1840–1960 (Cambridge, Eng., 1964); Bernard Semmel, *Imperialism and Social Reform, 1895–1914* (Cambridge, Mass., 1960); Ronald Robinson and John Gallagher, *Africa and the Victorians* (New York, 1961); G. B. Pyrah, *Imperial Policy and South Africa, 1902–1910* (Oxford, 1955); R. L. Tignor, *Modernization and British Colonial Rule in Egypt, 1882–1914* (Princeton, 1966). For France: Stephen H. Roberts, *History of French Colonial Policy, 1870–1925,* 2 vols. (London, 1929); Henri Brunschwig, French Colonialism, *1870–1914: Myths and Realities* (New York, 1966); J. Ganiage, *L'Expansion coloniale de la France sous la IIIᵉ République* (Paris, 1968), is a good factual survey based on the author's lectures at the Sorbonne. For Germany: Mary E. Townsend, *The Rise and Fall of Germany's Colonial Empire* (New York, 1930), is a standard work; Harry I. Rudin, *Germans in the Cameroons, 1884–1914* (New Haven, 1938), is a model case history; also W. O. Henderson, *Studies in German Colonial History* (Chicago, 1962). Two important studies of a major colonial problem are Jacques Willequet, *Le Congo Belge et la Weltpolitik, 1894–1914* (Brussels, 1962), and Ruth Slade, *King Leopold's Congo* (London, 1962); another area of European interest is treated in Edward M. Earle, *Turkey, the Great Powers, and the Bagdad Railway* (New York, 1923). For a general appraisal of Europe's impact on Asia see G. M. Beckmann, *The Modernization of China and Japan* (New York, 1962); H. Gollwitzer, *Die Gelbe Gefahr* (Göttingen, 1962), history of a slogan; Victor Purcell, *The Boxer Uprising* (Cambridge, Eng., 1963), a reexamination.

On nationalism the works of C. J. H. Hayes, Hans Kohn, K. S. Pinson, and Boyd C. Shafer are familiar to most students and need not be listed here. Additional studies of importance are: Edward M. Earle (ed.), *Nationalism and Internationalism* (New York, 1950); F. Chabod, *L'idea di nazione* (Bari, 1961); Eugen Lemberg, *Nationalismus,* 2 vols. (Hamburg, 1964); Francis S. L. Lyons, *Internationalism in Europe, 1815–1914* (Leiden, 1963), on international organizations; Calvin D. Davis, *The United States and the First Hague Peace Conference* (Ithaca, 1962). On the Pan-movements: Hans Kohn, *Pan-Slavism, Its History and Ideology* (Notre Dame, Ind., 1963); Alfred Kruck, *Geschichte des Alldeutschen Verbandes, 1890–1939* (Wiesbaden, 1954); Mildred S. Wertheimer, *The Pan-German League, 1890–1914* (New York, 1924).

Militarism and the role of force in international relations are dealt with in these works: Quincy Wright, *A Study of War,* 2 vols. (Chicago, 1942), truly monumental; also Theodore Ropp, *War in the Modern World* (Durham, N.C., 1959); Alfred Vagts, *A History of Militarism,* 2d ed. (New York, 1959); Gordon A. Craig, *The Politics of the Prussian Army 1640–*

1945 (New York, 1965); W. Goerlitz, *History of the German General Staff* (New York, 1953); Karl Demeter, *The German Officer-Corps in Society and State, 1650–1945,* 2d ed. (New York, 1964); Martin Kitchen, *The German Officer Corps, 1890–1914* (Oxford, 1968), is lacking somewhat in objectivity; Gerhard Ritter, *Staatskunst und Kriegshandwerk,* Vol. II, *Die Hauptmächte Europas und das wilhelminische Reich, 1890–1914* (Munich, 1960). For the Austrian military the best source is the papers of Conrad von Hötzendorf, *Aus meiner Dienstzeit, 1906–1918,* 5 vols. (Vienna, 1921–25), supplemented by Oskar Regele, *Feldmarschall Conrad* (Vienna, 1955); the only solid work on the Austrian navy is Walter Wagner, *Die obersten Behörden der k. und k. Kriegsmarine, 1856–1918* (Vienna, 1961).

British military history focuses on the navy, and for this period the correspondence and papers of Sir John Fisher are of primary importance: Arthur J. Marder (ed.), *Fear God and Dread Nought: The Correspondence of Lord Fisher of Kilverstone,* 3 vols. (London, 1953–59); also Marder, *The Anatomy of British Sea Power* (New York, 1940), and *From the Dreadnought to Scapa Flow,* Vol. I, *The Road to War, 1904–1914* (New York, 1961); Franklin A. Johnson, *Defence by Committee: The British Committee of Imperial Defence* (London, 1960); the most influential antiwar book of the period was Norman Angell's *The Great Illusion* (London, 1910); a rare kind of study is I. F. Clarke, *Voices Prophesying War, 1763–1984* (London, 1966).

The political role of the French army is the theme of Paul-Marie de la Gorce, *The French Army* (New York, 1963); a more scholarly treatment of civil-military relations is David B. Ralston, *The Army of the Republic, 1871–1914* (Cambridge, Mass., 1967); Richard D. Challener, *The French Theory of the Nation in Arms, 1866–1939* (New York, 1955); Henry Contamine, *La revanche, 1871–1914* (Paris, 1957), is a work of greater scope and scholarship than the title suggests; Raoul Girardet, *La société militaire dans la France contemporaine, 1815–1939* (Paris, 1953).

CHAPTER II: THE PEOPLE AND THE LAND

Deeply concerned with population problems, the French have cultivated intensively the field of demography. The most recent comprehensive work is Marcel Reinhard, André Armengaud, and Jacques Duparquier, *Histoire de la population mondiale* (Paris, 1968); Adolphe Landry, *Traité de démographie,* 2d ed. (Paris, 1948), is a reliable introduction; A. M. Carr-Saunders, *World Population: Past Growth and Present Trends* (Oxford, 1936), is still useful. Two monographs dealing with France's problems are: Wesley D. Camp, *Marriage and the Family in France since the Revolution*

(New York, 1961); Joseph J. Spengler, *France Faces Depopulation* (Durham, N.C., 1938).

The standard work on population movements is Walter F. Willcox (ed.), *International Migration*, 2 vols. (New York, 1929–31); the following general and specialized works refer to the pre-1914 years: Brinley Thomas (ed.), *Economics of International Migration* (London, 1958); Harry Jerome, *Migration and Business Cycles* (New York, 1926); Robert F. Foerster, *The Italian Emigration of Our Times* (Cambridge, Mass., 1924). The mass exodus of Jews from eastern Europe to western Europe and the United States is dealt with in these informative works: S. M. Dubnow, *The History of the Jews in Russia and Poland*, 3 vols. (Philadelphia, 1916–20); Samuel Joseph, *Jewish Immigration to the United States from 1881 to 1910* (New York, 1914); Jerome Davis, *The Russian Immigrant* (New York, 1922); Lloyd P. Gartner, *The Jewish Immigrant in England, 1870–1914* (Detroit, 1960); S. Adler-Rudel, *Ostjuden in Deutschland, 1880–1940* (Tübingen, 1959).

On agriculture the standard survey is N. S. B. Gras, *A History of Agriculture in Europe and America*, 2d ed. (New York, 1940), supplemented by M. Augé-Laribé, *La révolution agricole* (Paris, 1955). An especially important source is the *Bulletin of the Bureau of Economic and Social Intelligence,* published by the International Institute of Agriculture in Rome. The most useful recent work with a European focus is Folke Dovring, *Land and Labor in Europe, 1900–1950* (The Hague, 1956). Lord Ernle, *English Farming Past and Present* (London, 1961), has now reached a sixth edition with an introduction which in itself is a bibliographical essay; Pierre Besse, *La crise et l'évolution de l'agriculture en Angleterre de 1875 à nos jours* (Paris, 1910), is a valuable contemporary study; John E. Pomfret, *The Struggle for Land in Ireland* (Princeton, 1930), is the best work on the Irish land problem. The agricultural policy of the French government is treated in M. Augé-Laribé, *La politique agricole de la France de 1880 à 1940* (Paris, 1960); also Eugene Golob, *The Méline Tariff* (New York, 1944); and Charles K. Warner, *The Wine Growers in France and the Government Since 1875* (New York, 1960). Benjamin S. Rowntree, *Land and Labor in Belgium* (London, 1910), indicates the lessons to be learned from a small neighbor. The agricultural problems of Italy and Spain are covered in Ghino Valenti, *L'Italia agricola dal 1861 al 1911* (Rome, 1911); and Pascual Carrión, *Los latifundios en España* (Madrid, 1932); Ruth Trouton, *Peasant Renaissance in Yugoslavia, 1900–1950* (London, 1952), examines peasant society and education.

The standard Von der Goltz, *Geschichte der deutschen Landwirtschaft*, does not cover the twentieth century; a satisfactory survey and discussion of contemporary problems is provided by Heinz Haushofer, *Die deutsche Landwirtschaft im technischen Zeitalter* (Stuttgart, 1963); also Hans W. Finck von Finckenstein, *Die Entwicklung der Landwirtschaft in Preussen und Deutschland, 1800–1930* (Würzburg, 1960); Johannes Nichtweiss, *Die ausländischen Saisonarbeiter in der Landwirtschaft der östlichen und mittleren Gebiete des Deutschen Reiches, 1890–1914* (Berlin, 1959); Frieda Wunderlich, *Farm Labor in Germany, 1810–1945* (Princeton, 1961), is unsatisfactory on the prewar decade; Franz Rehbein, *Das Leben eines Landarbeiters* (Jena, 1911), is a realistic picture of the agricultural laborer.

The modernization of Russian agriculture, amounting to an agrarian revolution, is treated in the general works, such as Mavor, Liashchenko, and Pares, as well as in many special studies. Geroid T. Robinson, *Rural Russia Under the Old Regime* (New York, 1932), is the major work on serf emancipation and the resultant peasant problems; other scholarly works are Launcelot A. Owen, *The Russian Peasant Movement, 1906–1917* (London, 1937); George A. Pavlovsky, *Agricultural Russia on the Eve of the Revolution* (London, 1930); V. P. Timoshenko, *Agricultural Russia and the Wheat Problem* (Stanford, 1932), is much broader than the title suggests; Alexis N. Antsiferov and Alexander D. Bilimovich, *Russian Agriculture During the War* (New Haven, 1930), treats fully the pre-1914 developments.

CHAPTER III: TECHNOLOGY AND ECONOMIC GROWTH

Of the numerous textbooks and surveys, Herbert Heaton, *Economic History of Europe* (New York, 1948), is one of the best. The *Cambridge Economic History of Europe,* Vol. VI, *The Industrial Revolution and After* (Cambridge, Eng., 1965), is valuable though uneven; A. Sartorius von Waltershausen, *Die Entstehung der Weltwirtschaft* (Jena, 1931), is a standard work; and Wilhelm Treue, *Wirtschaftsgeschichte der Neuzeit* (Stuttgart, 1962), emphasizes the last two centuries. On the theme of economic growth the following are basic: W. W. Rostow, *The Stages of Economic Growth* (Cambridge, Mass., 1960); Charles P. Kindleberger, *Economic Growth in France and Britain, 1851–1950* (Cambridge, Mass., 1964); and P. Studenski, *The Income of Nations, Past and Present* (New York, 1958). Joseph Schumpeter, *Business Cycles,* 2 vols. (New York, 1939), is both theoretical and historical.

On the national economies the following are recognized standard works: J. H. Clapham, *An Economic History of Modern Britain,* 3 vols. (Cambridge, Eng., 1930–38); Phyllis Deane and W. A. Cole, *British Economic Growth, 1688–1959* (Cambridge, Eng., 1962); Hermann Levy, *Monopolies, Cartels and Trusts in British Industry* (London, 1927); Charles H. Wilson,

The History of Unilever: A Study in Economic Growth and Social Change, 2 vols. (London, 1954), traces the development of one of Britain's largest trusts; a recent work of great value is Rondo E. Cameron, France and the Economic Development of Europe, 1800-1914 (Princeton, 1961); Shepard B. Clough, France: A History of National Economics (New York, 1939), is a standard survey; the same author's Economic History of Modern Italy (New York, 1964), emphasizes the slow but steady progress of the Italian economy since unification; basic works in Italian are: L'Economia italiana dal 1861 al 1961 (Milan, 1961), a centennial study by Italian economic scholars; a great factual collection is E. Corbino, Annali dell' economia italiana, 1861-1914, 5 vols. (Città di Castello, 1931-38). Two standard works on the German economy are: A. Sartorious von Waltershausen, Deutsche Wirtschaftsgeschichte, 1815-1914 (Jena, 1923); and Heinrich Bechtel, Wirtschaftsgeschichte Deutschlands im 19. und 20. Jahrhundert (Munich, 1956); in English may be cited: Gustav Stolper, German Economy, 1870-1914 (New York, 1940); and Werner F. Bruck, Social and Economic History of Germany from William II to Hitler (London, 1938); there are revealing portraits of two financial tycoons in Carl Fürstenberg, Lebensgeschichte eimes deutschen Bankiers (Berlin, 1930), and Karl Helfferich, Georg von Siemens, 3 vols. (Berlin, 1923).

For Austria-Hungary there is a sore lack of sound economic studies; these may be cited: Hans Mayer (ed.), Hundert Jahre oesterreichischer Wirtschaftsentwicklung, 1848-1948 (Vienna, 1949); Heinrich Benedikt, Die wirtschaftliche Entwicklung in der Franz-Joseph-Zeit (Vienna, 1958); Peter Sugar, The Industrialization of Bosnia-Herzegovina, 1878-1918 (Seattle, 1963).

For Russia: P. I. Liashchenko, History of the National Economy of Russia to the 1917 Revolution (New York, 1949), is an abridged translation of Istoriia narodnogo khoziaistva SSSR, 3 vols. 2d ed. (Moscow, 1950-56), a work that meets the highest standard of Leninist orthodoxy; another Soviet study is P. A. Khromov, Ekonomicheskoe razvitie Rossii v XIX-XX vekakh, 1800-1917 (Moscow, 1950); a non-Marxist treatment is James Mavor, An Economic History of Russia, 2 vols. (London, 1925), of which Vol. II treats the post-emancipation period. Modernization of the Russian economy is the theme of Theodore von Laue, Sergei Witte and the Industrialization of Russia (New York, 1963); Margaret S. Miller, The Economic Development of Russia, 1905-1914 (London, 1926), emphasizes Russia's economic progress; a recent Marxist view is J. Notzold, Wirtschaftliche Alternativen der Entwicklung Russlands in der Ära Witte und Stolypin (Berlin, 1966).

On capital export and foreign trade, see A. Sartorious von Waltershausen,

Das volkswirtschaftliche System der Kapitalanlage im Auslande (Berlin, 1907), one of the first systematic works on foreign capital investment; Herbert Feis, *Europe, the World's Banker, 1870–1914* (New Haven, 1930); Harry D. White, *The French International Accounts, 1880–1913* (Cambridge, Mass., 1933); Alexander K. Cairncross, *Home and Foreign Investment, 1870–1913* (Cambridge, Eng., 1953); S. B. Saul, *Studies in British Overseas Trade, 1870–1914* (Liverpool, 1960); A. R. Hall (ed.), *The Export of Capital from Britain, 1870–1914* (London, 1968), a symposium. Rogert W. Liefmann, *Cartels, Concerns and Trusts*, Eng. trans. (London, 1932), is a standard work; E. Maschke, *Grundzüge der deutschen Kartellgeschichte bis 1914* (Dortmund, 1964), is a recent evaluation; and Rudolf Hilferding, *Das Finanzkapital* (Vienna, 1910), extended Marxist analysis to explain trusts, cartels, investment banking, and capital export.

Applied science and technology gave a mighty thrust to the European and world economy at the turn of the century; revolutionary in their impact were industrial chemistry, electricity, petroleum, and the internal combustion engine. The quarterly journal *Technology and Culture* (1959 ff.), published by the Society for the History of Technology, is invaluable for its bibliographical services; Charles Singer and others have edited an encyclopedic *History of Technology* in five volumes, of which Vol. V, *The Late Nineteenth Century, 1850–1900* (New York and Oxford, 1958), provides a background for our period; Thomas K. Derry and T. I. Williams, *A Short History of Technology* (Oxford, 1960), and Thomas P. Hughes, *The Development of Western Technology* (New York, 1964), are useful concise surveys.

On specific industries and entrepreneurs these works are significant: Malcolm MacLaren, *The Rise of the Electrical Industry During the Nineteenth Century* (Princeton, 1943), technical rather than socioeconomic; Georg Siemens, *History of the House of Siemens,* Eng. trans., Vol. I, *1847–1914* (Munich, 1957), is objective and scholarly; Harold F. Williamson and Arnold R. Daum, *The American Petroleum Industry, 1859–1899* (Chicago, 1959), is the best single volume on the American and world petroleum industry; Frederik C. Gerretson, *History of the Royal Dutch,* Eng. trans., 4 vols. (Leiden, 1953–57), covers twenty-five years of the history of the Royal Dutch Company, including the merger with the Shell Company and the bitter competition with Standard Oil; Robert J. Forbes and D. R. O'Beirne, *The Technical Development of the Royal Dutch Shell, 1890–1940* (Leiden, 1957), is a thorough account of technology in the oil industry and Shell's contribution through the Shell Development Company; Ralph W. Hidy, *History of the Standard Oil Company* (New Jersey), Vol. I, *Pioneering in Big Business, 1882–1911* (New York, 1955), and Vol. II,

The Resurgent Years, 1911–1927 (New York, 1956), give a detailed picture of Standard's international operations; Robert D. Henriques, *Bearsted: A Biography of Marcus Samuel* (New York, 1960), is a good study of the founder of the Shell Trading and Transport Company; Glyn Roberts, *The Most Powerful Man in the World: The Life of Sir Henri Deterding* (New York, 1938), is inflated but not without value.

Ludwig F. Haber, *The Chemical Industry in the Nineteenth Century* (New York and Oxford, 1958), covers the subject to 1914, giving due attention to economic and business factors as well as advances in chemistry; John J. Beer, *The Emergence of the German Dye Industry* (Urbana, Ill., 1959), is an excellent monograph which treats the subject broadly; Eduard Faber (ed.), *Great Chemists* (New York, 1961), somewhat uneven biographical sketches of more than 100 notable chemists; by the same author, *The Evolution of Chemistry* (New York, 1952), is good on theoretical and experimental developments; Carl Duisberg, *Meine Lebenserinnerungen* (Leipzig, 1933), memoirs of the leading figure in the German chemical industry and organizer of I. G. Farbenindustrie.

The development of oil- and gas-burning engines, which made possible the motorcar and the airplane, is authoritatively told in Eugen Diesel and others, *From Engines to Autos: Five Pioneers in Engine Development and Their Contributions to the Automotive Industry* (Chicago, 1960); the five inventors are N. A. Otto, Gottlieb Daimler, Karl Benz, Rudolf Diesel, and Robert Bosch. Theodor Heuss has written an excellent biography of the Stuttgart industrialist, *Robert Bosch, Leben und Leistung* (Tübingen, 1946); there are two good studies of Rudolf Diesel: W. Robert Nitske and Charles M. Wilson, *Rudolf Diesel: Pioneer of the Age of Power* (Norman, Okla., 1963); Eugen Diesel, *Diesel: Der Mensch, das Werk, das Schicksal* (Hamburg, 1940).

For the development of the airplane and controlled power flight the basic source is Marvin W. McFarland (ed.), *The Papers of Wilbur and Orville Wright*, 2 vols. (New York, 1953); Charles H. Gibbs-Smith, *The Invention of the Aeroplane, 1799–1909* (New York, 1966), concentrates on the period 1900 to 1909, with a wealth of technical detail; Claude Grahame-White and Harry Harper, *The Aeroplane, Past, Present and Future* (London, 1911), is a cooperative work by aviation authorities and flyers; Charles Dolfuss and Henri Bouché, *Histoire de l'aeronautique*, rev. ed. (Paris, 1942), is semi-popular but comprehensive.

CHAPTER IV: KNOWLEDGE AND SOCIETY

The intellectual climate, which is the theme of this chapter, is brilliantly portrayed in Gerhard Masur, *Prophets of Yesterday* (New York, 1961), and

H. Stuart Hughes, *Consciousness and Society* (New York, 1958). Browsing in the contemporary scholarly journals of philosophy and psychology also yields many nuggets. For the nonexpert the best introduction to recent and contemporary European philosophy is Michele F. Sciacca, *Philosophical Trends in the Contemporary World,* Eng. trans. (Notre Dame, 1964); Étienne Gilson and others, *Recent Philosophy—Hegel to the Present* (New York, 1966), is organized by countries and stresses national contributions; the older histories of philosophy by Wilhelm Windelband and Harald Höffding provide essential background. On Herbert Spencer the *Autobiography,* 2 vols. (New York, 1904), and David Duncan, *Life and Letters of Herbert Spencer,* 2 vols. (New York, 1908), provide all the essential facts; Walter M. Simon, *European Positivism in the Nineteenth Century* (Ithaca, 1963), explains its declining position. The late Philipp Frank, a prominent physicist, wrote a good treatise on *The Philosophy of Science* (Englewood Cliffs, N.J., 1957), and John Macquarrie, *Twentieth-Century Religious Thought* (New York, 1963), relates philosophy and theology. The popular philosophy of "as if" is best presented by its inventor, Hans Vaihinger, *The Philosophy of 'As If,' a System of the Theoretical, Practical and Religious Fictions of Mankind,* Eng. trans. (London, 1924).

The most scholarly and balanced study of Nietzsche is Walter Kaufmann, *Nietzsche: Philosopher, Psychologist, Antichrist,* 3d ed. (Princeton, 1968); Crane Brinton, *Nietzsche* (Cambridge, Mass., 1941), traces the growth of a posthumous reputation and places Nietzsche in the current of our time; two famous existentialists have explored Nietzsche's thought: Martin Heidegger, *Nietzsche* (Pfüllingen, 1961); and Karl Jaspers, *Nietzsche: An Introduction to the Understanding of His Philosophical Activity* (Tucson, 1965). Ian W. Alexander, *Bergson* (London, 1957), and Thomas Hanna (ed.), *The Bergsonian Heritage* (New York, 1962), serve to introduce the most popular philosopher of the day, although he is probably best approached through his own works. Ralph B. Perry, *The Thought and Character of William James,* 2 vols. (Boston, 1935), is a model biography of a cultural hero. G. N. Orsini, *Benedetto Croce, Philosopher of Art and Literary Critic* (Carbondale, Ill., 1961), is the most recent treatment; the memoirs of the Russian émigré scholar Fedor Stepun mirror all the philosophical trends of the pre-1914 era: *Vergangenes und Unvergängliches,* 3 vols. (Munich, 1947)—also abridged as *Das Antlitz Russlands und das Gesicht der Revolution* (Munich, 1961).

Useful surveys of the development of psychology are: John C. Flugel, *A Hundred Years of Psychology* (New York, 1934); Gardner Murphy, *Historical Introduction to Modern Psychology* (New York, 1949); Robert Watson, *The Great Psychologists* (Philadelphia, 1963); the most scholarly work is Edwin G. Boring, *A History of Experimental Psychology,* 2d ed. (New York, 1950); Binet's work is best presented in Edith J. Varon, *The Development of Alfred Binet's Psychology* (Princeton, 1935); on Pavlov's contribution see Y. P. Frolov, *Pavlov and His School* (London, 1937). The early Freudian movement is best followed in the authorized biography by Ernest Jones, *The Life and Work of Sigmund Freud,* 3 vols. (New York, 1953–57). The literature of interpretation and appraisal is immense and much of it uncritical; the following are sound works: Philip Rieff, *Freud: The Mind of the Moralist* (New York, 1959); J. A. C. Brown, *Freud and the Post-Freudians* (London, 1963); and Lancelot L. Whyte, *The Unconscious Before Freud* (New York, 1960). For Freud's co-worker and later rival see Carl G. Jung, *Memories, Dreams, Reflections* (New York, 1963).

The most intelligible statement on historicism—Dilthey, Meinecke, Troeltsch, and Croce—is H. Stuart Hughes, *Consciousness and Society,* especially Chap. VI, "Neo-Idealism in History." On history and historians generally see: Heinrich Ritter von Srbik, *Geist und Geschichte vom Deutschen Humanismus bis zur Gegenwart,* Vol. II (Munich, 1951); Maurice Mandelbaum, *The Problem of Historical Knowledge* (New York, 1938); William Kluback, *Wilhelm Dilthey's Philosophy of History* (New York, 1956); Theodor Schieder (ed.), *Hundert Jahre Historische Zeitschrift* (Munich, 1959). Two recent works of historiography are: John R. Hale, *The Evolution of British Historiography* (Cleveland, 1964), and Leo Valiani, *L'Historiographie de l'Italie contemporaine* (Geneva, 1968).

Preferring *Festschriften* to autobiographical writing, historians have modestly refrained from composing many memoirs. Some exceptions are: B. Croce, *An Autobiography* (Oxford, 1927); H. Koht, *Education of an Historian* (New York, 1957); F. Meinecke, *Erlebtes, 1862–1919* (Stuttgart, 1964); G. P. Gooch, *Under Six Reigns* (London, 1959).

A good introduction to sociological thought is Georges Gurvitch and Wilbert E. Moore (eds.), *Twentieth Century Sociology* (New York, 1945); Harry Elmer Barnes and Howard Becker, *Social Thought from Lore to Science,* 2 vols. (New York, 1961), is an encyclopedic survey of the development of sociology in all major countries. The briefer statements by Floyd N. House are still useful: *The Range of Social Theory* (New York, 1929), and *The Development of Sociology* (New York, 1936). Talcott Parsons has been the principal transmitter of the ideas of Max Weber, the German giant of social theory. A convenient summary of Weber's work is Reinhard Bendix, *Max Weber: An Intellectual Portrait* (New York, 1960); also, Julien Freund, *The Sociology of Max Weber,* Eng. trans. (New York, 1968); Marianne Weber, *Max Weber: Ein Lebensbild* (Heidelberg, 1950), is a work of high quality and interest. Harry Alpert, *Emile Durkheim and*

His Sociology (New York, 1939), is adequate but not inspired; Kurt H. Wolff (ed.), *Essays on Sociology and Philosophy by Emile Durkheim* (New York, 1964); and another sociologist whose stock is rising, Kurt H. Wolff, *Georg Simmel, 1858–1918: A Collection of Essays* (Columbus, Ohio, 1959). Of the many works explaining Georges Sorel, two of the best are James H. Meisel, *The Genesis of Georges Sorel* (Ann Arbor, 1961); and Richard D. Humphrey, *Georges Sorel, A Study in Anti-intellectualism* (Cambridge, Mass., 1951); Hans A. Schmitt, *Charles Péguy, the Decline of an Idealist* (Baton Rouge, La., 1967), is a searching evaluation of an elaborately cultivated reputation. Fritz Stern, *The Politics of Cultural Despair* (Berkeley, 1961); Walter Laqueur, *Young Germany: A History of the German Youth Movement* (London, 1962); and George L. Mosse, *The Crisis of German Ideology* (New York, 1964), deal with the "generation gap" and the emergence of a new ideology in Germany.

CHAPTER V: THE CULTURAL ENVIRONMENT

For the principal reference works and encyclopedias on religion see Hayes, *A Generation of Materialism*, pp. 363 ff. The starting point for any study of religion at the turn of the century must be the detailed and scholarly work of Kenneth S. Latourette, *Christianity in a Revolutionary Age*, 5 vols. (New York, 1958–61), covering the nineteenth and twentieth centuries. Other standard studies are: Heinrich Hermelink, *Das Christentum in der Menschheitsgeschichte*, Vol. III, *Nationalismus und Socialismus, 1870–1914* (Stuttgart, 1955); James H. Nichols, *History of Christianity, 1650–1950* (New York, 1956), is a balanced survey; Thomas P. Neill and Raymold H. Schmandt, *History of the Catholic Church* (Milwaukee, 1965), is a substantial work by Protestant scholars with Catholic collaboration. Volume III of Josef Schmidlin, *Papstgeschichte der neuesten Zeit*, 4 vols. (Munich, 1933–39), covers the reigns of Pius X and Benedict XV (1903–1922). The modernist movement is treated adequately by Alexander R. Vidler, *The Modernist Movement in the Roman Church* (Cambridge, Eng., 1934), but should be supplemented by the memoirs of the leader of the movement in France, Alfred Loisy, *Mémoires pour servir à l'histoire religieuse de notre temps*, 3 vols. (Paris, 1930–31).

On religion in the British Isles the following general works and special studies are noteworthy: George S. Spinks, *Religion in Britain Since 1900* (London, 1952), covers the principal developments; Roger B. Lloyd, *The Church of England in the Twentieth Century*, 2 vols. (New York, 1946–50); Donald O. Wagner, *The Church of England and Social Reform Since 1854* (New York, 1930); Kenneth S. Inglis, *Churches and the Working Classes in Victorian England* (London, 1963); Edward R. Wickham,

Church and People in an Industrial City (London, 1957), is a sociological study in depth.

For France the standard work is Adrien Dansette, *Religious History of France*, Eng. trans., 2 vols. (New York, 1961); supplemented by Émile G. Léonard, *Le protestant-français* (Paris, 1953). Gabriel Le Bras is the leading sociologist of religion; two of his principal works are *Études de sociologie religieuse*, 2 vols. (Paris, 1955-56), and *Introduction à l'histoire de la pratique religieuse en France*, 2 vols. (Paris, 1942-45). On church-state relations the definitive work is Lucie V. Méjan, *La séparation des églises et de l'état* (Paris, 1959); also Stuart Schram, *Protestantism and Politics in France* (Alençon, 1954); Mildred J. Headings, *French Freemasonry under the Third Republic* (Baltimore, 1949), stresses anticlericalism.

Elsewhere with regard to church and state we have: S. W. Halperin, *The Separation of Church and State in Italian Thought from Cavour to Mussolini* (Chicago, 1937); Arturo C. Jemolo, *Chiesa e stato in Italia dal Risorgimento ad Oggi* (Turin, 1955); John S. Curtiss, *Church and State in Russia, 1900-1917* (New York, 1940). On the leading prophet of the age, see Stanley R. Hopper (ed.), *Lift Up Your Eyes: The Religious Writings of Leo Tolstoy* (New York, 1960); and a related development, Nicolas Zernov, *The Russian Religious Renaissance of the Twentieth Century* (London, 1963).

On education the standard reference work is Paul Monroe (ed.), *A Cyclopedia of Education*, 5 vols. (New York, 1926-28). There are numerous surveys of the history of education, of which these represent a selection: Ellwood P. Cubberley, *The History of Education* (Boston, 1920); Harry G. Good, *A History of Western Education*, 2d ed. (New York, 1960); William Boyd, *The History of Western Education*, 7th ed. (New York, 1965); Robert Ulich, *The Education of Nations*, rev. ed. (Cambridge, Mass., 1967); a comparison of three leading nations is Hermann J. Ody, *Begegnung zwischen Deutschland, England und Frankreich im höheren Schulwesen seit Beginn des 19. Jahrhunderts* (Saarbrücken, 1959). Friedrich Paulsen was Germany's most famous educator, and his memoirs, *Friedrich Paulsen: An Autobiography*, Eng. trans. (New York, 1938), is valuable for the contemporary scene. Thomas N. Bonner, *American Doctors and German Universities, 1870-1914* (Lincoln, Neb., 1963), and E. C. Helmreich, *Religious Education in German Schools* (Cambridge, Mass., 1959), are two well-documented studies. Some recent works on the history of educational policies are: Andreas Kazamias, *Politics, Society and Secondary Education in England* (Philadelphia, 1966); Vernon Mallinson, *Power and Politics in Belgian Education, 1815-1961* (London, 1963); William H. E. Johnson, *Russia's Educational Heritage* (Pittsburgh, 1950); Paul Ignatiev (ed.),

Russian Schools and Universities in the World War (New Haven, 1929), is actually a detailed treatment of the period 1905-17, sponsored by the former Russian minister of education.

In the study of literature two reliable guides are available: Horatio Smith (ed.), *Columbia Dictionary of Modern European Literature* (New York, 1947), and Wilhelm Schuster (ed.), *Weltliteratur der Gegenwart, 1890–1931*, 2 vols. (Berlin, 1931). More interpretative and a pleasure to read are: J. B. Priestly, *Literature and Western Man* (New York, 1960); Edmund Wilson, *Axel's Castle: A Study in the Imaginative Literature of 1870–1930* (New York, 1931); René M. Albérès (pseud. René Marill), *Histoire du roman moderne* (Paris, 1962); Amy Cruse, *After the Victorians* (London, 1938). Works that guide rather than overwhelm are: Josef Nadler, *Geschichte der deutschen Literatur,* 2d ed. (Regensburg, 1961); Hermann Friedmann and Otto Mann (eds.), *Deutsche Literatur im 20. Jahrhundert,* 4th ed., 2 vols. (Heidelberg, 1961); Arthur Eloesser, *Modern German Literature* (New York, 1933); Gerald Brennan, *The Literature of the Spanish People* (Cambridge, Eng., 1951); Marc Slonim, *Modern Russian Literature: From Chekov to the Present* (New York, 1953); Henri Peyre, *The Contemporary French Novel* (New York, 1955); Victor Brombert, *The Intellectual Hero: Studies in the French Novel, 1880–1955* (Philadelphia, 1961). Two important works on popular literature and the "common reader" are: Desmond Flower, *A Century of Best Sellers, 1830–1930* (London, 1934), and Richard D. Altick, *The English Common Reader: A Social History of the Mass Reading Public* (Chicago, 1957). Significant memoirs and biographies: Carter Jefferson, *Anatole France: The Politics of Skepticism* (New Brunswick, N.J., 1965); Halvdan Koht, *Life of Ibsen,* Eng. trans., 2 vols. (New York, 1931); Ernest J. Simmons, *Leo Tolstoy* (Boston, 1946), and *Chekhov* (Boston, 1962); H. G. Wells, *Experiment in Autobiography* (New York, 1934); Stefan Zweig, *The World of Yesterday* (New York, 1943); Thomas Mann, *A Sketch of My Life* (Paris, 1930). Gerhard Masur describes Mann's *Buddenbrooks* and John Galsworthy's *The Forsyte Saga* as "the mirrors of an epoch."

The increasing importance of another popular medium of communication—the motion picture—is fully documented in Georges Sadoul, *Histoire générale du cinema,* 6 vols. (Paris, 1947–54).

On the history of the newspaper press the bibliography by Karl Bömer, *Internationale Bibliographie des Zeitungswesens* (Leipzig, 1932), although much in need of revision and expansion, is still useful; Sell's *Dictionary of the World's Press* is a convenient reference work. The only general history of the press is also dated: Georges Weill, *Le Journal* (Paris, 1934). The massive treatise on the German press by Otto Groth, *Die Zeitung,* 4 vols.

(Mannheim, 1928–30), has an extensive bibliography; Emil Dovifat, *Die Zeitungen* (Gotha, 1925), is a brief survey; Max Grünbeck, *Die Presse Grossbritanniens,* 2 vols. (Leipzig, 1936), is a good scholarly work; and Vol. III of *The History of 'The Times'* (London, 1947), treats in depth the years 1884–1912; Adolf Dresler, *Geschichte der italienischen Presse,* 2d ed. (Munich, 1933), is barely adequate. Some important biographies and memoirs: Hamilton Fyfe, *Northcliffe, An Intimate Biography* (London, 1930); J. L. Hammond, *C. P. Scott of the Manchester Guardian* (London, 1939); Harry F. Young, *Maximilian Harden, Censor Germaniae* (The Hague, 1959); Arthur Meyer, *Ce que mes yeux ont vu* (Paris, 1911).

CHAPTER VI: THE BREAKTHROUGH TO MODERN ART

An immensity of books on art, architecture, and the theater confronts the student; they are widely divergent in value and often capricious in judgments. Only those works the author has found to be directly useful and informative are listed here.

We lack a comprehensive and meaningful history of museums, although there are histories of many individual museums. Alma S. Wittlin, *The Museum: Its History and Its Tasks in Education* (London, 1949), is less than adequate, and David Murray, *Museums—Their History and Their Use,* 3 vols. (London, 1904), is antiquated; *H. von Tschudis Gesammelte Schriften zur neureren Kunst* (Munich, 1912) is an interesting collection of the papers of a great museum director.

General assessments and interpretations of the arts in this period are: Arnold Hauser, *A Social History of Art,* 2 vols. (New York, 1951); Hans Sedlmayer, *Verlust der Mitte* (Salzburg, 1948), Eng. trans., *Art in Crisis* (New York, 1958); G. Cassou and others, *Gateway to the Twentieth Century: Art and Culture in a Changing World* (New York, 1963); Roger Shattuck, *The Banquet Years—the Arts in France, 1885–1918* (New York, 1958), is a sparkling study. Significant works on aesthetics and style are: Frances M. Blanshard, *Retreat from Likeness in the Theory of Painting* (New York, 1949); Wilhelm Worringer, *Abstraction and Empathy* (London, 1953); Wassily Kandinsky, *On the Spiritual in Art* (New York, 1946).

There is no end to the publication of "coffee table art books" masquerading as period histories of art, and these can be dismissed. The following are serious treatises: Carl Einstein, *Die Kunst des 20. Jahrhunderts,* 2d ed. (Berlin, 1920), Vol. XVI in the excellent *Propyläen-Kunstgeschichte;* John E. Canaday, *Mainstreams of Modern Art* (New York, 1959); Werner Haftmann, *Painting in the Twentieth Century,* 2 vols. (New York, 1961); René Huyghe (ed.), *Histoire de l'art contemporaine: La peinture* (Paris,

1935), a mine of facts and the source of hundreds of popularizations. Other surveys are: Christian Zervos, *Histoire de l'art contemporaine* (Paris, 1938); Bernard S. Meyers, *Modern Art in the Making* (New York, 1950); Herbert Read, *A Concise History of Modern Painting* (New York, 1959); and Milton W. Brown, *The Story of the Armory Show* (New York, 1963), which narrates in detail America's first encounter with modern art. Also worthy of mention is Wolf Stubbe, *Graphic Arts in the Twentieth Century* (New York, 1963).

Of many works on schools and trends the following are worth noting: Robert Schmutzler, *Art Nouveau* (London, 1964); Georges Duthuit, *The Fauvist Painters* (New York, 1950); John Golding, *Cubism: A History and an Analysis, 1907–1914* (London, 1959); Lothar-Günther Buchheim, *Die Künstlergemeinschaft Brücke* (Feldafing, 1956), and *Der Blaue Reiter und die Neue Künstlervereinigung München* (Feldafing, 1959); Bernard S. Meyers, *The German Expressionists—A Generation in Revolt* (New York, 1957); Raffaele Carrieri, *Pittura, scultura d'avanguardia in Italia, 1890–1950* (Milan, 1950).

The best survey of architecture is Henry Russell Hitchcock, *Architecture: Nineteenth and Twentieth Centuries* (London, 1958), in the Pelican History of Art Series; Siegfried Giedion, *Space, Time and Architecture* (Cambridge, Mass., 1941), is a unique interpretive work; Arnold Whittick, *European Architecture in the Twentieth Century*, 2 vols. (London, 1950–53), deals with structure and materials as well as design; N. Pevsner, *Pioneers in the Modern Movement: From William Morris to Walter Gropius* (London, 1936), traces the emergence of the twentieth-century style; Carroll L. V. Meeks, *Italian Architecture, 1750–1914* (New Haven, 1967), is a major contribution to architectural history. Frank Lloyd Wright's achievements are presented in F. Gutheim (ed.), *Frank Lloyd Wright on Architecture—Selected Writings* (New York, 1941); and Wright's *Modern Architecture* (Princeton, 1931).

On contemporary music the standard reference work is *Grove's Dictionary of Music and Musicians*, 5th ed., 9 vols. (New York, 1954); Nicolas Slonimsky, *Music Since 1900*, 3d ed. (New York, 1949), is a chronology with contemporary comments on musical figures and events; Joseph Machlis, *Introduction to Contemporary Music* (New York, 1961), is a safe guide. Other surveys are: Norman Demuth, *Musical Trends in the Twentieth Century* (London, 1952), is tilted toward French and English composers, while Karl H. Wörner, *Musik der Gegenwart* (Mainz, 1949), and *Neue Musik in der Entscheidung* (Mainz, 1954), emphasizes the German contribution; Howard Hartog, *European Music in the Twentieth Century* (London, 1957); Paul Collaer, *La musique moderne, 1905–1955* (Paris,

1955), Eng. trans., *A History of Modern Music* (Cleveland, 1961); Otto Daube, *Die Wege zur neuen Musik, von Debussy bis Schönberg,* 2 vols. (Dortmund, 1950).

The music of particular countries and composers is treated in Martin Cooper, *French Music from the Death of Berlioz to the Death of Fauré* (London, 1951); Dika Newlin, *Bruckner, Mahler, Schönberg* (New York, 1947); Hans H. Stuckenschmidt, *Arnold Schönberg* (New York, 1960); Eric W. White, *Stravinsky: The Composer and His Works* (Berkeley, 1966).

The theater arts flourished under an Edwardian sun, but their history is not well tended. Sheldon Cheney, *The Theater: Three Thousand Years of Drama, Acting and Stagecraft* (New York, 1929), deals with the modern theater in the later chapters; Oscar G. Brockett, *History of the Theatre* (Boston, 1968), is comprehensive with bibliographies; J. G. Zamora, *Historia del teatro contemporáneo,* 4 vols. (Barcelona, 1961), treats in detail all aspects of the twentieth-century theater; Joseph Gregor, *Weltgeschichte des Theaters* (Zurich, 1933), emphasizes national and individual contributions; Martin Hürlimann (ed.), *Das Atlantisbuch des Theaters* (Zurich, 1966), presents individual authorities on the various national theaters including the Chinese and Japanese; Gordon Craig, *On the Art of the Theater* (London, 1905), is the work of a pioneer who revolutionized stage design. Two works by Hans Rothe deal with Max Reinhardt: *Die Spielpläne Max Reinhardts, 1905-1930* (Munich, 1930), and *Max Reinhardt: 25 Jahre deutsches Theater* (Munich, 1930); *The Stage Yearbook* (London) annually appraised the Continental as well as the English theater.

Memoirs and biographies are fairly numerous but uneven in value; the following are samples: Frank Lloyd Wright, *An Autobiography* (New York, 1943); Paul Nash, *Outline: An Autobiography and Other Writings* (London, 1949); Felix Klee (ed.), *The Diaries of Paul Klee, 1898-1918* (Berkeley, 1964); E. Erdmann-Macke, *Erinnerungen an August Macke* (Stuttgart, 1962); Igor Stravinsky, *An Autobiography* (New York, 1958); Alma Mahler Werfel, *Gustav Mahler, Memories and Letters* (New York, 1946); and Alma Mahler's singular autobiography, *And the Bridge Is Love* (New York, 1958). Born Alma Schindler, she was successively the wife of Mahler, Walter Gropius, and Franz Werfel.

CHAPTER VII: THE SCIENTIFIC REVOLUTION

Most of the general histories of science terminate with the end of the century, leaving the complexities of the ensuing years to be presented by the historians of the separate branches of science. A successful attempt to synthesize and extract meaning from it all is Charles C. Gillispie, *The Edge of*

Objectivity (Princeton, 1960); treating contemporary developments is René Taton (ed.), *Histoire générale des sciences,* Vol. III, part 2, *La science contemporaine, le XXᵉ siècle* (Paris, 1964); and the standard work by Sir William Dampier, *A History of Science and Its Relations with Philosophy and Religion,* 3d ed. (Cambridge, Eng., 1942). Two additional books in this category should be mentioned: George Gamow, *Thirty Years That Shook Physics: The Story of Quantum Theory* (New York, 1966); and Werner Heisenberg, *Physics and Philosophy: The Revolution in Modern Science* (New York, 1958). Of the encyclopedias of science, the newest and most comprehensive is William H. Crouse (ed.), *McGraw-Hill Encyclopedia of Science and Technology,* 15 vols. (New York, 1960).

The authoritative work on the "new physics" is Sir Edmund Whittaker, *A History of the Theories of Aether and Electricity,* 2 vols. (New York and London, 1951–53, Vol. II, *The Modern Theories, 1900–1926;* historically important is Ernst Mach, *Science of Mechanics in Its Historical Development* (Chicago, 1902); Bernard Jaffe, *Michelson and the Speed of Light* (New York, 1960), is a popular account of the "greatest of all negative results" in experimental physics; I. Bernard Cohen, *The Birth of a New Physics* (New York, 1960), and Alfred Romer, *The Restless Atom* (New York, 1960), are reliable popularizations.

The biographical and memoir literature is of special value: Otto Glasser, *Wilhelm Konrad Röntgen and the Early History of the Röntgen Rays* (Springfield, Ill., 1934); Eve Curie, *Madame Curie: A Biography* (New York, 1937); Sir J. J. Thomson, *Recollections and Reflections* (New York, 1937); Philipp Frank, *Einstein: His Life and Times* (New York, 1947), the best biography; H. Hartmann, *Max Planck als Mensch und Denker* (Munich, 1958); Max Planck, *Erinnerungen* (Berlin, 1948); Sir James Chadwick (ed.), *Collected Papers of Lord Rutherford* (New York, 1962), of which only the first volume has appeared; Ruth E. Moore, *Niels Bohr: The Man, His Science, and the World They Changed* (New York, 1966); Willy Ley (ed.), *Otto Hahn: A Scientific Autobiography* (New York, 1966); Tobias Danzig, *Henri Poincaré: Critic of Crisis* (New York, 1954); G. L. de Haas-Lorentz, *H. A. Lorentz: Impressions of His Life and Work* (Amsterdam, 1957). The institutionalizing of science is illustrated in Max Planck, *25 Jahre Kaiser Wilhelm-Gesellschaft,* 3 vols. (Berlin, 1936); and Maurice de Broglie, *Les premiers congrès de physique Solvay et l'orientation de la physique depuis 1911* (Paris, 1951).

None of the comprehensive histories of biology is very helpful on the period after 1900, but these may be mentioned: Erik Nordenskiöld, *The History of Biology* (New York, 1928), antiquated in its presentation of evolution and natural selection; Friedrich S. Bodenheimer, *The History of*

Biology: An Introduction (London, 1958); Benjamin Dawes, *A Hundred Years of Biology* (London, 1952). The centennial of Darwin's *Origin of Species* produced a harvest of books and articles, of which the following are representative: Loren Eiseley, *Darwin's Century* (New York, 1958); Samuel A. Barnett (ed.), *A Century of Darwin* (Cambridge, Mass., 1958); Gertrude Himmerfarb, *Darwin and the Darwinian Revolution* (New York, 1959), which is subtly hostile; Sol Tax (ed.), *Evolution After Darwin*, 3 vols. (Chicago, 1960); Gerhard Heberer and Franz Schwanitz (eds.), *Hundert Jahre Evolutionsforschung* (Stuttgart, 1960), is the best of the German centenary books.

Alfred Russel Wallace, the "forgotten man" in the history of evolutionary theory, lived until 1913. A social reformer and something of a crank, he was withal a sound naturalist. On his life see *Studies, Scientific and Social*, 2 vols. (London, 1900); and *My Life: An Autobiography*, 2 vols. (London, 1905).

On the Mendelian revival and the development of genetics the following are important: William Bateson, *Mendel's Principles of Heredity* (Cambridge, Eng., 1909), and *Problems of Genetics* (London, 1913); Conway Zirkle, *The Beginnings of Plant Hybridization* (Philadelphia, 1935); James A. Peters, *Classic Papers in Genetics* (Englewood Cliffs, N.J., 1959); Leslie C. Dunn (ed.), *Genetics in the Twentieth Century* (New York, 1951). M. L. Gabriel and Seymour Fogel, *Great Experiments in Biology* (Englewood Cliffs, N.J., 1955), is a useful selection from original research papers; and Ruth E. Moore, *The Coil of Life: The Story of the Great Discoveries in Life Science* (New York, 1961), represents the best in popular science writing.

The biographical material, while not too abundant, is illuminating: Beatrice Bateson, *William Bateson: Naturalist* (Cambridge, Eng., 1928); Egon S. Pearson, *Karl Pearson: An Appreciation of Some Aspects of His Life and Work* (Cambridge, Eng., 1938); Carl Correns, *Gesammelte Abhandlungen* (Berlin, 1924), is a collection of the scientific and professional papers of Germany's leading geneticist; Richard B. Goldschmidt, *In and Out of the Ivory Tower* (Seattle, 1960), gives a rare view of the scientific world before 1914; Hugo Iltis, *Gregor Johann Mendel: Leben, Werk und Wirkung* (Berlin, 1924), is the standard work on Mendel; the English translation, *Life of Mendel* (New York, 1932), is severely abridged.

Patents and profits made chemistry the most secretive of the sciences; doctoral candidates were sometimes sworn to secrecy when admitted to a professor's laboratory. This may account, in part, for the paucity of satisfactory histories. Sir William A. Tilden, *Chemical Discovery and Invention in the Twentieth Century*, 6th ed. (London, 1936), is the standard survey with a British focus; Archibald and Nan Clow, *The Chemical Revolution*

(London, 1952), treats practical applications; Ludwig F. Haber, *The Chemical Industry During the Nineteenth Century* (Oxford, 1958), is the best work on the development of industrial chemistry; three semipopular works by Eduard Faber are useful: *The Evolution of Chemistry* (New York, 1952); *Nobel Prize Winners in Chemistry* (New York, 1953); and *Great Chemists* (New York, 1961); John J. Beer, *The Emergence of the German Dye Industry* (Urbana, Ill., 1959), illustrates well the linkage of science and technology. From the memoir and biographical literature these may be cited: Emil Fischer, *Aus meinem Leben* (Berlin, 1921); Morris H. Goran, *The Story of Fritz Haber* (Norman, Okla., 1967); and Grete Ostwald, *Wilhelm Ostwald—Mein Vater* (Stuttgart, 1953), which succeeds in being both worshipful and informative.

Medical science is covered by Richard H. Shryock, *The Development of Modern Medicine* (New York, 1947); Charles Singer and E. A. Underwood, *A Short History of Medicine,* 2d ed. (New York, 1962); Ralph H. Major, *A History of Medicine,* 2 vols. (Springfield, Ill., 1954).

Erich Schwinge, *Welt und Werkstatt des Forschers* (Wiesbaden, 1957), is an original attempt to explore the mental, physical, and environmental situations in which men of science operated.

CHAPTER VIII: REFORMISM AND SOCIALISM

Among theoretical works dealing with political parties and social reform the following are either original in viewpoint or standard in the field: Joseph Schumpeter, *Capitalism, Socialism, and Democracy,* 3d ed. (New York, 1950); Robert Michels, *Political Parties,* Eng. trans. (London, 1916), exposes the oligarchical tendencies in political parties; Sigmund Neumann (ed.), *Modern Political Parties* (Chicago, 1956), uses a comparative approach, extensive bibliographies; Michael P. Fogarty, *Christian Democracy in Western Europe* (South Bend, Ind., 1957), covers a century's developments; Ralf Dahrendorf employs a sociological approach in *Gesellschaft und Demokratie in Deutschland* (Munich, 1965), Eng. trans., N.Y. 1967.

Electoral reform, a stirring political issue, is treated in many of the national histories cited in the first part of this essay. Additional studies worth noting are: Peter Campbell, *French Electoral Systems and Elections, 1789–1957,* 2d ed. (New York, 1960), mainly statistical; Walter Gagel, *Die Wahlrechtsfrage in der Geschichte der deutschen liberalen Parteien* (Düsseldorf, 1958); George D. Crothers, *The German Elections of 1907* (New York, 1941); Jürgen Bertram, *Die Wahlen zum deutschen Reichstag vom Jahre 1912* (Düsseldorf, 1964); William A. Jenks, *The Austrian Electoral Reform of 1907* (New York, 1950), is a well-documented monograph; John A. Scott, *Republican Ideas and the Liberal Tradition in France, 1870–1914*

(New York, 1951), finds that France was still basically liberal and republican.

Administrative history occupies a prominent place in German political science and historiography. Fritz Hartung, *Deutsche Verfassungsgeschichte,* 6th ed. (Stuttgart, 1964), and *Staatsbildende Kräfte der Neuzeit* (Berlin, 1961), serve adequately to introduce the subject. These recent studies also should be mentioned: Lysbeth W. Muncy, *The Junker in the Prussian Administration under William II, 1888–1914* (Providence, R.I., 1944); Emmeline W. Cohen, *The Growth of the British Civil Service, 1780–1939* (London, 1941); Robert C. Fried, *The Italian Prefects: A Study in Administrative Politics* (New Haven, 1963).

Conservatism in various forms was still a live option in western Europe. Some of the principal scholarly works are these: Robert B. McDowell, *British Conservatism, 1832–1914* (London, 1959); Janet H. Robb, *The Primrose League, 1883–1906* (New York, 1942); Samuel Osgood, *French Royalism under the Third and Fourth Republics* (The Hague, 1960); Eugen Weber, *Action Française: Royalism and Reaction in Twentieth Century France* (Stanford, 1962); and a parallel study, Edward R. Tannenbaum, *The Action Française: Diehard Reactionaries in Twentieth Century France* (New York, 1962). For Germany: Graf Kuno Westarp, *Konservative Politik im letzten Jahrzehnt des Kaiserreiches,* 2 vols. (Berlin, 1935); Karl Bachem, *Vorgeschichte, Geschichte und Politik der Deutschen Zentrumspartei,* 9 vols. (Cologne, 1927–32).

The liberal parties of western Europe between 1900 and 1914 embraced social as well as political reform. Charles W. Pipkin, *Social Politics and Modern Democracies,* 2 vols. (New York, 1931), treats in detail the politics of social reform in France and Britain; Bentley B. Gilbert, *The Evolution of National Insurance in Great Britain* (London, 1966), examines the origins of the welfare state and shows how the Liberals became the party of social progress; Hugh A. Clegg and others, *A History of British Trade Unions Since 1889,* Vol. I, *1889–1910,* (Oxford, 1964), replaces the older study by the Webbs; Henry Pelling, *A History of British Trade Unionism* (London, 1963), is an excellent brief survey. Margaret Cole's *Story of Fabian Socialism* (Stanford, 1961) and the critical appraisal by A. M. McBriar, *Fabian Socialism and English Politics* (Cambridge, Eng., 1962), supersede the older accounts. G. D. H. Cole, eminent historian of socialism and the British labor movement, has contributed an enlightening survey, *British Working Class Politics, 1832–1914* (London, 1960); Henry Pelling, *A Short History of the Labour Party* (London, 1961), is a good brief account; and an American view is presented in Philip P. Poirier, *The Advent of the British Labour Party* (New York, 1958). Satisfactory biographies of Keir Hardie and Ramsay MacDonald are lacking, but there is a good biography of the leader of the English Marxists: Chüshichi Tsuzuki, *H. M. Hyndman and British Socialism* (London, 1961).

The politics of social reform in Germany is the theme of Karl E. Born's *Staat und Sozialpolitik seit Bismarcks Sturz, 1890–1914* (Wiesbaden, 1957); the role of the German liberal party is examined in Theodor Eschenburg, *Das Kaiserreich am Scheideweg: Bassermann, Bülow und der Block* (Berlin, 1929); Hedwig Wachenheim, *Die deutsche Arbeiterbewegung, 1844 bis 1914* (Cologne, 1966), is an objective survey of both the labor movement and the evolution of socialism; the triumph of nationalism over liberalism is the subject of Friedrich Sell, *Die Tragödie des deutschen Liberalismus* (Stuttgart, 1953); the results of social politics are surveyed factually in William H. Dawson, *Social Insurance in Germany, 1883–1911* (New York, 1912).

Urban growth and development raised problems that have persisted through the century. Adna F. Weber, *The Growth of Cities in the Nineteenth Century*, published in 1899, had its latest reprinting in 1963; William B. Munro, *The Government of European Cities* (New York, 1927), introduces most of the urban problems; Ebenezer Howard, *Garden Cities of Tomorrow* (London, 1898), latest edition 1965, is a landmark in the history of town planning; other works on the same subject are: Dugald Macfadyen, *Sir Ebenezer Howard and the Town Planning Movement* (Manchester, 1933); Hans Kampffmeyer, *Die Gartenstadtbewegung*, 2d ed. (Leipzig, 1913); Patrick Geddes, *Cities in Evolution*, rev. ed. (London, 1949); William Ashworth, *The Genesis of Modern British Town Planning* (London, 1954). Charles Klapper, *The Golden Age of Tramways* (New York, 1961), treats interestingly the key factor of transportation in urban development.

The literature on socialism, trade unionism, and the labor movement in general could fill many libraries and cannot be cited here at great length. Edouard Dolléans, *Histoire du mouvement ouvrier*, 3 vols. (Paris, 1936–53), surveys broadly western Europe, Russia, and the United States from 1830 to 1945; Carl Landauer, *European Socialism*, 2 vols. (Berkeley, 1960), deals mainly with ideas and policies; G. D. H. Cole, *A History of Socialist Thought*, 4 vols. (London, 1953–56), is in fact a comprehensive history of socialism. A number of special studies deal competently with socialism as an international movement: Milorad M. Drachkovitch (ed.), *The Revolutionary Internationals, 1864–1943* (Stanford, 1966); James Joll, *The Second International, 1889–1914* (London, 1955); Patricia A. van der Esch, *La Deuxième Internationale* (Paris, 1957); Julius Braunthal, *History of the International, 1864–1943*, Eng. trans., 2 vols. (New York, 1967), although nonobjective, is probably the fullest treatment.

Despite the emphasis on internationalism the socialist movement showed great regional variation, hence the national histories: Aldo Romano, *Storia del movimento socialista in Italia,* 3 vols. (Rome, 1954–55), complemented by Daniel L. Horowitz, *The Italian Labor Movement* (Cambridge, Mass., 1963); Émile Vandervelde, *Le Parti Ouvrier Belge, 1885–1925* (Brussels, 1925), and his valuable memoirs, *Souvenirs d'un militant socialiste* (Paris, 1939); Ludwig Bruegel, *Geschichte der österreichischen Sozialdemokratie,* 5 vols. (Vienna, 1922–25), narrative and documents; Victor Adler, *Briefwechsel mit August Bebel und Karl Kautsky* (Vienna, 1954); Fritz Giovanoli, *Die sozialdemokratische Partei der Schweiz—Entstehung, Entwicklung, Aktion* (Bern, 1948); Carl E. Schorske, *German Social Democracy, 1905–1917* (Cambridge, Mass., 1955), is the best study of developments in the pre-1914 era; Peter Gay, *The Dilemma of Democratic Socialism* (New York, 1952), deals brilliantly with the revisionist movement; Erika Rikli, *Der Revisionismus, 1890–1914* (Zurich, 1936), treats the same subject in depth; the clash of socialism with nationalism is the theme of Hermann Heidegger, *Die deutsche Sozialdemokratie und der Nationalstaat, 1870–1920* (Göttingen, 1955); Guenther Roth, *The Social Democrats in Imperial Germany: A Study in Working-Class Isolation and National Integration* (Totowa, N.J., 1963), has made an original sociological contribution to this subject. Three interesting memoirs on growing up in the Social Democratic party are: Joseph Buttinger, *In the Twilight of Socialism* (New York, 1953); Julius Deutsch, *Ein Weiter Weg* (Zurich, 1960); and Wilhelm Hoegner, *Der schwierige Aussenseiter* (Munich, 1959). Other important biographies and memoirs are: Philipp Scheidemann, *Memoirs of a Social Democrat,* 2 vols. (London, 1929); Georg Kotowski, *Friedrich Ebert, eine politische Biographie* (Wiesbaden, 1963); R. Jansen, *Georg von Vollmar* (Düsseldorf, 1958), an important south German figure; J. P. Nettl, *Rosa Luxemburg,* 2 vols. (London, 1966); Z. A. B. Zeman, *The Merchant of Revolution: The Life of Alexander Israel Helphand* (London, 1965); Rosa Luxemburg, *Briefe an Karl und Luise Kautsky, 1896–1918* (Berlin, 1922).

On socialism and the labor movement in France the following are reliable surveys: Alexandre Zévaès, *Le socialisme en France depuis 1904* (Paris, 1935); Daniel Ligou, *Histoire du socialisme en France, 1871–1961* (Paris, 1962). Two good monographs are Val R. Lorwin, *The French Labor Movement* (Cambridge, Mass., 1954), and Aaron Noland, *The Founding of the French Socialist Party, 1897–1905* (Cambridge, Mass., 1956); Harvey Goldberg's biography of Jean Jaurès is almost a history of the socialist party for the period 1900–1914. Anarchism, of which France was the generating center, is treated definitively in Jean Maitron, *Histoire du mouvement anarchiste en France, 1880–1914* (Paris, 1951); and Victor Serge, *Memoirs of a Revolutionary, 1901–1941* (New York, 1963), is the interesting testimonial of an apostle.

The origins of the Russian revolutionary movement have been studied ad infinitum; some significant contributions are: Stuart R. Tompkins, *The Russian Intelligentsia: Makers of the Revolutionary State* (Norman, Okla., 1957); Allan K. Wildman, *The Making of a Worker's Revolution: Russian Social Democracy, 1891-1903* (Chicago, 1967); George Fischer, *Russian Liberalism, from Gentry to Intelligentsia* (Cambridge, Mass., 1958); Victor Leontovitsch, *Geschichte des Liberalismus in Russland* (Frankfurt, 1957), especially detailed for the years 1904-1907; Jacob Walkin, *The Rise of Democracy in Pre-Revolutionary Russia* (New York, 1962), emphasizes institutional factors. Two complementary studies of the origins of Bolshevism are: Leopold Haimson, *The Russian Marxists and the Origins of Bolshevism* (Cambridge, Mass., 1955); and Donald W. Treadgold, *Lenin and His Rivals: The Struggle for Russia's Future, 1898-1906* (New York, 1955).

The firsthand observations of Bernard Pares during the 1905 revolution are given in *Russia and Reform* (London, 1907); Sidney Harcave, *First Blood: The Russian Revolution of 1905* (New York, 1964), is an excellent brief study; Solomon Schwarz, *The Russian Revolution of 1905* (Chicago, 1967), a scholarly presentation by a prominent Menshevik; Anna M. Pankratova, *Die erste russische Revolution von 1905 bis 1907* (Berlin, 1953), trans. of *Pervaia russkaia revoliutsiia 1905-1907,* 2d ed. (Moscow, 1951), the official Bolshevik account; a good study of the working of the Russian assembly is Alfred Levin, *The Second Duma—A Study of the Social Democratic Party and the Russian Constitutional Experiment* (Hamden, Conn., 1966); Theofanes G. Stavrou (ed.), *Russia Under the Last Tsar* (Minneapolis, 1969), presents eight excellent papers on controversial or crucial topics. Some of the political groundswells of the revolution have been given special study: Donald W. Treadgold, *The Great Siberian Migration* (Princeton, 1957); Ivar Spector, *The First Russian Revolution: Its Impact on Asia* (Englewood Cliffs, N.J., 1962); Leo Stern (ed.), *Die Auswirkungen der ersten russischen Revolution von 1905-1907 auf Deutschland,* 2 vols. (Berlin, 1955-1956), is an important collection of documents; Wilfrid H. Crook, *The General Strike* (Chapel Hill, N.C., 1931); Elsbeth Georgie, *Theorie und Praxis des Generalstreiks in der modernen Arbeiterbewegung* (Jena, 1908).

CHAPTER IX: THE DIPLOMATIC REVOLUTION

AND

CHAPTER X: THE ARMED CAMPS, 1907-1914

No aspect of European history since 1870 has been studied more intensively than the diplomacy of the great powers. The circumstances of the outbreak of war in 1914 and its shattering denouement in 1918 intensified public as well as scholarly debate over the diplomatic origins of the catastrophe. Revolution and punitive peace settlements raised the *Kriegsschuldfrage* (war guilt question) to the level of a major international issue. Under such pressure the governments concerned began to publish in multivolume series the records of their diplomatic relations, extending these publications in some instances back to 1870. A generation of scholars—even though all did not participate directly—felt the impact of this heated inquest upon the origins of the great war. Documents, self-serving memoirs, scholarly monographs, and massive treatises were published in great profusion. The *Kriegsschuldfrage* has not ceased to be a matter of considerable interest even though a second world war has intervened and other fields now attract young scholars.

Most governments today—since fifty years have elapsed—permit direct access to their diplomatic records, but the official published collections have not been thereby totally devalued, and in some cases they constitute the only available documentary record. The most important of the published collections are: *Die Grosse Politik der europäischen Kabinette, 1871–1914,* ed. by Friedrich Thimme and others, 40 vols. (Berlin, 1922–26); *Die Deutschen Dokumente zum Kriegsausbruch, 1914,* 4 vols. (Berlin, 1927); *British Documents on the Origins of the War, 1898–1914,* ed. by G. P. Gooch and Harold Temperley, 11 vols. (London, 1926–38); *Documents diplomatiques français, 1871–1914,* 41 vols. (Paris, 1929–59), published by the French foreign ministry; *Österreich-Ungarns Aussenpolitik von der Bosnischen Krise 1908 bis zum Kriegsausbruch 1914,* ed. by Ludwig Bittner and others, 8 vols. (Vienna, 1930); *Diplomatische Aktenstücke zur Vorgeschichte des Krieges 1914* (28 June to 27 August, 1914), 3 vols. (Vienna, 1919), Eng. trans., *Austrian Red Book* (London, 1920). An extensive series from the Russian diplomatic archives has been planned and some volumes published: *Mezhdunarodny otnosheniia v epokhu imperializma: Dokumenty iz arkhivov tsarskogo i vrenennogo pravitel'stv 1878–1917;* no volumes have been published in Series I, 1878–1899; only three volumes in Series II, 1900–1913; and ten volumes in Series III, 1914–1917; most of these have been published in German translation, ed. by Otto Hoetzsch: *Die internationalen Beziehungen im Zeitalter des Imperialismus: Dokumente aus den Archiven der zaristischen und der provisorischen Regierungen* (Berlin, 1931–42). The most important documentary publication undertaken since World War II is *I Documenti Diplomatici Italiani* (Rome, 1952 ff.), for the years 1861–1943; series 3 and 4 are assigned to the two decades before World War I, but there seems to be no logical schedule for editing and publication.

The most helpful guide to the outpouring of books, articles, and monographs on international relations between 1900 and 1914 is the *Foreign Affairs Bibliography*, published by the Council on Foreign Relations, in 4 vols. (New York, 1933–64), covering the years 1919–1962. The semiofficial German periodical *Die Kriegsschuldfrage* (later *Berliner Monatshefte*), although propagandistic in its objectives, published valuable lists, reviews, and documents. During the twenties and thirties the Russian periodical *Krasnyi Arkhiv* published sporadically selected documents from the foreign ministry records; a very helpful digest of Vols. 1–130 has been prepared by Leona W. Eisele, *A Digest of the Krasnyi Arkhiv—Red Archives*, 2 vols. (Cleveland and Ann Arbor, 1947, 1955).

Among a great number of works on diplomatic history the following are considered standard: R. J. Sontag, *European Diplomatic History, 1871–1932* (New York, 1933); A. J. P. Taylor, *The Struggle for the Mastery of Europe, 1848–1918* (Oxford, 1954); the masterly volumes by W. L. Langer, *European Alliances and Alignments, 1871–1890*, 2d ed. (New York, 1950), and *The Diplomacy of Imperialism, 1890–1902*, 2d ed. (New York, 1951); and the volume by the eminent French historian Pierre Renouvin, in *Histoire des relations internationales*, Vol. VI, *De 1871 à 1914; l'apogée de l'Europe* (Paris, 1955).

Major studies focusing on the origins of the war are: Sidney B. Fay, *The Origins of the World War*, 2 vols. (New York, 1928); Bernadotte E. Schmitt, *The Coming of the War, 1914*, 2 vols. (New York, 1930); G. P. Gooch, *Before the War: Studies in Diplomacy*, 2 vols. (London, 1936–38); Erich Brandenburg, *From Bismarck to the World War* (London, 1927). These works, in depth if not in scope, have been to a degree superseded by the massive volumes of Luigi Albertini, *Le origini della guerra del 1914*, 3 vols. (Milan, 1942–43), Eng. trans., *The Origins of the War of 1914*, 3 vols. (London, 1952–57); ill-proportioned—two volumes on the 1914 crisis—and tediously detailed, the work nevertheless deserves the appellation "monumental." Shorter interpretative studies are: Gordon A. Craig, *From Bismarck to Adenauer* (New York, 1965); Laurence Lafore, *The Long Fuse* (Philadelphia, 1965); and the brief but perceptive presentation by Joachim Remak, *The Origins of World War I* (New York, 1967).

The autobiographical and memoir literature is voluminous, as diplomats and policy makers after the war sought to clear their reputations or to cast blame on others. The principal biographies of William II, the memoirs of Chancellor Von Bülow, and Norman Rich's solid biography of Holstein have been previously cited. Other diplomatic memoirs and biographies of value for this period are: Friedrich Rosen, *Aus einem diplomatischen Wanderleben*, 2 vols. (Berlin, 1930–31), contains interesting material on the Moroccan crisis; Richard von Kühlmann, *Erinnerungen, 1867–1914*

(Heidelberg, 1948); Ernst Jäckh, *Kiderlen-Wächter, der Staatsmann und Mensch*, 2 vols. (Stuttgart, 1925); Graf Anton Monts, *Erinnerungen und Gedanken* (Berlin, 1932), ambassador in Rome; Bogdan von Hutten-Czapsky, *Sechzig Jahre Politik und Gesellschaft*, 2 vols. (Berlin, 1936), important political and social memoirs; Erich Lindow, *Freiherr Marschall von Bieberstein als Botschafter in Konstantinopel, 1897–1912* (Danzig, 1934); Isaac Don Levine, *Letters from the Kaiser to the Czar* (New York, 1920), for the years 1894–1914.

Some important British memoirs and biographies are: Lord Newton, *Lord Lansdowne: A Biography* (London, 1929); Harold Nicolson, *Sir Arthur Nicolson, First Lord Carnock: A Study in the Old Diplomacy* (London, 1930); G. M. Trevelyan, *Grey of Fallodon* (Boston, 1937), supplementing Grey's memoirs, *Twenty-five Years, 1892–1916*, 2 vols. (London, 1925); Viscount Esher, *Journals and Letters*, 4 vols. (London, 1934–38); Sir Cecil Spring-Rice, *Letters and Friendships, a Record*, 2 vols. (London, 1929). For France: Charles W. Porter, *The Career of Théophile Delcassé* (Philadelphia, 1936); Keith Eubank, *Paul Cambon, Master Diplomatist* (Norman, Okla., 1960), and Cambon's *Correspondence*, 3 vols. (Paris, 1940–46); M. Paléologue, *Three Critical Years, 1904–1906*, Eng. trans. (London, 1935); Joseph Caillaux, *Agadir: Ma politique extérieure* (Paris, 1921); Leon Noël, *Camille Barrère, ambassadeur de France* (Paris, 1948), played a major role in Rome; Maurice Bompard, *Mon Ambassade en Russie, 1903–1908* (Paris, 1937). For Russia: A. P. Izwolski, *Recollections of a Foreign Minister* (New York, 1921), covers only to 1906; F. Stieve, *Der diplomatische Schriftwechsel Iswolskis, 1911–1914*, 4 vols. (Berlin, 1924); B. von Siebert (ed.), *Graf Benckendorffs diplomatischer Schriftwechsel*, 3 vols. (Berlin, 1928), dispatches to and from the Russian embassy in London; Serge Sazonov, *Fateful Years, 1909–1916* (London, 1927); Sergei Y. Witte, *Vospominaniia. Tsarstvovanie Nikolaia II* [memoirs of the reign of Nicholas II], 2 vols. (Berlin, 1922). Italy and Austria-Hungary: Giovanni Giolitti, *Memoirs of My Life* (London, 1923); Luigi Albertini, *Venti anni di vita politica*, 5 vols. (Bologna, 1950–53), valuable memoirs by the editor of *Corriere della Sera* (Milan); A. von Musulin, *Das Haus am Ballplatz: Erinneringun eines österreich-ungarischen Diplomaten* (Munich, 1924); Hugo Hantsch, *Leopold Graf Berchtold*, 2 vols. (Graz, 1963).

Public attitudes and opinions in the shaping of foreign policy have been treated in a number of studies: Pauline R. Anderson, *The Background of Anti-English Feeling in Germany, 1890–1902* (Washington, D.C., 1939); Oron J. Hale, *Publicity and Diplomacy, with Special Reference to England and Germany, 1890–1914* (New York, 1940); E. Malcolm Carroll, *French Public Opinion and Foreign Affairs, 1870–1914* (New York, 1931), also

Germany and the Great Powers: A Study in Public Opinion and Foreign Policy (New York, 1938); and the *Festschrift* in honor of Professor Carroll: L. P. Wallace and William C. Askew (eds.), *Power, Public Opinion, and Diplomacy* (Durham, N.C., 1959); another study worth noting is Gilbert Ziebura, *Die deutsche Frage in der öffentlichen Meinung Frankreichs von 1911–1914* (Berlin, 1955); and Henry Cord Meyer, *Mitteleuropa in German Thought and Action* (The Hague, 1955).

The estrangement of Britain and Germany and the consequent diplomatic revolution have been examined in their many stages and from various points of view: William L. Langer, *The Diplomacy of Imperialism*, II, Chap. XV; Oron J. Hale, *Publicity and Diplomacy*, Chaps. VII–X; Friedrich Meinecke, *Geschichte des deutsch-englischen Bündnisproblems, 1890–1901* (Munich, 1927); Norman Rich, *Friedrich von Holstein*, Vol. II, Chaps. XL–XLIX; Ross J. S. Hoffman, *Great Britain and the German Trade Rivalry, 1875–1914* (Philadelphia, 1933); Baron von Eckardstein, *Ten Years at the Court of St. James', 1895–1905* (London, 1921); Ian H. Nish, *The Anglo-Japanese Alliance: The Diplomacy of Two Island Empires, 1894–1907* (London, 1968); John A. White, *The Diplomacy of the Russo-Japanese War* (Princeton, 1964), is an excellent reassessment; Joseph J. Mathews, *Egypt and the Formation of the Anglo-French Entente of 1904* (Philadelphia, 1939); Eugene N. Anderson, *The First Moroccan Crisis, 1904–1906* (Chicago, 1930); Maybelle K. Chapman, *Great Britain and the Bagdad Railway, 1888–1914* (Northampton, Mass., 1948); John B. Wolf, *The Diplomatic History of the Bagdad Railroad* (Columbia, Mo., 1936); H. Bode, *Der Kampf um die Bagdadbahn, 1903–1914* (Breslau, 1941); R. P. Churchill, *The Anglo-Russian Convention of 1907* (Cedar Rapids, Iowa, 1939); J. M. Goudewaard, *Some Aspects of the End of Britain's 'Splendid Isolation'* (Rotterdam, 1952); another aspect of Britain's policy is treated by Bradford Perkins in *The Great Rapprochement: England and the United States, 1895–1914* (New York, 1968). The most important recent study of British policy is George Monger, *The End of Isolation: British Foreign Policy, 1900–1907* (London, 1963); it is a low-keyed but penetrating analysis based on the foreign office archives and the papers of cabinet members and diplomats. Noteworthy also is S. R. Williamson, *The Politics of Grand Strategy, 1904–1914* (Cambridge, Mass., 1969).

On Anglo-German naval rivalry and the security issues involved see the authoritative works of Arthur J. Marder, cited in Chapter I; Jonathan Steinberg, *Yesterday's Deterrent: Tirpitz and the Birth of the German Battle Fleet* (London, 1965); the excellent study by Eckart Kehr, *Schlachtflottenbau und Parteipolitik, 1894–1901* (Berlin, 1930); Walter Hubatsch, *Die Ära Tirpitz, Studien zur deutschen Marinepolitik, 1890–1918*

(Göttingen, 1955); E. L. Woodward, *Great Britain and the German Navy* (London, 1935).

The Bosnian crisis, the Agadir crisis, and the Tripolitan and Balkan wars have been subjects of monographic treatment. Two valuable studies of the Bosnian imbroglio are: B. E. Schmitt, *The Annexation of Bosnia, 1908–1909* (Cambridge, Eng., 1937); M. Nintchitch, *La crise bosniaque et la puissances européennes,* 2 vols. (Paris, 1937); W. M. Carlgren, *Iswolsky und Aehrenthal vor der bosnischen Annexionskrise, 1906–1908* (Uppsala, 1955); Wayne S. Vucinich, *Serbia Between East and West, 1903–1908* (Stanford, 1954); Oswald Wedel, *Austro-German Diplomatic Relations, 1908–1914* (Stanford, 1932); on the second Moroccan crisis, Ima C. Barlow, *The Agadir Crisis* (Chapel Hill, N.C., 1940); H. E. Enthoven, *Van Tanger tot Agadir* (Utrecht, 1929); William C. Askew, *Europe and Italy's Acquisition of Libya* (Durham, N.C., 1942), is a solid study; E. C. Helmreich, *The Diplomacy of the Balkan Wars, 1912–1913* (Cambridge, Mass., 1938), has not been superseded by Edward C. Thaden, *Russia and the Balkan Alliance of 1912* (University Park, Penn., 1965), which minimizes Russia's role in the formation of the Balkan League; Hans Uebersberger, *Österreich zwischen Russland und Serbien* (Graz and Cologne, 1958), is based on the Serbian diplomatic archives. Two Soviet studies covering these years are: I. V. Bestuzhev, *Bor'ba v Rossi po voprosam vneshnei politiki 1906–1910* (Moscow, 1961); and P. N. Efremov, *Vneshniaia politika Rossii, 1907–1914 gg* (Moscow, 1961).

CHAPTER XI: THE CRITICAL THIRTY-NINE DAYS—1914

A collection of diplomatic documents selected from the 1914 "Rainbow Books" is available in James B. Scott (ed.), *Diplomatic Documents Relating to the Outbreak of the European War,* 2 vols. (New York, 1916), published by the Carnegie Endowment for International Peace. The most recent collection, drawn from the later published documentary series, is Imanuel Geiss, *Julikrise und Kriegsausbruch 1914,* 2 vols. (Hanover, 1963); a one-volume abridgment has been published in translation entitled *July 1914* (New York, 1967). The appearance of Geiss' volumes and the controversy that has developed around Fritz Fischer's *Germany's Aims in the First World War* (New York, 1967) mark the beginning of a new phase of the *Kriegsschuldfrage.* An excellent anthology on the Fischer controversy is Graf Ernst W. Lynar, *Deutsche Kriegsziele 1914–1918* (Berlin, 1964).

The works of Fay, Schmitt, Gooch, Brandenburg, and Albertini, cited in the bibliographies for Chapters IX and X, also treat in detail the crisis of 1914. To these should be added Pierre Renouvin, *The Immediate Origins of the War* (New Haven, 1928), and Alfred von Wegerer, *Der Ausbruch des Weltkrieges,* 2 vols. (Hamburg, 1939). A degree of special pleading or national bias blemishes many of these works. A younger generation of historians has begun to speak on this subject. Representative of their work are the ten articles on important aspects of the pre-1914 scene and the current controversy over war aims published in *The Journal of Contemporary History,* Vol. I, No. 3 (1966).

On Sarajevo and its immediate antecedents the latest major work is Vladimir Dedijer, *The Road to Sarajevo* (New York, 1966), which emphasizes the Bosnian background; Joachim Remak, *Sarajevo: The Story of a Political Murder* (New York, 1959), tells the story graphically and emphasizes Serbian responsibilities; Hans Uebersberger, *Österreich Zwischen Russland und Serbien* (Graz and Cologne, 1958), presents material from the Serbian archives not hitherto available; an older, very pro-Serb work is R. W. Seton-Watson, *Sarajevo: A Study in the Origins of the Great War* (London, 1926); Richard Krug von Nidda, *Der Weg nach Sarajevo* (Vienna, 1964), is a popular account. The best biography of Franz Ferdinand, comprehensive and based on the private and public archives, is Rudolf Kiszling, *Erzherzog Franz Ferdinand von Österreich-Este* (Graz, 1953); Georg Franz, *Erzherzog Franz Ferdinand und die Pläne zur Reform der Habsburger Monarchie* (Vienna, 1943), is a definitive treatise on this much debated subject.

On the reaction in Vienna, besides the Austrian Red Book, the Hantsch biography of Count Berchtold, and the published papers of Conrad von Hötzendorf, the following add something to the picture: Roderich Gooss, *Das Wiener Kabinett und die Entstehung des Weltkrieges* (Vienna, 1919); Freiherr von Musulin, *Das Haus am Ballplatz* (Munich, 1924), memoirs of the official who drafted the ultimatum to Serbia; Baron Wladimir Giesl, *Zwei Jahrzehnte im nahen Orient* (Berlin, 1927), Austrian minister in Belgrade in 1914; Josef Redlich, *Schicksalsjahre Österreichs, 1900–1919,* 2 vols. (Graz, 1954)—Redlich's extraordinary diary breathes the war spirit of 1914.

Besides the documentary record in the relevant published collections, the following monographs and memoirs shed light on Russia's actions during the crisis: W. Cyprian Bridge (ed.), *How the War Began in 1914, Being the Diary of the Russian Foreign Office* (London, 1925), from the daily log kept by Baron Schilling, cited often as "Baron Schilling's Diary"; S. D. Sazonov, *Fateful Years, 1906–1916* (New York, 1928), written in exile without notes or documents; Sergei K. Dobrorolski, *Die Mobilmachung der russischen Armee 1914* (Berlin, 1922), important for Russian military measures, by the former chief of the mobilization section of the Russian general staff; W. A. Sukhomlinow, *Erinnerungen* (Berlin, 1924), memoirs of the minister for war; Gunther Frantz, *Russlands Eintritt in den Welt-krieg* (Berlin, 1924), Russian military documents on preparations and mobilization; Maurice Paléologue, *An Ambassador's Memoirs,* Eng. trans., 2 vols. (London, 1924-26), highly colored and unreliable; Sir George Buchanan, *My Mission to Russia,* 2 vols. (London, 1923), not very reveal-ing; Graf Friedrich Pourtalès, *Meine Verhandlungen in St. Petersburg Ende Juli 1914. Tagesaufzeichnungen und Dokumente* (Berlin, 1927), very valuable; Gustav Lambsdorff, *Die Militärbevollmächtigten Kaiser Wil-helms II am Zarenhofe, 1904-1914* (Berlin, 1937).

Among German publications shedding light on the crisis one should also note the Berlin reports of the ministers of Bavaria, Baden, and Württem-berg: Pius Dirr (ed.), *Bayerische Dokumente zum Kriegsausbruch und zum Versailler Schuldspruch,* 3d ed. (Munich, 1925); August Bach (ed.), *Deutsche Gesandtschaftsberichte zum Kriegsausbruch* (Berlin, 1937); Theobald von Bethmann Hollweg, *Reflections on the World War* (New York, 1920); Gottlieb von Jagow, *Ursachen und Ausbruch des Weltkrieges* (Berlin, 1919), apologetic and defensive; Wilhelm Freiherr von Schoen, *Memoirs of an Ambassador* (London, 1922), German ambassador in Paris; Hans-Günter Zmarzlik, *Bethmann Hollweg als Reichskanzler, 1909-1914* (Düsseldorf, 1957); Clemens von Delbrück, *Die wirtschaftliche Mobil-machung in Deutschland* (Munich, 1924), vice-chancellor and secretary of state for the interior; Prince Lichnowsky, *Heading for the Abyss* (London, 1928), sharply critical of his government; Edward F. Willis, *Prince Lichnowsky, Ambassador of Peace* (Berkeley, 1942), a sympathetic study; Theodor Wolff, *The Eve of 1914* (New York, 1936), a commentary by the editor of the liberal *Berliner Tageblatt;* Helmuth von Moltke, *Erinner-ungen, Briefe, Dokumente, 1887-1916* (Stuttgart, 1916); Alfred von Tirpitz, *My Memoirs,* 2 vols. (London, 1919); Gerhard Ritter, *The Schlieffen Plan,* Eng. trans. (London, 1958), a masterly critique with full texts of the ill-starred military plan that led Germany to invade Belgium and attack France; Walter Kloster, *Der deutsche Generalstab und der Präventivkriegsgedanke* (Stuttgart, 1932).

France had few options in 1914, and the relevant literature is not exten-sive: Georges Michon, *La préparation à la guerre; la loi de trois ans* (Paris, 1935); Gordon Wright, *Raymond Poincaré and the French Presidency* (Stanford, 1942); Marshal Joseph J. C. Joffre, *Mémoires du Maréchal Joffre, 1910-1917,* 2 vols. (Paris, 1932); Auguste Bréal, *Philippe Berthelot* (Paris, 1937), senior official of the foreign ministry; Jean-Baptiste Bienvenu-Martin, "Mon interim de chef de gouvernement (15-27 juillet 1914)," *Revue de France, XIII* (Aug. 15, 1933), 639-52, acting foreign minister in the absence of Poincaré and Premier Viviani; Sir Francis Bertie, *The Diary of Lord*

Bertie of Thame, 1914–1918, 2 vols. (London, 1924), British ambassador in Paris.

Notable for depth and balance is the study of how Britain entered the war by Ernst Anrich, *Die englische Politik im Juli 1914* (Stuttgart, 1934); on the scope of Britain's commitments, John E. Tyler, *The British Army and the Continent, 1904–1914* (London, 1938); and on mobilization of the navy, Winston Churchill, *The World Crisis, 1911–1914* (London, 1923). Besides Grey's memoirs these should be mentioned: H. H. Asquith, *The Genesis of the War* (New York, 1923); Richard B. Haldane, *Before the War* (London, 1920); Viscount John Morley, *Memorandum on Resignation* (New York, 1928); Sir Horace Rumbold, *The War Crisis in Berlin: July–August 1914,* rev. ed. (London, 1940); Austen Chamberlain, *Down the Years* (London, 1935), shows how the Conservative-Unionist leadership rallied to support the interventionists in the Liberal cabinet.

The dilemma of socialism in 1914 is illustrated by these accounts: Milorad Drachkovitch, *Le socialismes français et allemand et la problème de la guerre, 1870–1914* (Geneva, 1953); J. J. Becker and A. Kriegel, *Juillet 1914; le mouvement ouvrier français et la guerre* (Paris, 1964); Jürgen Kuczynski, *Der Ausbruch des ersten Weltkriegs und die deutsche Sozialdemokratie* (East Berlin, 1957); William H. Maehl, *German Militarism and Socialism* (Lincoln, Neb., 1968).

For the currents of opinion, the role of the press, and the temper of Europe in 1914, these studies are valuable: Jonathan F. Scott, *Five Weeks: The Surge of Public Opinion on the Eve of the Great War* (New York, 1927); Anton Jux, *Der Kriegsschrecken des Frühjahrs 1914 in der europäischen Presse* (Berlin, 1929); Walter Zimmermann, *Die englische Presse zum Ausbruch des Weltkrieges* (Berlin, 1928); Ladislas Singer, *Eine Welt bricht Zusammen—Die letzten Tagen vor dem Weltkrieg* (Graz, 1961); George M. Thomson, *The Twelve Days, 24 July to 4 August 1914* (New York, 1964); Geoffrey Marcus, *Before the Lamps Went Out* (London, 1965).

INDEX

← pocket inside

RACIAL DISTRIBUTION IN CENTRAL and EASTERN EUROPE—1914

Teutonic
Latin
Slavonic
Letts & Lithuanians
Ural-Altaic Stock
Greeks
Albanians

Slavonic

East Slavs
West Slavs
South Slavs